Elephant Life

FIFTEEN YEARS OF HIGH POPULATION DENSITY

FRONTISPIECE This huge bull portrays Herculean strength, courage, and beauty as he strides through optimal habitat. (*Photograph by G. L. Smuts*)

Elephant Life
FIFTEEN YEARS OF HIGH POPULATION DENSITY

Irven O. Buss

IOWA STATE UNIVERSITY PRESS / AMES

IRVEN O. BUSS was professor of wildlife biology, Department of Zoology, Washington State University. He received a Fulbright appointment as Senior Scholar in Wildlife Research in Uganda, Africa, in 1958–1959. He returned to Uganda in 1961–1963 to study the African elephant *Loxodonta africana* on a National Science Foundation Grant.

© 1990 Iowa State University Press, Ames, 50010
All rights reserved

Manufactured in the United States of America
⊗ This book is printed on acid-free paper.

First edition, 1990

Library of Congress Cataloging-in-Publication Data
Buss, Irven O., 1908–
    Elephant life : fifteen years of high population density / Irven
O. Buss.—1st ed.
      p. cm.
    Includes bibliographical references.
    ISBN 0–8138–0139–7
    1. Elephants. 2. Mammal populations. I. Title.
QL737.P98B87 1990
599.6'1—dc20   89-77431

Contents

Foreword

PROFESSOR IRVEN O. BUSS is a product of the late Aldo Leopold who held the chair of Wildlife Management at the University of Wisconsin until his death in 1948. Leopold was internationally recognized as the father of wildlife management, and his writings and philosophies are monuments to this recognition. His book, *Game Management,* published in 1936, stands a half century later as the bible of wildlife management unmatched by a half dozen other books on this subject.

Evidently some of the teachings of Leopold rubbed off and stuck to Professor Buss, for he reflects this in both his teaching and his writing. Some of his graduate students are among the top leaders in the field today including Robert D. Nelson, presently director of Fish and Wildlife, U.S. Forest Service. Buss served as chief of wildlife research for the Wisconsin Conservation Department (now the Department of Natural Resources) until accepting his position at Washington State University in 1948. His philosophy until retirement, 30 June 1973, has been quality, not quantity.

Soon after getting settled into his new environment and looking over opportunities for research, he evidently reflected back to his youthful interest in the African elephant and soon had grants to support elephant studies in Uganda in East Central Africa. After publishing over 100 technical reports (36 on elephants), he has written this book covering his most important findings. Some have been published, but they are now synthesized and in a more readable style than when previously published.

One of the best-written reports I encountered about the research of Professor Buss was made by Dr. Henry Grosshans, a Rhodes Scholar, who was serving as editor of the Washington State University *News Bulletin* when one of the first articles written by Buss came across his desk. This article, "Elephant Census—III," was published in *Uganda Wild Life and Sport,* Vol. 1, No. 5, 1959. After reading the article, Dr. Grosshans wrote as follows:

> Some years ago, a well-known commentator wrote: "Towns are full of people, houses full of tenants, hotels full of guests, cafes full of customers, consulting rooms of doctors full of patients, theaters full of spectators, and beaches full of bathers. What previously was in general no problem, now begins to be an everyday one, namely, to find room." Since that time, it has become more and more apparent to more and more of us that, if in no other way, the extent of our religious feelings can be measured by our demonstrated allegiance to the old Biblical precept to increase and multiply.
>
> It is, however, one of the sad jokes of nature that this exercise in fruitfulness by one species threatens the existence of fellow creatures. In the understandable attempt to find room in which to catch his breath (and this, I am told, may in the near future be more than a mere figure of speech), man is forced to impinge upon the territories of others. No one is safe, and even that monument to size and strength, the elephant, has a doubtful future.

Professor Buss points out that the African elephant belongs to a group of animals that formerly occupied most of the land areas of the earth and included over 300 kinds.

> At the present time, the African and Asian elephants are the only survivors of
> this large group, and the present range and numbers of the African elephant are
> but a small fraction of their former magnitude. . . . It is entirely possible that
> there will be no African elephant living in natural environments by the end of
> another century; by that time they may be existing only in relatively small
> numbers under seminatural conditions in National Parks.

Professor Buss had no trouble in identifying the major threat to the African elephant. It
is "the erupting human population with its continued spread of habitation and cultivation
into lands previously occupied by elephants. Thus the elephant is forced to retreat and
live under restricted conditions available to him."

Because he is dedicated to the general principle of wildlife conservation, Professor
Buss is concerned over the fate of the African elephant. Yet one of the most important
arguments he makes is what may strike even those relatively uninterested in wildlife as
such a unique but practical attitude toward the decline of the elephant. He writes that the
elephant "could be conserved and become one of Africa's most valuable resources."

Numerous "new" problems on elephant management surfaced after Professor Buss
wrote his 1959 report. Both old and new problems are discussed and suggestions offered
for solving them in the last chapter, Looking Ahead.

Many years ago I checked out *The Physiology of the Elephant* by Francis G. Benedict, published in 1936, by the Carnegie Institution. Benedict was director of the Nutrition Laboratory of Carnegie Institution at that time. I notice that Professor Buss has
referred to some of Benedict's findings in his chapter Structure and Function, supporting
the philosophy that once reliable information is published, regardless of publication time,
it will be used.

I was really thrilled to visit Kenya and observe the animals there, including the
elephants. At the Masai Mara I observed a very large herd of elephants for a prolonged
time; I ceased observing them only when my arms were too tired to hold my field glasses.
Professor Buss destroys many legends with scientific facts that he and his associates
developed, not in a short visit like mine, but by extensive field studies. His four trips to
Africa between 1958 and 1971 included 27 months of field research and then shipment
home of nearly 3 tons of specimens for study in laboratories at Washington State University (and a few other laboratories).

As a physiologist I believe the information in this book will stand the test of time.
Who has delved into a study of mineral requirements of wild elephants and found that
they travel considerable distances to eat manganese- and cobalt-laden soil? Who has
discovered gallstones in an elephant when they don't even have a gall bladder? Professor
Buss has come up with information on both subjects. New insights and knowledge are
presented that will benefit elephants and the people who work with them and who have
responsibility for their welfare and management.

I am pleased that Professor Buss manifests sensitivity and concern for this remarkable beast.

LEO K. BUSTAD
Dean Emeritus and Professor, Veterinary College,
Washington State University

Preface

MY EXPERIENCE with wildlife began as a preschool youngster with mosquito- and ant-bitten bare feet and legs from watching young woodchucks playing about their den under a large old pine stump just off the edge of our farm orchard in northwest Wisconsin. Life continued through years of fur trapping and hunting and through extended years of study and research, which guided me through a rather erratic evolution from trapper to biologist and university professor.

How does one become interested and excited about elephants when living on a midwestern farm? I first encountered elephants in my youth while attending a circus with my parents. The elephants excited me very deeply; I never forgot them as I worked my way to a university professorship.

Where I lived on the old farm in northwest Wisconsin I learned, not only from my father but from some of the neighbors as well, that livestock was raised within the limits of available annual forage. My father put it this way: "Son we can control the number of cattle we feed, but we can't control the climate." Later I met the same principle while studying under Professor Aldo Leopold at the University of Wisconsin; his teaching was related to deer and elk, rather than cattle. Still later when I was a biologist working for the Wisconsin Conservation Department I learned that the state had a huge deer problem: whitetails were overabundant and white cedar had been browsed excessively, occurring mostly on an Indian reservation where deer were hunted throughout the year.

A state-wide study of deer damage to forest reproduction showed that if the National Forest Service should present a bill to the State Conservation Department for this damage, the department would become bankrupt. Deer were far above carrying capacity; they had to be reduced in number, which was not easy. When plans for deer reduction were made public, more problems became evident. After more than a few attempts to increase the deer harvest, success was finally achieved. By 1948 the deer harvest reached 45,000; by 1983 the kill reached an estimated 197,600; and in 1984 a record of 256,000 deer were taken in Wisconsin, excluding the harvest by Indians on their reservation.

Biologists realized what was happening: the deer were responding to the "Inversity Principle," which was first pointed out in the United States by the late Dr. Paul L. Errington from Iowa. He showed that there was an inverse relationship between population density and reproductive gain in bobwhite quail. Biologists in various areas began finding that mammals also responded to this principle. In the state of Maine deer began breeding before reaching a year in age. This was particularly the case in the rich croplands of southern Maine. Elk in two western states also showed responses to this principle. Would this also occur with elephant populations? I would watch for an opportunity to study this important problem.

Although the aerial counts of elephants conducted in Kabalega Falls National Park, Uganda, are of historic value, they provided additional information. Data on distribution and migratory behavior in relationship to annual rainy and dry seasons were obtained.

PREFACE

Even more important in my judgment was the opportunity to demonstrate that elephants do respond to the principle of inversity.

Up to 1963–1964 aerial counts were made of elephants in Kabalega Falls National Park, which was a single contiguous parcel of land. At that time, however, two additional units of land were added to enable a comparison of calf production on these three units that were known to have variable population densities. The three units were (1) Ruwenzori National Park, (2) the Tangi-Karuma and Elephant Sanctuary, and (3) the South Kabalega area. Comparison of percentages of calves with densities of elephant populations on these three areas showed that annual increment was inversely related to population density during the period of this study.

When I reached Uganda in 1958 I learned that among the various goals of my study was one of high priority, namely, to collect and study up to 200 elephants, all outside the national parks of Uganda. This request seemed like a full-time assignment and caused me a bit of concern. What would readers believe when they read that a scientist who claimed to like elephants killed over a hundred of them? Through reading, however, I learned that elephants were above carrying capacity on some of their East African ranges. The research findings of Shants and Turner and also Buechner and Dawkins were related to me by my colleague Dr. H. K. Buechner. Both studies showed the role of elephants in destruction of woody vegetation in the same area where I would be working. Also, before I started collecting, I flew, drove, and hiked over parts of the area where I would be working and saw much evidence of overutilization. Finally, Dr. H. K. Buechner's aerial counts suggested that collection of 200 elephants would reduce the population in Kabalega Falls National Park by less than half of its annual increment. Collectively, these considerations and observations helped set my mind at ease about collecting elephants for study purposes.

During my four trips to Africa, starting in late May 1958 and ending on 18 August 1971, I spent 27 months in the field gathering nearly 3 tons of material, which were shipped to the laboratories at Washington State University where I would spend much more time analyzing these materials. Selecting advanced graduate students who were qualified to assist in particular phases of analyses and who were interested in working jointly with me on elephants proved doubly beneficial to the student; both the experience gained in techniques of analyses and writing were of high educational value. However, the total time required to complete the analyses was greater than anticipated. Some qualified students were reluctant to participate for very few could complete their doctorate in less than 4 years. Also, some were not interested in studying elephants because they questioned the job opportunities in a country with no wild elephants. The record shows, however, that those who did participate in this study had no difficulty with placement in excellent positions.

Previously published material that appears herein has been modified and updated. Statistical analyses have been reduced to facilitate reading and to hold the interest of a wider audience. All work cited can be found in the References.

Acknowledgments

ACKNOWLEDGMENT is made for the support provided to this study through a Fulbright appointment as a Senior Scholar on Wildlife Research in Uganda, and by National Science Foundation Grant GB-53. The study was also supported by funds from the New York Zoological Society, and from Medical and Biological Research Fund, Washington State University. The Rockefeller Foundation provided funds for two years of field work in East Africa for Dr. Norman S. Smith who collaborated in reproduction studies.

I am grateful for the extensive support and cooperation of the Uganda Forest Department. The original impetus given to the three-year Forest Study by the chief conservator of forests, W. E. M. Logan, was strongly supported by his successors, George Webster and M. L. S. B. Rukuba. The government of Uganda supplied most of the funds for staff and labor, as well as some equipment. Arnold Beaton, regional forest officer, Western Region, generously supported the field work, and Michael Philip, conservator (research) for the Forest Department, gave valuable technical suggestions in planning the study. A. B. Katende, assistant forester, and L. K. Kimarakwija, forest ranger, both of the Forest Department, provided much valuable assistance in gathering data.

I am also grateful to the Game Department (successor to the Game and Fisheries Department) for its generous support and cooperation throughout this study. Major Bruce G. Kinloch, chief warden, was receptive to practically all new ideas suggested and helped provide funds, personnel, and advice when needed. Special acknowledgment is made to Senior Game Guard Camelo Rwakaikara who served faithfully supervising Ugandan labor forces and demonstrated exceptional skill in locating elephants on many occasions. Lawrence Tennant, chief warden (successor to Major Kinloch) of the Uganda Game Department, and members of the Uganda National Parks gave support to the field work whenever possible.

Special acknowledgment is made to my former graduate students who collaborated with me in the various phases of this project; they are now: Dr. James A. Estes, wildlife biologist, U.S. Fish and Wildlife Service, and adjunct professor in biology and marine sciences, University of California, Santa Cruz; Dr. O. W. Johnson, professor of biological sciences, Moorhead State College, Moorhead, Minnesota; William A. Kumrey, originally biologist, Wildlife Cooperative Research Unit, Southern Illinois University, Carbondale; Dr. Thomas F. Ogle, professor of physiology, Medical College of Georgia, Athens; and Dr. Norman S. Smith, professor of wildlife ecology, University of Arizona, Tucson.

I am deeply indebted to William O. Pridham and John J. Heppes, formerly district supervisors of the Uganda Game Department, who assisted with much of the rigorous work involving the collection of elephants. I owe special thanks to C. D. Margach of Kinyala Estates, Masindi, Uganda, for his generosity in providing use of his Stinson Voyager airplane at cost and serving as pilot on six aerial counts. R. F. Newton, then of the Uganda Game Department, made reconnaissance flights prior to the study, helped initiate the aerial counts, served as pilot on the first and a subsequent count, and loaned his Auster to the study at cost. I am indebted to the East African Wildlife Society for providing use of its Piper Cruiser at cost for the last four aerial counts.

Dr. U. de V. Pienaar and his staff in the Kruger National Park, South Africa, were exceptionally cooperative in every conceivable way; an official park Landrover was provided along with lodging for three weeks. Harold Braach served as my driver and assistant biologist. Dr. G. L. Smuts, then in charge of elephant research in the park, assisted in planning the collection of reproductive tissues and provided photographs. Dr. Anthony Hall-Martin also provided a large number of photographs of his elephant drawings. Dr. S. C. J. Joubert, control research officer, provided information on the impact of anthrax on park mammals.

I am grateful to Dr. Thomas S. Russell, statistician at Washington State University, for statistical assistance, and acknowledgment is made to the Royal Botanic Gardens for assistance in furnishing proper scientific names of plants.

W. R. Bainbridge, chief game officer of Zambia Game and Fisheries, and Dr. J. Hanks were instrumental in furnishing valuable specimens from Luangwa Valley, Zambia.

ACKNOWLEDGMENTS

Leslie H. Squire, Reed College, generously provided information on the elephants in the Washington Park Zoo, Portland, Oregon. Douglas R. Wise, Cambridge University, assisted with field work in Uganda for three months.

The Nuffield Unit of Tropical Animal Ecology provided support and assistance in conducting aerial counts of elephants in Ruwenzori National Park.

I am grateful to Elsie A. Newhouse, Rights and Permissions, Alan R. Liss, Inc. for granting permission to republish two articles from *The Anatomical Record.* Also I am grateful to Richard N. Denney, Executive Director of the Wildlife Society, for allowing me to republish in part material that I had authored and had printed in *The Journal of Wildlife Management,* and to publish modified and updated material, which was published as Wildlife Monograph No. 19, 1970, entitled *Elephants and Forests* by Larry D. Wing and Irven O. Buss. On the matter of republishing, I am grateful to Elmer C. Birney, managing editor, *Journal of Mammalogy,* Bell Museum of Natural History, University of Minnesota, Minneapolis, for permission to use material from any or all of the six articles I had published in the *Journal of Mammalogy.* Dr. Jean Dorst, member of the institute, Museum of National Natural History, Paris, kindly granted permission to republish all the information in my papers published in the museum's journals.

Vicki Croft, head librarian, Veterinary Medical/Pharmacy, Washington State University, Pullman, was always very helpful in obtaining references to elephant health problems. Also Albert J. Zimmerman, medical librarian/editor, in the large medical clinic, Marshfield, Wisconsin, with the assistance of James S. Vedder, M.D., on several occasions helped locate important references to elephant health problems.

I thank Dr. Richard M. Laws, formerly director of scientific research, Nuffield Unit, Ruwenzori National Park, Uganda, for allowing me to combine some of his published data on elephant growth form with similar data I had collected in the same area, thus complementing both sets of data, and also allowing me to use the figure he had published on molar characteristics.

I am deeply grateful to Carol Borden for typing the final copy of this report.

Introduction

THE UNMISTAKABLE TONES of a steam calliope drifted faintly out of the east on a light summer breeze. Although this was over a half century ago, I remember it as though it were yesterday. I was a youngster living on our farm 4 km west of Menomonie in northwest Wisconsin. Leaning on the old lawn-mower handle and listening, an unforgettable picture came into sharp focus and a lump rose in my throat. Ringling Brothers, Barnum, and Bailey Circus had arrived in town, and this was the first day of their stop-over. Their arrival was proclaimed annually to all within earshot of their music machine.

A year previous when I attended my first circus with my family, there was a parade headed by a steam calliope. Then came clowns and wagons with many kinds of animals, and last came the elephants. They were in a long single file with a large old cow leading, closely followed by others of mixed sizes and ages. Some held on to their leader's tail, others followed free-lance. (In reflecting back on my early experience, I am reminded of Jay Reed's [1981] feelings expressed so forcefully when hearing "for the first time in [his] life the howl of a genuine, wild timber wolf" while camped on the White Moose River in northern Saskatchewan, Canada.)

There on the streets of Menomonie I saw, for the first time in my life, a live elephant!

Upon meeting my first African elephant, I saw eloquence, power, and cunning. (*Drawing by R. W. "Mike" Carroll*)

Seeing these giants really did things to me, surely much like Reed's wolf music did to him. Those swaying giants, huge and powerful, were a key to every door there ever was. A new kind of fear was born, yet at the same time a greater joy than I had ever known welled up within me. I envisioned Herculean strength, courage, and confidence as the great beasts moved down the street in saintly stride. Six jockey-sized mahouts (drivers) were individually perched on the heads of the largest elephants, talking to their charges in "elephant language" and guiding them with hooked sticks.

In the following half dozen years, I obtained my parents' permission to volunteer as a temporary laborer when the circus came to town. My work included helping carry trunks and boxes, cleaning up and carrying animal dung to a repository, and moving food from box cars to animal feeding stalls. My apparent reward was a ticket to the performance in the "big tent"; my actual reward was working where I could admire and learn a little about elephant care and behavior.

Following my early circus experience, I acquired an ever increasing burden of responsibilities, mainly of educational nature. Completing grade school in the country, I had to travel 4 km to Menomonie for high school and undergraduate college training. Each day was full and long. Upon rising in darkness I slipped a flashlight into my pocket and a 22-caliber single shot Stevens Crackshot rifle over my shoulder and set off to attend my trap line. Any furbearers I was able to outsmart were temporarily cached in an empty rain barrel. Soon after morning chores, I was off to school on my Ranger bicycle purchased from Sears Roebuck. During those years when the weather proved most cooperative, I was able to ride my bike until Christmas; thereafter I hiked regardless of snow depth or other weather conditions. After classes and football practice, I hiked or peddled home, skinned any animals I had cached, and helped with evening chores. Then I studied until 8:30 P.M., which was my bedtime.

Each day followed a similar pattern until I completed undergraduate training at the University of Wisconsin-Stout. Then came graduate training under Aldo Leopold at the University of Wisconsin-Madison, two stints in the Navy, various jobs, and finally in 1948 an appointment as head of wildlife biology at Washington State University.

In 1950 I worked under a grant from the Arctic Institute of North America conducting wildlife research in the Yukon Territory. This was tremendously interesting and stimulating, but not enough to override my interest in elephants. Consequently, when an opportunity arose in 1958 to work with elephants in Uganda, I immediately applied for the assignment and in a short time was on my way to Africa.

Africa, 1958–1959

Soon after arrival in Africa I learned that my first year there, mid-May 1958 to the end of June 1959, would be spent almost entirely in Uganda. An early joint meeting was held in Entebbe, then the capital of Uganda. Representatives of the East African Virus Institute, the Uganda Game Department, the Uganda Forest Department, and the Uganda national parks attended to plan and establish a program involving my work with the African elephant. An inventory or aerial count of elephants in Kabalega Falls National Park (then Murchison Falls National Park) ranked high among the problems that needed study, thus a continuation of the aerial counts of elephants made in the park by the late

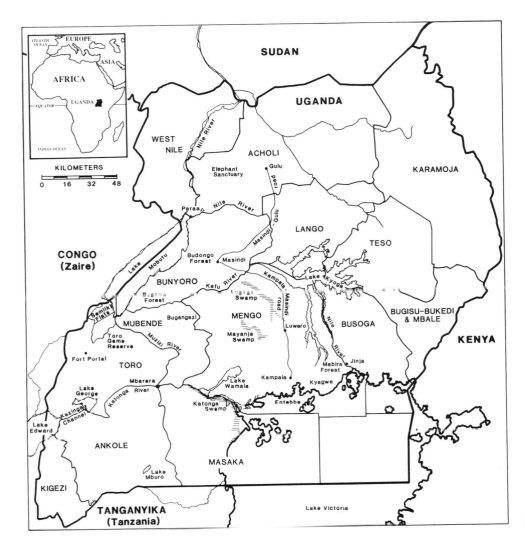

Map of Uganda.

Dr. Helmut (Hal) K. Buechner, my colleague and predecessor to Uganda, was quickly agreed upon as first priority.

Second in importance was a need for information on the annual reproductive increase compared with the annual mortality rate. This would be accomplished by collection and field examination of up to 200 elephants, all to be collected outside of Uganda's national parks. Information also was needed on movements and history of elephants in Uganda. Obtaining this information would not be difficult for in 1925 the Game Department began recording, in the headquarters of each district, the location and date of all elephants shot on control operations. The assistant district commissioner would upon request allow me to use these records. They, together with the locations of elephants seen on aerial counts and plotted on maps, would provide information on distribution, seasonal movements, and range of the animals. Any additional information related to these problems that I could obtain would depend on my interest and judgment.

My friend Major Bruce Kinloch, chief game warden, informed me that a house had been selected for me and my wife Kay in Masindi in western Uganda where both the

Game and Fisheries departments had their Bunyoro District offices. Masindi was about 89 km from Paraa, the headquarters of Kabalega Falls National Park. There were plenty of elephants between Masindi and the park boundary for my study, as well as a rich profusion of other faunal species sharing this range with the elephants.

Little time was lost getting settled into our new home before our first field trip into elephant country. On Friday 13 June 1958 Hal Buechner and I set off from Masindi in his Landrover bound for the park. Close to the park boundary and below the rim of the escarpment were two adult bull elephants and a subadult bull, my first close-up view of wild African elephants; we stopped abruptly to observe them. Although they saw us, little apparent concern was paid to our presence. Nevertheless, they probably were registering every movement and sound we made; I noticed that at least one animal directed his attention toward us at all times. The lack of bulbous foreheads gave them a more streamlined appearance than the Asian circus elephants I had seen as a youngster. They impressed and inspired me more than any other animal I had ever met in the wild—I saw eloquence, power, and cunning. Hal added that rhinos, lions, and buffaloes give way before them—they dominate wherever they go. I witnessed this dominance and courage on more than a few subsequent occasions. As we drove off, a few champagne bubbles still danced up and down my spine.

Time passed inexorably. Our aim was to acquaint me with the areas where and people with whom I would be working. During mid-June Hal, his daughter Nancy, and I drove to Ruwenzori National Park where we visited with Dr. William Longhurst before proceeding to Bill's hippopotamus study area. Then we were off to Semliki Plain and the headquarters of Hal's Uganda Kob Study below the western rift about 56 km by road west of Fort Portal, where we spent considerable time since we agreed on a reciprocal plan: Hal would turn over a collection of teeth from elephants shot on control in 1947 by Game Department personnel; I in return would extend his observations and collections of the kob.

Soon after returning to Masindi, Hal and I drove to Budongo Forest scouting and discussing some of the elephant-forest problems. Robin Knight, superintendent of Budongo Forest, which is classified as a medium-moist semideciduous forest, served as pilot on several aerial counts conducted in Kabalega and made several suggestions for improving techniques planned for the elephant project. Following the trip to Budongo Forest, I accompanied the Buechner family to Entebbe where they started their flight to the United States after 20 mo in Africa. My orientation was over.

A second meeting was held on 26 June at the Ministry of Natural Resources headquarters in Entebbe with Peter Bleakley as the ministry representative in charge. Also in attendance were Sandy Haddow, East African Virus Institute; Major Bruce Kinloch, chief game warden representing the Game Department; Allen Brooks, biologist of the Game Department; and John Heppes, game warden in charge of the Game Department District Office in Misindi. The purpose of the meeting was to finalize arrangements for my elephant project.

On 14 July I received a note stating that Bruce Kinloch had shot an elephant near the road to Kabalega. Allan Brooks, my wife Kay, and our porter Pedro left Masindi to collect the dead elephant—the first collected for my study; I would now test the techniques planned for measuring, dissecting, and weighing the elephants to be collected for my study.

On 25 July 1958 I made my last trip to Semliki Plain to fulfill my obligation to Hal

A bull herd in Kabalega Falls National Park. (*Photograph by Roger Wheater*)

Buechner and his kob study. With me were my wife, my headman and senior game guard Camelo Rwakaikara, and our porter Pedro. The 311-km route to Fort Portal was over an unimproved, tortuous, and bumpy road; thus we were happy to stop at Bill and Margaret Pridham's house before arriving at our destination in Fort Portal.

Bill came to Uganda in 1932, when he was not quite 20 yr old. He became a professional elephant and buffalo hunter in Toro District, apprenticing himself to one of the old pioneers by the name of "Red" Vivers, who also taught him the art of prospecting for alluvial gold in the streams that flowed through the dense rain forests of Toro and western Ankole. He joined the Game Department in 1946, and a bit more than 4 yr later, as game warden, took responsibility for Toro, Ankole, and Kigezi districts of western Uganda.

After a hearty breakfast, we set off for the last leg of our trip to Semliki Plain via Fort Portal. Our camp on Semliki was close to the game guard's camp and the Wasa River, on an extensive savanna of grass and forest remnants in the Western Rift Valley. Our camp was close to the site where Bill previously had camped with Bruce Kinloch and Mike Holmes (Bill's understudy) and which Bruce described as

the flat, grassy plains on the Toro Game Reserve in the broad valley of the Semliki River. To the south of us towered the northern peaks of the Ruwenzori. Across the Semliki, to the west, the dark mass of the Ituri—home of pygmies and the rare okapi—sprawled in a dense, dark green carpet over the hills of the Congo [Zaire]. On every side of us, as far as the eye could see, the chestnut-colored forms of Uganda kob dotted the landscape. In the rivers hippos grunted, while high overhead white-headed fish eagles wheeled and soared filling the air with their yelping, laughing cries.

As night fell the occasional roar of a lion echoes across the rolling plains. . . . From nearby, in a clump of thorn scrub, came the deep sawing of a hunting leopard and in the tall rushes by the river an elephant trumpeted loudly. . . . We rolled into our sleeping bags under the velvety, star-studded canopy of an African night (Kinlock 1972).

Out of our Semliki camp I not only collected kob for Hal's study, I also used it as a base for studying elephants. By 4 October 1958 I had collected 17 elephants, some of which were of the forest subspecies *Loxodonta africana cyclotis,* having moved to Semliki Plain from the Congo.

After 4 October my main base of operations was in Masindi; from there I continued collecting until 4 June 1959, by which time I had collected 127 elephants. Of these, 104 (50 males) were taken in Bunyoro District (savanna subspecies *L. a. africana*). Of the remaining 23 elephants (12 males), which were collected in Toro District, 16 were from Semliki Plain and 7 were taken close to Ruwenzori National Park.

Elephant No. 28, collected in Toro District, was collected at night under rather harrowing circumstances. Bill Pridham called me in Masindi during mid-November requesting that I meet him at his home near Fort Portal. Cotton growers in Mubuku were complaining of nightly elephant raids on their cotton fields, and Bill was the logical official to alleviate the problem. Would I help him shoot some of the night raiders? Well yes, almost anything that would add specimens to my collection was fine. I left for Fort Portal the following day. Upon meeting Bill, I was promptly briefed on the problem and informed of his plans. We would camp close to Mubuku and inform the cotton growers of the location. They would come to our camp and tell us when the elephants were in their cotton fields.

This happened shortly before midnight on our second night of encampment; we assembled our gear quickly and headed for the raiding scene. A warm south breeze pushed heavy dark clouds over a large moon at irregular intervals. At one moment visibility was almost as good as at midday, the next moment all was dark. The cotton field was studded with termite mounds, which we envisioned as safeguards in the event of elephant charges. That was almost correct. We moved slowly, straining eyes and ears for the raiders. Once I thought I saw an elephant ahead, but before many steps my elephant became a termite mound. We moved on. Then a large dark cloud closed the entire field in darkness; quickly I stepped closer to a termite mound. The cloud kept moving, and I felt like I was standing very much alone in the moonlight; this time there was no termite mound close to me. The mound was actually an elephant that had moved completely out of sight. A little farther I saw Bill standing very still. I moved closer toward him, and without even whispering he pointed ahead and nodded. There, now plainly visible, were 11 elephants. We moved more cautiously now, watching the moon as much as the field ahead. The intervening distance between us and the elephants seemed to close rapidly, too rapidly. The elephants were approaching. Fortunately termite mounds are perfect for an ambush. No sooner had we gained the safety of a mound when the elephants were well within gun range. When our shooting ended, we had one very dead bull elephant; being closest of the approaching group, we had both selected the same target. The other 10, probably all bulls, lost no time leaving the field, and neither did we. The time was 11:45 P.M.

We stayed in the Mubuku Valley for five more days, collected six more elephants, and then returned to Fort Portal.

Before leaving Fort Portal for Masindi I had a question for Bill. How do elephants living in the park several or more miles from the cotton fields know almost exactly when the cotton bolls open? Shaking his head, he smiled and said, "I think of that each year when it happens and I was just about to ask you the same question."

After returning to Masindi, from that night collecting trip, I continued collecting operations by driving up the tortuous track to the park border. Driving slowly enough to assemble a volunteer labor crew, we watched for elephants or for any fresh signs of elephants having crossed the road recently. This proved entirely successful; subsequently my limitations were not in finding plenty of elephants, but rounding up enough volunteers for each working party. Once a crew obtained elephant meat (their payment for services), they stayed at home and ate until they had no more meat. If I had an exceptionally lucky day and collected five or six elephants, I soon learned that the following morning I would have difficulty rounding up a reasonable-sized crew. Thus on such days I alternated collecting at Mobutu Flats, which proved equally successful. Usually I camped at Mobutu for up to 10 days, then returned to Masindi where I prepared tissues for shipment back to the states, and prepared for the next day's trip to Kabalega.

June marked the end of my first year in Africa. I ceased elephant studies and packed up my massive assortment of tissues and personal gear in readiness for our return to Washington State; I shipped 2268 kg of collected elephant tissues to the Zoology Department at Washington State University. These materials, from the 127 elephants collected in Uganda, would keep me and some of my graduate students busy for at least several years. Then I would probably return to Africa for further studies.

International Union for Conservation of Nature and Natural Resources, 1961

The International Union for Conservation of Nature and Natural Resources met in Arusha, Tanganyika (Tanzania), during 5–12 September 1961. Since I was scheduled to present a report on my elephant studies, I decided to allow enough time to enjoy a few short tours of wildlife areas in the countryside about Arusha. Thus I left Pullman, Washington, on 16 August via air transport.

Soon after arriving in Arusha I learned that I was to stay in the New Arusha Hotel with Uganda's first chief game warden, Captain Charles R. S. Pitman. After getting settled under our mosquito nets for the night, we usually talked about elephants and elephant hunting. Pitman related that in 1923 when the government of Uganda initiated its elephant control work, the first man on this assignment was B. P. ("Samaki") Salmon. F. G. ("Deaf") Banks and Pete Pierson (both colorful old hunters) were added in 1924. Pitman did not like Samaki very well complaining that he shot too many elephants and that he was an exhibitionist who was on the lookout for big ivory, which he shot and

The variation in sizes of individuals in this tightly grouped herd is typical for family groups and herds. (*Photograph by John H. Blower*)

cached away, selling it gradually to the Indians. The government got on to this and warned him, but Samaki persisted. At one time Samaki had to turn in 90 tusks to the government. He had intended to sell them gradually but got caught before they were disposed of. Samaki delighted in getting right into the middle of a herd of elephants, stirring them up, and when they got excited and started to charge he shot them with deadly precision ending up with a ring of dead animals surrounding him.

My report, written in collaboration with Allan Brooks, then biologist for the Game Department of Uganda, was on "Observations of Number, Mortality, and Reproduction of Elephants in Uganda" and was the sixth report listed for presentation. Completing the report early in the 8-day meeting allowed considerable time to discuss wildlife problems with numerous individuals, one of whom was Sir Julian Huxley. He asked if I had been to Ngorongoro Crater at the site where elephants use their tusks to gouge out soil and eat it. When I assured him that I had never even heard of it, he responded that I should get there before I left the conference. He then contacted my good friend Major Bruce Kinloch who had become Tanganyika's chief game warden in 1960. Bruce kindly drove me to the crater during one of the last days of the conference set aside for various field trips. This was the highlight of the conference for me, particularly since I could talk about elephant behavior with Bruce who had experienced many field trips in Uganda specifically on elephant problems. The soil samples we collected and which I packed back to the laboratories of Washington State University, were analyzed and are described in Chapter 6 under "Mineral Utilization."

African Plans, 1963–1964

In April 1963 I presented some of the highlights from my 1958–1959 elephant study in Uganda to a Zoological Society meeting in Portland, Oregon, illustrating the presentation with a movie on elephant behavior. Following the presentation I met and chatted with Dr. James Metcalfe, cardiologist at the University of Oregon Medical School. He asked several questions about elephant behavior that needed more illucidation than could be comfortably given with the mob of questioners about us. Finally, when most questions had been given reasonable attention, we left and headed for his office where we expounded more leisurely about some of his questions.

In a nutshell, he and his associates were studying the affinity of mammalian red blood cells for oxygen. There was wide and general knowledge that mammals (including humans) living at, or moving to, high elevations developed larger hearts and more red blood cells to compensate for reduced available oxygen. What was not known was that a given volume of red cells at high elevations developed or had a greater affinity for oxygen than the same volume of red cells at low elevations. Metcalfe's team made this discovery by studying the llama at high elevations, the yak at medium elevations, and the camel at low elevations. Therefore, as Dr. Metcalfe listened to my presentation, the most important question that concerned him was, exactly where do wild elephants live in relation to elevation? Do they live at low elevations, are they more inclined to spend most of their time at medium elevations, or do they prefer higher elevations? Or even better, do they ever migrate through various elevations? Yes, elephants occasionally migrate through variable elevations. For example, from Ruwenzori National Park elephants made trips as high as 2,745 m and probably higher into the Ruwenzori Mountains, living temporarily in *Hagenia-Rapanea* and *Ericaceae-Stoebe* vegetation associations of the moist Montane Forest and high Montane heath vegetation types respectively. Then they migrated back down to conspicuously lower elevations to the grass and wooded savannalands in the park environs. In other words, these elephants moved up and down through variable elevations. Dr. Metcalfe envisioned the elephant as possibly being the ideal animal to complement their research findings.

The following morning Jim Metcalfe called to ask me to join him at breakfast to talk a little more about elephants. I assured him that I had plenty of time before my plane departed and I indeed would like to join him.

Jim told me that after our discussion the previous night he had given a lot of thought to elephants, and wondered that if he and his research team came to Africa, could I collect two or possibly three pregnant females so that he and his team could collect matched samples of fetal and maternal blood without mixing them? I told him I could not promise to do this, but if he could give me a time when his team would arrive in Masindi, I may then be able to locate elephants that typically have wide seasonal movements and set up a strategically located camp. I would also have to know how long his team could stay, and how many pregnant females would meet minimal requirements? With this information I could guesstimate chances for success. He proposed a 10-day to 2-wk trip in late November, and he preferred three pregnant females. Under those conditions, I projected a 95% probability for getting the animals. His broad smile told his answer better than words, and he added that under such circumstances they would definitely try to make arrangements to be at my scene of operations during late November.

On 17 June 1963 my wife and I departed from New York to Fort Portal, our African home for another year. En route we stopped in London and made a trip to the University of Cambridge where we met and talked to Dr. Roger V. Short in the Unit of Reproductive Physiology and Biochemistry, Department of Veterinary Clinical Studies. We talked about elephants and some of their reproductive phenomena; eventually our discussion settled on a cooperative study on progesterone level in the elephant. Dr. Short suggested that we might employ the services of one of his students, Douglas R. Wise. If we could provide local travel, board, and a place for Douglas to sleep, he would be of considerable help on our study. To this we quickly agreed.

Our study involved collecting pregnant females, removing their ovaries, and dissecting corpora lutea from these ovaries for freezing and subsequent laboratory study. As soon as a pregnant female was identified in the field, I would attempt collection, and Douglas would start making dry ice for fixing the ovarian tissues. Slices from corpora lutea would quickly be placed in a small plastic sack, placed between two discs of dry ice, and slipped into a thermos flask. As the thermos filled with samples, a cable would be sent to Dr. Short alerting him that a parcel would arrive in London via a named airline and flight number, on a given date and time. Dr. Short would meet the airline, pick up the thermos, and take it to his laboratory for analysis—primarily for the progesterone content. Hopefully, at least some of these pregnant elephants could also be used for blood studies by Dr. Metcalfe's team.

Most big cities leave me pretty cold, and London was no exception. I wanted to get back into elephant country and away from concrete, asphalt, and brick-lined canyons. After a bit of pushing, coaxing, and subterfuge we finally caught a limousine on 20 June from our hotel and headed for the airport. Departing in the early evening, by the time we were over the Alps the low sun was painting the west-facing mountain slopes in soft pale pastels; the east slopes fell off into dark somber depths. In a matter of seconds the mountains began losing their color, gradually becoming a vast expanse of gray. The twilight of evening had come and faded in surprisingly short time. I pulled the window shade, tilted back my seat, and closed my eyes.

We arrived in Entebbe, Uganda, at 6:05 A.M. not expecting anyone to meet us at that early hour, but there was John Heppes, bright-eyed and looking very sharp. We left the airport and headed to John's residence where we cached our gear and settled in to wait for Douglas Wise, who agreed to send a cable via the Game Department telling of his arrival time.

Meanwhile we thoroughly enjoyed the hospitality of John and Peggy Heppes, who we knew very well from our stay in Masindi during our first year in Africa, and appreciated their continued guidance and encouragement in getting along with the African way of life. In late afternoon John drove me back to the airport; a short distance of perhaps 30–50 m off the north end of the landing strip we saw six sitatunga (antelopes). Evidently they had just emerged from the nearby cover and started feeding. Six of these elusive creatures were more than I had seen during my entire first year in Uganda.

We stayed with John and Peggy about a week waiting for Douglas, and swapping experiences about elephants and other African wildlife. We learned about local bird life, the vegetation, and also a few things about elephants. John told about a creeper, *Arborus* sp., with red berries that may be lethal to elephants. He found a fairly large number of dead elephants during December 1960 and February 1961 on Mobutu Flats along water courses that they had evidently been following. The dead elephants occurred in groups and were believed to have moved downstream from the escarpment to Lake Mobutu and then died on their return from the lake. Deaths occurred each year, always in the dry season, and apparently were higher some years than in others. Rangers working for the Game Department reported finding dead elephants in the Karuma Falls area approximately 71 km upstream from Kabalega Falls. Dr. John Lock, Pharmacology Department,

Makerere University College Medical School, Kampala, Uganda, examined material from some of the dead elephants and found one positive to anthrax. He believed anthrax probably caused the deaths, but John Heppes believed they died of poison from *Arborus* sp. Later, Allan Brooks (then a biologist for the Uganda Department of Game) told me that perhaps as many as a thousand elephants had died on Mobutu Flats between December 1960 and February 1961. He made no reference to either Locke's belief or that of Heppes.

Douglas arrived in the forenoon of 27 June, and we completed packing our gear into Landrover UF 66 (Uganda Forest Department). We left the Heppeses' residence the next forenoon for Ruwenzori National Park, where we stayed overnight. During the following forenoon on our way out of the park, we counted and classified into size-age classes 106 elephants while driving along the so-called "Channel Track" (an unimproved road) that followed the Kazinga Channel for 29 km. We reached Fort Portal at noon, just in time to eat with Sandy and Larry Wing; Larry served as my competent assistant for over 2 yr.

Fort Portal, which was the district and regional headquarters of the government Forest Department, was also our headquarters and home for another year. For the Wings this was their second year in Fort Portal, having worked the past year in nearby Kibale Forest Reserve, which was the main setting for our forest study. Kay, Douglas, and I moved to our house about two city blocks beyond the Wing's place.

Larry had his team of forest workers operating smoothly, so we decided that Douglas Wise and I would provide the most valuable service to our program by continuing to collect elephants in order to obtain (1) blood samples for Dr. Metcalfe's team, (2) corpora lutea tissue samples for progesterone study with Dr. Short, and (3) temporal gland tissues for our continued study. For these studies 19 additional elephants (5 males) were collected bringing the total number collected to 146. We also agreed to conduct a study on elephant defecation rate for the forest study.

At the end of the 2-yr forest study, George Webster, chief conservator of forests, suggested that, in view of the relatively low elephant damage our study showed to trees in the forest, we might consider continuing the study for a third year. The weather during both years had been without drought, which might have been a major factor in our findings. Mr. Webster further suggested that since the team of men working in the forest was well trained and experienced, the study could be continued for a third year with reduced supervision, which could well be carried on by personnel of the Forest Department. Larry and I agreed wholeheartedly. The third year of study was also without drought and supported the 2-yr findings without modifying them appreciably.

Kruger National Park, 1971

My fourth trip to Africa was made by serving as tour leader for Club Tours, which operates out of New York City. When President John Rothschild called to inquire as to whether I was interested in serving as leader for his conservation tour to Africa, I responded by saying I would be if an arrangement could be made that would allow me to stay in Africa and work when the tour ended and after I saw all tour participants safely aboard their flight back to New York. After discussing the matter with Sabena Airlines officials, Mr. Rothschild called me back the next day asking if 45 days would be satisfactory. I agreed and on 6 July 1971 I flew to New York to meet Mr. Rothschild and his very efficient secretary Barbara Morgan, and the tourists. The following day the group was briefed on various details governing the tour. The small, 13-member heterogeneous group was from the eastern United States with one thing in common—all were interested in conservation. I liked them all; they represented a broad spectrum of interests and helped maintain high enthusiasm throughout the entire tour.

Sabena Airlines provided travel to Brussels, Belgium, and after a brief stop there continued on to Athens, Greece, for refueling and rest. Then on to Entebbe, Uganda, where we transferred to three new VW minibuses operated by Hunts Travel Service. Our African tour was underway. We visited many exciting places: 14,826-ha (hectare) Mayer Ranch about 48 km from Nairobi; Nakuru and the many flamingoes; Masai Mara Game Reserve; Serengeti National Park; Seronera Safari Camp; Ol Duvai Gorge of Dr. Leaky fame; Ngorongoro Crater where I obtained soil samples in 1961; Tarangire, in Tanzania; Arusha National Park. Then on to Tsavo in Kenya, and Kilanguni Lodge; Mzima Springs; Momasa Beach Hotel; Mnarani Club; Marine National Park; Kilifi; Gedi, an ancient ruined Arab city; and back to Nairobi via Moshi for an excellent view of Kilimanjaro.

On 27 July I bid the tour group smooth sailing for New York, and then I left for Johannesburg where I picked up supplies and my rented pickup truck. I then headed for Kruger National Park.

Driving slowly, to readjust to right-hand driving and having to take several directional "starts" to get on the right road out of Pretoria, I rolled into Middleburg where I spent the night. The following morning, I headed eastward toward Kruger National Park, completing the 507-km one-way trip from Johannesburg to Skukuza on 29 July. I soon met Dr. U. de V. Pienaar, assistant warden, who, after taking one look at the pickup, assigned an official Landrover and driver to me to prevent any insurance problems in case an ill-tempered elephant took out his feelings on my pickup. My driver, Harold Braach, was more than a driver—much more—and so were all the others who worked with Dr. Pienaar. No one could possibly expect more or better cooperation than I received while working in Kruger. Harold's wife Tony, a competent laboratory worker, kindly helped prepare glutaraldehyde for electron microscopy. Dr. G. L. (Butch) Smuts, then in charge of elephant research in Kruger, spent considerable time with me discussing elephant problems. Identifying pregnant females and securing their ovaries before the 24-man ground crew eviscerated all the collected specimens in readiness for transport to the abattoir would be particularly problematic. Mr. Peter van Wyh outlined the large-mammal count, conducted by aerial and ground counts annually soon after completion of the collecting program for that year. Finally, Dr. V. de Vos, state veterinarian, briefly discussed his buffalo project with me.

On 1 August Harold Braach and I left Skukuza in the Landrover for Tsende Camp about 71 km north and a little west of Letaba. Tsende Camp is located on a high river bank. On the north side of camp and across the river a troop of baboons claimed headquarters on a nearly sheer rocky cliff, and bushbucks were occasional visitors there. In the river lived catfish, some of which Harold caught and prepared for our eating pleasure. Tilapia and a dozen crocodiles were also in the river. To the south a short distance from camp a rocky hill with a lone baobab tree and impala-flower shrubs created a setting for three klipspringers.

From this splendid campsite we conducted daily trips into elephant-occupied areas. We mostly drove to Ted and Sue Whitfield's residence near Mahlangene not far from the

A family bull follows the matriarch and eight other family members but will soon be driven from the unit. (*Photograph by I. O. Buss*)

confluence of the Little and Greater Letaba rivers. This was at the western edge of Kruger and was the starting point for elephant culling operations. Ted Whitfield was a well-experienced district supervisor in charge of all culling. He too proved very cooperative and arranged to have me fly with him on some of the collecting flights. We saw elephants, buffaloes, lions, greater kudus, and sable on these flights. All collecting was conducted far from surfaced roads that are maintained for tourists; they never even knew about the collecting operations, which could be reached only via unimproved service roads, and these were closed to all general traffic. Between 2 and 13 August 62 elephants were collected. From the 17 adult and 7 subadult females collected I fixed plenty of corpora lutea tissue for subsequent study.

On 14 August Soloman C. J. Joubert, who was studying roan antelope, told me that in this species there is a dominance order for males entirely separate from another order for females. According to my observations this is probably also true for elephants. Dr. Joubert went on to state that in roan antelopes the dominant male chases and reminds subordinate males who is boss. When a subordinate roan enters water, however, the chase ends; water is out of bounds and provides a means of escape for inferior or subordinate males.

On 17–18 August Harold and I participated in the annual big-game count. Our count was conducted on a 129-km route northeast of Pretoriuskop, which is in southern Kruger.

On 19 August I started my return trip to Washington State via air to Luanda, in north Angola; Brussels, Belgium; New York City; and finally to Minneapolis where I stopped for a rest after 46 hr of almost continual flying with only bits of uncomfortable sleep.

Helgard Griesel, Information Officer, National Parks Board, South Africa, standing by immobilized elephant. (*Photograph by A. M. Harthoorn*)

Elephant Life

FIFTEEN YEARS OF HIGH POPULATION DENSITY

Behavior

Early Records

In 1962 Allan C. Brooks, then a biologist working for the Uganda Game and Fisheries Department, and I published a report on past and present status of the elephant population in Uganda. Most of the information for that report was taken from records maintained by the Game and Fisheries Department. The records showed that before 1925 there was only an Elephant Control Department (ECD) in Uganda. The primary responsibility of that department was to protect landowners and operators from hazards and crop depredations by elephants. When a complaint was made, particularly by someone living at the frontier of a large resident herd or migratory route, a member of the ECD was sent to the area with orders to shoot one or more of the marauding elephants.

In 1925 the ECD broadened its objectives and became the Game and Fisheries Department. Annual reports on the elephants were then published. The reports included data on the number of elephants taken by control operations, tusks found outside national parks, and tusks confiscated following violations of the Game Ordinance. These records were extracted from the annual reports for the period 1926–1958 and analyzed to learn (1) whether changes occurred in population numbers throughout the protectorate during these years—changes by time, and (2) whether population changes of similar magnitude occurred in each district of Uganda— changes by place. Records of elephants shot on control operations were not maintained on a district basis during the war years of 1940–1944, but they were maintained continuously on a protectorate-wide basis throughout the period 1926–1958.

The distribution and migration pattern of elephants in Uganda were studied and recorded from three sources: observations presented orally by district rangers and other officials of the Game and Fisheries Department, observations published in the annual reports, and direct sightings of elephants or evidence of their presence that I and my team observed.

CONTROL OPERATIONS 1926–1958. Elephants were shot throughout the protectorate, but the number shot during control work at a particular time or place was influenced by human proximity to resident herds and migratory routes. Since the largest herds required the most intensified control efforts, the number of elephants shot provided evidence of their relative abundance by time and place.

In conducting control operations in Uganda 31,966 elephants were shot during the period 1927–1958, an average of 999 animals per year. In addition licensed hunters shot approximately 8,170 elephants during this period. Although a combination of these data indicates that an average of approximately 1,235 elephants were shot annually for over 30 yr, the number shot annually for control purposes showed a decreasing trend. During the period 1927–1942, 18,581 elephants were shot compared to the period 1943–1958 when 13,385 animals were taken; thus 5,196 more elephants were shot during the first 16 yr of control operations than in the last 16 yr.

Most of the 31,966 elephants had small tusks, because a policy was in effect throughout the 32-yr period to shoot individuals with small tusks whenever possible. The average weight of 62,766 tusks from these 31,966 elephants, regardless of sex and age, was 6.1 kg with a range in yearly average tusks weights that varied from 5.1 kg in 1938 to 7.6 kg in 1956.

The distribution of weights for 51,988 tusks from elephants shot between 1932 and 1958 showed that 47% (24,651), or nearly half, of the tusks weighed less than 4.5 kg and less than 2% (910) of the tusks weighed 22.7 kg or more.

When tusk weights were placed in weight groups and combined into 5-yr periods, the percentage of tusks that occurred in respective weight groups remained conspicuously similar throughout the period of 1930–1958. These data suggested that tusk weight based on elephants shot during control operations did not change appreciably. The data also suggested that a relatively small percentage of large tusks was taken on control operations. For any 5-yr period the percentage of tusks weighing 22.7 kg or more never exceeded 4.1%. Although an unknown percentage of heavy ivory taken on control had, by devious means, occasionally been declared as trophy ivory by licensees, the relative percentage of such tusks is probably of minor significance.

Sex determinations for 31,362 of the elephants indicate a ratio of 65.2% (20,460) males to 34.8% (10,902) females. Since females have smaller tusks than males and since small-tusked elephants were shot selectively on control operations, I assumed that most of the elephants shot on control were adult cows and relatively young animals of both sexes.

Perry (1953, 103) also studied the data for elephants shot on control operations in Uganda, which were reported in the annual reports. His comments imply that the disproportionate sex ratio is not indicative of actual ratios, pointing out that game guards engaged in control work frequently erroneously recorded a bull when a cow was actually shot.

Although the sexes of approximately 8,170 elephants shot as trophies by licensed hunters between 1925 and 1958 were not recorded, the average weight of tusks from these elephants suggests that a high percentage of these tusks came from bulls. There is a more or less unwritten law that the licensed elephant hunter will shoot a bull, and most hunters prefer bulls. There

is also general recognition, however, that some cows were shot, particularly between 1930 and 1951 when the minimum legal tusk weight was 5 kg.

Considering the high percentage of males reported for elephants shot on control operations and the additional number of bulls shot for trophies, one would expect a residual sex ratio considerably favoring females. Unpublished data in my files, however, suggest a nearly balanced sex ratio for populations studied during 1958–1959 and 1963–1964 in Bunyoro and Toro districts of Uganda. Thus the sex ratio derived from the 31,966 elephants shot on control was very probably erroneous and highly inaccurate.

Of the 31,966 elephants shot during control operations, 1,108 were recorded as single tusked and 29 were reported as tuskless. These data indicate a low percentage of single-tusked individuals and an even lower percentage of tuskless animals. The accuracy of the percentages, however, is considered unreliable since there was wide recognition, particularly among Game and Fisheries Department personnel, that occasionally game guards assigned to control work shot a tuskless elephant, substituted the tusk from another elephant shot or found dead, and declared two single-tusked animals.

Elephants shot on control were studied by districts. For convenience the 14 districts were grouped into the same 10 units used in studying trends in tusk size from elephants shot by licensed hunters in Uganda (Brooks and Buss 1962b).

The 10 districts were arranged according to the total number of tusks taken on control operations during the 1926–1958 period. Bunyoro, Mubende, Mengo, and Toro districts, adjacent to each other on the western border of Uganda, assumed the top-ranking positions. Approximately 67% of the tusks came from these 4 districts. Variation in the number of elephants shot annually within each district was primarily a result of changes in intensification of control work. Three instances of intensified control were notable: in Mubende-Mengo, 4,155 tusks (35% of total removal) were recorded between 1933 and 1936; in Bunyoro, 2,995 tusks (24% of the total removal) were reported taken between 1935 and 1938; and in Kigezi District, where control operations were usually comparatively moderate, 367 tusks were taken in 1938, nearly 29% of the total recorded in this district during the 33-yr period.

Changes in emphasis of control operations in the various districts were noted when the years preceding World War II (1926–1939) were compared to the postwar years (1945–1957) and to a later year (1958). During the 14-yr period preceding the war 61% (30,257) of the tusks were taken; only 39% (19,035) were taken in the 14-yr postwar period, indicating the extent to which control work had been curtailed.

Reduction in control work was particularly acute in Mubende-Mengo where an average of 657 tusks were taken during the prewar period in contrast to an average of 187 taken during the postwar period, a decrease of approximately 71%. Control operations continued to decrease in Mubende-Mengo; in 1958 only 100 tusks were recorded, or about 9% of the total tusks taken in Uganda that year. Although control work decreased in most districts, it increased in Kigezi and Busoga districts during the postwar period as a result of an expanding agriculture and establishment of resettlement schemes. Lastly, the data showed that Bunyoro became the major area for control work in Uganda

TUSKS FOUND OR CONFISCATED OUTSIDE NATIONAL PARKS. The number of tusks found outside the national parks and game reserves of Uganda between 1929 and 1958 (records were not available before 1929), and those confiscated following violations of the Game Ordinance during the same years, averaged approximately 250/yr. No attempt was made to analyze the data from these two sources separately or to analyze the data on a district basis.

Most of the ivory found or confiscated was small. Data on weight of 5,380 tusks recorded between 1929 and 1958 indicate that 84.6% (4,571 tusks) weighed less than 13.6 kg, 12.7% (683 tusks) weighed 13.6–26.8 kg, 2.2% (119 tusks) weighed 27.2–40.4 kg, and 0.5% (16 tusks) weighed at least 40.8 kg.

Assuming that the 5,389 tusks represented the same proportion of single-tusked (3.5%) and tuskless (0.1%) elephants as the tusks taken on control operations, the number of elephants accounted for by tusks found or confiscated between 1929 and 1958 totals approximately 2,800.

Some tusks were recovered from inside the national parks. Prior to establishment of the Uganda national parks, tusks recovered from the two areas now demarcated as parks were recorded in the annual reports. Since their establishment in 1952, however, the national parks have maintained all records of tusks recovered in the parks. These records show that 502 tusks weighing 4,352.8 kg were recovered in Ruwenzori National Park and 468 tusks weighing 4,876 kg were recovered in Kabalega Falls National Park.

The average number of tusks (84.4) recovered annually from Ruwenzori National Park between 1955 and 1959 suggests that an annual mortality of probably 50 elephants occurred in the park during that time. The average number (93.6) recovered annually from Kabalega Falls National Park between 1955 and 1959 suggests that probably 55 elephants died annually of unknown causes during those years. Reasons for the increase in number of tusks found annually are unknown.

Some elephants probably died of infirmities related to old age. This belief is based on direct observations of at least 14 old elephants that lived in relative seclusion and subsequently were found dead (reported verbally by Frank Poppleton, then senior warden, Uganda national parks). Their tusk weights ranged between 31.8 kg and 71.7 kg on each side.

The average weights of tusks recovered in both parks were 8.7 kg and 10.4 kg respectively. These weights certainly suggest small elephants. There is a high probability that such elephants represented cripples that escaped from control operations outside the parks. Why do I believe this? Elephants with small tusks would seldom be crippled by licensed hunters searching for large tusks, and since elephants with small tusks are relatively young they would also tend to be healthy and not as vulnerable to disease as old individuals.

DISTRIBUTION AND MIGRATION. Distribution of elephants in Uganda for the years 1929 and 1959 is presented graphically in Figures 1.1 and 1.2 respectively. (Some records varied up to 4 yr from these dates.)

In 1929 approximately 70% of all the land in Uganda was occupied by elephants; in 1959, however, only about 17% was occupied. The leading fundamental cause for this drastic decrease in distribution was the great increase in human population, which climbed from about 3.5 million in Uganda in 1929 to about 5.5 million in 1960 (Cole et al. 1962). As natives spread and infiltrated into occupied elephant ranges, crop depredations became inevitable and human activities were subjected to increased hazards. Consequently elephant control operations followed agricultural frontiers and gradually restricted the animals to diminished ranges. In some areas elephants were completely extirpated by persistent and concentrated control efforts.

Several forces of lesser magnitude also contributed to the reduction of the elephants' habitable range. Intensive hunting ended the seasonal visitations of elephants to the shortgrass–thorn tree woodlands in the Ankole

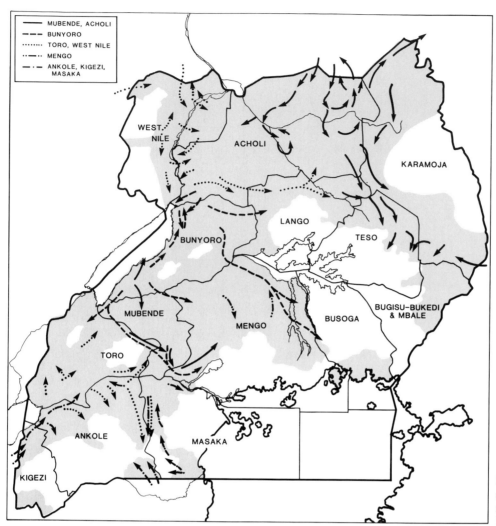

FIG. 1.1. Distribution (gray area) and direction of movements (arrows) of elephants in Uganda, 1929.

and Karamoja districts. Competition for forage by livestock in these areas and elimination of large mammals by the Tsetse Control Department in the Lango District and parts of Ankole and Acholi districts contributed to the reduction in elephant distribution.

The distribution of elephants in Uganda from 1957 to 1972 showed a remarkably close relationship to protected areas. If Figure 1.2 is super-imposed on a map that includes all national parks, game reserves, crown forest reserves, and sleeping sickness zones, one would readily see that approximately 95% of the elephant population in 1959 was confined to these protected areas. Notable exceptions were eastern Acholi, a part of western Acholi, and northern Singo and Bulemezi counties in Mengo.

One of the most significant changes in the 1929 dis-

tribution of elephants in Uganda was effected by changing or arresting migrations. The major migration routes followed by elephants, before and up to 1959, are shown in Figures 1.1 and 1.2, where arrows indicate the direction of the migrations. When elephants were widely distributed (Fig. 1.1) there probably was considerable mixing and interchange of individuals among herds. By 1959 a number of elephant populations such as those of Mount Elgon in Bugisu-Bukedi District, southern Busoga, and the Malabigambo and Tero forests of southeast Masaka District were completely isolated from major populations. Also, various populations once linked with each other along a broad front were by 1960 in contact at a narrow corridor. The Katonga Valley, the Buruli-Kafu (eastern Bunyoro) corridor, and the Attiak-Aswa (northwest Acholi) corridor are notable examples of

BEHAVIOR

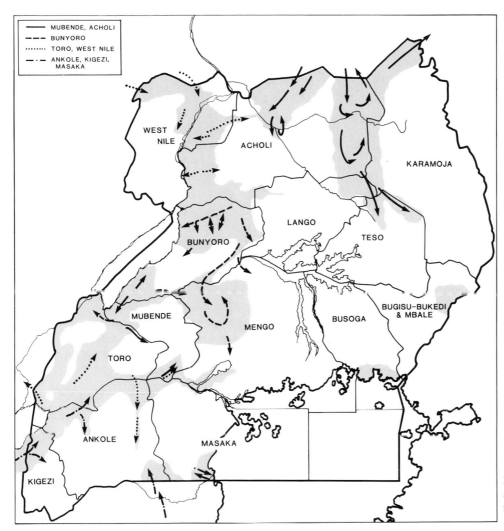

MUBENDE, ACHOLI
BUNYORO
TORO, WEST NILE
ANKOLE, KIGEZI, MASAKA

WEST NILE

ACHOLI

KARAMOJA

LANGO

TESO

BUNYORO

BUGISU-BUKEDI & MBALE

MUBENDE

MENGO

BUSOGA

TORO

ANKOLE

MASAKA

KIGEZI

FIG. 1.2. Distribution (gray area) and direction of movements (arrows) of elephants in Uganda, 1959.

such restrictions (Fig. 1.2). The herds of Bufumbiro (southern Kigezi) were in contact with the north Kigezi herds through the Congo.

Bunyoro District. Between 6,000 and 7,000 elephants were shot on control operations in Bunyoro District during the period 1927–1958. The consistently high numbers shot during these years are indicative of the relatively dense population that occurred in this district. There was wide recognition that the elephant population in the area that became Murchison Falls National Park and more recently Kabalega Falls National Park increased in numbers since 1912 when the area was closed to settlement as a Sleeping Sickness Area. In 1926 this area was designated a game reserve, and in 1952 it became a national park.

Changes in patterns of elephant movement in Bunyoro during the period 1929–1959 resulted in part from changes in population density within Kabalega (or comparable area prior to 1952). With the onset of rains in late March 1925–1935, a well-known migration of elephants started southeastward from the park, generally crossed the Masindi-Gulu road near Kiryandongo and Kigumba, and proceeded southeastward. During the late 1930s the movement across this road was temporarily arrested by control operations. After a lapse of about a decade, however, the elephants resumed this seasonal movement, crossing the Masindi-Gulu road during the rainy season, crossing the Masindi-Kampala road between 19.3 km and 40.2 km east of Masindi, and eventually crossing the Kafu River into northern Singo and Bulemezi counties of Mengo. Some of the Bulemezi herds lived temporarily in and between the Mayanja and Lugogo swamps; in 1959 a few herds foraged eastward into Buruli County (northeast of Mengo) to a point 16 km west of Luwero. Between 1925 and 1935 some of the herds dispersed through Buruli County into the Sezibwa Swamp of eastern Mengo going south to Kyagwe and Bombo, east on the Bugerere Peninsula (eastern Mengo) to the Nile River, and then southeast to contact the herds of the Mabira Forest (southeast Mengo). C. R. S. Pitman, the game warden in Uganda from 1925 to 1950, informed me (personally and by letter of March 1960) that the northern Bunyoro herds in their migrations during the 1930s probably contacted the southern Busoga herds via the Mutai Forest and Sezibwa Swamp. Such a migration would involve crossing the Nile River from Bugerere Peninsula into the Mutai Forest (immediately north of Jinja in western Busoga).

Nearly all available records for this migration indicate that the elephants returned over the same routes, and that the return movement generally occurred during the early part of the dry season in late October through November. On 23 July 1958 I accompanied Dr. W. M. Longhurst, a Fulbright Scholar conducting wildlife investigations in Uganda, to a point approximately 17.7 km east of Masindi where freshly made elephant tracks crossed the Masindi–Kampala road from south to north. Eight km east of this point elephant tracks crossed the road going southward. The variable age of droppings, trails, and browsings north of the road indicated that a herd of perhaps 50 elephants had lived there for at least several weeks. Natives living in the area informed us that this herd had lived there seasonally for several years but always disappeared when it got dry.

Prior to 1930 elephants from north Bunyoro migrated eastward into Lango fording the Nile River near Fowera and joined herds from Lango and southern Acholi.

Elephants from the Bugoma Forest (south Bunyoro) dispersed southward during the onset of rains in late March or early April following two routes. The first route crossed the Hoima–Fort Portal road between kilometer 40 and the Nkusi River at kilometer 60 into Bugangazi County (northeast Mubende) then either eastward into Bulemezi (northwest Mengo) or southward along the Bugangazi–Singo boundary. There some of the Bugoma migrants probably contacted herds from north Bunyoro that crossed the Kafu River. Prior to 1934 some of the Bugoma herds contacted the Lake Wamala herds in southwestern Mengo.

The second route crossed the Nkusi River west of the Nkusi bridge 59.5 km (Hoima–Fort Portal road) into

Mubende and southeastward along the Muzizi River, swinging southward around Mubende Township (Buwekula County) and finally reaching southern Gomba County. Reports indicate that elephants traveled over this route in June 1960 and that some of the Bugoma herds contacted Katonga migrants and herds from Lake Wamala.

Bugoma herds along the lower Muzizi River probably came in contact with the Kibale-Buyaga herds of Toro, and small herds from the Bugoma population occasionally moved down to Kaiso and Bukuka flats (southeast edge of Lake Mobutu). A widely known movement of elephants to Mobutu flats south of the Mobutu-Masindi road was arrested in the late 1930's.

A southward movement of elephants from the Bugungu Elephant Sanctuary and Kabalega Falls National Park occurred between April and September. This route generally followed the western edge of Budongo Forest into the southern part of the forest and across the Masindi-Mobutu road into the Siba Forest (in the Waki Triangle). Although this movement was arrested before World War II by intensified control operations, elephants temporarily reestablished their movements over this route after 1957.

This resumption of elephant migrations, temporarily arrested in Bunyoro, probably was a direct consequence of the increase and intraspecific competition of elephants in Kabalega Falls National Park.

Mengo District. In the late 1920s elephants occurred throughout Mengo District except near Lake Victoria and in the environs of Kampala.

During the early 1930s there were seasonal movements of elephants in Bugerere Peninsula, into southern Buruli, Bulemezi, and Singo counties, and into the Lake Wamala area (see discussion under "Early Records," "Bunyoro"). Also during this time, herds from Katulikire (north Bunyoro), the Bugoma Forest, and Bugangazi (northeast Mubende) migrated to the Lake Wamala area (about 16.1 km west of Kampala) where they joined herds that followed the Katonga River. There was a large resident herd in north Bulemezi between the Mayanja and Lugogo swamps.

In 1934 control work was intensified in Buruli and Bulemezi counties. Between 15 and 19 July, B. P. ("Samaki") Salmon of the Game and Fisheries Department shot 66 elephants, and from 20 August to September he killed 403 additional elephants. After his cease-fire, Salmon reported that there was not an elephant in Mengo east of the Lugogo Swamp.

A few small herds that still resided near Lake Wamala and in Muzizi Valley were infrequently bolstered in numbers by migrants. In June 1960 a herd of 243 animals was seen near Kasanda (approximately 16.1 km northeast of Lake Wamala); reportedly this herd had migrated via the Muzizi and Katonga watersheds from the Bugoma Forest, south Bunyoro. The last occurrence of elephants on the Bugerere Peninsula was recorded in 1947, and the last observations for Mira were recorded in 1951. In June 1960 elephants caused damage to Lukoma Gombolola, 42 km from Kampala on the Hoima road. Two bulls were shot and the native inhabitants, many of whom had never seen an elephant, flocked to the carcasses.

Ankole District and Masaka District. Until the early 1930s elephants moved southward from the Katonga River on a broad front to Lake Mburu (about 31 km) southeast of Mbarara. Some of the elephants spread into Kabula County (western Masaka) contacting herds that had moved northwestward from Tero and Malabigambo forests (southeast Masaka) into the swamps along the Maska-Ankole border.

Between 1925 and 1930 there were regular reports during the rainy seasons of Tanganyika (Tanzania) herds moving from the Bushenya and Nyakabadzi forests, about 16.1 km and 8 km respectively, south of the Masaka border into southeast Ankole and southwest Masaka where they contacted resident herds of the Tero and Malabigambo forests. There were reports that some of these elephants migrated to Lake Kijanebalola (29 km north of the border in southwest Masaka) where they joined herds from Kabula and Mawogola counties (northwest Masaka).

In 1960 elephants were reported frequently near the Tanganyika border. A herd of 100–200 animals moved back and forth across the border, spending most of its time in Tanganyika. There were no records for Kabula County in 1950, and only a few observations (reported as Katonga migrants from Lake George area) were recorded in Mawogola County.

Reports of elephants near Mbarara during the early 1930s probably represented migrants from Kalinzu and Kashoya forests (approximately 24 km southeast of the Kazinga Channel connecting Lake George to Lake Edward). By 1960 there were only local migrations restricted to the area between southern Kashoya and Kalinzu forests and the Kazinga Channel.

Resident herds of the Chambura River flats (south edge of the Kazinga Channel) probably contacted herds from the watersheds of the Mpanga and Katonga rivers in southern Toro.

The Bunyaruguru County migrations of northwest Ankole (near Lake Edward) were by 1960 restricted to local movements between Kalinzu and Kashoya forests and the Maramagambo Forest of northern Kigezi.

Reports of 1960 indicate that 1,000–1,500 elephants moved into west Mawogola County and later returned along the Katonga River into southern Kibale County of Toro. Herds that totaled from 200 to 500 elephants were recorded in north central Ankole (Mitoma County), the Lake George-Kazinga Channel flats (Buhweju County), the Chambura River area (exclusive of Ruwenzori), and the Kalinzu Forest area (Bunyaruguru County).

Kigezi District. Complaints of elephant damage in Kigezi District began in the early 1930s. Control operations that followed were directed primarily to forest areas where elephants damaged bamboo. During the early 1950s reports of elephants in bamboo forests ceased, and control emphasis shifted to agricultural areas in northern Kigezi, necessitated by resettlement schemes in this area.

In 1960 a resident herd estimated at 200–500 elephants lived in and foraged from the Maramagambo Forest (their movements have been discussed above). In Bufumbira Gorilla Sanctuary (southwest Kigezi) a resident herd of about 40 elephants migrated seasonally into the Congo (Zaire).

By 1960 the north Kigezi herds were largely restricted to the southwest corner of Ruwenzori National Park and Maramagambo Forest. These herds, which moved freely into the Congo, mixed with larger herds that occurred in the park below the Kichwamba Escarpment about 11.3 km south of Kazinga Channel.

Mubende District. Early reports indicated that elephants abounded throughout most of Mubende District, and between 1927 and 1936 an average of 270 elephants were taken yearly on control work. This average dropped to 36 for the years 1946–1955 and averaged 70 for four subsequent years. During the 1940s and 1950s there were numerous reports of elephants migrating between the Bugoma Forest and Muzizi Valley; some herds probably mixed with the Katonga River elephants and with herds from north Bunyoro (see discussion under "Early Records," "Bunyoro" and "Mengo").

In 1960 five or more herds (about 700 elephants) were reported in western Mubende; some of these animals probably came from the Toro Game Reserve bordering the southern tip of Lake Mobutu. Six additional herds (approximately 1,200 elephants) ranged from

Bunyoro into northern Mubende and intermingled with resident groups varying from 6 to 30 individuals (about 500 total). Farther east in Mubende, two herds totaling about 200 elephants migrated from Bunyoro along the Mubende-Mengo border during the rains. In the southeast region of Mubende, two herds (about 200 elephants) moved in from the Katonga River, and another herd of about 100 entered the region from the Muzizi Valley.

Toro District. Very few counts of elephants or even estimates of herd size were recorded for Toro District during the 30 yr preceding this study. Extensive forests and interspersed grasslands in the district concealed the elephants so effectively that direct appraisal of their numbers was virtually impossible.

Although statements published in the annual reports indicate that control work in Toro was more difficult than in any other district of Uganda, persistent shooting accounted for approximately 4,500 elephants between 1927 and 1959. Introduction of a special control scheme resulted in a kill of over 600 elephants in 1936. The consistently high kill under these conditions suggests that the number of elephants in Toro remained at a relatively high level or even increased over the 30 yr preceding this study.

According to W. O. Pridham, district ranger of Toro, there were five rather distinct elephant areas or populations in 1960. Two of these were in north Toro: (1) herds of the small Toro Game Reserve (at the south end of Lake Mobutu) that moved locally during the rainy season—some groups migrated east to the Muzizi Valley (Toro-Mubende border) and some moved west into the Ituri Forest of the Congo; (2) the Muzizi Valley herds moved northeastward and joined migrants from the Toro Game Reserve and herds from Mugoma Forest of south Bunyoro. There were three areas or populations of south Toro: (1) elephants from Ruwenzori National Park that migrated, at least until 1965, in the Ruwenzori Mountains frequently moving across the Fort Portal–Kasese highway about 13 km northwest of Lake George; in November 1958, seven elephants were collected close to Lake Mobutu near the highway and about 9.7 km north of Kasese; (2) Ruwenzori National Park population (Lake George area) that is in contact with the Park Albert Ruwenzori, and Kibale-Mpanga populations; some herds migrated between the park and Kibale Forest, which is about 35 km northeast of Lake George, and from there some migrated east and north to the Muzizi Valley where they interspersed with herds from north Toro and south Bunyoro; and (3) the Kibale-Mpanga

herds (part of the Ruwenzori National Park population) that traveled around the east side of Lake George and eastward into the Katonga Swamp (bordering the Katonga River). Some of these elephants dispersed into northern Ankole, others migrated east into Mawogola County of northwest Masaka and Gomba County of southwest Mubende. Some herds probably moved northeastward to the Muzizi Valley. The western extension of a railway line across southern Toro to Kasese partly suppressed the Kibale-Mpanga migrations, but some herds braved the railway line in their annual movements.

Busoga District. Before 1928 the elephants in southern Busoga District were in contact with herds of the Mabira Forest, about 32.2 km northwest of Jinja, and until the late 1930s elephants were recorded in the Mutai Forest on the east bank of the Nile River immediately north of Jinja. Before World War I these herds ranged toward the east and north and were in contact with Mount Elgon herds. By 1959 the Busoga herds were reduced to a single group of about 150 elephants that lived in the South Busoga Sleeping Sickness Area; they occurred only in the dense bush near Lake Victoria.

Bugisu-Bukedi and Mbale District. In 1925–1930 there was a seasonal movement of four resident herds (150–300 elephants) down the slopes of Mount Elgon to the adjacent plains of Bukedi. By 1950 there were no further reports of elephants moving down the mountain, and in 1959 only two small groups were reported in Suam and Bukwa valleys.

Teso District. Only five elephants were shot on control operations in Teso District after 1927. Although migratory herds of Acholi elephants that used to arrive in Teso during the early part of the dry season were reputedly arrested, records obtained between 1950 and 1954 suggest that a remnant of the southbound herds still existed.

Lango District. Until the early 1920s elephants crossed the Nile River from Bunyoro into western Lango District where they mixed with migrants from Acholi and Karamoja (see discussion under "Early Records," "Bunyoro"). Since then control operations increased until practically all migrations in Lango ended. In 1959 a small resident group inhabited the Ngeta Hill area (north central Lango) and Moroto (Aswa) Valley in northeast Lango. There the herd mingled with a few elephants from Acholi and Karamoja.

Karamoja District. In 1929 elephants from the slopes of Mount Elgon, from Acholi, and from northern Karamoja District met and mingled on the plains of southern Karamoja. The last record of Mount Elgon herds in Karamoja was published in 1935. By 1953 the herds from the Sudan and Acholi were greatly reduced in numbers and also greatly restricted to the extent of southward movements, and by 1959 Karamoja elephants were limited in casual herds entering the district from the Sudan and Acholi during the wet seasons.

Acholi District. The number of elephants (about 3,500) shot on control in Acholi District between 1929 and 1959 indicates that this district supported a relatively high elephant population during this period. Between 1915 and 1935, in the wake of sleeping sickness epidemics and the establishment of an Elephant Sanctuary and Game Reserve near Gulu, elephants increased markedly, particularly near the Nile River entering and also leaving Lake Mobutu. In 1959 there were four rather distinct populations in the district: (1) the Nile River population in western Acholi, (2) the Nile River or eastern Kabalega Falls National Park population of northern Acholi that migrated seasonally into the Sudan, (3) the Agago-Terrentenia population of northeast Acholi that associated with (4) a small population of about 200–250 elephants in western Karamoja.

West Nile District. At the beginning of this century when West Nile District was part of the Lado Enclave leased to King Leopold of Belgium, the region bordering the western bank of the upper Nile was famous for its big ivory. This was then the poachers' paradise, and among the well-known ivory hunters who hunted there were W. D. M. ("Karamoja") Bell, F. G. ("Deaf") Banks, and Pete Wilson. In 1933 Banks and his game guards shot 450 elephants in the district; he judged that there were more elephants in West Nile at that time than 25 yr previously. Intensified control and excessive poaching gradually reduced the herds until about 1950 when elephants reached their lowest numbers. Since 1950 there appeared to have been a general increase in elephants in northern West Nile. Transients from the Sudan and Congo tended to concentrate with resident elephants near the Nile during the rainy seasons when the total district population reached 1,500 or more animals.

Summary. Game guards and other control workers in Uganda shot 31,966 elephants during the period

The West Nile was famous for its "big ivory," like this old bull with tusks estimated at 59 kg. (*Photograph by John H. Blower*)

1926–1958. In addition trophy hunters shot approximately 8,170 tuskers in this same period, for a total of 40,136 elephants, an average of approximately 1,235 elephants shot annually for over 30 yr. Most of the 31,966 elephants shot by game guards and control workers carried small tusks that averaged 6.1 kg and varied from 5.1 kg to 7.6 kg; 47% of the tusks weighed less than 4.5 kg, and about 2% weighed 22.7 kg or more.

A district analysis of elephants shot on control shows that 67% of the animals were shot in three districts: Bunyoro, Mubende, and Toro. Control work decreased in most districts, but it increased in Kigezi and Busoga after World War II as a result of an expanding agriculture and the establishment of resettlement schemes.

When data based on distribution and migration of elephants in Uganda were plotted graphically, they showed that in 1929 approximately 70% of all the land in Uganda was occupied by elephants; however, 30 yr later only about 17% was occupied.

One of the most significant changes in the 1929 distribution of elephants in Uganda was effected by changing or arresting migrations. Some of the smaller populations became entirely isolated from major populations, and in some areas elephants were completely extirpated.

These drastic changes in distribution and migration were primarily and fundamentally attributable to the great increase in human population. As natives spread into occupied elephant ranges, crop depredations and hazards to human activities became inevitable. These observations forced the conclusion that the 1960 diminished ranges were still shrinking, and the best hope for preserving this large beast appeared to be by scientific management within the national parks and other reserves of Uganda and elsewhere in Africa.

Mortality

Every female elephant calf is a potential leader on its birthday, but achieving leadership typically extends over a long period of learning. Experiences during these years are unique for each calf, being fraught with innumerable hurdles and pitfalls. During the first year or two there is mostly play among youngsters and close guardianship by tolerant and patient mothers, but even then the mother occasionally employs early disciplinary action. The calf learns the meaning of respect and obedience early in life. Thanks to the mother's unmitigable discipline practiced resolutely throughout her life, the calf does not repeat its mistakes—repetition of a mistake might spell doom. When there are multiple calves in a family, or in a herd, there is much playful pushing, scuffling, and wrestling by both sexes. Mothers and closely related adult females stand nearby or even surround the youngsters during such playful encounters, ever watchful of danger.

Despite the outstanding guardianship mortalities do occur. In fact losses are highest during the first year of life (Bourliere and Verschuren 1960). Their low estimate was about 3% with about twice that for young animals compared to adults. I assume this places infant or very early-life mortality at about 6%. In contrast, Allan Brooks and I studied mortality rates in the vicinity of Kabalega Falls National Park during the lush populations between 1957 and 1960 and found a 36% mortality rate in calves up to a year old. This rate decreased rapidly thereafter until elephants reached an age of 12 yr by which time there was about a 3% annual mortality. Laws and Parker (1968) studied elephants in about the same area and reported mortality rates for up to 2 or 3 yr of age as 24% on the North Bank and 38% for the South Bank where our studies were conducted. Laws (1969b) in Tsavo, basing his studies on found jaws, estimated a

mortality of 36% for the first year of life, 10% for juveniles between 1 yr and 5 yr of age, and 2–3% for both sexes between 6 yr and 45 yr of age. These estimates are indeed very close to ours. How Laws estimated the number of additional deaths in the early age classes and which he added to his Tsavo estimates is rather vague. We knew there was a rapid decrease in mortality between 1 yr and 12 yr, and we also knew that the rate dropped to 3% during adult life; what we did not know, however, was when and how much the mortality declined during various intervals among elephants of 1 yr to 12 yr of age.

A second report of much lower mortality, particularly for the first year, was published by Douglas-Hamilton (1973) for elephants in the Lake Manyara area; for the first year of life he reported 10% and thereafter between 3% and 4% annually. This is closer to the rates reported by Bourliere and Verschuren (1960) than those reported to us by Laws and Parker (1968) and by Laws (1969a). Do the very low rates reported by Douglas-Hamilton and Bourliere and Verschuren reflect miraculously high-quality habitats, inaccurate or varying techniques, or both? I suspect that highly variable techniques were used to obtain these rates.

Mortality is more important to the maintenance of elephant population levels than reproduction, yet less is known about mortality, particularly quantification of its causes and functions. Even quantification of the mortality factors in early life are furtive and need considerably more study. Hanks (1979, 106) agrees and groups these mortality factors under the headings of predation (excluding humans), disease and parasites, accidents, drought, starvation, stress, hunting and poaching, and old age and fighting. I can add only one additional factor, snake bites.

Bere (1966) reports that in Uganda not more than two-thirds of the elephants survive the first year in spite of the maternal care; this reflects a 33% mortality, which is also very close to our estimate of 36% mortality from birth to 1-yr-olds.

I personally witnessed three cases of mortality to elephant calves: one by tumbling into a hole dug by mining prospectors, a short distance off the south edge of Kabalega Falls National Park; the second was attributed to lion predation. The late David Sheldrick and I were in Tsavo National Park (East), Kenya. Vultures flushed about 60 m from the road and examination showed much fresh blood and trampled vegetation; obviously a desperate struggle had occurred. Drag marks led to three skull fragments, a lower jaw, pieces of elephant skin, and several lion feces. A lion had fed on an elephant calf there

Despite guardianship by mother elephants, mortalities do occur. (*Drawing by R. W. "Mike" Carroll*)

very recently. About 20 m further and under another bush was the carcass minus the head but otherwise mostly intact; rigor mortis had not yet set in. We immediately suspected a lion or lions nearby and hurried to the Landrover and drove about the site trying to flush a lion or more, but none were. They probably skulked into the tall dense grass and shrubbery about the site or had sneaked off at the sound of our Landrover. We were convinced that more than one lion was involved. The trampled arena was nearly 70 m wide and twice as long. The calf had been dragged across one end of the oval-shaped area on top of the elephant tracks suggesting that while the mother was being harassed (decoyed) by one or more lions, another lion killed the calf and dragged it away from the distracted elephant(s). We agreed that such predation probably could succeed only in a small elephant family.

The third death was caused by drowning. During mid-afternoon, John Milton of the American Conserva-

tion Foundation, New York City, and I were driving along the north shore of Lake George close to the mouth of the Kamulikwezi River when we came upon two family units close to the water's edge. Each family had an exceptionally tiny calf. The nearest family detected us and shuffled off rather hurriedly toward the lake into tall and tangled herbaceous vegetation close to and in the lake. I was amazed to see the mother of the tiny calf walk deliberately and unhesitatingly into belly-deep water, thus forcing her baby to swim. At one moment I saw an intermediate-sized elephant swim from behind an adult, and the tiny calf swam for several minutes before going behind its mother and out of sight. I never saw the baby elephant again. Because the calf remained out of sight for nearly 25 min, we were unable to learn how long it actually survived. When the family finally emerged from its watery hideout and headed into shrubbery bordering an acacia woods, the tiny calf was conspicuously absent. The little tike never made shore, perhaps getting entrapped by tangled vegetation in the deep water from which it could not escape, or swimming to exhaustion.

I tried to rationalize the behavior of the calf's mother: Why had she gone into water that forced her calf to swim, and while she was there, why did she not recognize the danger to her calf as it swam close about her? Did the calf remain silent? Why did she remain outwardly calm with no indication of excitement when she left the lake without her calf? The entire episode was completely contrary to what I had witnessed of a mother elephant's deep concern, close guardianship, efficient detection, and aggressive response to any danger threatening her calf. Today this observation remains completely inexplicable!

Other infant mortalities are doubtless attributable to snakes and crocodiles. I never witnessed such losses, but Game and Forest Department rangers reported seeing elephant calves killed by these reptiles. I noticed that among adult elephants that spent considerable time along the Nile River there appeared to be an unusually high percentage with shortened tails that allegedly had been bitten off by crocodiles. A stretch of the Nile upstream from Paraa to Kabalega Falls supported an exceptionally high population of crocodiles at that time. Although I saw elephants along this stretch of the Nile many times, I never saw them swim there, but I saw them belly deep feeding on emergent vegetation on more than a few occasions.

In discussing elephant calf mortality Hanks (1979, 112) tells of finding a very young calf stuck in mud at the edge of a pan in Wankie National Park in 1973. He

Mother elephants typically show deep concern, efficient detection of danger, and aggressive response to any danger threatening their calves. (*Drawing by R. W. "Mike" Carroll*)

Youngest members of an elephant group nearly always appear to enjoy bathing more than oldsters. Sometimes, however, youngsters expose themselves to crocodile predation when bathing. (*Photograph by G. L. Smuts*)

was with Frank Thomas, an RTV cameraman. "With a bit of struggle" the calf "managed to pull itself clear and came out and stood next to me." Thomas rushed to join Hanks and started filming as quickly as he could. "The miserable creature followed me around wherever I went. As darkness fell, we had to return to camp, leaving the elephant where it was, on its own." The film was presented on the air that evening, and the following morning several very irate telephone calls were received inquiring how he (Hanks) could possibly be so heartless toward such a poor, defenseless animal! The following week Hanks went on the air to explain that "two African game guards who camped nearby reported that during the night a herd of elephants came to drink. The abandoned calf joined . . . them and by morning all had disappeared back into the bush." Hanks postulated on why the calf was abandoned, and included the possibility that its mother might have died soon after it was born, and it could have been adopted by another cow. If the following observation from Kruger National Park has significance, perhaps the calf's mother (or close relative) was alive and in the herd reported by the two game guards.

While studying in Kruger National Park in 1971, I had several opportunities to talk about elephants with a district supervisor who had spent many years in the heart of Kruger's prime elephant ranges. On 9 August we were discussing calf mortalities when he related the following experience gained from rounding up elephants with a helicopter for culling; my field notes read as follows: "On one occasion all members of a family unit were darted except a calf that was driven to a nearby family for adoption. There the calf was thumped and pummeled severely and eventually forced to leave. Later it was found dead." This is only one such fatality, which is wholly insufficient for postulating a conclusion. Why did this happen? We know that an adult or subadult female in a true family will adopt and even suckle a calf born of another female from the same family if the biological mother is killed or incapacitated to raise her calf. Such a case was witnessed on 12 September 1958 near Butuku in northwest Toro District. There we shot two medium-sized females; all others from the group ran away except a large cow and a tiny calf. We assumed the large cow and tiny calf were mother and daughter, but the large cow was the calf's grandmother; the biological mother was unable to produce milk for her calf (see dis-

Elephants were seen many times belly-deep in water, feeding along the edges of the Nile River between Paraa and Kabalega Falls. (*Photo by John Savidge*)

cussion under "Matriarchal Organization," "Bonding or Fidelity of Families").

Evidently elephants are relatively free from at least some diseases that can result in serious mortality. For example, in some ranges of the African elephant, anthrax (an infectious and often fatal bacterial disease) has been involved in serious losses of elephants, whereas in some other ranges the elephants apparently do not suffer serious losses from this disease. Pienaar (1961) in Kruger National park reported finding a dead male and two dead females killed by anthrax in a 5-mo period in 1960. During this same period 771 greater kudu, 75 waterbuck, 58 buffalo, 41 roan antelope, 28 nyala, plus lower numbers of individuals for 16 additional mammals were found dead, a total of 1,054 anthrax victims. Pienaar (1961) reported that of the larger cloven-hoofed species, only eland, sable, tsessebe, and blue wildebeest escaped the scourge entirely. Government veterinarians checking for diseases at collection sites in the park, particularly anthrax and hoof-and-mouth disease in elephants and buffaloes, never found an elephant with either disease. However, out of some 80 buffaloes collected by park officials in 3 days, the veterinarians found 7 that were infected with hoof-and-mouth disease; these carcasses were stacked in piles, drenched with gasoline,

and burned in an attempt to prevent spread of the disease.

One disease that does affect elephants as well as other wild species is cardiovascular disease. McCullagh and Lewis (1967), studying arteriosclerosis in the African elephant, described lesions similar to those occurring in humans even though elephants do not feed on animal fats. Sikes (1971) concluded that cardiovascular disease was correlated with degradation of habitats associated with overpopulations and was not found in elephant populations living in balance with their food resources. Despite her detailed study Sikes (1971) reported finding no relationship of cardiovascular disease to age. However, Hanks (1979) and Dillman and Carr (1970) reported that arteriosclerotic lesions increased in number and in calcification with age, particularly in female elephants, yet there was no evidence that the elephants showed a loss of condition, even those with the heaviest arteriosclerotic lesions. McCullagh (1972) confirmed that the extent of the disease in the aorta was dependent on age but concluded that death from occlusion of the main coronary arteries must be extremely rare in the wild elephant. Perhaps Sikes used too few numbers.

Laws (1978) reported that of 2,000 elephants

16

sampled in Murchison Falls National Park (now Kabal-ega Falls National Park) in 1966, almost all the mature individuals (aged 13–14) were suffering from stress-induced diseases of the cardiovascular system.

Fighting

EARLY EXPERIENCE. Playful tussles of baby elephants within family units and herds occur frequently, appear to involve much fun, and initiate a life-long period during which experience is acquired in fighting. Nevertheless, these playful games, however they are stimulated, gradually become more competitive, and each encounter involves learning both offensive and defensive fighting tactics. Some youngsters appear more forceful and eager than others to seek and promote these playful encounters; such youngsters are both playful and devilish. Occasionally the most aggressive youngsters, after wearing down their subordinates, resort to a quixotic behavior of substituting bushes and other inanimate objects for youngsters in their continued attacks. These tussles among youngsters continue even after the calves grow older and young males reach puberty. At this stage the young females' fighting tendencies appear to wane, although if young females are jostled into combat they usually respond positively but clearly with less aggression than is demonstrated by males.

After reaching puberty, encounters among bulls are almost always of a mock, sham, or ritualistic fashion—head butting, tusk sparring, and head-to-head pushing. With rare exceptions this kind of fighting was seen only among adults and subadults gathered into bull herds; such fighting continues through life. While camped at a site where the Kamulikwezi River entered Lake George, the Kamulikwezi Area, we observed bull herds spending considerable time loafing and indulging in ritualistic fighting. Occasionally when several bull herds occurred there simultaneously, one could see two or even three pairs dueling at one time. Frequently a large bull was challenged by a smaller subordinate bull. Two different bull herds were followed and studied for frequency of fighting activities under conditions that appeared to be without tension. The first subadult, in a bull herd of 7 individuals, challenged adults four times in a half day; the other subadult, in a bull herd of 16 individuals, challenged adults five times in the same length of time. Neither subadult was challenged by dominant bulls during these observation periods.

Youngsters are both playful and devilish. (*Drawing by R. W. "Mike" Carroll*)

17

Young bull in a typical charging position—ears spread, head high, tusks parallel to ground. (*Photograph by Anthony Hall-Martin*)

Subadults invited larger bulls to fight by approaching frontally with ears spread forward and trunk either extended forward with tip curved downward or backward over the head. If the trunk extended forward, one or both bulls moved slowly forward until their trunk tips nearly touched, pausing as though deciding whether to attack or retreat. If the head and tusks were raised and the trunk curved backward, or particularly if the tusks were held in a horizontal position, attack followed. These positions are even assumed by captive elephants (Kühme 1963). If the trunk moved to either side without lifting the head, however, the challenger retreated. After retreating, a challenger either retired temporarily or approached another large bull without delay and repeated the threat postures. Encounters nearly always were brief, and the subadult was usually retired quickly.

Four encounters among subadults of equal-appearing size were observed, and regardless of the duration of their encounters, the intensity of dueling was relatively mild. Only a few challenges by high-ranking bulls were seen. Perhaps these dominants challenged to reassure and assert their dominance.

Why do young subordinate bulls challenge old dominant bulls? More than likely, the young bulls are trying to raise or increase their dominance. Such contests not only relegate individuals into relative rank order, but provide valuable experience in fighting. Combatants need not win a duel to gain valuable experience. In fact, a lost encounter might result in a never-to-be-forgotten experience that would probably not be repeated, at least not in the same way. Even if the bull knows or expects he is going to lose, when a youngster challenges an older bull, he probably challenges to see if his defense or offense has improved, thus allowing him to advance to higher dominance and respect among other elephants. Only through experience can an inferior bull advance in dominance. These observations entirely support those of Valerius Geist for mountain sheep studied in the northern wilds. Geist (1975) concluded that "in these sporting, sparring, or clashing matches, the rule is that, although the dominant may solicit the fight, it is the subordinate who starts and ends it. Why? Because it is the only way such contests could exist; with a reluctant subordinate, no combat can develop, and a dominant forcing a fight will only frighten off the subordinate."

The male African elephant mostly acquires rank in dominance by displaying tusks and by ritualistic fighting, and almost always while in a bull herd. Thus the species is assured that the characteristics that support or help foster survival are thereby maintained.

While ritualistically fighting in bull herds, elephants occasionally smell an opponent's vomeronasal organ located in the dorsal part of the mouth. (*Photograph by Roger Wheater*)

FIGHTING AND EROTICISM. Wildlife of the Kamulikwezi Area was very abundant, and particularly high in species diversity. Hippopotami came from Lake George to feed near and on shore and waterbucks, bushbucks, Uganda kobs, warthogs, and lions were common. Occasionally a situtunga appeared stealing through the emergent tangles off shore, bands of buffalo moved through the area from adjoining lands, and birds of many species added to the faunal diversity. Elephant families and herds fed on the abundant emergent vegetation in the shallow water of the littoral zone. They paused there to drink and bathe as well. Bull herds were very common and could be depended on to appear soon after 9:00 A.M. After drinking, bathing, and selective feeding, they loafed on the open shore where they could be readily studied in detail. There we first observed ritualistic fighting and the development of sexual stimulation as their sporting jousts advanced.

After several ritualistic bouts, bulls began to show sexual arousal; penises were partly unsheathed and readily visible. Sexual stimulation appeared to increase as fighting continued, and by the time a half dozen or more encounters were completed penises were prominently out full length. Both challenger and challenged seemed to become stimulated to equal degrees at any stage of an encounter. However, we noticed the swelling of male genitalia in dominant elephants, but never withering of the genitalia in defeated subordinates.

Elephants are not the only mammals subject to such erotic arousal by fighting. In the outskirts of Masindi, Uganda (our headquarters), and along the main roads leading out of Masindi, there are many shambas (small farms). Nearly every owner had at least a few goats, and as we drove to and from elephant lands near

After several ritualistic bouts, bulls began to show sexual arousal. (*Drawing by R. W. "Mike" Carroll*)

After completing a half dozen or more ritualistic bouts, penises were prominently out full length. (*Drawing by R. W. "Mike" Carroll*)

Kabalega Falls National Park, goats would occasionally be seen fighting. In all cases the participants were males, frequently with penises extended and tumescent. These bouts did not appear to be sporting or ritualistic, but vigorous all-out fights for establishing or asserting dominance; perhaps some were sparring matches following establishment of dominance.

Since sexual arousal tends to dull pain, it could serve as a reward and thus encourage aggressive engagements. Such interactions would foster improved defensive and offensive fighting techniques assuring that contestants would be better prepared for further fighting.

More important, these studies suggest that aggression and sex are closely linked in the elephant. As shown by a study of testosterone, once the elephant reaches puberty the testosterone level goes through a cycle from high to low. What is not known is the duration of any one phase of this cycle. What raises their testosterone level? We know that when elephants are in bull herds their mean testosterone levels are relatively low. We also know that ritualistic fighting is closely associated with bull herds, and that their frequent indulgence in these interactions causes sexual arousal and stimulation. Perhaps the continuation of such ritualism starts testosterone on its upswing, and once the level reaches a certain threshold the elephant leaves the bull herd in search of an estrous female.

I suspect that fighting among elephants is stimulated and occurs more frequently during periods of high than low population density. On Semliki Plain, where I spent considerable time studying elephants and where density was relatively low on the vast unrestricted range, I never observed elephants fighting, either ritualistically or violently.

INFLUENCE OF AN ESTROUS COW. Usually upon arising in the June-August dry season, I was greeted by a peach-colored eastern sky, but on 18 August 1958 the entire eastern sky was filled with dark clouds. We were nearing the end of the dry season, which is often accompanied with strong winds and rain. Today, however, there was no perceptible breeze, and the temperature remained relatively high. My wife Kay, our teenaged neighbor Gordon Martin, and I would make our planned trip to Paraa, the headquarters in Kabalega Falls National Park; the one-way distance then was about 89 km over a tortuous unimproved road.

Approximately 0.4 km inside the entrance and escarpment at the southern edge of the park, we rounded a bend and came upon five large elephants in a gully within 75 m of the road.

Four bulls, each estimated at 3,600–4,100 kg and with tusks, each approximately 11–18 kg, showed special interest in an adult cow. Although the four were of similar body and tusk size, one was slightly larger and obviously dominated the other three. Rain began falling and although I had no rain gear, I decided to follow the elephants and study their behavior.

With binoculars and camera I set off leaving instructions for Kay and Gordon to stay in place until I returned. I had no idea how long I would be gone. In fact the only thing on my mind was following the elephants that were slowly moving away.

The largest and dominant bull stayed closest to the cow. Occasionally he chased away one of the subordinates when it crossed his threshold of tolerance. Once when he was challenged, the sound of head butting and tusk clashing indicated the intensity of the encounter. Eventually the dominant bull moved close to the cow and, with trunk and tusks held lengthwise on the cow's back, attempted to mount. The attempt was unsuccessful as the cow moved ahead slowly with no visible response to the attempt. As the bull attempted to mount, the bull in apparent second dominance bellowed and rolled on the ground as though completely frustrated from having repeatedly challenged the dominant one to get closer to the cow. All was to no avail, the dominant bull maintained his top position throughout my vigil.

In spite of the rain now falling steadily, a light wind rising, and heavy clouds suggesting an approaching thunderstorm, I continued to follow the elephants. Forty minutes after the first mating attempt, the dominant bull mounted the cow and achieved coitus. The female's movements were slow throughout the 2-hr period of my observations; she remained passive during copulation. The entire act was accomplished in less than a minute. While the dominant bull was mounted the three male followers again showed increased excitation and the second in dominance again rolled on the ground. Time, distance from Kay and Gordon, and nearness of the storm impulsively urged me to turn back, which I did reluctantly.

While completing our trip I pondered the mating observations, particularly the relative aggressiveness of the four bulls. The dominant bull was slightly larger in body and tusks, but most important in my belief was a high testosterone level, which probably was paramount to his behavior. The second most dominant bull, which challenged and rolled, was the smallest of the four bulls, but why did he dominate over the other two followers? I could only speculate, but nothing fit the picture better than testosterone levels. I had seen similar behavior among bulls that were followed and studied before collecting them for a testosterone study (Buss and Johnson 1967), and each time the most dominant bull had the highest testosterone level of those collected from the group. If I could have followed this group farther, perhaps at least one of the three lower-ranking bulls might have been observed mating. My experience suggested that once a bull succeeds in mating, he leaves the scene quickly; elephants are not monogamous animals.

VIOLENT FIGHTING. Physical encounters among adult bull elephants occur commonly but vary widely in their vigor. Ritualistic head butting, tusk sparring, and pushing are most common; violent struggles, sometimes for estrous cows, are rare yet occasionally terminate in death. Evidence that some encounters do terminate in death is provided by the following observations.

Accounts of two fights (personal letter), each ending fatally for one combatant, were provided by R. J. Wheater, the former warden of Kabalega Falls National Park, where both incidents occurred. Visitors camped north of the main lodge heard screaming and trumpeting before dawn, and daylight revealed a dead bull in an area heavily trampled with torn-out shrubs and small trees. Park rangers tracked the conqueror and reported that he was large and was also badly wounded. Four years later elephant bones still remained at the site of this battle. On another occasion, a confrontation ended with one of the animals being so badly injured by a tusk wound in its neck that it was unable to regain its feet and was, therefore, shot by the warden.

Another fatality resulting from a fight occurred in Ruwenzori National Park and is recorded in the Uganda national park's quarterly report for the quarter ending 31 March 1964.

An extremely violent fight that terminated in death to one of the combatants was related to me by the late David L. W. Sheldrick, warden of Tsavo National Park (East), Kenya, after we had studied elephants at Mudanda Rock, a granitic formation adjacent to and overlooking a large water hole in the park. Park rangers observed a small group of elephants drinking when five others approached the pool, which is used regularly by large numbers of elephants during the dry season. Evidently a cow in the group was in or near estrus, for two bulls indicated interest in her. The bulls began sparring, apparently to determine dominance and "possession" of the cow. The sparring increased in tempo

Victim of the Mudanda battle. The three tusk holes were made by the enraged victor after the victim's death. (*Photograph by David Sheldrick*)

until a full-scale fight developed. After the battle had raged for a few minutes, one bull lunged viciously, driving one of his tusks through the roof of his opponent's mouth; the other tusk penetrated the chest from the front. The tremendous power behind the thrust lifted the stricken animal's forelegs off the ground. The wounded bull tried desperately to disengage the tusks, but in doing so exposed his flank, which proved fatal, for the aggressor was quick to seize the advantage and plunged both tusks into the doomed animal's body just behind the shoulder. The victim staggered a few paces and fell dead. After a brief pause, the victor, who was bleeding profusely from several gashes on the trunk and forequarters, walked slowly back to the pool and drank. When he had his fill he returned to the battle site. On viewing the body of his erstwhile challenger, he appeared to be seized by a blind rage, and trumpeting loudly charged, ramming his tusks full length into the dead animal's head. The two park rangers, still witnessing the drama, claim that the infuriated bull managed to turn the body completely over so that it was facing the opposite way. Encountering no opposition, the bull moved off and stood in the shade of some nearby trees. For the next 6 hr he mounted guard over the dead elephant, chasing off several groups of elephants coming down to drink and forcing them to detour a considerable distance to the pool.

The contest was fought viciously with no indication of which bull might win until the moment the victim received a tusk in his mouth. Both bulls had massive tusks of similar dimensions and weight; the tusks of the dead bull weighed 51.3 kg each and were curved very little more than those of the victor. The somewhat straighter tusks of the winning bull possibly gave him a little more "reach," thus a slight advantage.

Although the victor of this fight was probably the superior individual, both bulls were of exceptionally high dominance and superb physical specimens of practically identical-appearing proportions. For the victorious aggressor, success was gained at too great a cost.

The battle was observed from beginning to end and rather clearly indicates some of the fundamental causes for the horrendous confrontation. The large body and tusk size of both bulls suggests that they were not young and had very probably reigned as top-ranking bulls in their respective home ranges for a long time. Displaying tusks raised to horizontal position, which they undoubtedly did many times in their long lives when preparing for a ritualistic encounter, would discourage most challengers confronted with such formidable weapons. As these bulls grew older and maintained their dominance

by repeated victories, they probably eventually came to believe they were dominant over all bulls in their respective home ranges.

Should two such large, old dominant bulls chance to meet as strangers at a waterhole shared by elephants from two adjoining home ranges, the chances are high they would engage in a sparring match. However, would they quickly start an all-out battle? Not really unless one or more additional causes were involved. I believe that testosterone is a mediating physiological factor involved in raising aggressiveness in bull elephants, particularly when estrous cows are involved. I have seen lone bulls upon meeting family units inspect each cow's vaginal opening with the tip of his trunk presumably searching for an estrous cow. If there was an estrous cow, the bull stayed in the family until the cow was receptive, at which time they bred. If there was no estrous cow, the bull showed no further interest and left the family unit. When testosterone level was low, however, elephants tended to congregate into bull herds and indulged only in ritualistic fighting. Individuals collected from bull herds showed average testosterone levels below those of bulls from other social groups and particularly lower than lone bulls. Those collected while engaged in ritualistic fighting were relatively low in testosterone. We saw families chance upon several very large bulls consorting together as a herd; usually the bulls paid no attention whatsoever to any of the family members. These observations of lone bull vs. bull-herd behavior and the battles recorded above suggest that aggressive behavior in the African elephant leading to violent fighting is mainly governed by testosterone.

R. W. Carroll reported additional all-out battles in Tanganyika, one of which resulted in death to both combatants.

I was on an elephant hunt with two friends, Trevor Tierney and Jack Carlyon. We were hunting from a temporary camp about 97 km from Mpanda, southern Tanganyika. This was excellent game country, large boogas (flat, extensive grasslands) interspersed with forested areas, a great deal of forage and water, providing ideal habitat for elephants.

There was a large elephant population resulting from seasonal rains, which temporarily flooded the boogas resulting in luxuriant stands of grass. Also at that time the adjoining area to the north, the Moalla Mountains, was a natural sanctuary. This district was bad "fly country." There had been a devastating sleeping sickness epidemic some 50 yr before and consequently no natives inhabited the entire mountain region. Sleeping sickness was still very prevalent in the surrounding areas in which we were hunting. The rough terrain of the mountains and bad fly area precluded hunting safaris as well. The moun-

"One Tusk" dropped and turned his head, which caused the opponent to strike high, thereby exposing his throat for a fatal thrust. (*Drawing by R. W. "Mike" Carroll*)

tains could only be penetrated by foot safari. We had left our camp at dawn. The Wandarobo trackers had found several large bulls east of the camp some 48 km distant.

The elephants were in foothill country, rolling and forested, not frequented at this time by relatively large family units. We proceeded by car till we were near the place the elephants were to be found, then we continued on foot. The "Darobo" pushed on ahead to scout the situation; we followed at a slower pace. In less than an hour they returned quite excited and informed us they had made contact with three large bulls and a smaller elephant. Needless to say, the pace was quickened and in half an hour we came up to them.

On stalking up to them we noted that the group consisted of one smaller bull, 15–20 yr of age, and three large bulls in the 45–55 age range. Two of the large ones were engaged in a mild shoving contest. As we watched, planning our strategy, the tussle grew more intense. We decided to watch them a bit more and see what might develop. The small bull and the other large one were feeding and paying no heed to the scuffle.

The scuffle soon escalated into a fight. Suddenly one bull made a vicious thrust; his tusk slid past his opponent's guard ripping the hide of his shoulder. At this the wounded bull made a deep roaring growl and quickly charged back almost knocking his opponent off his feet. The tussle was now a full-scale

battle. The two by-standers at this time began moving away. Trevor followed them and shot the large one. He was no more than 0.4 km away and the sound of the shot was very clear, but the contestants either did not hear the shot or ignored it.

The noise made by the two contestants was terrific. The battleground was about an acre in extent. They continued charging each other, parrying with their tusks, growling, and screaming. The brute force of the charges was amazing. At the end of a seemingly long time, both bulls were bloody from the wounds about their heads, necks, and shoulders, but nothing seemed very debilitating. That they could carry on seemed incredible. They indeed carried on for still another long period without any let up or showing any signs of fatigue.

Then once again they crashed together, and as their tusks engaged one gave a mighty twist with his head, catching his opponent's tusk about midlength and broke it off. This seemed to give one bull an advantage, but it did not deter "One Tusk" although he thereafter took a great deal of punishment, losing much blood from two large wounds in his chest.

Sparring continued but was uneven and difficult with just the one tusk, but suddenly he dropped his head, turning it at the same time, thus aiming his tusk at his opponent's throat. Dropping his head allowed his opponent's tusks to go high on his head, tearing a terrible gash above his eye and ripping a great hole in his ear. But that one tusk thrust home and caught his opponent in the throat, going deep. With a tremendous heave One Tusk raised his head, lifted the impaled bull off his front feet, and ripped a great hole in his neck. As he caught his balance his guard dropped, and again the one tusk went home, this time through the trunk and deep into the head. Both elephants went down to their knees.

The one tusker immediately arose, tossed his head, and again thrust his tusk deep into the head of his opponent. With this blow the stricken bull went over on his side, feet flaying the air. One Tusk quickly stepped around and repeatedly drove his tusk into the fallen bull's back, all the while trumpeting and screaming.

After the last thrust he backed away several steps, turned still trumpeting, and started to move away. Although he was bleeding badly from chest wounds, he suddenly turned and charged back to the fallen victim, repeatedly goring him. This goring continued for nearly an hour—going off, then turning and rushing back to again savage the downed bull, trumpeting loudly. He was now bleeding profusely from his chest wounds, and after the last attack he turned slowly and started toward a small stream. He entered the stream, drank deeply, and sprayed himself with water. After a few minutes of this, he started up a rather steep incline from the stream. On reaching the level above he stumbled, went to his knees, struggled to gain his feet, took several faltering steps, and fell dead.

Both bulls were large adults. The tusk of the one weighed 34 kg, and the broken-off piece weighed 18 kg. The tusks of the other weighed 35 kg and 34 kg.

Geist (1975) suggested that as long as rivals with dangerous weapons are likely to get tit for tat, there is natural selection for those individuals who settle dominance by means other than the use of their weapons and who relegate fighting to extreme occasions only. There is, then, selection for the cautious rather than the foolhardy, for the bluffer rather than the fighter. In place of fighting, one sees elaborate displays of strength and might, but only where dangerous weapons are matched against poor physical defense. The first and major reason, though not the only one, that combatants escape injury, is their great skill in defense. This is exactly the situation with African elephants with low testosterone levels—elephants in bull herds.

Circumstances under which the above violent battles occurred apparently were very similar: bulls were large with large tusks; a cow in or near estrus probably helped trigger the fights; and more important, the combatants, at meeting time, probably had high testosterone levels, which raised their aggressiveness above that of bull-herd elephants. The combination of such circumstances probably (and thankfully) is rare, if the low num-

ber of such known violent battles are indicative of the frequency of such fighting. Finally, an extrinsic factor might also have been involved in the circumstances: two large bulls could live separately as strangers on adjoining home ranges where numerous temporary watering sites were available during wet seasons. During a dry season, however, there would be a low but definite probability of their meeting at a permanent watering site should it occur on or near the perimeter of their home ranges. There also is the possibility of at least some other battling bulls having been in musth (a state of excitation marked by a viscous secretion from the temporal glands).

Although a victor usually emerged from most of the violent battles, both combatants appeared superb physically. Theoretically, these superior attributes included inheritable characteristics of high survival value acquired through a long period of inheritance. Transmission of such characteristics to future generations by both bulls would obviously be desirable. Death of either bull, therefore, would appear to mitigate against survival and contradict the purpose of fighting for dominance. Dominance determination should, seemingly, be a rigorous contest to establish superiority without reducing the opportunity for transmitting characteristics of high survival value.

Moss (1983), in studies of estrous behavior and fe-

Was this big bull injured in a violent battle? Note the prominent back bone, short tail, and deep ear laceration. (*Photograph by John Savidge*)

How do elephants get "lop-eared"? The broken tusk of this bull suggests that perhaps a violent fight caused his ear problem. (*Drawing by R. W. "Mike" Carroll*)

male choice in the African elephant, states that "nonmusth males compete for oestrous females, but they are always subordinate to males in musth (Poole 1982)." Short (1966) in Uganda observed a female elephant throughout most of its estrus during which time she was mated by many different bulls. Initially there was little competition among bulls for the cow, but as estrus wore on, fighting broke out and eventually one bull established dominance, driving the others away. This bull showed no discharge from its temporal gland.

Matriarchal Organization

BONDING OR FIDELITY OF FAMILIES. Recognition of an elephant family was reported more than 100 yr ago. Sir J. Emerson Tennent in his book *The Wild Elephant*, published in 1867, reported that "a *herd* of elephants is a family, not a group whom accident or attachment may have induced to associate together." Very little new information on the concept of an elephant family was published during the following one-half century, primarily because very little research was conducted on elephants during that time. Thereafter as research on both the African and Asian elephants progressed, knowl-

edge of elephant family life gradually accumulated. Today we recognize that the elephant's longevity of over 50 yr provides for a long period of development and learning in which members develop lasting and tightly bonded families. Loyalty and devotion are paramount among family members, setting an example for today's human society.

The closest bonding seems to exist between the dam and the first two filial generations, with a mother's attachment to her daughter or son being no stronger than to her grandchildren. For example, I saw a matriarch exhibit exceptionally aggressive behavior when I collected her subadult son (probably her first progeny), and 17 days later she showed equally aggressive behavior when I collected her grandchild.

My wife, my headman Camilo, and the six other members of my seven assistants were with me when we first contacted this aggressive leader and her family. We were hunting for our 35th elephant as we headed for the south entrance of Kabalega Falls National Park via the Masindi-Paraa road. The narrow 89-km unimproved road meandered through excellent elephant range of grasslands interspersed with woodlands bordering the south side of the park. Streams throughout this range provided year-round water for all animal life. This was my main collecting area. Most of the 104 elephants collected in Bunyoro District between July 1958 and June 1959 were taken from this area. On days when all went well, I collected at least one and up to six elephants, depending mostly on how many villagers lined up on their bikes behind my Landrover. They represented my labor force. A half dozen villagers meant that I could collect two or three elephants, if I could find the elephants early enough to allow reasonable time to complete measuring, dissecting, weighing, recording data, and fixing tissues. With about 25 villagers, five or six necropsies could be completed. My seven-man crew could supervise a maximum of 25 laborers; more merely added confusion. The men had their meat sacks and pangas (large chopping knives) neatly secured to the carrier over the bike's hind wheel with a rubber binder fashioned from an inner tube. Thus prepared the bike was ready for its owner to leap aboard and fall in behind my Landrover. When I asked my crew how these men knew I was coming, they simply replied that "the bush telegraph works well," meaning that signals were sent ahead by drum beats like a true telegraph system—the message was, "Bwana tembo happa" (Sir elephant here). The system worked well indeed.

The villagers' interest was to fill their meat sacks with as much elephant meat as their bikes would support (occasionally a bit more). Meat was their payment for services rendered. However, no matter how hot the sun beat down or how late they worked, no one was allowed to take his share until all necropsies were completed and Camilo gave them the word that all was completed. Then the pangas really flew! Some of the men cut wooden stakes and poles about 1–2 m long and improvised racks for curing their meat, which involved part smoking and part roasting until 23 kg of raw meat was reduced to about 9 kg. The meat was then sacked and lashed to the bike carriers. Some men carried a sack of meat on their heads; little protein was left behind. I often wondered how the vultures and hyenas sustained themselves.

As we drove close to the park boundary on the Masindi-Paraa road, we saw a small group of elephants in shoulder-high grass less than 200 m from us. Camilo and I left Kay and the crew in the Landrover while we started our approach to the elephants. This was easy for the tallgrass provided excellent cover to within 25 m of the family of five. Nevertheless, we carefully watched the small sack of ashes (upepo, Swahili for wind) that Camilo used for testing wind direction (two flicks of his wrist produced two puffs of smokelike ashes that drifted downwind). We kept the very light breeze in our faces. I slowly pointed to a subadult bull and nodded; Camilo understood my signal—that was the bull we would shoot. My instructions on all but emergency situations were that I would shoot first, and if the elephant did not drop dead on the spot Camilo would then shoot. At the crack of my rifle the bull dropped in his tracks. The large matriarch then put on one of the most aggressive demonstrations of charging that I ever saw, posturing over the dead bull, trumpeting, and trying to lift the bull to his feet. Most impressive was her furious charges in three different directions. The third charge was headed directly at us. Fortunately there was a termite mound that we both reached in perhaps three long strides.

After what seemed a long time, we retreated to a safer distance and watched her continued performance for perhaps another 10 min. We then returned to the Landrover and our crew.

We drove slowly toward the dead bull, watching carefully to be sure the matriarch had departed with her survivors. We paused briefly to look and listen before getting out to obtain the information that we recorded for all collected elephants.

The bull's weight was 2,767 kg, height at shoulders was 250 cm, and the status of his fourth molars suggested an age between 10 and 12 yr. He was definitely a family bull that had not yet been driven out of the unit.

About 2 wk later we chanced upon the four remain-

ing elephants of this family within 1.6 km of their position when first sighted. The same crew was with me. I decided to try collecting all four survivors.

Camilo and I moved up until we could study the elephants in detail. We identified the old matriarch and two somewhat smaller females, but the sex of a calf could not be identified in the dense ground cover. We decided to shoot the two smaller females first, then the matriarch, thus allowing the old cow to put on whatever display this might provoke. I shot one of the females; Camilo shot the other, leaving the leader and the calf. The matriarch quickly rushed to the female shot by Camilo, displaying the same behavior shown when the subadult bull was shot earlier. Her first charge was nearly straight at us. The calf started to follow her but suddenly disappeared completely from our sight by tumbling into a hole about 2 m deep. We had the impression that the matriarch was so intent on what was ahead that she did not notice the disappearance of the calf until she started her return from the charge. She then found the calf and frantically tried to pull it from the hole. Even after circling completely around the entrapped calf, she seemed unable to get hold of the youngster with her trunk. The only result was caving in soil and debris at the hole's edge so that the calf became progressively more securely wedged in. Evidently she knew the calf was alive for she raced back and forth between the dead female and the calf, with continued and equally aggressive behavior at each site. Excitement and stress stimulated activation of her temporal glands, which were now secreting rather copiously. We decided that instead of extracting the calf she would soon have it buried alive, so we shot her. Digging out the calf was a slow and laborious job we had not anticipated. The calf was a female and was added to our collection (No. 48).

The first female shot (No. 45) weighed 1,529 kg, measured 211 cm at the shoulder, and had not yet bred according to the very small size of her uterus, udder, mammary glands, and the absence of corpora rubra. She was not lactating.

The second female shot (No. 46) weighed 2,132 kg, measured 234 cm at the shoulder, and had given birth. Her uterus weighed 5 kg, her udder 8.6 kg, and she was lactating freely and copiously. This obviously was the mother of the calf that tried to follow its grandmother but fell into a hole. (I was later informed that mining prospectors had dug such holes in their explorations across Uganda.)

The matriarch (No. 47) weighed 3,026 kg, measured 259 cm at the shoulder; she was not lactating, and her mammary glands showed no recent use. Examination of her uterus revealed a fibrous dark mass of regressing tissue about one-fourth the size of a football, which was never positively identified. Possibly this was an embryo in terminal stage of resorption, but fixation in formalin and subsequent examination at the College of Veterinary Medicine in Kampala resulted in negative identity. Possibly this unidentified tissue affected her temperament, but my belief is that she was innately an exceptionally aggressive elephant.

Obviously the large cow was most concerned about her daughter (No. 46) and grandchild (No. 48) that weighed 313 kg, measured 124 cm at the shoulder, and was estimated at 23 mo of age. Following collection of the first two females, the matriarch showed interest only in her daughter and the calf, but was not observed going to the other female (No. 45). The relationship of this intermediate-sized or juvenile female to the family remains a completely inexplicable enigma. More important was that the matriarch demonstrated that she was bonded as closely to the offspring of the second generation as to the offspring from the first generation, if one can use aggressive and defensive behavior as valid criteria for this conclusion.

Another case of close bonding within a family unit was observed in September 1958 near Butuku in northwest Toro District of Uganda. Our group of 10, which included Camilo and 4 of my regular 7-man crew, was sleeping soundly when Camilo reported approaching elephants. We lost very little time getting dressed and into our Landrovers in pursuit of the elephants. Camilo directed us ahead of the elephants to an ideal crossing site where he believed the elephants would pass, and they did.

Two medium-sized females, No. 12 weighing 1,481 kg and No. 13 weighing 1,361 kg, were collected from the tail-end of the group of 22. The rest departed quickly, except a large, old cow that stood close by one of the dead females (No. 12) and refused to leave. The defensive behavior this cow showed for the younger female suggested that the large cow was the dead female's dam. Again this behavior proved to be typical of an adult female for any immediate member of her family. All attempts to drive the cow from the dead female failed, and finally the cow had to be shot. We then discovered that a very recently born calf (No. 14) was with her in the surrounding tallgrass. We assumed that the large cow was the calf's dam, particularly since she was lactating and her turgid nipples were clean and pink indicating very recent nursing.

To our surprise, dissection and examination of the old cow that weighed 2,536 kg revealed a fetus, which weighed 77.6 kg; the nursing calf (No. 14) weighed 78.5 kg. Obviously the large cow, with a fetus estimated very close to parturition, was not the calf's mother, yet she was nursing and protecting it. Evidently she was either lactating when the calf (No. 14) was born or was subsequently stimulated to lactation by the presence of the hungry calf.

Dissection and examination of the young female (No. 12), which the old cow refused to leave, revealed a 35-kg uterus with the endometrium only partially healed from recent calving. In contrast, the uterus of No. 13, a nulliparous female of nearly the same age, weighed only 0.45 kg. No milk could be expressed from the mammary glands of No. 12, and dissection of her udder showed that she was not producing milk. Her right ovary weighed 50 g and contained two corpora lutea, which measured 22 mm and 25 mm in diameter; her left ovary weighed 28.3 g and had no corpora lutea. There was no corpus rubrum (a brick-colored corpus atreticum) or developing follicle in either ovary. We were forced to conclude, therefore, that this young female had given birth very recently to her first calf, and that the calf was nursing its pregnant grandmother.

Female No. 12 weighed 1,481 kg and measured 206 cm at shoulder height. The molariform status indicated she was approximately 9–10 yr old. Subtracting 22 mo for gestation results in an age at first breeding of roughly 7–8 yr for this elephant.

If we had not collected these four elephants, and the pregnant cow had passed through parturition and allowed both calves to nurse, a very confusing and misleading situation could have occurred. Anyone observing two similarly sized calves nursing only the large cow would have strong evidence for reporting them as twins.

Was this large group of 22 elephants a herd or a clan? Although there was no opportunity to study group behavior before or after making the collections, I believe this was a herd. I have seen family units of 10 members, but they were always closely bonded together. Regardless of age or sex of any individual collected from a family, the others stayed close to the matriarch that was foremost in aggressive behavior, showing close bonding of her family. The unhesitating departure of most survivors from this group and the aggressive behavior of the cow over her daughter while nursing her grandchild provide evidence that this group consisted of two or more families, in other words a herd. There is an outside chance that this was a clan, but how can one claim descent from a common ancestor without having at least some members of each family tagged or marked by a technique assuring individual recognition?

Another incident of familial fidelity occurred in March 1959. A family of 10 elephants was feeding and walking very slowly down the middle of a wooded valley. A second family of 9 elephants approached from the opposite side of the valley, and the meeting was casual and amicable. Some individuals paused briefly, lifted their trunks slightly, then relaxed and continued eating and meandering down the valley. In less than 5 min all the elephants had intermingled and were feeding and moving together as a single herd. They continued down the valley until an intermediate-sized male of 726 kg was collected. In an amazingly short time, the other animals reorganized into two groups; one family of 8 ran down the valley, the other family of 10 departed on a diverging course for the opposite side of the valley. Apparently the animals had re-formed into their original families.

The following week a group of 24 elephants was observed converging upon a family of 10 elephants on a savanna 3.2 km south of the park boundary. Their behavior upon meeting was very similar to the behavior of the elephants in the two families observed earlier, except that both groups were traveling rather fast and pausing to eat only infrequently. I was stationed with Camilo in a small clump of combretum directly downwind from the approaching herd. Luckily the herd was not massed closely as the animals shuffled past us. Soon after the leading elephant passed us they detected our scent and bolted with snorts and a few restrained screams. Some of the trailing elephants crisscrossed very close to us as they reorganized into the family of 10 and the group of 24 and ran out of sight toward the park.

While working in Kruger National Park during 1971, I had numerous opportunities to discuss elephant problems and exchange field observations with personnel working on culling operations. Ted Whitfield, who darted many of the elephants rounded up with helicopters, reported that elephants in a herd split into their respective family units when a helicopter is low over them, and an entire family is easily driven close to a roadway for darting.

These field observations of various kinds of herd disturbances provide evidence of the degree of family bonding. Detection of human scent by any member of a herd, shooting an elephant from a herd, or flying low over a herd with a helicopter caused family members to split from herds and regroup into their original family units. Bonding was too strong, however, for either of these disturbances to cause intrafamily splitting.

Bonding endurance within family units was forcefully shown during the period of 1970–1971 when a critical drought in Tsavo caused over 6,000 elephants to weaken and die. Calves were first to weaken thus restricting family movements. Bulls were not as critically affected since their family bonding is relatively loose and temporary; mostly they moved to other sites. Soon after waning water and food supplies neared exhaustion, older females also weakened. However, the close bonding among family members prevented oldsters from moving without their youngsters that were too weak to travel, thus entire families died.

Although large bulls remain in families only as long as one of the cows is in or near estrus, bulls do aggregate into bull (or bachelor) herds with individuals coordinated in their activities. Bonding in these bull herds is on a very low level, particularly when compared to members of a true family. Evidently bulls leave bull herds when testosterone increases to a relatively high level, at which time they start searching for estrous cows. There is wide recognition that when a family-unit bull reaches breeding status, and a cow in the family comes into estrus, the young bull is driven from the family by one or more old cows. This, however, is not the only way such bulls become separated from their families. In May 1959 about 3.2 km south of Kabalega Falls in Kabalega Falls National Park, we watched a large invading bull viciously attack a family bull repeatedly, driving it farther from the family at each attack before the young bull accepted defeat. On at least two occasions we saw them butt heads and thrust forward vigorously. Throughout the encounter the large bull dominated and pursued the smaller family bull when there was a retreat. We believe there was an estrous cow in the family of eight members, for the large invading bull guarded her closely during our period of observation.

The many observations obtained on bonding or fidelity of family members illustrate the degree of variability witnessed. On 10 September 1963 a family of 10 elephants was observed in Ruwenzori National Park. This family was readily recognizable by having 4 adult females of almost identical size; 1 had no tusks, another had one tusk, and the other 2 had tusks of practically equal size. Six of the members ranged in size from nearly full grown individuals to a youngster about 2 yr of age. No adult bulls were seen in the unit.

Thirty-five days later these same elephants were encountered at close range near the original site of observation. There was the adult tuskless cow and the one with a single tusk, but now the original family had increased to 23 elephants. There were 11 adults of which 3 were large bulls. The other 12 included 5 subadults, 6 intermediate-sized individuals ranging down to about a year old, and a calf less than a year old. The increase in

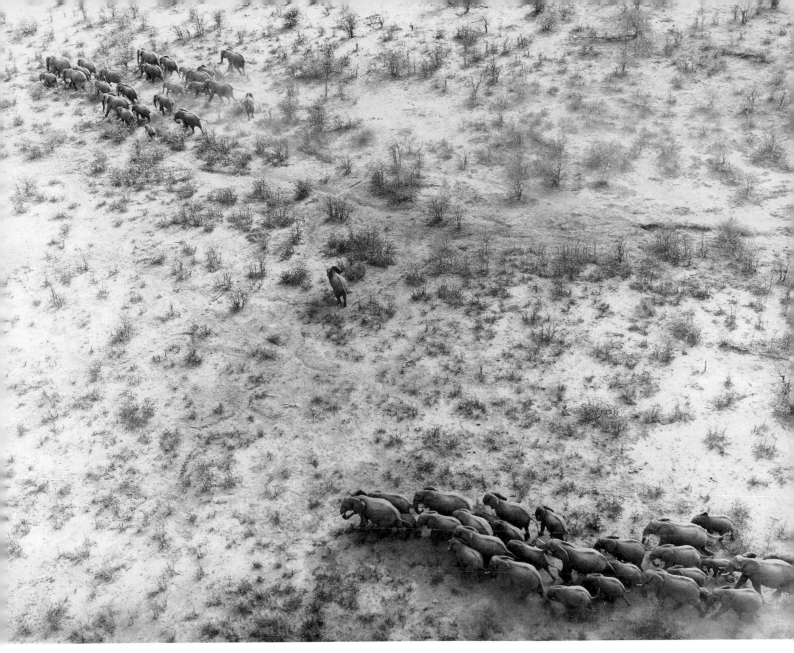

Splitting of a large herd into smaller units in Kruger National Park. (*Photograph by Anthony Hall-Martin*)

group size occurred in a relatively short time, probably resulting from coalescing of two family units plus addition of the three large bulls.

During the relatively high and dense populations of the 1960s and particularly on extensive ranges, when our records of family integrity were obtained, we noticed a wider scope of variability than some other writers reported. However, some families tended to remain intact. A second family of 10 elephants was also studied in Ruwenzori on 10 September 1963 in which there was a very large matriarch with a unique combination of identifiable physical characteristics. She had no right tusk, her left tusk was slender and very long, and about one-third of

her tail was missing. She was in a family of 5 adult cows, 3 subadult elephants, and 2 calves. On 14 September and again on 16 October this family was seen near the original site of observation. The short-tailed cow was present on both occasions, and the number and size of all individuals in the unit remained the same.

An unusual group of seven elephants seen during midafternoon of 30 November 1963 on the bank of the Joliya River close to the main road leading to Kabalega Falls National Park headquarters at Paraa. The family consisted of six adult females and a nursing juvenile estimated between 1 and 2 yr of age. The second largest cow was tuskless and nursed by the juvenile. The largest cow was pregnant and had crossed tusks estimated at approximately 9 kg each. Her left tusk appeared normal and curved upward; her right tusk also curved upward, but about 61 cm from the gum, it turned medially, close under the left tusk at nearly a right angle. The upper side of the transverse section was distinctly concave, being worn down at least one-fourth by her trunk. Four months later the tuskless cow accompanied by her youngster and the large cow with crossed tusks, now also with a youngster, were seen as a group of 12 at exactly the same spot (Wing and Buss 1970).

On 15 October 1963 a group of 22 elephants (6 adults, 8 subadults, 6 intermediates, and 2 calves) was encountered feeding at the edge of an acacia forest on the Kamulikwezi Area near Lake George. The 6 adults included 3 large bulls. One adult cow had no tusks and was in prominent musth. A very large cow, which proved to be the matriarch of a family within this group, guarded a 2.5-yr-old youngster and a calf with utmost care. On the following day I saw this same group going to water about 1.6 km from their feeding site of the previous day. Now there were 19 elephants in the group, which was conspicuously without any adult bulls. On 17 October I saw this group leaving nearby Lake George and slowly meandering toward a nearby acacia forest where they were first seen two days previously. On this third day there were 25 elephants present, of which 9 were adults. Sexes were not ascertained accurately, but the large size and head contours of several adults suggested that these were bulls that had joined the others. The elephants were kept under observations for nearly 40 min by which time two newcomer bulls approached and joined the group. Within the next 10 min the wind shifted slightly carrying human scent toward the elephants causing them to increase their pace. By the time they had traveled about 500 m, both newcomer bulls deserted and departed singly into bush cover, whereas the rest of the elephants continued into the forest.

Perhaps fidelity of family members should be expected to remain higher in small and isolated populations; however, families tend to remain intact. The elephants studied in both Ruwenzori and Semliki had relatively unrestricted movements at the time of my studies there. I would expect that there is greater opportunity for interfamily mixing and shifting where high density populations occur.

SECOND IN COMMAND OF FAMILY. Rain fell during the night and on 11 December 1963 when we left the hotel, oppressive fog shadowed the roadway leading northward out of Fort Portal. Two Landrovers

were used to transport our gear and crew. We were hoping to complete collection of pregnant elephants for the special study on uptake of oxygen by the red cells. When we reached Semliki Flats below the escarpment we stopped at the game ranger's camp and added two men to our crew, one of whom positioned himself topside sitting close to the front edge serving as lookout.

From the game ranger's camp the road headed generally northward. Just after we crossed the Wasa River a family of 9 elephants started across the road about 0.4 km ahead of us. As the Landrovers rolled to a halt we adjusted binoculars and quietly watched as the last members of the family shuffled across the road and continued eastward out of sight. Staying downwind we followed with the Landrovers at a distance no closer than about 60 m to 70 m.

Evidently the elephants were headed toward a swampy forest about 3 km ahead. They forged ahead until reaching a fringe of scattered palms bordering the forest, where they paused. The family leader, or matriarch, was the largest and probably the oldest cow in the group, but she tended to remain near the right flank rather than a more typically forward position in the family. A second female, nearly as large and carrying tusks of nearly equal size as the assumed matriarch, stayed closer to the center of the unit.

Upon reaching the forest edge the matriarch slowed to a halt, and so did all the others. There they shuffled about, and a few easy-to-reach branches were tugged off with trunks and eaten, particularly by the youngsters. The feeding and shuffling continued, but obviously the group as a whole was going nowhere at the moment. The leader and two other large elephants stood quietly testing the air with their very sensitive and multipurpose trunks. (With this fantastic appendage an elephant can smell humans at least 1.6 km distant; signal visually while testing the air with the trunk up like a periscope; trumpet an audio danger signal; use it for snorkeling, drinking, or bathing (water and dust); tug out choice herbs and shrubs; reach through a large clump of papyrus and select tender young shoots without seeing the opposite side; or break limbs up to 20 cm in diameter from growing hardwood trees, and bash over living *Lonchocarpus capassa* trees up to 38 cm in diameter.)

Stopping the Landrovers at the top of a gradually sloping embankment about 60 m downwind from the elephants, we again trained our binoculars on the elephants. The matriarch remained in her position near the right flank, whereas the second largest cow tended to move about more but returned to near the center of the

The entire group forged ahead until reaching a fringe of palms bordering the forest. (*Drawing by R. W. "Mike" Carroll*)

family. We began postulating about the role of these two cows. Was the leader the large old flanker cow, or was it the next largest cow positioned more centrally? We noticed that when the second largest cow moved about freely and widely, the others seemed not to follow; when the flanker cow moved, however, the others appeared to follow unhesitatingly regardless of distance or direction of her movements. She therefore must be the matriarch, but was she pregnant?

Identifying a pregnant elephant in the wild is not simple, particularly one in early stage of pregnancy. One of the criteria for pregnancy is whether a youngster from about 2 yr to 4 yr of age accompanies a cow. Assuming 2–4 yr represents a post partum period, she should then probably have conceived again. In the family we were observing, there were two intermediate-sized youngsters, just a little larger than calves and a little smaller than subadults, or breeding-age elephants. Their size and apparent age suggested that their mothers might be pregnant. Now, which cows were their mothers? Although the old flanker cow had neither of the intermediate youngsters close to her during our period of observation, we nevertheless decided to collect her.

At the first shot, the cow went down instantly and was quickly surrounded by all the other elephants. The two intermediates remained close to their mothers, one of which was the second largest cow, and the other a medium-sized subadult. Our collected cow had no youngster, at least not of nursing age. The surrounding elephants were highly excited and tried to lift the dead cow with tusks pressed low against each side of her body. This was to no avail—she slipped off with repeated attempts. The second largest cow was most excited; at one time, with both front feet on the dead cow, she extended her trunk in various directions as though trying to pick up scent of the enemy. Finally she screamed, circled the dead one, and trumpeted loud blasts in quick succession. This was a typical demonstration of behavior that I had seen on numerous collecting trips. If that dead cow was actually pregnant, we had to get blood quickly, and right now our chances did not look good. Without much hesitation we decided to charge the excited, milling mob on foot. With much shouting, clapping of hands, and shooting we closed in, which only further enraged the elephants and caused them to charge, leaving no question about their intention. We turned as quickly as possible with some of the elephants in hot pursuit; the others remained close to the dead cow. Fortunately the pursuing elephants soon gave up their chase, and we stopped. Quickly, we scrambled into one of the Landrovers and charged while shouting, beating on the sides of the vehicle, and shooting into the air or into the ground close enough to the elephants so that debris and clods of earth ricocheted against the surging beasts. This kind of charge was successful; the elephants began leaving, which bolstered our confidence and spurred us into greater effort with more shouting and continued shooting.

As the elephants left the scene, we noticed that the second largest cow that showed exceptionally high excitation and was observed staying near the center of the family was now leading the others away; she, with her youngster close at heel, was serving as leader. I believe she was the oldest daughter of the cow we had killed, if I interpreted her behavior correctly while she demonstrated about the dead cow. We watched the new leader and the departing elephants until they were out of sight and then started our examination of the old cow (No. 141).

Weight, measurements, and all observations were recorded. Before necropsy, we noticed that the udder was large, weighing 7.4 kg; she was lactating freely, but the nipples showed no recent use. Necropsy squelched our hopes for blood samples—the cow was not pregnant. We also found a 56-g right ovary with two corpora lutea that measured 14 mm and 15 mm in diameter; the left ovary weighed 64 g and contained no corpora lutea; both ovaries contained numerous developing follicles up to 10 mm in diameter. The small, 5.9-kg uterus was unusual in several ways: Although without adhesions, a hyperemic area of 1.5 cm in width occurred over the fundus where the cornu divide; there were three constrictions—one on each cornus and the opening into the uterus was constricted enough to resist insertion of a finger. The endometrium of the uterus appeared glistening, exuberant, and hyperplastic. The large corpora lutea and the appearance of the uterus suggested that she had aborted. The small uterine opening and relatively small but edematous status of the uterus did not support early postnatal or early infant mortality. I believe the loss of her fetus was attributable to abortion; there is a remote possibility, however, that an extra-uterine pregnancy caused the anomalous situation.

Both eyes were defective. The very thin, amber-colored, shriveled, and irregularly edged lens of the right eye indicated blindness. The lens of the left eye was also abnormal, being slightly smaller (mostly thinner) than normal with an irregular edge. The center of the left lens had a milky appearance suggesting a cataract. She probably could see from her left eye, but not well.

We did not obtain blood samples from this old female, but several new observations emerged. Evidently the blindness in her right eye and the poor visibility in her left eye caused her atypical right flank position in the family unit. For there she could probably best see all members of the family and thus facilitate her leadership role. Perhaps she was getting assistance from her daughter, the second in command, which possibly increased as time went by. After all, in a matriarchal system assistance in training of the young is exercised by practically all but the very youngest members in the family. That is, each elephant is trained by all the older members, not only by the leader; therefore it seems very reasonable to assume that there is a second-in-command in family units.

I believe there is a high probability that most or all families do have a subleader or second-in-command for leadership. In addition to the experience of the partially blind old cow that was collected, I collected entirely healthy leaders and subsequently searched for the residual family members. When I was fortunate enough to find such a group, I followed them and tried to ascertain whether they were actually under leadership; in each case they were! The second-in-command was a female and oldest of the survivors.

ASSISTING WOUNDED OR DYING ELEPHANTS.

Numerous popular reports have been published of elephants coming to the assistance of a wounded or dying elephant, apparently trying to protect or help it escape. I witnessed more than a few such episodes, of which two were exceptional.

The first case of unusual behavior associated with an injured elephant occurred in November 1958 close to the Sonso River on Lake Mobutu Flats. We were searching for an elephant to collect and the crew of 10 was sandwiched with our gear into two Landrovers. We were returning from Sonso Falls and were about 6.5 km downstream from the falls on the north side of the river when we heard and then saw a huge aggregation of elephants on the south shore traveling slowly, feeding, and milling about. Evidently this area is a traditional stronghold of the African elephant—both in numbers of animals and size of the ivory. Gatherings of over 1,200 strong are not uncommon (Kinloch 1972).

We studied our herd for 3 hr, during which time there was hardly a moment without trumpeting, rumbling, grunting, or purring. We stopped and climbed nearby trees to facilitate observing, particularly counting. There were at least a thousand elephants, the largest herd I had seen. When they turned and started across the river toward us, we scrambled down from

32

the trees and took positions behind termite mounds. The elephants continued milling about, drinking from the river, and then started back up the river. As the last were leaving, I decided to collect a subadult bull, the very last elephant in the herd. John Heppes, the Bunyoro District game warden, and I opened fire almost simultaneously, but the bull did not go down. As he stumbled toward the river, several large cows quickly came to his assistance closing in tightly about him, thus preventing further shooting. As the cripple and his assistants crashed into the river, several screams sounded from the herd as it thundered off in a great cloud of dust. The bull and assisting cows plunged completely out of sight, leaving me with very uncomfortable thoughts and standing helplessly on the bank. Rolling, swirling water and a few bloody bubbles surfaced over the submerged beasts. Much to my surprise the whole mass of elephants heaved to the surface, moved toward the opposite bank, staggered ashore, and disappeared into the thickets. Again there was no chance to shoot. John, Camilo (my head man), and two porters took off on the track, but they returned within a half hour and reported no luck. The wounded elephant left a bloody track for only a short distance, then his tracks merged with the others and further following became a more difficult problem. The herd was headed toward the escarpment close to Sonso Falls, and ultimately probably the Budongo Forest, another 1.6 km ahead beyond the falls. We held a brief discussion, selected two of the most experienced and dependable porters, and gave them orders to follow the elephants until they found the dead one. They would return to our base camp only after recovering the two tusks. That happened 2 days later; the bull had traveled a long distance, ending up in the deepest and most remote part of Budongo Forest.

The second case occurred in July 1963 when one of the first attempts was made to immobilize an elephant using Etorphine (M-99), a concentrated form of morphine. With me was Dr. Cecil P. Luck, professor of physiology, Makerere College, Kampala, Uganda, who would do the immobilizing. The syringes, loaded for a small elephant, would be shot from a crossbow.

We left camp on the lower reaches of the Waisoke River of Mobutu Flats in early morning and headed upstream in search of a small family unit with at least one small elephant. We found three family units before noon, but all were too large. Finally we came upon a family of 14 elephants, about 9.6 km east of Lake Mobutu, all gathered closely into the shade of a large fig tree close to the river. We decided to move downwind and across the river to the opposite bank from the ele-

phants and work our way within darting range near the top of the riverbank. Our position was about 5 m above and 25 m from the elephants. A small elephant on our side of the family was the first target.

The first syringe-carrying arrow (dart) was shot at a small elephant, but a subadult female lowered her head just in time to be struck in her forehead. She went down in 6 min, got up 3 min later, went down again in 30 min, after which she stayed down in an immobilized status for 1 hr and 45 min; I saw no more ear movement, she was dead.

Two intermediate or juvenile elephants were also darted soon after the cow was accidentally struck with the first dart. No. 2 was struck about midway between its head and tail, 20 cm to one side of its backbone; its weight was estimated at 907 kg. This youngster went down in 7 min, gained its feet in 4 min, and 1 hr later went down again for 1 hr and 10 min; it finally struggled to its feet and mingled with the other elephants.

No. 3 was darted low in the hind leg and not observed to go down. This was a female estimated at approximately 2,268 kg. One of the crew members reported seeing this elephant standing alone showing symptoms of partial immobilization; she had apparently received an under-dose.

Immediately after going down, the other family members surrounded and closely guarded the fallen elephants. When the subadult cow fell, the behavior of a huge cow indicated that she was the family leader—she screamed, raced to the fallen female, stood over it with trunk extended, ears cocked out, and tail lifted stiffly. The darted cow, with a small calf beside her, was evidently the leader's daughter. On frequent occasions the leader trumpeted and charged viciously to about 50 m in various directions. On three occasions the elephants started to depart, but each time the leader brought them charging back with much screaming and subsequent posturing over the immobilized cow.

The afternoon was quiet and hot with an ambient temperature of 35°C, and the elephants showed unmistakable indications of becoming exceptionally warm. The leader was particularly warm, and temporal gland secretion became evident 45 min after the first elephant went down. At the end of 1 hr and 45 min when the darted cow died, the temporal gland secretion darkened an area about 2.5 cm wide at its upper end (immediately below the pore in each gland) and at least 10 cm wide near the lower edge of the matriarch's lower jaws. Evidently high ambient temperature and stress of protracted excitement stimulated or triggered activation of

33

the matriarch's temporal glands. After 1 hr and 16 min of continual excitement and activity, she blew a small cloud of moisture resembling an aerosol spray from her trunk onto her left ear. Moisture dripped from the lower edge of her ear, and watery-appearing exudate continued running from her temporal glands.

At the exact moment when the darted cow dropped her head and stopped her ear action, the huge leader stopped her intense protective behavior, and the entire group of elephants appeared to relax and stood quietly about the dead animal. Without perceptible hesitation, the leader used her trunk to tug out grass and gather other vegetation with which she covered her daughter's head and shoulders. The other elephants stood quietly nearby. Ears, trunks, and tails now tended to hang nearly straight down; there were no fast movements. Also we detected no further behavior that would indicate concern for one of the family members.

After the leader completed covering her daughter's head and shoulders, she slowly turned and led the unit to a distance of about 366 m at which point she stopped all the elephants. Lifting her head rather abruptly, the huge leader turned back and came to the side of the dead cow. Her grandchild was still standing close to its mother. A large trunk gently nudged the calf toward her, but twice the youngster escaped, returning to its

The grandchild was still standing there close to its dead mother. (*Photograph by I. O. Buss*)

mother. The third attempt was successful; the huge leader with her grandchild safely between her forelegs returned to the waiting elephants. Slowly the family walked down the river valley.

To me the most notable deduction from our attempt at immobilizing an elephant was the almost instantaneous change in behavior of all the elephants in the group when the darted cow died. The final flap of her ear was like switching off an electric circuit. Did

After the matriarch completed covering her daughter, she slowly turned and led her family away. (*Drawing by R. W. "Mike" Carroll*)

the leader, which was closest to the darted cow, give some kind of low audio signal that was out of human earshot? Whatever the cue for the reversal in behavior, the elephants responded abruptly, ending their excitement and thus their concern for a family member.

As I pointed out in the Introduction, I was berthed with Captain C. R. S. Pitman, Uganda's first chief game warden, during the September 1961 IUCN Conference. While discussing assisting wounded elephants Pitman related that authoritative testimony of many reliable and competent observers, in Uganda and other areas, substantiates this remarkable and touching trait of elephants succoring a wounded elephant. Most of the recorded cases concern the efforts, not always successful, of cows attempting to help a wounded bull; in only a few cases did bulls come to the assistance of another bull, and in only one case did other elephants try to help an injured cow.

Bere (1966) agrees on this remarkable trait, and Temple-Perkins (1955), who spent over 30 yr in the Colonial Administrative Service in East Africa, reported having seen other bulls come to the assistance of a wounded or dead companion many times.

In 1950 Bruce Kinloch was to conduct an elephant control operation about 65 km southwest of Entebbe in the Lake Wamala and Katonga River swamp. After carefully organizing his trip, and taking two assistants, he set off on safari. After 5 days of rugged cross-country travel and search in the huge swampy area, the elephants were finally located. By climbing about 4 m up into the straggling branches of the nearest combretum, Bruce studied the herd with his binoculars. "Under one big fig tree there was a tightly packed group of eight elephants dominated by a very tall, very old cow. The old cow's head drooped, her ears were tattered, her features were gaunt, and her wrinkled, weathered skin hung in loose folds on her ancient bony frame like a damp, well-worn blanket draped over a hard, wooden clothes horse."

Beyond them were more elephants. "Some were just standing; others were shifting slowly and ponderously into the long grass and out again, occasionally idly plucking . . . a choice bunch of leaves, or a juicy tuft of grass. The latter they tapped fastidiously on their forelegs to remove the clinging earth before leisurely stuffing the carefully selected morsel into their cavernous mouths . . ." Nearby another group of six big bulls was seen under a lone kigelia, or sausage tree.

Since it was late afternoon, there was no time to lose, for some of the elephants were starting to show signs of moving out. Very cautiously Bruce moved

closer. The old cow was already on the move, at her heels a well-grown bull calf approaching maturity. She was clearly the herd leader, for the other elephants, apart from the six large bulls, were slowly beginning to converge on her. The whole concourse was swinging into formation to move up wind away from where Bruce was crouched at the edge of the long grass. The six bulls remained where they were; in due course they would follow, behind or to one flank, but with dignified independence and at their leisure.

Three elephants were shot and killed; a fourth one was shot in the neck and not killed. The herd was followed and again seen from a point overlooking the valley.

There, far below us, was the herd streaming across the papyrus swamp in a long extended line. Leading the column, wading steadily through the reeds and shallow water, was the old cow. At the end, and far behind the rest, was a small group of five elephants moving at half the pace of the others. I sat down on a termite mound, rested my elbows on my knees, and trained my binoculars on them.

As the picture swam into focus, my eyes were greeted with a picture that few people, even experienced elephant hunters, have ever actually seen. In the middle of the lone group of elephants was the injured bull. There was no mistaking him for he towered above the others. On either side of him, leaning inwards to support him with their powerful shoulders, were two big cows. Behind him, their massive foreheads against his rump, were two more cows. The whole group was moving slowly but steadily through the water . . .

I watched, fascinated. Only once before had I seen a similar sight. On that occasion it had been at night . . . on the Kenya coast. We had caught a small herd of bulls raiding a maize shamba in pitch darkness, and in the dim light of our torches [flash lights] we had seen them lift a mortally wounded bull to his feet and attempt to carry him away. Now I was being lucky enough to observe another gallant elephant rescue, but this time in the broad light of day. And all I could do for the moment was to watch and see what the herd could do once it had crossed the swamp (Kinloch 1950, 141–42).

We tracked down the wounded bull and put him out of his misery.

Observations indicate that hereditary relationship of the stricken elephant to the assisting elephant(s) is of paramount importance. Close bonding among members of a family unit is also of high importance. Since the matriarchs or oldest cows of families have had the longest time for developing the highest degree of bonding, the frequency of large cows observed in assisting stricken elephants is not surprising. The lower frequency of bulls observed assisting stricken elephants of either

Two large old cows assist a stricken elephant. (*Drawing by R. W. "Mike" Carroll*)

sex suggests a lower degree of bonding among bulls; they have a social grouping entirely separate from that of females. The members of bull groups are integrated functionally, but they lack the high level of bonding among family members. Why? Because studies show that testosterone fluctuates among individual bulls, and when individuals reach relatively high testosterone levels they leave the bull herd and start searching for estrous cows. In other words, bulls that have assembled into groups separate from families are more fluid and have lower bonding levels than do family members.

DISADVANTAGES OF MATRIARCHAL ORGANIZATION. Overpopulation and concurrent overutilization of habitat are more apt to occur in matriarchal than in territorial organization. An example is the severe drought of 1970–1971 in Tsavo (East) where an estimated 6,000 elephants and over 300 black rhinos weakened and died. This is a rare example of bonding strength mitigating against, rather than for, survival. Calves were first to weaken when water and food supplies neared exhaustion. Soon thereafter older females weakened, but close bonding prevented them from moving without their calves that were too weak to travel; thus entire families perished. Much of this, of course, could have been avoided by adjusting the population to fit drought or other severe climatic conditions. Is starvation of 6,000 elephants less repugnant

than shooting them? How much is lost when that many elephants and rhinos starve? We should sensitize ourselves to seemingly sparse populations as well as abundant ones. No population can maintain relatively dense numbers indefinitely!

Matriarchal organization lacks the "built-in" population regulation of territorial organization. When extrinsic factors such as drought, floods, fires, and erosion abruptly reduce the carrying capacity of elephant ranges, there would be a delay before self-regulatory mechanisms would start functioning and decrease population numbers to the reduced carrying capacity. The elephant's exceptional longevity would further delay change to a homeostatic status. Should adverse conditions continue retrograding on restricted ranges, preventing movement of elephants to higher-quality range, carrying capacity for them might very well shrink to zero. The key to scientific management is range status. If more forage is eaten or destroyed than is grown in a given unit of time, the range is overpopulated. On some ranges one elephant per unit of space might be too many; on other ranges of equal size three might not be too many. In other words, managers should study range conditions and obtain annual counts of elephants living on those ranges. Observations of decreased fertility, increased calving interval, or increased juvenile mortality are important. These are symptoms, infallible indicators of populations above carrying capacity; these are self-regulatory mechanisms in action indicating that the range has suffered serious degradation for an appreciable time.

Intraspecific competition is higher in large groups than in small ones living in territories. All animals in a large group are limited to the same quality and quantity of habitat while providing maximum competition, which is particularly acute when habitat is limiting. Such competition, as pointed out above, could result in decreased population size through increased mortality and/or decreased fecundity (lower birth rate through reduced egg or sperm production). There also could be a lower physiological status of the elephants that survive.

In respect to security from enemies, most mammals with relatively extensive home ranges are at a disadvantage when compared to territorial species that have an advantage of security based on highly familiar surroundings and detailed knowledge of escape routes. This might or might not be a disadvantage to the elephant.

ADVANTAGES OF MATRIARCHAL ORGANIZATION. Evidently the matriarch of an elephant family makes very few mistakes. She and the other family members can ill afford mistakes. The late David Sheldrick believed that matriarchs not only knew the locations of practically all watering sites within the family's home range but they knew precisely when the sites dried up. He had observed daily a family of eight elephants, including a very young calf, that drank regularly at a watering site until the dry season caused the water to evaporate from the pan. On the day that the pan dried up, the old matriarch did not bring her family to the site. She apparently knew there would be no water; she and the family were found several hours later at another watering site nearly 3.5 km distant. David believed the sage old cow would not lead the young calf to a waterless site, check the site, and upon discovering there was no water attempt to go on to another site. The calf probably would not have survived to the next watering site. She did not make this mistake; she went directly to the new site. When dry seasons are protracted into drought status and water is no longer available above ground, the last resort is for the matriarch to seek a river bed and tusk out a hole to reach water. After the family members slake their thirst, other animals utilize the water hole, a good example of mutualism. However, even these diggings sometimes fail; the upshot is usually heavy population mortality.

The story of the matriarch shifting from a dried up watering pan to one with water fits the matriarchal type of social organization perfectly. This organization does not lend itself as well to rigidly patterned behavior of lower animals. The matriarch must be able to do more than react to a situation in a mechanical manner. General flexibility of leadership organization lends itself well to higher mammals that have well-developed nervous systems, like humans, apes, predators, and certain ungulates. According to Odum (1971, 207) "aggregations may increase competition between individuals for nutrients, food, or space, but this is often more than counterbalanced by increased survival of the group. Individuals in groups often experience a lower mortality rate during unfavorable periods or during attacks by [predators and] other organisms than do isolated individuals." This might apply to mammals in general, but not entirely so for elephants. Although elephants congregate and form large aggregations (herds), if disease attacks, high mortality can result. Anthrax, a contagious bacterial disease, is such an organism and could have been responsible for the death of up to 1,000 elephants on Mobutu Flats in western Uganda between December 1960 and February 1961.

The observed elephant predation by lions in Tsavo (East) (see discussion under "Early Records") very probably would not have occurred if a herd of elephants had been involved. My guess, however, is that such predation is of minor if not insignificant effect to an elephant population.

Matriarchal organization leads to higher development of individual characteristics than territorial organization. The long period of growing up provides for increased training during the developmental period of young elephants. Experiences are not limited by territorial boundaries. The matriarch, being the oldest and most experienced member of the family, is the most important animal in a family in training the young; however other members also assist. Although in nearly all families there are several or more elephants present to learn from, on at least two occasions I have seen one cow with a calf—the start of a new family. Obviously, matriarchal organization allows for some degree of social specialization.

Matriarchal organization is spatially fluid as opposed to the spacial stability of territories. Elephants are free to move widely for food and other life requisites. Matriarchs not only know the location of watering sites within their family home ranges, they also know where adequate food is available; they can move their families whenever requisites become limiting. During mid-November of 1963 I was camped a short distance south of the Kabalega National Park boundary within 3.5 km of Igisi Hill waiting for the arrival of a team of physiologists. I had agreed to collect several pregnant elephants from which matched samples of fetal and maternal blood would be obtained for studying oxygen uptake by red cells taken from the blood samples. The dry season was at that time merging into the long rainy season. The mornings were mostly clear, even sunny, but by noon the sun was behind clouds and rain followed very certainly. One clear and sunny morning, I asked my top game guard Camilo, where could we find elephants that day. He slowly turned, tilted his head, raised his right arm, and pointed straight south where a thunder and lightning storm had occurred during the night; the storm had attracted the elephants, and the large old matriarch had led them to the rains. We went there and, true to Camilo's prediction, found several family units. The elephants had moved to satisfy some of their life requisites.

A hierarchy of social position is provided by the matriarchal organization; this tends to reduce fighting among individuals (see discussion under "Fighting," "Early Experience"). Once the order of dominance has been established, conflict among family members is mostly limited to ritualistic fighting. These social positions within a family are not easily disrupted by strangers trying to join a family.

Since there are both territorial and nonterritorial types of animal organization functioning successfully today, one might logically ask why have these two types through millenia of evolution not merged into a single social organization best for all animals? Theoretically, the best type of animal organization in a long-term evolutionary sense depends on which gives the greatest long-term advantage. Considering the great species diversity within the animal kingdom, from single-celled protozoans to complex vertebrates, the present two types probably provide the best long-term advantages to the animals living under them.

Bull Behavior

ASSERTING DOMINANCE. Dust drifted up from a thicket among shrub-dominated range, floated slowly skyward, thinned, and then blended from sight. A white-browed coucal called softly from nearby, and a half dozen white egrets winged about the upper thicket level, moving steadily closer. Elephants were coming. Without a sound the leading edge of the thicket parted, exposing the head and trunk of an enormous bull bearing

magnificent ivory. Closely about him were 14 elephants, all bulls and mostly large.

David Sheldrick and I were headed for Mudanda Pond in Tsavo National Park, Kenya. The rains had ceased and the dry season had already laid a thick layer of dust almost everywhere. We were about 8 km south of our destination when we saw the rising dust and white egrets topping the expansive thicket. We decided to pause and watch the elephants, which were probably headed for Little Rock Pond close to us. Luckily our position was downwind and there was an almost imperceptible breeze—we would probably not be detected.

On came the elephants without breaking stride. A layer of reddish dust lay heavily on each beast attesting to a long dry trek. Most impressive were their dark eyes, which appeared black and unusually large in contrast to their dusty coats. When reaching a distance of roughly 40 m from the pond, the smell of water apparently sparked their enthusiasm, for I noted a slight increase in nodding of heads and quickening of strides. They spread out and entered the pond. The larger bull was not the first to reach water, but on his way there he reminded several subordinates inadvertently blocking his way; to show that he was the dominant boss he gave each one a husky jab in the rump. The subordinates would not make that error again.

Obviously this was the Alpha or most dominant of all the bulls, for he unhesitatingly walked, drank, and bathed where he chose; the others recognized and honored his choices at all times. Nevertheless, throughout our period of watching there was considerable head butting, tusk clashing, and head-body pushing as subordinates were maintained in their respective positions while drinking; seemingly the subordinates were being reminded of their low rank. At no time did we see smaller bulls at choice drinking sites.

Their thirst supported our original belief that they had undergone a long trek. After the initial jousting and all the bulls were relegated to their proper sites, drinking continued until all were completely satisfied.

These observations differed from those of bulls seen loafing and intermittently feeding on the Kamulikwezi Area near Lake George, Uganda, where the subordinates usually challenged dominants; here we never saw a subordinate challenge. Dominant bulls do occasionally assert their dominance or remind subordinates of their lower rank, but this is different from establishing rank. Within a given home range most bulls are well aware of their rank. For example, watching three adult bulls about 1.5 km from our camp on the Kamulikwezi, I noted that the largest bull was closest to us and faced us for nearly 15 min while feeding. At one time the other two bulls walked close to the largest bull that stood facing them. The largest one made no overt movements or postures that I could detect, yet the bull coming closest to him definitely turned aside slightly, showing he was second in dominance to the large bull. I have seen these subtle kinds of dominance indictors several times; apparently elephants have a keen sense of their rank even within relatively large herds. The smaller the herd, the more clearly dominance is reflected.

For a long time I had suspected that in the African elephant there is a separate dominance order for males entirely apart from that among females. This suspicion originated while following and studying elephants for a study on testosterone levels in bulls. On these occasions groups of elephants, including large bulls, were followed for more than a day to be sure they were accurately classed into one of four social categories (lone bull, family unit, herd, bull herd); certain family units and herds were most difficult to identify validly. Collection of the bulls to measure testosterone was only made after social groups were positively identified. If darkness intervened before positive identification was made, no collections were made that day. While following and studying these groups, more than a few observations suggested that bulls had a dominance order completely separate from one for females (Buss and Johnson 1967).

A rather typical example was in a herd of 22 elephants close to the Chambura River, off the west side of Ruwenzori National Park. The group consisted of 14 adults (4 large bulls), 2 subadults, 4 intermediates, and 2 calves. After following this group from early morning until late afternoon, the close guarding behavior of the largest bull for a cow suggested that she was close to estrus. If by chance this cow and the large bull rounded a clump of shrubs and suddenly came close to another bull, there was immediate interaction with the large bull driving the other bull a "safe" distance from the cow. At no time was a cow involved in an aggressive interaction with another cow or a bull.

Another example of bulls asserting dominance was observed in Ruwenzori. In a family unit of nine elephants, two adult males became involved over an adult female in estrus. When first sighted the two bulls were involved in a mild fight. The bulls appeared equal in size and both carried approximately 11-kg tusks. One lighter-colored bull seemed to dominate the other; the cow occasionally butted either one. Fighting subsided, but 5 min later it began with renewed vigor. The cow

began to feed, but after 4 min she stopped feeding and approached the fighting bulls. The dominant bull soon mounted her but was promptly "unseated" by the other. Fighting was renewed and the subordinate bull was driven away. He retired about 25 m and had a dust bath, leaving the light-colored bull and cow facing each other butting heads and entwining trunks. The light-colored bull now had his penis extended and erect. The cow seemed only partially receptive; however, the bull finally positioned his tusks lengthwise along her back and, after following her about 10 paces, mounted and achieved coitus. Within 2 min all the elephants in the family unit were feeding peacefully. The six elephants not involved in the interactions remained passive throughout the observation period.

The only aggressive cow-bull interaction that I observed also occurred in Ruwenzori. A bull at the edge of the Kazinga Channel repeatedly attempted to mount a small cow that would not stand still. After pursuing the cow for about 4 min, the bull gave up and began to drink from the channel. The cow, meanwhile, moved rapidly away from the water and toward the channel embankment. Part way up the slope she met another bull coming toward her. This second bull also attempted to mount her but she fled. He then chased her for about 2 min during which time he made several semimounts. At this point, a third elephant, then of unknown sex, intervened. This elephant appeared to be a female since no extended penis was visible. She chased the second bull away from the small cow, which then escaped. After the bull left, the intervening elephant became passive, and was easily approached for positive identification as an adult female.

There were observations of single bulls happening upon family units or herds. At such occasions, the lone animal inspected each cow's vaginal opening with the tip of his trunk, even if a cow had a small calf. Although the cow objected to this behavior, she only tried to escape without showing aggression. In a family the matriarch maintains dominance throughout her life over all other family members, but not over invading large bulls searching for estrous cows.

As I continued these studies, my early suspicions were bolstered; eventually I became convinced that there must be two separate dominance orders among African elephants.

Finally, Bruce Kinloch's detailed report of a control operation conducted in the Katonga River swamp gives a clear picture of separate social organizations for cows and bulls (see under "Matriarchal Organization," "Assisting Wounded or Dying Elephants").

THE GRAVEYARD MYTH. Large cumulus clouds developing over the hills were blocking out the last vestiges of late afternoon sunshine. Tempestuous westerly winds from across the Nile pushed the clouds threateningly close and bounced our Piper Cruiser without respect for machine or body. Concentrating on aerial counting became progressively more difficult as the light waned, yet we had planned to complete the count today in the Elephant Sanctuary bounding the north side of the Kabalega Falls National Park. We were in the remote northeast sector of the sanctuary, our fuel was getting dangerously low, and our landing strip near park headquarters was about 81 km southwest of us. Thus our return flight would be with a quartering to head-on wind. The full force of the storm might very well hit us before we could land. We had counted elephants since early morning and were desperately anxious to complete the count for the day— we had committed ourselves to flying the cruiser the next day to Ruwenzori National Park for further counting of elephants.

We slowly climbed to a higher altitude to allow for better long-range visibility and a better chance for selection of an emergency landing site if that became a necessity. Soon after crossing to the south side of the lower Tangi River I looked back and down and saw what I thought might be bones of an elephant under a large tree. We descended and circled the tree; we agreed that they were indeed elephant bones, including a very large set of tusks. We marked the spot as best we could and then headed toward the landing strip. When we landed the fuel gauge read empty.

Early the next morning an attempt was made in the Landrover to locate the large tree and bones that had been spotted the previous evening, but neither the tree nor the bones could be found. On the day following the trip to Ruwenzori National Park, a short flight was made to an arbitrarily selected point on the Tangi River, which luckily put the plane over the large tree. The tree was marked more carefully, and the second ground trip proved successful. Practically all the bones including the two tusks from a very large bull were lying undisturbed, with the exception of a few bones that had evidently been dragged short distances by hyenas or other scavengers. The jaws with teeth and the tusks were loaded into the Landrover and brought to park headquarters at Paraa.

At Paraa a metal tag stamped with No. 165 was wired to one of the jaws, and both lower jaws were placed inside an enclosure with other jaws and skulls.

The enclosure was protected by a 2-m-high woven-wire fence and a locked gate to prevent losses to predators, primarily hyenas. Examination of the lower jaws and skull showed that the alveolar pocket, where all of the elephant's teeth develop, was filled with a honeycomb-like bony material, which is typical for old elephants that have completed development of their sixth and last set of teeth—there would be no more. The six sets of teeth, all of which develop in this pocket, move progressively forward in the jaw in orderly fashion. Even while being used, the teeth continue to move forward until becoming worn beyond further use, by which time the first five sets, in order, have reached the ultimate forward position and are dropped from the elephant's mouth as eroded remnants. After the sixth set of teeth is worn out and about half its original length remains, the animal can no longer masticate food adequately and it dies. This tooth replacement process is remindful of an operating Caterpillar tractor. When the tractor (say with six lugs, or six sets of teeth) is started and set into forward motion, the six lugs move progressively forward until the sixth or last one reaches ground level. The lugs move until the tractor is shut off. So it is with an elephant; its teeth move forward until the elephant dies.

In the case of No. 165, only about half of the sixth set of lower teeth were left in the jaws. On the left side six laminae remained; on the right there were eight. The sixth tooth typically has 11 or 12 laminae, each capped with an enamel "loop" for mastication. The most anterior or forward loops were relatively smooth and only faintly visible. The teeth were extremely wide attesting to the bull's large size—the left tusk weighed 49 kg, the right one tipped the scale at 51 kg. This old bull probably died a natural death.

Among the large and old bulls that have been accounted for in the Tangi River area was one known as the Tangi bull. Soon after the big bull died, his skull including teeth and tusks were removed from the rest of the carcass and transported to park headquarters at Paraa. There the tusks, teeth, and skull were carefully cleaned and measured (later the skull and tusks were mounted and placed in the museum at park headquarters).

The left tusk measured 3 m on the curve, 55 cm in girth at the widest point, and weighed 72 kg. The smooth constriction near its end was made by the animal's trunk in the course of many years. The right tusk measured 2.9 m long, 50 cm in girth, and weighed 66 kg. These tusks were the second heaviest recorded from the national parks of Uganda, and ranked among the heaviest known. The elephant stood 3–3.1 m at the shoulder.

The two very large, old bulls that died in the Tangi River area generated interest in the possibility of an elephant "graveyard." When I confronted park authorities they smilingly responded with, "Well we don't know about the graveyard bit, but this has long been recognized as a dominantly old bull area." I never questioned other park employees or anyone else about this matter. The "seed" of doubt lay dormant briefly, then germinated, and then grew when nourished by the following observations.

In August 1963 a third dead elephant was found in the Tangi River area. The skull with its sixth set of teeth was recovered, labeled No. 46, and added to the growing collection at Paraa. The lower left tooth had 12 laminae; the lower right tooth was presumed to be the sixth since it had 11 laminae, but the alveolar pocket behind this tooth contained 4 additional laminae that were nearly completely developed but not fused. This was very probably the beginning of tooth number seven. The left tusk weighed 36 kg, the right one weighed 34 kg. This was an old elephant though he carried smaller tusks than some elephants of his age.

The jaws with teeth from a fourth old bull were recovered from the Tangi River area some time before the Tangi bull's death. This must have been another very large and old bull judging from the appearance of his sixth or last set of teeth. Nine laminae of the sixth tooth

The Tangi bull with his attendant bull. Note the large sunken hollows over eyes, the protruding backbone, and the weathered, wrinkled skin that hangs loosely over his huge bony frame. (*Drawing by R. W. "Mike" Carroll*)

This huge tusker and attendant were seen near the Tangi River where 19 other bulls were seen during aerial counts during 1963–1964. (*Drawing by R. W. "Mike" Carroll*)

remained in each lower jaw; there was much wear on the surface of the anterior three loops on both sides, and the teeth were exceptionally wide. The left tusk weighed 54 kg, the right one was 51 kg.

In addition to the four large bulls that died in the Tangi River area, supporting evidence of their affinity for this area was obtained by sightings of large living bulls in this area while conducting aerial surveys. Between June 1958 and May 1964 I participated in eight aerial counts of elephants, all of which included the Tangi River area. Large and old bulls (judging by body and tusk size) were seen on each flight—never less than two and twice there were four large bulls with tusks well over average size.

Seeing large bulls in the same area on every aerial count caused me to ponder the idea of an elephant graveyard. There was the story told by W. D. M. Bell, the great elephant hunter, about the time he was hunting in

the Akipi country east of Lake Chad, when he came upon a great number of elephant skeletons. He believed the elephants were migrating from a devastating drought and when they reached this area, drank from the numerous natron springs and were poisoned. An old caravan route was nearby and the caravan people on seeing the skeletons allegedly helped spread the story.

Another story told by an old hunter friend, involved an elephant slaughter in the Bangui-Chari country in southwest Central African Republic. The native Balubbas set fire around a large area containing hundreds of elephants. The slaughter was terrible—hundreds of carcasses were found after the fire.

Louis S. B. Leakey (1969) relates that during the nineteenth century many Arab traders roamed East Africa in search of ivory and slaves. Africans living near these trade routes would collect ivory and hide it in some thicket near their huts. White men, who found such a collection misinterpreted it, and assumed that the tusks survived while the bones had crumbled to dust, may have told the first tales of an elephant graveyard. Moreover, at a few sites in East Africa poisonous gases were sometimes vented from volcanic rock. At certain times these escaping gases would suffocate any creature that came near one of these places, particularly if it was in a small valley or depression. Possibilities for a graveyard? Perhaps, but they remain only as possibilities suggesting how the graveyard myth might have originated.

Getting back to the Tangi River area. Whether this really is an elephant graveyard rests partly on semantics. How many elephants must die in how large an area in how much time for the area to qualify as a graveyard? Since this term and its concept is currently viewed with raised eyebrows, the safest policy is not to use the term

at all. One thing is sure: the lower Tangi River area held a very strong attraction for large old bulls. Why not cows? No one really knows. Nevertheless, several components and characteristics of the area suggest why it attracted old bulls.

Also, think of hunter impact. An elephant hunter nearly always is after a large bull carrying heavy tusks. The dream is to shoot a specimen with at least 45-kg tusks. He had read many stories of big bulls, but what he probably does not realize is that probably less than 1% of all the elephants he will see carry 45-kg tusks. So he strikes out for the bush with high aspirations and searches diligently among many elephants seeking the "trophy." Time moves on. He continues searching, sweating, struggling, and cursing tsetse flies until one day he begins to realize that there aren't many big bulls

An old bull and young attendant in the Tangi River area. Note the prominent backbone and wider, deeper depression above eye of the old bull. (*Photograph by John Savidge*)

with heavy tusks like he had always dreamed of. Should he shoot one of about 36 kg? First he has to find one that large! Time continues inexorably, and now there is a little less than half of the time left for finding and shooting that bull. He continues searching, approaching and studying elephant groups cautiously. Mostly more elephants see and watch him than he appreciates. Then one day he realizes there is not much time left at all to get his big bull. He is now down to specimens with 18- to 23-kg tusks, about enough ivory to pay for his license (in those days). Even 18-kg tusks are not that common, but finally he finds an elephant that appears to have those 18-kg tusks; he shoots it only to discover that they weigh close to 14 kg.

The relevance of this experience is that there was such highly differential harassment between cows and bulls that bulls eventually learned they were being followed. To some bulls this was initial training; to others with previous experience this was enhancement education—an education that ceases only upon death. My close friend John Heppes, who served as assistant warden of Uganda's Game Department and who took me on many field trips into elephant country, once told me that some bulls with 14- to 18-kg tusks probably get looked over a hundred times before getting shot to fill a license. There is no wonder then that bulls, particularly old bulls that have escaped bullets or sustained wounds, develop a strong aversion to humans. Cows practically never undergo such stressful experiences from hunters.

So the older bulls carry their experiences and scars into seclusion, remote from roads and human activity. Such areas are not abundant; however, the lower Tangi River area qualified in every known respect. This area was one of the most remote and inaccessible of any in the park, excluding certain sections of the Elephant Sanctuary, which is outside but adjacent to the north park boundary. Green foods growing along the lower Tangi River, particularly in the swamp sections, are available throughout the most critical dry seasons. The surrounding grass savanna supports scattered borassus palm, tamarind, and desert date. Just as important, the Tangi provides a permanent source of water for drinking and bathing. Thus in an area like the lower Tangi River an elephant could satisfy all its life needs in a relatively small area and have minimal disturbance by the number one enemy—humans.

WATER CONSUMPTION. While watching a thirsty bull herd at Little Rock Pond in Tsavo National Park (East), Kenya, David Sheldrick and I noticed that three large bulls of similar size were drinking while standing in easy-to-observe locations. We counted the number of times each bull (Nos. 1, 2, and 3) filled and emptied its trunk. They filled their trunks 18, 21, and 22 times respectively, emptying the trunkful of water into their mouths after each filling. No. 3 that filled his trunk 22 times dribbled considerable water as he lifted his trunk toward his mouth the last two times, and then squirted some of the residual water outside and behind his mouth allowing the surplus to run down his neck and front legs.

How much water is consumed by an elephant filling his trunk a known number of times? Three Asian elephants (*Elephas maximus*), trained for circus per-

Table 1.1. Water consumption by three Asian elephants

Animal	Water Taken per Trunk Filling (L)[a]		Time Taken from Moment of Sucking to Complete Drinking of One Trunk Filling (sec)		No. of Trunk Fillings	Total Water Consumed and Time Taken (L/sec)	Average Water per Trunk Filling (L)
	Minimum	Maximum	Minimum	Maximum			
Male Asian elephant, 4,445 kg, 37 yr of age[b]	5	10	5	25	25	212/282	8
Female Asian elephant, 2,955 kg, 16 yr of age[c]	2	4	4	6	17	60/84	4
Female Asian elephant, 1,364 kg, 8 yr of age[c]	2	4	4	10	11	32/84	3

Note: Test was conducted at Michigan State Fairgrounds, Detroit, Michigan, 28 March 1982. Weights of elephants are approximate.
[a] Environmental temperature at the Coliseum was 21° C, and water temperature was 9° C.
[b] This elephant was not watered for 15 hr prior to testing.
[c] These elephants were not watered for 17 hr prior to testing but were given a small amount of water 7 hr earlier in the day.

Three bulls drinking at Little Rock Pond in Tsavo National Park. (*Drawing by R. W. "Mike" Carroll*)

forming, were used by Shoshani (1982) at the Michigan State Fairgrounds to test their water consumption.

On the basis of nasal-passage volume of Asian elephants, Shoshani applied these volumes to three Asian circus elephants (Table 1.1). He reports finding among other details that a 37-yr old bull, consumed 212 L of 9°C water in 25 trunk fillings, or an average of 8 L per trunk filling. He was not watered for 15 hr prior to testing.

Considering water spillage during the 21st and 22d uptake of water by No. 3 when observed at Little Rock Pond, 18, 21, and 21 trunk fillings are used here to estimate maximum total water consumed by the three African bulls.

I do not know whether the nasal-passage volume of equal-sized African and Asian elephants is the same, nor do I know how long the African bulls had gone without water. The wild bulls, however, were estimated from 4,000 kg to 4,500 kg in weight, which is in the same weight class as the 37-yr-old Asian bull, estimated at 4,445 kg. Despite the two unknown factors, a rough approximation of total water consumed by each of the three wild African bulls can be obtained by multiplying the average of 8 L times the number of trunk fillings, which is 152 L for 18 fillings, and 178 L for each of the two bulls with 21 fillings.

Responses to Other Animals

ANTAGONISM. A troop of about 25 baboons set up a veritable din of barking at the north end of Mudanda Pool, three white-throated bee-eaters flew southward over the pool, and a female knob-billed goose near the center of the pool uttered a creaking whistle. Something was approaching from the north. A tawny patch hove into view among the tangle of shrubs moving closer until a large lioness came into full view and headed straight toward the pool.

David Sheldrick and I were positioned on the long granite rock bordering the west edge of the pool, hoping to study elephants usually coming to drink during late afternoons. We were watching two large bull elephants on the opposite side of the pool when the lioness moved in from the north. She walked straight in without stopping despite the din of barking and scolding. While the lioness was drinking the two bulls walked northward along the east shore, detected the cat's scent, and followed it to a bush about 10 m from the water's edge where the cat tried to hide. They lined to the bush and drove the big cat out; she retreated begrudgingly. The bull on the pool side of the bush thrust his head into the bush and thrashed as though to assure that the cat had left. They continued driving her along shore; at one

The two bulls walking northward along the east shore detected the cat's scent.
(*Drawing by R. W. "Mike" Carroll*)

point she was forced into the water against her wishes. She obviously resented being driven away from the pool, but this did not deter the bulls from their determination. The baboons barked and scolded continually during the entire time from the cat's approach until she reached a point about 50 m from the troop. Evidently the bulls had driven the lioness across the threshold of baboon safety for suddenly and in unison they stopped barking, retreated, and were heard no more.

David told me that he had seen bulls drive off lions on previous occasions, but cows coming to the north end of the pool to drink and catching scent of lions there immediately retired to the south end of the pool.

Obviously, elephants and lions do not share a mutualistic relationship. The lion is born a predator, the elephant an herbivore. Lions, like most other predators, are opportunists and occasionally succeed in killing young elephants despite the close guardianship of their mothers. Elephants, however, are basically defenders and ex-

cel in this role, thus their losses to lions are indeed low. Each time the lion succeeds in killing a young elephant the mother becomes a better defender, and each time the elephant prevents a lion from attempting to kill a young elephant, the more clever that lion becomes. Thus predator and prey become progressively more efficient in their conflicting species role; each tends to improve the skills of the other. Coexisting on many ranges throughout Africa, the lion and elephant have fulfilled their species' way of life very successfully; both should be managed to maintain this relationship.

My good friend R. W. (Mike) Carroll observed the following response of elephants to the presence of crocodiles in the Rungwa River in south central Tanganyika. September usually is well into the dry season and this year was no exception. The river was reduced to large pools 3–3.7 m deep. Wild animals were watering from the pools: a group of 28 elephants (including two small calves, one about 1 mo old and the other about 3 mo old) was watering daily; there was a large crocodile population, including some very large ones; and the usual hippo mob.

One morning the elephant herd came for their drink and bath at a large pool close to camp. They played in the water for about a half hour, with the usual cavorting by the younger ones. The old matriarch was in the water over her knees; her 3-mo-old calf was nearby in the water. Two other cows, one with the 1-mo-old calf, were a bit apart from the rest and just in the water's edge.

There was a sudden commotion, a great splashing about, and one of the cows trumpeted loudly in a high-pitched piercing tone. The old matriarch swung toward the bank with something in her trunk. There was such splashing it was difficult to see what she was up to.

When she got onto the beach she was carrying a very big croc, about 5 m long; her trunk was wrapped around its tail about midway between the tip and hind legs. The croc was twisting, snapping, and roaring all the time. The other cows became very agitated, trumpeting and moving about. The din was terrific!

She swung the croc high over her head and repeatedly smashed him to the ground; the croc, much worse for it all, was still alive. She moved farther up the bank and began flailing him against the bole of a large tree for about 5 min. The other elephants milled about watching. The cow then threw the croc on the beach and began to stomp it. Another big cow joined the fun. This continued for about 10 min or so. Finally, the rest of the group gathered around to inspect what was left of the croc.

The matriarch swung the croc high over her head and smashed him to the ground.
(*Drawing by R. W. "Mike" Carroll*)

Still holding the croc by the tail, the bull stomped on the head and stretched the croc; another bull joined the fray. (*Drawing by R. W. "Mike" Carroll*)

After completing inspection, they gradually drifted back to the bush. Anyone would have had difficulty telling that the grizzly remains had ever been a crocodile. A croc that big would weigh at least 680 kg, yet she had used him like a flail. What provoked this incident? Perhaps it was the cow's protective instinct aroused by the croc's proximity to the small calves.

On another occasion two bulls killed a croc. A group of five bulls was bathing, rolling, and playing about in the river. One big bull came up on the bank dragging a large croc by the tail. On reaching solid ground, the bull stomped on the croc. Then, still holding the croc by its tail, the bull put his foot on its head and pulled up mightily stretching the croc out. At this time another big bull left the water and joined in the fray. They stomped on the croc, and then grasped the croc in their trunks and played tug of war with it. Soon they pulled it apart. With a final stomp, they returned to the river. Had the croc tried to bite the bull, or had the croc come too close and the bull just took offense?

Bill Pridham, with whom I spent considerable time studying elephants in Toro District, told me about an ele-

phant response to a waterbuck. He was watching a rather large bull drinking at a waterhole west of the Chambura River, a short distance off the west edge of Ruwenzori National Park. A waterbuck unhesitatingly trotted over the bank and down to the water approaching within trunk's length of the bull. That was a mistake! The bull lashed out with his trunk striking the thirsty buck in the rib cage, smashing him against the slope with a single fatal blow. The bull slowly turned and with head held high and trunk swinging strode away from the scene.

I believe this was an atypical interaction. Had the waterbuck not approached so directly and suddenly, this interaction might not have occurred. On several occasions I saw elephants and waterbucks on the Kamulikwezi Area drinking within 10 m of each other; they appeared relaxed, and both species drank their fill peacefully.

TOLERATION. Not all responses to other animals are of an antagonistic nature. In fact elephant responses to avian associates appear diametrically opposite to the responses discussed above for relatively large and mostly predatory associates. That is, elephants appear completely tolerant of birds, even when they ride on the elephant's back and feed on ticks or flies. Most people who have spent time in Africa know or soon learn that egrets are closely associated with elephants and buffaloes. The clouds of white birds swirling over the African veldt are typical indicators of nearby elephants or buffaloes, usually under the egrets.

These egrets, which use the large mammals as moving platforms to observe frogs, insects, and other living food items, have an advantage over egrets that seek and find such foods without this back-riding advantage. Some biologists found that the ultimate size and weight of elephant-riding egrets are greater than those seeking their food independently and not cohabiting with large mammals.

Egrets are not the only avian species to associate with elephants and other large mammals for food-seeking advantages. I have seen both yellow-billed and red-billed oxpeckers, or tick birds, perched on elephants, presumably utilizing ticks and flies for food. McLachlan and Liversidge (1958) and Williams (1963) report that both species are indeed associated with domesticated stock and the large game animals.

Spinage (1962), however, reports that although elephants carry their fair share of ticks, mainly behind

Wild elephant herd on the Ruamputo, Mozambique, shows egrets closely associated with elephants. (*Photographer unknown*)

the ears and in the inguinal region, they are never attended by the tick bird or oxpecker. In northern Uganda, the place of the tick bird is taken by another bird called the piapiac. Though the oxpeckers, or tick birds, feed primarily on ticks, the piapiacs, like the egrets, are not specialized feeders; they are general insect-eaters, and their main interest lies in the insects disturbed by the animal's feet as they move along.

In both Tsavo and Kruger National parks David Sheldrick and I also saw fork-tailed drongos riding on elephants and buffaloes. David believed that these birds gave early warning of approaching vehicles, signaling with a rasping metallic call as they launched from an elephant. Oxpeckers, however, appeared to move away from our approach by shifting to the elephant's side away from us, leaving only when our approach was too close. We occasionally saw piapiac birds perched on or closely following elephants in Tsavo. I also saw them occasionally in Kabalega. Based on the limited number of my observations, these birds were accepted by elephants and were presumably feeding from them.

These responses to other animals were not acquired by the elephants in a few years of time. Almost surely lions and crocodiles preyed upon young elephants for millennia, whereas avian associates have enjoyed a mutualistic life with elephants, perhaps also for a very long time. The birds, which relieve the large beasts of pestiferous insects, are enhanced by a ready source of food. For some of the large mammals with shorter vision than that of birds, the birds communicate early warning of impending danger by call notes usually given at early detection and again at their departure time. Thus the elephants and other large mammals eventually learn who is friend and who is foe; over centuries these responses become fixed as inheritable behavior patterns. To some readers this may seem like a dogmatic statement. Let it be clearly understood, however, scientists discovered long ago that behavior patterns, along with morphological forms and physiological responses are the primary inheritable characteristics.

The varied responses to certain cohabiting animals make the elephant a much more exciting personality. The aggressions toward some of these animals and acceptance of others have not been recently acquired; instead they constitute an old and well-established behavior. Certainly this behavior clearly indicates the elephant's superior intelligence in the struggle for survival, and to me adds considerable charm.

DEAD ANIMALS. Cotton has a special attraction for elephants, particularly when the bolls start to open. Unfortunately, where cotton fields are available to elephants, depredations occur frequently and control of the marauding animals is necessary. During November 1958 William O. Pridham, district ranger in Toro District, received complaints of elephants raiding cotton fields at night in the Mubuku River area near Kilembe Mines on the eastern border of Ruwenzori National Park. From 22 to 28 November I accompanied Bill on safari to this area, where we succeeded in collecting 7 elephants. The first one, a 4,000-kg bull was shot at night while feeding with a band of 11 elephants in a cotton field where extensive damage to cotton had occurred (see description in Introduction under "Africa, 1958–1959"). The following afternoon at 5:00 P.M. we started searching the park boundary for elephants and trails leading toward the cotton fields. At 6:30 P.M. a family of 5 was seen about 0.4 km inside the park boundary, headed out of the park; hence we hid and watched them until 7:40 P.M., by which time they had crossed the railroad track that forms the park boundary and were shuffling toward the cotton fields. At that time we shot a 2,830-kg bull; the remaining 4 elephants bolted and ran back into the park.

On the next afternoon, we returned to the same site to watch for other elephants that might leave the park and start for the cotton fields. At 5:50 P.M. a family of nine was feeding and meandering toward the boundary, over precisely the same route taken by the family of the previous day. This family consisted of three adults, three subadults, two intermediates, and a calf less than a year in age. At 6:30 P.M. they reached the railroad track exactly where the family had crossed the previous night; a subadult male was in the lead and followed closely by a very large cow that evidently was the matriarch, and much more cautious and wary than the young bull. Just as the young bull stepped over the first rail, both he and the large female apparently caught the scent remaining from the bull shot during the previous day. Both animals turned immediately and retreated with the herd into a thicket about 25 m from the track. The young bull was first to return to the track and attempt to cross the second time; the large female followed but very cautiously and farther behind than the first time. The entire herd advanced slowly, several steps at a time. They were tense, with ears and tails lifted slightly and held rigidly, trunks lifted and tested the air continuously, and each step was slow and deliberate. The young bull and large cow walked parallel to

50

the track for about 20 m as though searching for another place to cross, but they returned to the original crossing where the young bull again started in the lead with the others following across the track. Before stepping across the first rail, he paused and tested the air from what appeared to be a very tense and strained position. Then he stepped across the first rail, stopped briefly, and walked slowly but directly to the site of the dead bull. The large cow followed in much the same manner, but she was even more cautious in her actions and appeared more reluctant to approach the site of the dead bull. Within 6 more minutes the rest of the herd crossed at the same place. After the last elephant was clear of the track, the herd began to relax. Tails and ears hung down loosely, there was much defecating and micturating, and most of the animals sniffed the ground where the bull was shot the previous day. Just as the herd started to leave, the young bull (2,073 kg) and the large cow (3,856 kg) were shot. The other seven elephants turned immediately, recrossed the tracks without hesitancy, and disappeared into the dusk and the thickets of the park.

2

Structure and Function

Body Temperature

In conjunction with a comprehensive study of the African elephant (*Loxodonta africana*), which I started in 1958, a restricted number of elephants were collected from Bunyoro and Toro districts, Uganda, for continued studies on reproduction between August 1963 and April 1964. Coincidental to the reproduction studies, information was obtained on body temperature from nine of these elephants and is presented here.

Standard clinical thermometers were inserted into the rectum to arm's length as soon as possible after the elephant was shot; at least three successive temperatures were taken from each elephant. When possible, the thermometer was inserted between the wall of the rectum and the adjacent fecal material. The highest reading was regarded as most representative of the body temperature and is recorded for each elephant in Table 2.1. The time lapsed from shooting to obtaining the highest temperature varied from 3 min to 35 min. A minimum of 3 min was allowed after insertion of the thermometer before temperature readings were taken. In three cases (Nos. 131, 133, and 134) one or two boluses, which restricted insertion of the thermometer, were removed to nearby shade and their temperatures compared with the rectal temperature. In one case (No. 143) intermuscular tem-

Table 2.1. Rectal and ambient temperatures for nine adult elephants, 1963–1964

Date Collected	Specimen Number	Sex	Time Shot	Time Thermom. Inserted	Rectal Temp. (°C)	Ambient Temp. (°C)	Remarks
				(A.M.)			
03 Jan. '64	143	F	8:20	8:37	36.7	19.4	Intermuscular 35.8°C, 9:00
30 Nov. '63	135	F	8:55	9:12	36.5	19.4	
28 Nov. '63	134	F	9:06	9:27	36.3	21.5	Bolus 36.5°C, 10:00
31 Aug. '63	133	F	9:30	10:00	36.6	23.3	Bolus 36.3°C, 10:30
29 Aug. '63	132	M	9:30	10:05	36.0	24.4	
22 Aug. '63	130	M	10:15	10:18	36.2	26.6	
23 Mar. '64	36	M	10:50	10:55	36.5	29.4	
				(P.M.)			
23 Aug. '63	131	F	12:12	12:29	36.3	31.6	Bolus 35.8°C, 1:27
06 Jan. '64	144	M	4:56	5:07	36.7	33.9	

Note. Samples arranged from earliest (8:20 A.M.) to latest time of day shot (4:56 P.M.).

peratures were taken from separate and equal-sized punctures made in the elephant's rump for comparison with rectal temperatures. Data obtained on oral and urethral temperatures were discarded, since they proved to be more variable and generally lower than rectal temperatures.

Data on rectal and ambient temperatures for nine adult elephants are presented in Table 2.1. The mean temperature of the nine readings is 36.4°C and ranged from 36° to 36.8°C. The range of 0.8°C represents individual variation in rectal temperatures of these nine elephants.

Arranging the elephants in Table 2.1 from earliest (8:20 A.M.) to latest time (4:56 P.M.) of day collected, shows that ambient temperatures increased progressively from the cool-time of morning to the warm-time of afternoon. The two highest rectal temperatures, however, occurred at both the lowest and highest ambient temperatures (19.4°C and 33.9°C).

Furthermore, when the elephants are arranged according to increasing rectal temperatures (Table 2.2), specimen Nos. 131 and 134 have equal rectal values (36.3°C), but ambient values are 31.6°C and 21.5°C respectively; this is next to the maximum range of ambient temperatures. Also, Nos. 135 and 36 have equal rectal temperatures of 36.5°C, yet the difference in ambient values for these two specimens is 10°C (29.4–19.4°C).

These preliminary observations suggest no relationship between rectal and ambient temperatures. To be certain, however, about the possibility of such a relationship not being present in these data, Dr. Thomas S. Russell, Chairman of Statistical Services at Washington State University, was asked to examine the data for such a possible relationship, emphasizing the use of the straight-line regression technique. He concluded that there was no relationship between rectal and ambient

temperatures based on these data. The calculated F value = 0.0011/0.23 < 1, which is nonsignificant at the 50% level of significance.

Both ambient and body temperatures were recorded from 11 African elephants immobilized with Etorphine (M-99) in the Luangwa Valley of eastern Zambia by Elder and Rodgers (1975). Body temperatures were taken by inserting a rapid-reading thermometer into the rump muscles, and these data show a highly significant relationship between body and ambient temperatures. Even when the temperature was taken after 0.5–4.0 hr recumbency, a positive correlation with ambient temperatures (P < .05) was evident (Pienaar et al. 1966).

An extensive study on body temperature of a female Asian elephant (*Elephas maximus*), including an impressive series of feces and urine temperatures, was reported by Benedict (1936). Benedict concluded that

the digest of this entire series of temperature measurements shows that the temperature of the freshly dropped feces of the elephant, although varying considerably in the course of twenty-four hours . . . can be considered on the average to be 36.5°C. In general the temperature of the urine is 0.7°C. lower than that of the feces. There is no significant difference between the temperature of the first bolus in passage of feces and the temperature of the third, fourth, or fifth (p. 149).

After completing a 10-day study on urine temperature, Benedict (1936, 142) concluded that "the temperature of the urine of the elephant is by no means constant. It may vary 2°C. in the same animal in ten days' time and not less than a degree and at times over one degree in the same twenty-four hours." He also stated that "since the temperature of the feces is higher than that of the urine, because of fermentation, it follows that the temperature of the urine is more nearly representative of the true body temperature" (p. 149).

Considering Benedict's findings, I have corrected the nine rectal temperatures of this study by subtracting 0.7°C from each of them, resulting in a mean body temperature of 35.7°C and a range of 0.1°C. This corrected mean body temperature (35.7°C) is close to the body temperature (35.1°C) reported for 11 African elephants studied by Elder and Rodgers (1975) in Zambia, and for 18 African bulls studied (and rectal temperatures corrected, 35.5°C) by Pienaar et al. (1966) in South Africa.

Comparative behavior prior to collection of elephants No. 144 and No. 143 helps rationalize the high body temperature of No. 144 but not the equally high temperature of No. 143 (Table 2.1). Bull No. 144 was estimated to be about 43 yr of age, was large (4,799 kg), very aggressive (testosterone level 27.9 µg/kg of body

Table 2.2. Rectal and ambient temperatures for nine adult elephants, arranged according to increasing rectal temperatures

Specimen Number	Rectal Temperature	Ambient Temperature
	(°C)	
132	36.0	24.4
130	36.2	26.6
131	36.3	31.6
134	36.3	21.5
135	36.5	19.4
36	36.5	29.4
133	36.6	23.3
143	36.7	19.4
144	36.7	33.9

weight), and with both very large temporal glands (left one 2.165 g) secreting copiously. The collection day was quiet with a very light north breeze and with a rather rapid afternoon rise in ambient temperature from 31°C at 3:30 P.M. to 33.9°C at 4:56 P.M., collection time. We were camped near the Chambura River, southwestern Toro District when we encountered a big bull (No. 144) in a herd of 22 elephants including 3 other adult bulls and a cow that appeared in or near estrus. The bull followed and closely guarded this cow and on four occasions drove away an intruding bull. We followed the herd for nearly 6 hr before making the collection, by which time No. 144 was flapping his ears vigorously.

At 5:11 P.M. the rectal temperature of No. 144 was 36.7°C; a second thermometer showed the same temperature, and 20 min later the rectal temperature was still the same. The protracted period of aggressive behavior, the copiously secreting temporal glands, the relatively high ambient temperature, and the rapid ear flapping support the high body temperature, corrected to 36.0°C. I believe the rapid ear flapping was significant in dissipation of heat.

Behavior of elephant No. 143 prior to collection was very different from that of No. 144. Number 143 was a young cow and was with a second and somewhat larger cow, the matriarch; both were accompanied by an intermediate-sized male and a calf. Ambient temperature was 19.4°C when No. 143 was first observed at about 7:50 A.M. This temperature did not change appreciably in the half hour prior to collection. The group was feeding on the bank of the Wasa River on Semliki Plain in Toro District; trees growing along the river provided partial shade. The elephants moved about slowly and at times stopped while feeding. The cow showed no evidence of aggression, no ear flapping, and her temporal glands were not visibly secreting. Necropsy showed that No. 143 weighed 1,814 kg, she was lactating freely, had a 23.6-kg uterus, and her ovaries contained six large corpora lutea varying in maximum diameter from 11 mm to 32 mm. She was the mother of the calf, probably her first.

At 8:41 A.M. rectal temperature of No. 143 was a surprising 36.7°C. We expected a lower rectal temperature since there was no aggressive behavior, there was partial shade, an ambient temperature of 19.4°C, slow movements, no observed ear flapping, and no visible secretion from her temporal glands. Collectively, these observations were in fact opposite to the behavior of bull No. 144, yet both elephants had the same body temperatures.

BOLUS TEMPERATURES. Two boluses (from Nos. 131 and 133), which were removed from the rectum and measured 60 min and 75 min respectively, following death, were only 0.33°C and 0.27°C less than the rectal temperatures taken 17 min and 30 min, respectively, after death. A bolus (from No. 134) removed and measured 54 min following death was 0.2°C higher than the rectal temperature taken 21 min after death. Evidently the higher bolus temperature reflects heat generated by fermentation and retained longer than in an evacuated rectum. I noticed that a rectum filled with fecal material tended to conserve heat, whereas the temperature of an empty one declined more rapidly. The relatively high temperatures retained by these boluses suggest that they can be used for obtaining reliable body temperatures provided readings are taken reasonably soon after defecation.

The highest of 22 successive intermuscular temperatures (36.2°C) was taken 40 min after death and was less than the highest of 22 successive rectal temperatures taken 20 min following death (Fig. 2.1). Both intermuscular and rectal temperatures were obtained at 5-min intervals from the same elephant.

The different boluses of one dropping varied considerably in their heat-retaining characteristics. A mucous seal tends to hold the bolus intact and prevents

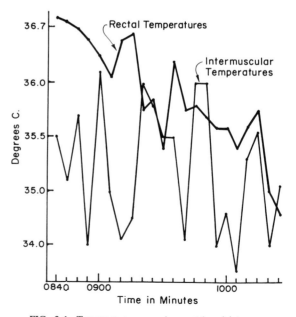

FIG. 2.1. Twenty-two successive rectal and intermuscular temperatures at 5-min intervals taken from an adult female elephant shot 3 January 1964 at 8:20 A.M.

cracking and accelerated loss of heat. The first few boluses extruded often fall on a hard or rough surface breaking this seal, whereas the last boluses extruded usually fall on the first ones and remain intact.

To study the rate of temperature decline following defecation, two large adult elephants (male and female) were followed until they defecated. After the animals left, temperatures were taken by using four thermometers inserted deeply into four different boluses; readings were taken at 5-min intervals. Temperatures presented in Figure 2.2 were taken from the last four boluses extruded, and each point represents the highest of the four temperatures obtained.

Although both curves of Figure 2.2 show a steady decrease in temperature, the average temperature for the first four readings was 36.4°C, the same as the mean uncorrected rectal temperature of the nine elephants used in this study. These data suggest that temperatures from droppings obtained within 15 min after defecation are valid indicators of the elephant's rectal temperature.

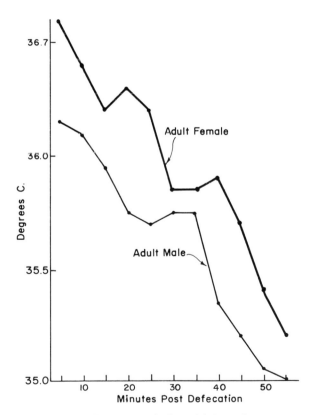

FIG. 2.2. Temperature decline of boluses from two adult elephants based on successive readings taken at 5-min intervals following defecation.

Temperatures were obtained from the droppings of 20 wild elephants as soon after defecation as possible, using the techniques described above. The mean for these 20 temperatures, taken from 1.0 min to 8.0 min postdefecation, was 36.4°C with a range from 36.0°C (3.0 min after defecation) to 36.7°C (1.0 min and 2.5 min after defecation). Both the average temperature and the temperature variations of these droppings are within 0.06°C of the respective measurements of rectal temperature shown above. Therefore, these 20 temperatures, when corrected by subtracting 0.7°C from each measurement, provided valid indicators of body temperature.

Age Estimation

REVIEW OF PREVIOUS STUDIES. Need for a field method for estimating the age of elephants has been recognized by many workers for a long time (Morrison-Scott 1947; Perry 1954; Frade 1955; Bourliere and Verschuren 1960; Johnson and Buss 1965; Laws 1966, 1967; Sikes 1966, 1968; Krumrey and Buss 1968; Hanks 1972; Sherry 1975; Smuts 1975; and Williamson 1976). All of these investigators were involved with elephant studies and needed such a technique; a few assumed that its development would be a rather simple matter, which soon proved otherwise. Fatti et al. (1980) pointed out that "uncertainties in these methods stem largely from the dearth of known-aged material, especially from free-ranging animals, and to the long life expectancy of elephants."

After examination of many fossil and museum elephant teeth, and studying various formulas and indexes previously suggested for obtaining measurements that could be used in identification of a particular molar, Morrison-Scott (1947) rejected most of them. Instead, he proposed the "laminary index" based on the maximum length of all complete lamellae, not including partly worn and terminal lamellae; this length, when divided by the total number of laminary units measured, provided the laminary index. He also proposed an "enamel loop index" based on tooth width and laminary index, thus providing the relative space encircled by a single enamel loop. The laminary index is his most valuable contribution to the problem of age estimation in the African elephant, since it is useful even today in helping to identify the six molars that develop during the life of an old elephant.

Bouliere and Verschuren (1960) gave ages for

eruption and loss of various teeth but only showed limited supporting evidence. Their supplementary field observations on shoulder height are useful, and their observations on tusk development are valuable for studying the age of calves. Sikes (1966, 285) supported this statement relative to calves, stating that "specimen 135 was a female calf of probably under six months old and still possessed a pair of milk tusks, as well as a distinct pair of permanent tusks developing behind them . . . Specimen 114 was a larger calf, which had already lost the milk tusks and possessed permanent tusks, 15 cm long which were still subcutaneous. . . ."

Sikes (1966) used "31 African elephants of both sexes, covering almost the complete potential age range of an elephant's life, and of known body condition, locality and size for constructing a reference chart of molar laminary age." There is wide recognition "that the African elephant, during its life, normally [acquires] six mo-

lars in each half-jaw, upper and lower, which move forward by linear progression towards the distal end of the jaw, where small fragments break off during wear and are lost" (Sikes 1966, 285) (Fig. 2.3). The first molar is the smallest, and each successive one normally increases in size and in number of laminae, although there is considerable variation in the number of laminae per molar. Abnormal seventh molars occur rarely. Sikes (1966) used the *foramen mentale* as a reference point for identifying and describing the laminary situation at a given tooth age. Having found that a maximum total of 57 laminae occur in the six molars (I/1–5; II/1–7; III/1–10; IV/1–10; V/1–12; VI/1–13), Sikes (1966) showed graphically the molar sequence, "showing the potential lifespan of an elephant as the period covered by the progression of the 57 laminae anteriorly past the *foramen mentale* of the mandible."

Probably one of Sike's most important observa-

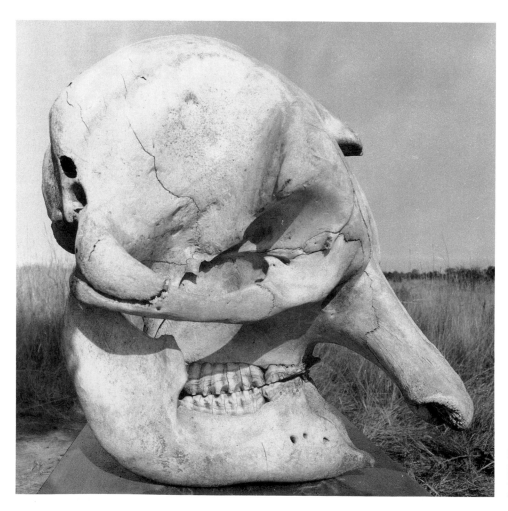

FIG. 2.3. Skull of African elephant with third and fourth molars in situ. (*Photograph by I. O. Buss*)

tions, is that "the whole concept of molar laminary age is based on a numbered laminary progression, not upon laminary or molar size. The measurement of molar length, width and weight are given only as a guide to the identification of the molar, or molars, currently in use."

The concept of molar progression, or molar replacement stage, was used before and after Sikes reported her work on age estimation. Molar replacement stage, rather than tooth size, was used by Johnson and Buss (1965) for estimating age, since replacement rate is probably more constant among various sized elephants of the same age than tooth size. In his second summary statement, Laws (1966, 1) stated that "thirty age groups are described and illustrated, which are related to the progress of eruption and wear of the six teeth in each side of the lower jaw."

Laws's (1966) study is based on a collection of 385 lower jaws of the African elephant (*Loxodonta a. africana* Blumenbach) from western Uganda, and he used molar length and width, number of lamellae per molar, and the laminary index (Morrison-Scott 1947) as a partial basis for molar identification. When Laws plotted molar length against molar width for the six teeth, the points fell into six well-defined groups, and had these measurements been plotted separately for each sex, he believed there was a high probability that six quite discrete groups of points would have resulted.

Fatti et al. (1980) state that "the system of age determination described by Laws (1966) has been used widely, but since 1971 four investigators who used this system have reported anomalous fluctuations in age distribution of cropped elephants (Hanks, 1972; Sherry, 1975; Smuts, 1975; Williamson, 1976)." They point out that three of these studies showing anomalous fluctuations were reported for "populations from Zambia, Rhodesia [Zimbabwe], and South Africa, despite different years of collection, different base years, and the absence of correlation of these peaks with rainfall." These fluctuations stimulated initiation of their project.

Fatti et al. (1980) used samples of female elephants, Nos. 230, 530, 227, 236, and 177, collected in Kruger National Park from 1970 to 1974. After studying age distribution of these females by use of cohorts, they state that

on the assumption that the female elephants cropped in Kruger National Park were a representative sample of the female population during the period 1970 to 1974, we concluded that the peaks and troughs in age distribution were artifacts on the method of age determination (Laws, 1966). [His] system of age determination enjoyed wide use as it is easy to implement

in practice. Future revision of methods of determining ages of elephants undoubtedly should involve use of analyses similar to those used in this report.

Very recently Lark (1984) compared the techniques used by Laws (1966) and by Sikes (1966; 1968) by applying them to the Perry Collection (1954), which is housed in the British Museum of Natural History. By using the Pearson's Product Moment Correlation Coefficient he obtained an apparent correlation value of 0.958 ($P < 0.001$) showing a significant correlation between the results from the two techniques. Currently there is rather wide recognition among biologists interested in elephants that both techniques have intrinsic weaknesses in assignment of absolute ages. Sikes (1966; 1968) assumes that each of the six molars has a constant number of lamellae, which is shown by both Laws (1966) and this study not to be true, thus significantly affecting dependability of absolute ages assigned. Laws's (1966) technique assigns absolute ages arbitrarily, resulting in an average overestimation in age of about 2–3 yr. The artificial peaks and troughs in age distribution curves resulting from use of Laws's (1966) technique is discussed above with a suggestion made relevant to technique improvement by Fatti et al. (1980).

UP-DATING EARLIER WORK. Since publishing information on molariform teeth of male African elephants with one of my graduate students (Johnson and Buss 1965), I have supplemented and refined our earlier work. Additional information is based on three sources: (1) extension of data published by Land (1980) on captive elephants (*L. a. africana*) of known age; (2) addition of data from three large bulls (Nos. 123, 124, and 144) and from four females (Nos. 31, 75, 134, and 136); and (3) discovery that our earlier work included two male forest elephants (*L. a. cyclotis*) (Nos. 8 and 89) collected on Semliki Plain, Toro District. Semliki Plain not only has both subspecies, but also a profusion of intergrades. How did this affect our earlier findings? Laws (1966, 32) studied the onset of puberty in both the forest and savanna elephants and found that the forest elephant, *L. a. cyclotis*, has an earlier average age (about 8 yr) at puberty. Considering this significant difference, there is no wonder that some of our early work on both estimating usage intervals of the six molars and in estimating average age of first breeding varied with information from studies of only typical *L. a. africana*.

Thus the threefold purpose here is to (1) supplement and refine earlier work published on age estimation in the African elephant, *L. a. africana;* (2) demonstrate that molars taken from the same regional population of elephants can be readily identified on a morphological basis if supplementary data, such as body weight and the status of the replacement molar, are available; and (3) relate dental characteristics to approximate age, body size, and growth cycle. Throughout this work, emphasis has been placed upon relative exposure of the replacement molar and the extent of tooth wear. Hopefully additional data, particularly from elephants of known age, will become available to supplement and further refine the present findings.

METHODS. Fifty-eight male elephants, from very young to very old individuals, were collected in western Uganda between July 1958 and May 1959. Three other males (Nos. 123, 124, and 144) were collected in May 1963 and replaced Nos. 8 and 89. The exposed teeth (right upper and lower) of each animal were removed, cleaned, and numbered. Additionally, any developing teeth in the alveolar pockets in the posterior horizontal ramus of the jaw also were saved. The study materials are stored in the Department of Zoology at Washington State University.

Body measurements were obtained as follows: (1) Total length was measured from the anterior end of the occipital crest to the posterior end of the anal flap; the steel tape was held to follow the contours of the center of the back of the recumbent animal. (2) Shoulder height was measured using a steel tape and measuring "from the edge of the sole of the foot to tip of scapula, in a straight line, with leg straightened by manipulation so that the joints lock. The point corresponding to the top of the scapula is fixed by sighting on the two scapulae (upper and lower) so as to bring their dorsal sides into line" (Laws 1966, 4). Initial shoulder measurements were made from the dorsal edge of the upper scapula, down the center of the forelimb, with leg relaxed, to the edge of the forefoot. Comparison of a sample measured by both methods showed up to a maximum increase of 10 cm for a large bull when leg joints were locked. (3) After the measurements were obtained, the entire weight of each elephant was secured by systematically weighing all parts of the carcass. Fluid loss was estimated by the method described by Johnson (1964). These same methods were used for 56 female elephants collected between November 1958 and May 1959 and for 4 females (Nos. 31, 75, 134, and 136) collected in 1963, which were added to the original specimens used in the report by Krumrey and Buss (1968) on age estimation of female African elephants.

GENERAL FEATURES OF THE TEETH. Tusks of an elephant are upper incisors; there are no canines, and each side (half) of the upper and lower jaw bears a series of six molariform teeth. In contrast to most other mammals, the cheek teeth (or molars) of an elephant appear successively during the life of the animal. This succession makes it difficult to homologize these teeth with the usual mammalian premolar and molar designations. Each of the six teeth of the African elephant consists of a variable number of compressed units known as laminae, or lamellae. Each lamina is composed of dentine bounded by enamel (Fig. 2.4). Cementum occurs between adjacent laminae and encompasses all of the external surface except for the apical ridges of the crown surface. The overall structure of the elephant molar is interpreted in two ways. Some workers (Driak 1937; Osborn 1936–1942) suggest that the laminae are not representative of individual teeth, but rather that the whole tooth is a single unit complicated by differentiation. Others (Thompson 1942; Perry 1954) consider the tooth to be a product of concrescence, so that each lamina actually represents a separate tooth with the entire molar being a composite structure. Bolk (1919), however, in studying the elephant embryo, found that the molar is formed by only one enamel organ, which supports the theory of a single tooth composed of many lamellae as suggested by Driak (1937) and Osborn (1936–1942).

Tooth movement appears to involve growth and root elongation posteriorly combined with root resorption beneath the old tooth (Verheyen 1960).

Since all the teeth (molars) in the living elephant are deciduous, they are referred to in this report simply as M_1 to M_6; the M_1 to M_3 are equivalent to mm_2 to mm_4 of Morrison-Scott (1947) and Perry (1954).

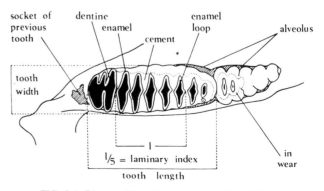

FIG. 2.4. Diagram illustrating measurements and terms for elephant dentition. (From Laws, 1966, Fig. 1, p. 3)

MOLAR IDENTIFICATION. Representative molars are shown in Figures 2.5 and 2.6. In Figure 2.6 the alveolus was opened to expose the entire sixth tooth and to show the proximal mass of porous bone, which proliferates to fill the pocket following complete exposure of the final molar. Each successive molar is larger than the preceding one and is normally composed of more laminae. Males and females have been analyzed separately in this study, probably helping a little in identification of molars. Plotting tooth length against tooth width, as done by Laws (1966), separates the six molars (M_1-M_6) into "six well-defined groups, only about five percent of the points falling in borderline positions." He goes on to state that "it is highly probable that had it been possible to sex the jaws, six quite discrete groups of points would have resulted for each sex because male jaws and teeth tend to be slightly more massive than female."

Using this technique on elephants in the Luangwa Valley of Zambia, Elder and Rodgers (1968) compared molars from 32 elephants of known sex to molars from 189 elephants of unknown sex. "Analyses of data from both groups showed very similar results: M_1, M_2, and M_3 were completely separable on the basis of measurement of either width or length; M_4 and M_5 showed much overlap in width, but almost none in length; M_5 and M_6 overlapped in both length and width, but less in length. Only 6 of 189 molars could not be separated on the basis of length alone." Data suggest that there is no difference in molar size between the two sexes. Otherwise, their findings are in complete agreement with those given by Laws (1966) for elephants in Uganda.

All molars from the 189 elephants used by Elder and Rodgers (1968) were from elephants killed during the first 2 yr of cropping operations in the Luangwa Valley. Hanks (1972) also worked in the Luangwa Valley, using 1,236 lower jaws from elephants killed between 1965 and 1969, evidently including those collected in 1965–1967 for the Elder and Rodgers study, but to which I found no reference. Hanks (1972) used the same technique used by Laws (1966) and by Elder and Rodgers (1968), and came up with essentially the same results. In respect to the number of lamellae Hanks (1972, 7) reported that "13 females and 7 males had eight la-

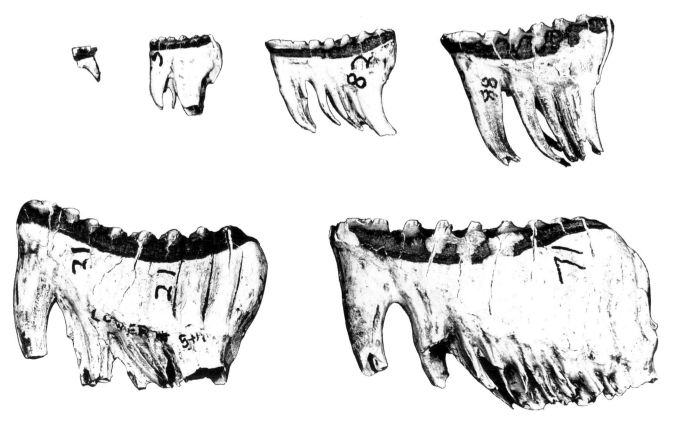

FIG. 2.5. The six molars of the African elephant. Numbers on teeth represent specimen numbers.

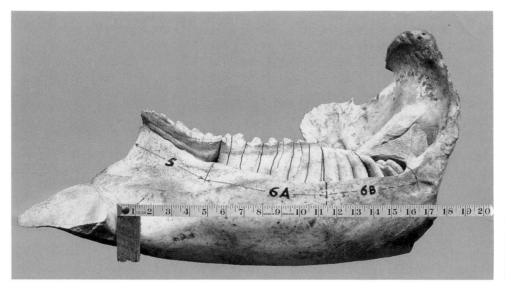

FIG. 2.6. Lower right mandible from a male elephant approximately 38 yr old. Of the 13 laminae comprising M_6, 7 were exposed and in use (6A), and 6 were still within the alveolus (6B).

mellae in M_2, and one male had nine lamellae." Laws (1966) reported finding a maximum of seven lamellae in M_2. I found from 6 to 8 lamellae in M_2, 8 or 9 lamellae in M_4, and among 11 males there were from 8 to 11 lamellae in M_5 (Tables 2.3 and 2.4).

The laminary index was also used in this study to identify the six molars. Practically the same results were obtained as those reported by Laws (1966), Elder and Rodgers (1968), and Hanks (1972). Minor difficulties were involved in distinguishing M_4 and M_5 in several cases. Final decision in these cases was made by reference to the replacement molar, body weight, shoulder height, and total body length.

ESTIMATING CHRONOLOGICAL AGE. There are only a very limited number of known-age ele-

phants, and nearly all of these are captive animals, which probably are not exactly comparable to free-living elephants. Also, as pointed out by Laws (1966, 17), "an approach involving animals marked as calves of known age is not feasible in such a long-lived animal. We should have to wait many years for results covering the adult span. Similarly, to determine the interval between the age groups by examination of the teeth at capture and subsequent recapture is not to be contemplated." The use of cohorts, as suggested by Fatti et al. (1980), is a valuable technique, provided an adequate sample of teeth is available.

Despite these difficulties, as pointed out by Laws, estimating chronological ages arbitrarily at least gives ages that can be refined in the future. Thus all or most information available was used in this study to estimate

Table 2.3. Dental characteristics and estimated ages of 21 male African elephants

Spec. No.	Molars Present (lower right mandible)			Estimated Age (yr)
	M_1	M_2	M_3	
60	Complete[a]; exposed and in use	Complete; 8 laminae but not yet exposed	Fragments present[b] in alveolar pocket	1
74	Complete; exposed and worn flat	Complete; 6 laminae, all exposed, slightly worn	Fragments in alveolar pocket, anterior fusion; first lamina stained[c]	1.5
	M_2	M_3	M_4	
51	Incomplete[d]; very worn fragment representing only 2 or 3 laminae	Complete; 9 laminae, all exposed, well worn	Fragments in alveolar pocket; 7 anterior laminae fused, 3 of which are exposed	4

Table 2.3. *continued*

Spec. No.	Molars Present (lower right mandible)			Estimated Age (yr)
	M₃	M₄	M₅	
95	Incomplete; 3 laminae remain	Complete; 9 laminae, 8 of which are exposed, moderately worn	Small fragments present in alveolar pocket	11
36		Complete; 9 laminae, all exposed, moderately worn	Large fragments present in alveolar pocket, some anterior fusion and staining	12
1		Complete; 9 laminae, all in use, anterior lamina well worn	Large, loose fragments in alveolar pocket, some anterior fusion and staining	13–14
76		Complete; 8 laminae, all exposed, well worn	Large laminae, at least 7 fused, 3 of which are exposed	16
104		Complete; 8 laminae, all exposed, well worn	Large laminae mostly fused, 3 laminae exposed	16–17
	M₄	M₅	M₆	
85	Incomplete; 3.5 laminae remain	Complete; 10 laminae, 5.5 of which are exposed		18
91	Incomplete; 3 laminae remain	Complete; 10 laminae, 6 of which are exposed		18–19
83	Incomplete; 3 laminae remain	Complete; 10 laminae, 6.5 of which are exposed		19
42	Incomplete; 3 laminae remain	Complete; 11 laminae, 8 of which are exposed	Small fragments in alveolar pocket	20
116	Incomplete; small fragment remains	Complete; 9 laminae, 8 of which are exposed	Small fragments present in alveolar pocket	20
119		Complete; 9 laminae, 8.5 of which are exposed, moderately worn	Large, loose fragments in alveolar pocket; 3 anterior laminae fused and stained slightly	21
121		Complete; 8 laminae, all exposed, moderately worn	Large, loose fragments present in alveolar pocket; 5 anterior laminae fused, 2.5 of which are exposed	23
25		Complete; 9 laminae, 8 of which are exposed, moderately worn	Large, loose fragments present in alveolar pocket; 6 anterior laminae fused, 2.5 of which are exposed	24
124		Complete; 9 laminae, all of which are exposed, anterior 2 well worn	Large, loose fragments in alveolar pocket; 7 anterior laminae fused, 3 of which are exposed	27
123		Complete; 9 laminae, all of which are exposed, well worn	Large, loose fragments in alveolar pocket; 7 anterior laminae fused, 4 of which are exposed	30
	M₄	M₅	M₆	
84	Complete; 9 laminae, all of which are exposed, well worn	Large, loose fragments in pocket, 6 anterior laminae fused, 4 of which are exposed		34
120		Incomplete; 5 laminae remain	Complete; 12 laminae, 7.5 of which are exposed	39
144		Incomplete; 4 laminae remain	Complete; 12 laminae, 8 of which are exposed and in use	43

ᵃ Complete indicates that the entire tooth was present.

ᵇ Newly forming teeth are first seen as laminary fragments in the alveolar pocket (see text), which later fuse together from anterior to posterior to form the definitive tooth.

ᶜ As a tooth nears eruption from the alveolar pocket, the anterior laminae lie close to the gum surface and become darkly stained.

ᵈ The term "incomplete" indicates that certain parts of a tooth were worn away and had been lost from the jaw.

Table 2.4. Dental characteristics and estimated ages of 35 female African elephants

Spec. No.	Molars Present (lower right mandible)			Estimated Age (yr)
	M_1	M_2	M_3	
67	Complete[a]; exposed and well worn	Complete; all 6 laminae exposed	4 fragments in alveolus partially fused	1.5
	M_2	M_3	M_4	
58	Complete; 7 laminae exposed and moderately worn	Complete; 9 laminae, 5.5 of which are exposed	4 unfused fragments in alveolus	3
134		Incomplete; 6 laminae remaining, plus fragment	5 laminae exposed and in use	8–9
112		Complete; all 8 laminae, anterior 3 are worn flat	Complete; 9 laminae, 3.5 of which are exposed	9
114		Incomplete; 4 well-worn laminae remaining	Complete; 9 laminae, 4 of which are exposed	9.5
97		Complete; 7 laminae of which anterior 3 worn flat	Complete; 8 laminae, 4.5 of which are exposed	10
	M_3	M_4	M_5	
45	Incomplete; 4 remaining are well worn	Complete; 9 laminae, 5.5 of which are exposed	Small fragments in alveolus	10.5
39	Incomplete; fragment remaining	Complete; 9 laminae, all of which are exposed	Fragment in alveolus larger than those of No. 45	11
103		Complete; 8 laminae, anterior 1 of which is well worn	Fragments in alveolus slightly fused	13
100		Complete; 9 laminae, anterior 1 of which is well worn	Fragments not available	13
136		Complete; 8 laminae, anterior 1 of which is well worn	Fragments in alveolus starting to fuse	14
88		Complete; 8 laminae, moderately worn	Fragments numerous; 3 large and well fused, anterior 1 appears near eruption	14
	M_4	M_5	M_6	
81	Complete; 8 laminae, anterior 2 of which are well worn	9 fragments; anterior 5 fused, 3.5 of which are exposed		15
63	Complete; 8 laminae, anterior 2 of which are well worn	9 laminae; anterior 7 fused, 3.5 of which are exposed		15
93	Complete; anterior 3 or 4 are well worn	Complete; 9 laminae, 3.5 of which are exposed		16
69	Complete; 8 or 9 laminae, anterior 2 of which are well worn	Complete; 10 laminae, 4 of which are exposed	Small fragments in alveolar pocket, none fused	16
108	Incomplete; fragment represents 4 laminae	Complete; 10 laminae, 4 of which are exposed	Small fragments in alveolar pocket, none fused	16
111	Incomplete; 5 remaining laminae are all well worn	Complete; 9 laminae, 4 of which are exposed	Small fragments in alveolar pocket, none fused	16
73	Incomplete; 6 laminae remaining	Complete; 10 laminae, 4.5 of which are exposed	Fragments not available	16
59	Incomplete; 4 laminae remaining, anterior 2 of which are well worn	Complete; 9 laminae, 6 of which are exposed	Larger fragments than those of No. 111	17
66	Incomplete; 4 laminae, anterior 2 of which are well worn	Complete; 10 laminae, 6.5 of which are exposed	Fragments present	18
92	Incomplete; 3 eroded laminae remain	Complete; 9 laminae, 6.5 of which are exposed	Large fragments in alveolar pocket	19
122	Incomplete; fragment of 3 laminae remaining	Complete; 9 laminae, 6.5 of which are exposed	Fragments, 2 of which are fused	19
68	Incomplete; small fragment remaining	Complete; 9 laminae, all of which are exposed	Fragments larger than those of specimen No. 122	20
21	Incomplete; small fragment remaining	Complete; 9 laminae in use, anterior 1 of which is well worn	Fragments larger than those of specimen No. 68	21
20		Incomplete; 8 laminae remaining, all of which are well worn	11 laminae, 9 of which are fused and 2 beginning to erupt	25

Table 2.4. *continued*

Spec. No.	Molars Present (lower right mandible)		Estimated Age (yr)
24	Incomplete; 6 laminae remaining, all of which are well worn	12 laminae, 6 enamel loops of which are exposed and in use	35
47	Incomplete; fragment of 3 or 4 laminae remaining	Complete; 12 laminae, 7 of which are exposed and in use	39
27	Incomplete; fragment of 3 or 4 laminae remaining	Complete; 12 laminae, 7 of which are exposed	39
117	Incomplete; fragment too small to distinguish laminae	Complete; 11 laminae, 9 of which are exposed and in use	45
105	Incomplete; fragments of 2–3 laminae; roots well eroded	Complete; 11 laminae exposed, anterior 2 of which are well worn	50
107[a]		Complete; 11 laminae exposed and in use, anterior 2 of which are well worn	50
75		Incomplete; 9 laminae, all of which are worn flat	50
49		Incomplete; 9 laminae, all of which are worn heavily	52
31		Incomplete; 8 laminae very heavily worn	55

[a] Complete means entire tooth was present. See footnote to Table 2.3 for additional comments.

and allocate ages of 35 female and 21 male African elephants (*L. a. africana*) collected from western Uganda where the elephants used by Laws were taken. The initial step in this endeavor was to decide on an ultimate age for the African elephant. Laws (1966, 17) obviously ferreted out considerable information related to longevity of both *L. a. africana* and *I. a. cyclotis*, which he used to estimate a "potential longevity of 60–70 years . . . for the African elephant, *L. a. africana*." Bosman and Hall-Martin (1986) report 60 yr for the

Typically tuskless female Addo elephants. (*Photograph by Anthony Hall-Martin*)

Bull showing small tusks of the Addo poplation. (*Photograph by Anthony Hall-Martin*)

nae in each molar. Since each successive molar is larger and normally has more laminae than its predecessor, time periods were proportionately adjusted for each molar-use period (Table 2.3). By considering the potential life span of the wild African elephant, considered here as 60 yr, time periods were arbitrarily allocated for each successive molar. Within each time period ages were allocated to individual elephants, emphasizing status of the replacement molar.

Tables 2.3 and 2.4 present dental characteristics and estimated ages of the 21 male and 35 female elephants studied. For some of the elephants in these two tables supplementary information was obtained (Table 2.5). When M_6 of male No. 144 (Table 2.3) is compared to M_6 of male No. 4 (Fig. 2.6) and to M_6 of male No. 6X (Fig. 2.7), they all appear highly similar, yet there is a difference. Molar M_6 of No. 4 had 13 laminae, 7 of which were exposed in use, 6 still in the alveolus, and 3 still not fused; M_5 still had 5 laminae remaining. The other two males (Nos. 144 and 6X) each had 12 laminae of M_6 with 8 fully exposed and in use and the 4 still in the alveolus were fused; only 3 or 4 laminae remained of molar M_5. My interpretation is that No. 4 was the largest of these three males, but progression of his sixth molar was behind that of the other two males; Nos. 144 and 6X were about 3 yr older but not quite as large as No. 4.

To supplement Tables 2.3 and 2.4, I made impressions of the grinding surface of teeth from four elephants of different ages (Fig. 2.8 A-D). The first elephant (No. 110) was a relatively small female, estimated to be 7–8 yr of age, weighing 1,923.2 kg and standing 236 cm at the shoulder. The maximum length of M_3 was 13.2 cm and the maximum width was 4.6 cm (Fig. 2.8A). The second elephant (No. 136) was also a female, estimated to be 14 yr of age, weighing 2,238.6 kg and standing 246 cm at the shoulder. The maximum length of M_4 was 16.5 cm and the maximum width was 6 cm (Fig 2.8B). The third elephant was a

longevity of Addo elephants they studied. Considering the paucity of known-age elephants (*L. a. africana*) that have reached even 50 yr and the dangerous application of known-age forest-type elephants to savanna-type African elephants, a potential longevity of 60 yr is assumed for the elephants used in this report.

The second step in this process of estimating chronological age was mostly an arbitrary assessment of a time scale for the duration of each molar. This was done by taking into consideration the number of lami-

Table 2.5. Molar-usage intervals

	Age When Lost (yr)				Erupt[a]	
M_1	M_2	M_3	M_4	M_5	M_6	References
1–2	3–4	9–10	19–25			Lang (1980), known age
2	6	13–15	28	43	30	Laws (1966)
2	5	12	22	39–40	28	Johnson and Buss (1965)[b]
2	5	11	20	40	27	Krumrey and Buss (1968)[b]
2	4–5				28–30	Sikes (1966)

[a] First appearance (eruption).
[b] Updated 1983.

FIG. 2.7. Lower left mandible of male elephant No. 6X. M_5 with 3–4 fragments left; M_6 complete with 8 laminae in use, 4 in alveolus fused, estimated 43 yr old (highly similar to No. 144, Table 2.3).

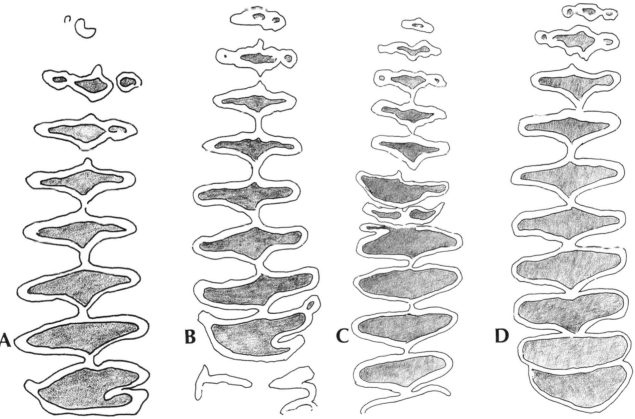

FIG. 2.8A–D. Impressions of the grinding surfaces of teeth from four elephants of different ages. **A.** M_3 from female No. 110; estimated age of 7–8 yr; full-scale length of tooth surface = 13.2 cm. **B.** M_4 from female No. 136; estimated age of 14 yr; full-scale length of tooth surface = 16.5 cm. **C.** M_5 and M_6 from large male No. 11X; estimated age of 36 yr; full-scale length of total grinding surface = 26.3 cm. **D.** M_6 from large male No. 10X; estimated age of 44 yr; full-scale length of tooth surface = 26.3 cm.

large male (No. 11X), estimated to be 36 yr of age, shot by a licensed hunter. The teeth consisted of about half M_5 and half M_6. The maximum length of the 11 laminae remaining from M_5 was 12.5 cm and the maximum width was 7.2 cm. The maximum length of the 7 laminae of M_6 was 13.8 cm and the maximum width was 6.3 cm. Molar M_6 had 7 laminae above the gum and in use, and 6 laminae were still in the alveolus; the posterior 2 laminae were not fused. The total length of grinding surface was 2.6 cm (Fig. 2.8C). The fourth elephant (No. 10X) was a very large male, estimated to be 44 yr of age, shot by the district warden while on control assignment. No evidence of M_5 remained, and there was no evidence of laminary fragments in the alveolus. The total length of M_6 was 25 cm and the total width was 7.3 cm (Fig. 2.8D). I found only one instance of anomalous molar growth among all the elephant teeth I examined; a female showed anomalous curving medially of M_4 (Fig. 2.9).

Evidence for the oldest elephant I obtained came by chance and a bit of luck on 11 March 1964. John Savidge, his wife Yvonne, and I were returning from an aerial count in the northeast sector of the Elephant Sanctuary, which bounds Kabalega Falls National Park on the north. As we approached the Tangi River at the border, elephant bones were seen under a large tree. When the skull, including both tusks, was recovered, examination showed that only about half of the sixth set of teeth remained in the jaws. On the lower left side six laminae of M_6 remained, on the right there were eight laminae. The tooth remnants were extremely wide attesting to the bull's huge size. The left tusk weight

FIG. 2.9. Anomalous growth of M_4 curving medially in a female elephant.

49.5 kg, the right one weighed 51.4 kg. Evidence where the skeletal remains were found, particularly the huge tusks, suggested that the bull very probably died a natural death. Later I pondered this old bull's history while trying to decide on the African elephant's longevity.

Still other elephants were a bit perplexing in establishing chronological age. Elephant No. 49 (Fig. 2.10A) was my second oldest female (Table 2.4), but when compared to No. 105 (Table 2.4), which had very impressive slanting roots and a remnant of its fifth molar (Fig. 2.10B), age criteria forced the conclusion that No. 49 was about 2 yr older than No. 105.

Female No. 107 weighed 3513 kg, was 290 cm high at her shoulders, which was our tallest female, and carried long tusks that weighed 12.7 kg on the left side and 14.1 kg on the right side. Although she had only her sixth molars with the anterior two laminae well worn, they did not show as much usage as those of three other females. If she had weighed more and shown a little more wear on her sixth molars she would have been the oldest female contacted. Since Laws (1966) used 65 yr as the potential life span of the African elephant, and provisionally assigned the same age to animals in his group XXX, there is a minor difference in our assigned individual ages as a result of my allocating 60 yr for the elephant's potential longevity.

Allocating individual ages generally fit the criteria without difficulties. A good example is female No. 31 (Table 2.4), which was our oldest and largest female elephant with molariform status fitting her measurements well. This cow was collected close to the east side of Ruwenzori National Park on 24 November 1958. Her shoulder height was 279 cm, her weight was 3,858 kg, and she carried tusks of 8.8 kg on both sides. As shown in Table 2.4, her sixth set of molars were incomplete with eight laminae well worn. She was judged as being 55 yr of age.

However, a few difficulties were encountered in the allocation of age to elephants having only their sixth set of molars. For example, a female elephant (No. 75, Table 2.4), which I collected close to the south border of Kabalega Falls National Park on 1 February 1959, posed such a problem. This old cow had both sixth lower molars worn completely flat, but her ovary showed that she was still ovulating, her shoulder height was 267 cm, her total body length was 325 cm, and her total weight was 2,736 kg. Her molars suggested an age of about 55 yr (Laws 1966, age group XXVIII); but her shoulder height, body weight, and tusk weights suggested an elephant of considerably

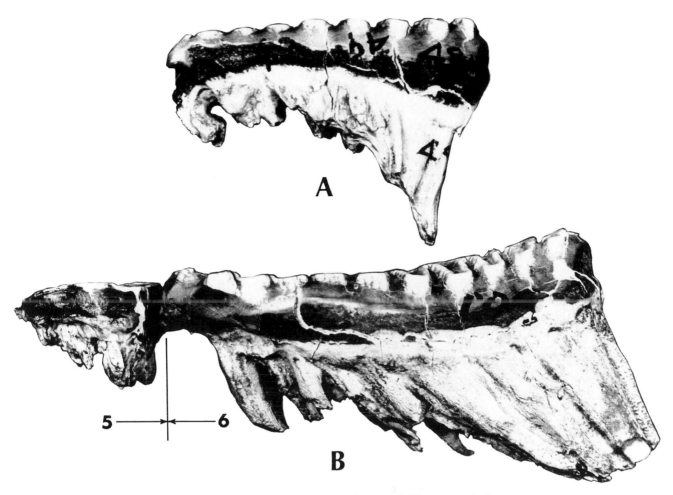

FIG. 2.10A, B. Molars from two female elephants of different ages. **A.** Incomplete M_6 of female No. 49 with 9 well-worn laminae; estimated 52 yr of age. **B.** M_5 fragment and M_6 of female No. 105 with 11 fully exposed and well-worn laminae; estimated 50 yr of age (approx. 0.2 actual size).

lower age. Thus the age suggested by the status of her molars was slightly modified to 50 yr.

USAGE INTERVALS. Estimation of usage intervals for each of the six molars was based upon the dental characteristics of known-age elephants (Lang 1980) and by comparison with earlier work (Johnson and Buss 1965; Laws 1966; Sikes 1966; and Krumrey and Buss 1968). These comparisons are presented in Table 2.5. Lang (1980) has updated information on elephants raised at the Zoological Garden in Basle, Switzerland, extending age data on three males (Omari, Katoto, and Tembo) and on three females (Idunda, Ruaha, and Beira). Weight and age at death of the three bulls was as follows: Tembo, 6600 kg, 25 yr; Katoto, 4280 kg,

20 yr; and Omari 3850 kg, 13 yr. Considering these additional data, including addition of seven specimens (Nos. 31, 75, 134, 136, 123, 124, 144) and deletion of two (Nos. 82 and 86), probably intergrades collected on Semliki Plain, molar usage intervals reported earlier have been altered as shown in Table 2.5.

As shown in the table, M_1 is lost at 2 yr, M_2 at 5 yr, M_3 at 11–12 yr, M_4 at 20–22 yr, M_5 at 39–40 yr, and M_6 appears at 27–28 yr. Although these data extend the usage intervals beyond those reported earlier, they are still not quite as far as the values reported by Laws (1966).

Weights reported by Lang (1980) on death of the three bulls are slightly higher than the wild bulls of similar age collected in western Uganda. Perhaps confinement and regular availability of food caused the captive elephants to be heavier than elephants of similar age living in the wild environment.

THE GROWTH CURVE. From measurements obtained on the 35 females presented in Table 2.4, shoulder heights were plotted against estimated ages (Fig. 2.11). The points show some scatter about the estimated mean growth curve, but are within the expected variation. The shoulder height for the 35 females shows an asymptotic height of about 274 cm, which is the same as Laws (1966) reported for females taken from practically the same area of western Uganda.

Measurements on shoulder height of the 21 males of western Uganda listed in Table 2.3 were also plotted against their estimated ages (Fig. 2.12). The points also show some scatter similar to that of the females. The curves for both sexes are strikingly parallel and show that growth in height continues for at least three-fourths of the elephant's life. The asymptotic height for the 21 males was 317 cm, again the same as Laws (1966) gives for 14 males from Kabalega Falls National Park. The growth curves suggest validity of the estimated ages assigned to elephants of both sexes.

RELATIONSHIPS AMONG BODY WEIGHT, SHOULDER HEIGHT, AND TOTAL LENGTH. Johnson (1964) found that close relationships exist between body weight and shoulder height, and body weight and total length in the male elephant. Similarly close relationships were found to exist in the female elephant. These relationships are best expressed as logarithmic functions (Fig. 2.13). The correlation coefficient between shoulder height and body weight is 0.99, and between body weight and total length is 0.97.

These values can serve as useful tools in the field. Since the body weight can be extrapolated with high confidence from either the shoulder height or total length, the laborious task of weighing the carcass is eliminated.

Utilizing this information, Douglas-Hamilton and Douglas-Hamilton (1975, 61–63) fashioned a photographic device with which they could obtain duplicate pictures on a single exposure (stereo photography principle), magnified them 25 times by projection on a screen, and with micro-manipulating servo-mechanisms were "able to pinpoint exact co-ordinates and record them to the nearest two microns on paper tape, which was then fed into a second computer that made the calculations and printed out the elephant's height and age."

Also, Leuthold (1976) in Tsavo National Park of

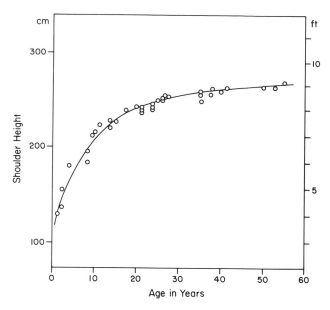

FIG. 2.11. Growth curve fitted to growth data on 35 wild female elephants, western Uganda.

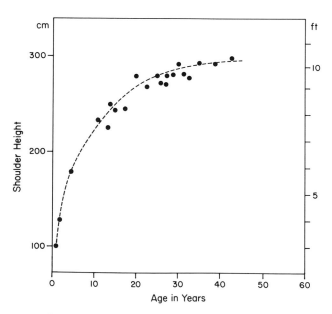

FIG. 2.12. Growth curve fitted to growth data on 21 wild male elephants, western Uganda.

Kenya, obtained aerial photographs of elephants from which he measured body length, extrapolated ages from the body lengths, and placed the elephants into 5-yr age groups for managements purposes.

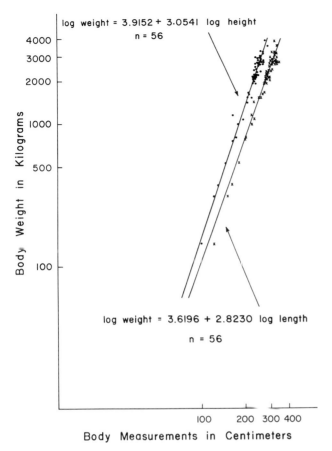

log weight = 3.9152 + 3.0541 log height
n = 56

log weight = 3.6196 + 2.8230 log length

n = 56

FIG. 2.13. Relationships between body weight and measurements of the female African elephant.

MORPHOLOGICAL TUSK CHARACTERISTICS.

Information on morphological characteristics of elephant tusks has a rather large number of practical applications. Elder (1970) in Luangwa Valley of Zambia studied elephant tusks and found that he could identify the sex of elephants with surprisingly high accuracy by only using the shape of tusks. He misjudged the sex of only two elephants by merely glancing at 60 tusks, and rationalized that "if sex of the animal from which a tusk was taken can be thus distinguished it would greatly enhance (1) chances of finding morphological differences [among] populations, (2) judging the age distributions of a harvest, and (3) determining mortality rates as pointed out by Laws (1966, 28)." After weighing and measuring large samples of tusks from Bechuanaland (Botswana), Zambia, Uganda, and the Congo (Zaire) in the Ivory Room at Mombasa, he concluded that "weights of tusks from Botswana are usu-

ally underestimated in the field because elephants of this population have tusks that are deeper rooted and larger in circumference than are tusks from other regions studied" (Elder 1970, 158). Seemingly, the more knowledge managers of hunting safaris have on tusk morphology, the better they would please their clients in selecting a trophy elephant in the field.

Numerous studies have reported on the morphological characteristics and growth rate of tusks of the African elephant: Humphreys 1926; Perry 1954; Colyer and Miles 1957; Foran 1960; Brooks and Buss 1962b; Deraniyagala 1963; Laws 1966, Owen-Smith 1966; Sikes 1971, and Parker and Amin 1983. No information was found, however, on volume of tusk pulp cavity and only limited information was found on statistical treatment of various parameters related to tusks. Thus the purpose was to study some of these parameters and amplify current knowledge of morphological and growth patterns of elephant tusks.

Methods and Materials. Tusks from 42 female and 39 male savanna-type African elephants (*Loxodonta a. africana*) were collected in western Uganda between July 1958 and May 1959 and used in this study. Ages were estimated by molar succession and laminae wear. Tusk measurements used are the length measured along the outside or convex curvature, girth or circumference measured at the gum line, weight, and volume and depth of pulp cavity. If two tusks were available, average measurements of both were used. Pulp cavity volume was obtained by filling the cavity heaping full with dry sand, scraping the sand level with the end of the tusk, and measuring the volume of sand that it held. Measurements of girth, length, and depth of pulp cavity were made using a standard steel tape. The mean value and standard deviation were calculated for all parameters of tusk growth.

Results. In Figure 2.14 age is plotted against tusk length for 16 males and 28 females. The figure shows that males have longer tusks than females of the same age. Evidently tusks grow throughout the life of both sexes, but the ultimate length of tusks from females is shorter than those of males. There also is a suggestion that females may experience a slowing of tusk growth relative to length at about 30 yr of age. From a sample size of 81 animals for which tusk length and sex, but not age, were known, the sample mean and standard deviation were computed (Tables 2.6 and 2.7). The mean and standard deviation of the average tusk length is 99.5 cm and 27.0 cm respectively for males, and 100.0 cm and 32.5

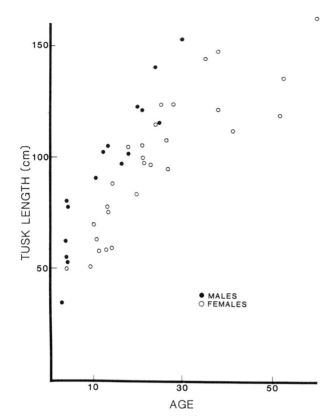

FIG. 2.14. Relationship between age and tusk length for 16 males and 28 females.

Table 2.6. Characteristics of male tusks

Parameters of Tusk Growth	n	$\overline{X}$	s
Age (yrs)	16	13.4	9.1
Body weight (kg)	38	2248.0	894.0
Left tusk			
Length (cm)	39	100.0	27.4
Girth, at gum level (cm)	39	26.6	6.1
Weight (kg)	39	5.8	3.4
Pulp cavity volume (cc)	39	1387.0	738.0
Pulp cavity depth (mm)	39	528.0	108.0
Right tusk			
Length (cm)	39	99.1	26.7
Girth, at gum level (cm)	39	26.5	6.1
Weight (kg)	39	5.8	3.3
Pulp cavity volume (cc)	39	1444.0	754.0
Pulp cavity depth (mm)	39	525.0	108.0
Average tusk			
Length (cm)	39	99.5	27.0
Girth, at gum level (cm)	39	26.6	6.1
Weight (kg)	39	5.8	3.4
Pulp cavity volume (cc)	39	1390.7	737.0
Pulp cavity depth (mm)	39	527.3	105.6
Longest tusk			
Length (cm)	39	101.3	27.5
Shortest tusk			
Length (cm)	39	98.0	26.4

Table 2.7. Characteristics of female tusks

Parameters of Tusk Growth	n	$\overline{X}$	s
Age (yrs)	27	24.9	14.3
Body weight (kg)	42	2266.4	677.3
Left tusk			
Length (cm)	42	101.0	33.6
Girth, at gum level (cm)	42	20.9	4.4
Weight (kg)	42	4.5	3.0
Pulp cavity volume (cc)	42	436.0	209.7
Pulp cavity depth (mm)	42	340.3	58.6
Right tusk			
Length (cm)	41	100.2	32.1
Girth, at gum level (cm)	41	21.1	4.2
Weight (kg)	41	4.5	2.9
Pulp cavity volume (cc)	41	441.0	216.9
Pulp cavity depth (mm)	41	334.2	63.5
Average tusk			
Length (cm)	42	100.0	32.5
Girth, at gum level (cm)	42	21.15	4.3
Weight (kg)	42	4.5	2.9
Pulp cavity volume (cc)	42	438.4	210.5
Pulp cavity depth (mm)	42	336.8	58.9
Longest tusk			
Length (cm)	41	102.9	34.0
Shortest tusk			
Length (cm)	41	97.8	31.8

cm for females. The small difference between the mean average tusk lengths of males and females is probably attributable to the younger age of males within the sample. Increased differences between right and left tusks of individuals were noted when comparing the shortest to the longest tusks in both sexes. This difference in differential wear probably suggests which tusk is the so-called "working tusk," since there is wide recognition that African elephants are either right or left tusked with a few being ambidextrous.

When volume of the pulp cavity is plotted against age, a distinct segregation between males and females becomes evident (Fig. 2.15). The pulp cavity of males is always larger than that for females of a given age. In females cavity size increases up to approximately 15 yr of age; thereafter the rate of cavity increase slows conspicuously, allegedly being correlated with puberty. The mean and standard deviation of the average of both tusks is 1390.7 cc and 737.0 cc respectively for males, and 438.4 cc and 210.5 cc for females.

A clear difference between sexes becomes evident

when pulp cavity volume is plotted against tusk length (Fig. 2.16). For males the relationship suggests that as pulp cavity increases in volume the tusk also increases in length. In females, however, the pulp cavity only increases in volume until the tusk reaches approximately

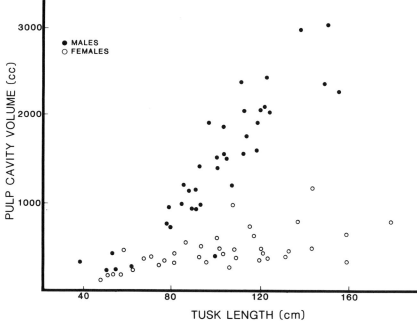

FIG. 2.16. Relationship between volume of tusk pulp cavity and total tusk length for 38 males and 37 females.

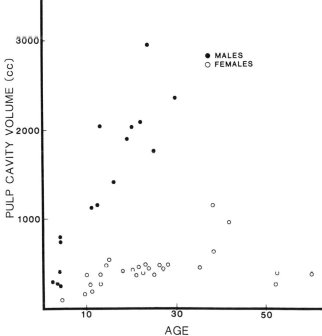

FIG. 2.15. Relationship between age and pulp cavity volume for 16 males and 27 females.

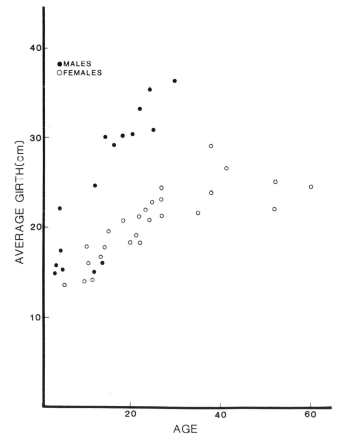

FIG. 2.17. Relationship between age and girth of tusks for 16 males and 26 females.

60 cm in length; then little or no enlargement of the pulp cavity occurs even though the tusk increases in length.

Figure 2.17 shows that there is a distinct difference between sexes regarding tusk girth with increasing age. Girth of male tusks appears to increase in linear fashion, whereas girth of female tusks appears to increase similarly until approximately 30–35 yr of age then ceases to increase almost entirely. The mean average and standard deviation of tusk girth is 26.6 cm and 6.1 cm respectively for males, and 21.1 cm and 4.3 cm for females.

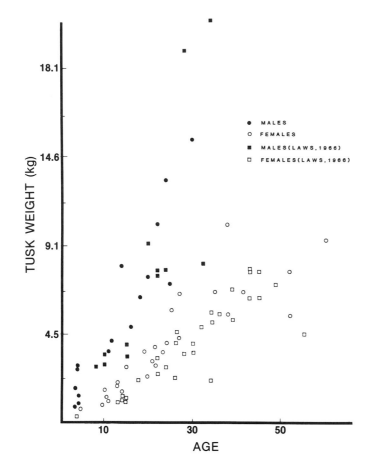

FIG. 2.18. Relationship between age and tusk weight for 16 males and 26 females from this study, and 12 males and 29 females from Laws (1966). Both sets of data were from western Uganda.

Laws (1966) disagrees, stating that "tusk growth in females is continuous and can be represented by a straight line, there is no cessation at puberty as suggested by Perry (1954) or any change in the rate of growth."

In this study, tusk growth of the female was continuous throughout life and appears to undergo a reduction in growth rate after approximately 30 yr of age. Other characteristics of tusk growth such as weight and girth also undergo a similar inflection point at a similar age. The pulp cavity increases in size until the animal is about 15 yr of age, or roughly puberty, and then decreases in volume while maintaining only a slight increase in depth in relation to total tusk length.

Growth of tusks in the male elephant is also a continuous process in which girth, length, weight, and pulp cavity volume also increase with advancing age. The exception is that the rate of increase in depth of the pulp cavity decreases significantly after a depth of approximately 500 mm is reached or 100 cm in total tusk length.

When comparing sexes, males and females both experience increases in growth of the tusk, but that of the male increases more so in girth and consequently also more in weight than that of the female. This gives the male tusk a more bulky appearance when compared to the female tusk. Also, the pulp cavity of the male elephant is significantly larger than those of females in all cases. The pulp cavity of males increases consistently throughout life, but those of the female cease increasing after puberty. Elder (1970) states that "the depth of the pulp cavity decreases with tusk size (age) in both sexes but this process sets in much earlier in females, probably at puberty." In this study this holds true for females, but for males cavity depth appears to increase throughout life.

When pulp cavity was plotted against tusk length, the relationship for males suggested that as pulp cavity increased in volume the tusk also increased in length. Tusk growth in males, therefore, can be represented by a straight line. I found no evidence of accelerated tusk growth rate in males of any age studied. In females, however, the pulp cavity only increased in volume until the tusk reached a length of approximately 60 cm; thereafter little or no enlargement of the pulp cavity occurred even though the tusk increased in length. We found no evidence of cavity closures among our females.

Figure 2.18 shows the relationship between tusk weight and increasing age. Data shown in this figure are from this study and from Laws (1966); both sets of data were collected from elephants in western Uganda. Again the data show a clear distinction between sexes. Both display a tusk weight to age relationship that appears to be a linear function although males seem to increase their tusk weight more rapidly than do females.

Discussion. There is wide and general recognition that female elephants do not grow tusks to the size grown by males (Elder 1970). Several writers state that tusk growth rates are similar in both sexes during early life, but change in the female upon reaching puberty. Perry (1954) stated that the "tusks of the female appear to cease growing soon after puberty, about the same time when growth of the body as a whole is slowed down."

Functional Significance of Pinnae Movements and Positions

After conducting laboratory studies at Makerere College in Uganda, Luck and Wright postulated that an important and controllable source of heat loss in *Loxodonta africana* is via the circulation in the pinna (ear). Arteries and veins are large, spaced alternately with wide separation and connected to a dense capillary bed. Using a special dye-dilution technique in immobilized wild elephants, they measured cardiac output and reported that the arteriovenous temperature difference reveals that a large part of the estimated metabolic output can be lost by this channel. In addition, Wright (personal communication) measured ear blood flow and found an arteriovenous temperature difference of up to 19°C under the conditions of the experiment (immobilized animals with ear hold still). The ear was shaded and there was a light breeze on each occasion. The magnitude of flow and heat loss, together with the anatomical arrangements and vascular control in the ear and the behavioral pattern of activity, convinced Wright that this is a "major controllable source of heat loss in this animal." In some of my field studies I also observed large, prominent circulatory vessels close to the relatively thin skin on the inner side of the ear of African elephants (Fig. 2.19).

Observations from my field study in Uganda in 1963 and 1964, which was conducted to obtain information on the function of ear movements and positions and their relationships to various influences, support the physiological observations of Luck and Wright. Temperatures were taken at the site of observations, nearly always by placing a thermometer in improvised shade approximately 5 ft above ground. Wind velocity near the observation site was measured with an anemometer placed on the roof of a Landrover, about 2 m high. With few exceptions, observations were obtained in the Kamulikwezi Area near the north shore of Lake George in the northern part of Ruwenzori National Park. Observations (generally with binoculars) on ear movements were recorded only if the elephants under observation showed no overt signs of detecting the observer. The term "ear flap" refers to the movement of pinnae, once forward and once back. If an elephant spread or flapped its ears when relaxed or unexcited, such positions and movements did not appear to elicit a response to danger by other elephants. However, when an elephant spread or flapped its ear in excitement and raised its head, such movements quickly evoked a response in other nearby elephants. When detecting danger a large elephant occasionally shook its head vigorously; its flapping ears resounded sharply and loudly, like the snap of a wet towel.

Data on the influence of temperature and wind ve-

FIG. 2.19. Large arteries and veins are conspicuously prominent under the thin skin on the inner side of the ear of an elephant. (*Photograph by I. O. Buss*)

When this African elephant detected danger, its head went up, its ears spread widely and rigidly, and its trunk bent downward from the base of the tusks. Nearby elephants quickly recognized such danger signals. (*Photograph by I. O. Buss*)

locity on ear movements and positions of 20 wild elephants are presented in Table 2.8. During the relatively cool periods between 7:00 A.M. and 11:00 A.M., rates of flapping for nine elephants were consistently low, varying from 0 flaps to 3.2 flaps/min. Wind velocity was low during this period, reaching a maximum average of 5.6 km/hr; temperature varied from 19°C to 25.5°C.

During relatively hot periods between 11:00 A.M. and 5:30 P.M., rates of ear flapping were highly variable. Seven of the 11 observations involved relatively low rates of ear flapping (1.3–4.5 flaps/min), which were associated with relatively high temperatures (27°–34°C) and with ear spreading. Elephants were observed with ears spread widely or angled away from their bodies when temperatures rose to 26.6°C, when winds reached a velocity of 4 km/hr, and when they faced or walked downwind. Apparently the air circulated fast enough about the ears to preclude the necessity for rapid flapping. The three highest rates (14.7, 20.7, and 22.8 flaps/min.) were observed when the temperatures were 36°–31°C and wind velocities were 8.5, 5.0, and 3.0 km/hr

respectively. These three elephants did not spread or angle their ears away from their bodies while they were under observation. One of the 11 elephants observed during this hot period flapped its ears 5.3 flaps/min but there was no ear spreading. Evidently the temperature of 26°C was low enough to preclude the necessity of ear spreading.

After 5:30 P.M. when temperatures declined and winds subsided, ears flapped at rates (1.6–3.5 flaps/min) similar to those recorded during the cool morning periods.

The relationships between rate of ear flapping and ambient temperature is shown in Figure 2.20. Excluding the seven individuals that spread their ears, a correlation coefficient of 0.85 (based on data from 13 observations in Table 2.8) was found in this relationship, which is significant at the 0.001 level.

By way of discussion, the seven elephants that spread their ears away from their bodies (Fig. 2.20) had conspicuously lower ear-flapping rates than elephants that did not spread their ears, although both kinds of

Table 2.8. The influence of temperature and wind velocity on pinnae movements and positions in elephants

Observation Time (min-sec)	No. of Flaps	Flaps/ Min	Ears Spread	Wind (mi/hr)	Temp. (°C)
Observations between 7:00 A.M. and 11:00 A.M.					
28-00	0	0.0	no	none	19.0
14-00	43	3.0	no	none	19.0
336-00	0	0.0	no	1.0	19.4
42-00	129	3.1	no	1.0	19.4
17-00	23	1.4	no	2.6	22.2
5-40	16	2.9	no	1.9	22.2
60-00	0	0.0	no	2.3	23.3
12-30	4	0.3	no	3.5	23.3
12-00	38	3.2	no	1.9	25.5
Observations between 11:00 A.M. and 5:30 P.M.					
10-00	53	5.3	no	5.9	25.5
239-00	309	1.3	yes	5.1	27.2
245-00	344	1.4	yes	2.5	27.7
10-00	45	4.5	yes	4.3	27.7
10-00	207	20.7	no	3.1	30.0
5-00	116	22.8	no	1.9	30.5
9-00	132	14.7	no	5.3	31.1
9-00	12	1.3	yes	8.0	31.6
5-38	20	3.6	yes	8.0	32.2
0-46	3	3.9	yes	5.5	33.8
15-00	29	1.9	yes	6.5	34.4

behavior frequently occurred under the same environmental conditions. These elephants presumably took advantage of the wind by spreading their ears and reducing ear movements.

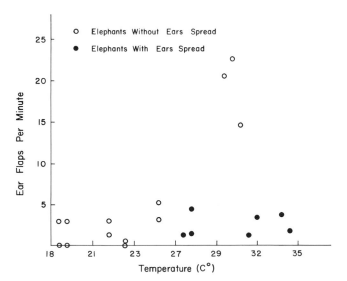

FIG. 2.20. The relationship between rate of ear flapping and temperature for 13 elephants without ears spread and 7 with ears spread.

During rains, particularly when there were accompanying winds, elephants generally ceased ear flapping and either spread their ears or held them close to their bodies. When 23 elephants were observed in a rather compact group walking into a cool breeze, about half of them flapped their ears at widely separated intervals. Approximately 15 min later the herd began stringing out into the wind, which reached a velocity of nearly 24 km/hr. When rain began falling all ear flapping stopped. Within the follow 4 min, the ears were folded close to bodies, and every elephant in the herd moved ahead with ears held continuously and closely against its body. Soon two big bulls joined and followed the herd through the rain for nearly a half hour; their ears also were motionless.

Elephants utilizing shade generally showed decreased rates of ear flapping; four adult bulls were observed standing under a large acacia tree at the edge of a forest at noon, two bulls were completely shaded and flapped their ears less frequently than two smaller bulls standing in partial shade. About 366 m from this site, two other bulls approached across a flat, open area where they were exposed to a 6.4-km wind. These two bulls each flapped their ears once for every 3–4 flaps recorded for the two partially shaded bulls under the acacia tree.

Various elephant activities preceding my observations probably affected body temperature, thus accounting for some of the variation in ear flapping under the same or similar environmental conditions.

Ear positions are used as danger signals. The following four observations illustrate the use of ear positions as signals or warnings of danger. A herd of 28 elephants moved slowly along the shoreline of Lake George during late afternoon. A rainstorm was developing, and a cool breeze swept across the lake. No ear flapping was observed until they reached a point downwind from the observers. At this point the animals showed excitement; paused briefly with trunks raised in "periscope" position; and, with much ear flapping and heads held high, turned and ran from sight into the nearest shrubbery.

A large cow accompanied by an elephant estimated at 4–5 yr of age and a calf about 1.5 yr of age were observed feeding in a marsh during the early afternoon. A sudden movement by the observer from a downwind position apparently caught the attention of the cow. She quickly turned to face the observer, lifted her head, cocked her ears rigidly, and held her trunk extended straight downward. Almost immediately the two accompanying elephants showed similar responses, looked in different directions, and then all three animals moved quickly from the marsh into the nearby forest.

A group of nine bulls fed and moved slowly through a marsh during the midafternoon. The elephants were well dispersed with a young bull following rather widely at one flank. Suddenly the young bull showed concern over a small group of marabou storks standing close to where he was walking. He raised his head, flapped his ears, and with tail raised, walked stiffly toward the rest of the herd. The other elephants stopped, lifted their heads, ceased all ear movements, and faced the young bull, which had stopped about 7 m from the nearest elephant. At this point the young bull turned, faced back toward the maribous, and lowered his head. Almost simultaneously the other elephants resumed feeding and continued moving slowly. Evidently lowering the head terminates the signal.

While David Sheldrick and I were approaching six big bulls in the remote area north of the Galana River, Tsavo National Park (East), Kenya, one of the bulls detected our approach. His head raised until the tusks were pointed nearly straight forward, his ears were partly spread, and his tail was held stiffly upward as he started walking off into the dense stand of trees and shrubs. Within a few seconds the other five bulls assumed practically identical postures and moved off with the first bull. An attempt was made to follow them, but the bulls made a complete circle without once permitting a close approach. Even when the bulls paused upwind under several large trees surrounded with dense shrub and vine cover, they appeared tense and gave the distinct impression of readiness to charge.

With one exception, these observations of wild elephants showed behavior similar to those reported by Kühme (1963), who studied behavior of three 11-yr-old East African bush elephants in an enclosure at Krönberg, Germany. In summarizing his observations on ear movements, Kühme stated that "these observations permit the conclusion that when the *a* animal flaps his ears because it is warm this is also understood as implying aggression." Although I did not observe this behavior, it could have occurred without my recognizing it, or perhaps (as Kühme stated) "this behavior may be a captivity phenomenon arising from living in a confined space with insufficient environmental stimuli."

Origin of Rumbling Sounds

A mild breeze whispered through the acacias, colorful starlings restlessly moved about reflecting metallic sheen of wings and tails, and a well-worn hippo trail led through the tallgrass to the lake beyond. Here was an ideal camp site.

A large bull in Ruwenzori National Park holding his ears outward about 30 cm thus exposing their inner side to a tail wind of 13 km/hr. Relative wind direction is registered by the bull's tail and the bending grass. (*Photograph by I. O. Buss*)

STRUCTURE AND FUNCTION

William O. Pridham, the ranger of Toro District, led us and his headman Uano to this site on 25 July 1958. I followed in our Landrover with my wife Kay, my headman Camilo, scout Lorentio, and his porter Pedro. Bill's campsite was about 500 m from Lake Kabalega and a small fishing village. An area was nearly cleared of tallgrass for tents and a cooking space when Pedro, completing the clearing operation, swung his panga close to a lion sleeping in grass under an acacia tree. With two or three muffled thumps the lion bounded up and sprinted out of sight down the hippo trail. Already the campsite was providing excitement. On the numerous occasions I traveled with Bill in elephant lands of Uganda, we never camped more than once on exactly the same spot. He insisted on clean ground for camping to reduce the potential of contacting disease-carrying organisms. I never disagreed with his philosophy.

That evening I asked Bill about elephant rumblings. Do elephants make rumbling noises in their abdominal cavities, their throats, or both? Opinions varied widely on this controversial subject ever since the writings of Pliny in the fifteenth century on the *Romance of Alexander* and the Anglo-Saxon *Epistola Alexandri ad Aristotelem*. More recent popular articles on elephants invariably refer to this phenomenon, notably Percival, *A Game Ranger's Note Book*, 1972, 173; Temple-Perkins, *Kingdom of the Elephant*, 1955, 46; Shebbeare, *Country Life*, 28 September 1961; and many others. To my knowledge no writer had supported Pliny's beliefs on the origin of these noises with convincing evidence.

While I was studying elephants in Uganda (1958–1959) at least six different hunters emphasized that rumbling noises are made when the elephants are unaware of the presence of humans, but with the first detection of approaching humans the rumbling ceases. Therefore, while stalking an elephant, a hunter knows when he has been detected and must be prepared to shoot. The hunters revealed no unanimity of opinion regarding the origin of the noises, but they all agreed that an elephant can start and stop the noises at will. With luck, Bill and I decided we might approach an elephant along the lake edge to within hearing distance of its rumblings.

On the following day we left camp with a two-fold objective: find and approach at least one elephant close enough to study possible rumblings; and collect an elephant for further scientific study. We were lucky, for I obtained my first observation of this rumbling phenomenon. A large bull was observed feeding from a clump of small trees at the swampy edge of Lake Kabalega. We approached very cautiously to listen for rumblings and possibly to collect the bull. At a range of about 50 m downwind, the bull's rumblings were heard clearly. This sound continued while the elephant fed and until we were 15 m from him. Then very abruptly the rumblings ceased, and the bull stopped feeding as he turned slowly in our direction. Evidently he heard us, turned to investigate the source of the sound, and thus exposed his head to a lethal shot. Although the job of measuring, dissecting, and weighing the carcass required the rest of the day, we had accomplished our objective.

Rumblings were observed on numerous subsequent occasions. Sometimes only one elephant was involved; on most occasions individuals were heard rumbling when there were up to 20 or 30 animals in a group. As discussed in Chapter 1 under "Assisting Wounded or Dying Elephants," I studied a herd of 1,000 at close range from 9:00 A.M. to 12:15 P.M. and during this time there was hardly a moment without trumpeting, rumbling, grunting, or purring.

In each experience I had with rumbling elephants, one facet of their behavior was notably constant—the stopping and starting of their rumbling was under perfect control.

The fact that these rumbling sounds are under voluntary control leads to a preliminary conclusion. In reviewing the functions of the mammalian nervous system, the reader is reminded that the autonomic nervous system innervates various internal glands and the smooth, nonstriated muscles of the body such as those in the walls of hollow organs, including the stomach and intestines. Since all activities regulated by the autonomic system are, with rare exceptions, involuntary, it becomes evident that functions of the stomach and intestines are not under voluntary control. There is a high probability that digestive processes within the elephant's stomach and intestines result in certain sounds, but one can safely assume that these are involuntary, irregular, and not of uniform pitch. Therefore, I conclude that the clearly audible, and rather continuous rumblings or purrings that an elephant makes under conditions described above do not originate in the stomach or intestines.

In 1961 elephant sounds were studied in a group of six captive elephants at the Basle Zoo, Switzerland, through the generous cooperation of Dr. Ernest M. Lang, director of the zoo. Five of the elephants (two males) were Africans, having been captured in Tanganyika in 1952, when they were about yearlings. The other one (a female Asian yearling) was obtained from India in 1956. For three days I accompanied and talked with Mr. Werner Behrens, formerly an elephant trainer and handler for Hagenbeck Circus, who had done an outstanding job rearing and training the Basle elephants.

While we were discussing the subject of sounds made by elephants, Mr. Behrens assured me that he could stimulate any of his elephants to make the sound I had described. One of the females was called and Mr. Behrens began to stroke her and talk to her in "elephant language," which I could not understand. Within a very few seconds, she lifted her head slightly, straightened her trunk and began rumbling or purring. There was an immediate response by the other five elephants that quickly closed in about us, squeezing us rather uncomfortably in their midst and forcing us to stop the experiment. We decided to continue the observations the following morning before the elephants were released from their chains.

At 8:30 A.M. the next day, while the elephants were still chained in their individual spaces in the elephant house, Mr. Behrens stimulated four of the elephants (two females, one Asian and one African, and two African males) to make the same kind of purring sounds I had heard in Uganda. In each case when the stimulated individual started to purr, the other elephants strained to the limit of their chains leaning toward the purring individual. While I held my right hand on one of the female's throat and my left hand over the tip of her trunk, Mr. Behrens stroked her udder. As she purred I could feel vibrations clearly and definitely in her throat; simultaneously and synchronously there were staccatolike exhalations of air from her trunk striking against my left hand.

Mr. Behrens was firmly convinced that these purrings or rumblings are a means of communication, and that the purring from his elephants conveyed a feeling of sexual pleasure. He believed the purrings aroused the other females to jealousy and the males to attempt exertion of their dominance. The male response was demonstrated by the two bulls, butting their heads together and attempting to push each other backward after we had retired from the yard.

Regardless of the functions of these purrings or rumblings, and recognizing that certain involuntary noises occur in the stomach and the intestines, I was forced to the conclusion that the most frequently heard rumblings are voluntarily controlled and originate in the throat area.

This account was originally published in *Wildlife and Sport* (1962, 3[1]:33–35), which is now defunct. A. J. E. Cave, formerly of St. Bartholomews Hospital Medical College in London, published a report on "Vocal communication in the elephant" in *Wildlife and Sport* (1963, 3[3]:15–19) employing an anatomical technique for his study of the rumblings produced by elephants.

His observations and conclusions wholly corroborate mine. He states the "two independent lines of inquiry demonstrated that the 'grumbling' noises made by elephants are the result, not of involuntary bowel action, but of voluntary, controlled, laryngeal activity."

An excellent demonstration was given by Mr. Sam Weller, Aberdere National Park, on the effectiveness of voice or sound communication employing the purring or rumbling by the African elephant. By using his hands cupped about his mouth, he imitated the laryngeal rumbling of an elephant, and called them close to him from distances claimed up to 0.8 km. This demonstration was presented by the National Geographic Special Report on the "Last Stand in Eden," which was aired on Public Television during March 1978. Weller was shown driving a Landrover in Kenya where land and air crews were attempting to drive elephants out of farmlands where their depredations were damaging crops. Near a wooded area, Weller stopped, got out taking two or three steps from his rig, imitated the rumbling, and soon had a group of obviously excited elephants coming in positively with tails and heads up, ears spread widely as though charging, and trunks swinging. Weller kept purring, and the elephants came very close. Then they paused and showed considerable surprise by turning and slowly retreating into the thickets and trees. The higher approach speed of the elephants contrasted to their lower departure speed clearly indicated the effectiveness of Weller's rumbling call.

In all three of the observations of different elephants described above, the rumbling or purring sounds were transmitted via the elephant's trunk. Seemingly each transmission of the purrings was interpreted differently by each group of elephants. However, friendship, pleasure, or safety might fit each situation. Elephant's "language" might have various connotations, all clearly understandable to elephants but not necessarily to humans.

In the Lake Manyara area of Tanzania, Iain and Oria Douglas-Hamilton (1975, 40) reported that "elephants are never silent whether resting or feeding." However, they also reported that "following our tracks, but unobserved by me, an elephant family had strolled down the path as silently as the clouds moved in the sky." Does this suggest that elephants have several levels of communication, and under certain conditions transmit signals inaudible to humans?

Although one cannot rule out that the elephant might be able to send and receive signals entirely inaudible to humans, I am not familiar with morphological structures suggesting such a communication system.

Seems that in '89 or '90, he'd know about Katie Payne's work with deep tones. When was that??

78

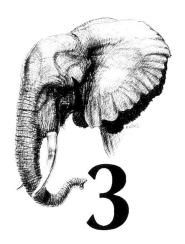

3

Numbers, Distribution, and Movements

Aerial Counts, 1957–1959

When this study was initiated in January 1957, elephants were approaching an unnaturally high density in the region of Kabalega Falls National Park in western Uganda as a consequence of a natural increase in the resident population, blocking of migration routes, and harassment outside the park combined with complete protection within the Elephant Sanctuary. Elephants apparently began increasing when the entire human population was evacuated from the region in 1912 because of sleeping sickness. This area was made into a game reserve in 1926 and converted into a national park in 1952. Although numerical data are not available to measure the actual increase of elephants over the past half century, the rise in population is reflected in conversion of arboreal vegetation to treeless grasslands as reported by Buechner and Dawkins (1961) in their study of vegetation change induced by elephants and fire in Kabalega Falls National Park, Uganda. Others also subsequently reported such changes. Also, the number of elephants shot annually during the period 1926–1958 (see Chapter 1, under "Early Records," "Control Operations, 1926–1958") reflected this trend.

The Bunyoro region, in which the southern part of the park is located, included one of the three most important concentrations of elephants in Uganda, as shown in this same report on early records.

The results of 12 aerial counts are discussed here to establish the numbers, distribution, and some migratory behavior of elephants in relation to annual rainy and dry seasons. Although use of sample plots, or strips, provide statistically reliable counts at relatively low cost, such techniques allow for no observations on distribution or migration. Thus attempts were made to obtain total counts. Hopefully this information, by providing better understanding of Kabalega and Ruwenzori parks on their elephant populations, would serve as a basis for effective conservation practices to preserve elephants in these and similar areas of Uganda (Fig. 3.1).

STUDY AREAS. Kabalega Falls National Park consists of 3,895 km² of relatively flat land 2° north of the equator. This area includes the park south of the Nile River and adjacent areas, which was divided into Blocks I, II, and III for convenience of counting and reference (Fig. 3.2). North of the river, arboreal vegetation, particularly in the northeastern part of the park, precluded accurate counts. South of the river the vegetation, except for Rabongo Forest consisting of seven patches of high forest covering about 284 ha, was sufficiently open to make counting feasible. Former woodlands and heavily wooded grasslands had progressed so far toward grassland that scattered trees did not interfere significantly with aerial observations. Occasionally a small group of elephants huddled in the shade of iso-

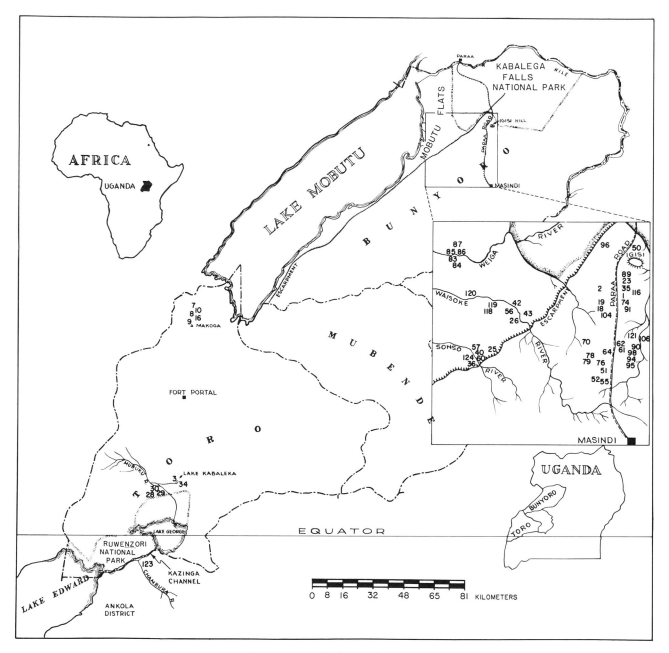

FIG. 3.1. Location of Kabalega Falls National Park in Bunyoro District and Ruwenzori National Park in Toro District.

lated trees, in which case it was necessary to circle low to disperse the animals and obtain a good count. Indeed, the study area was selected in part because of the ease with which elephants could be counted from the air. Also important in selection of the area was the significance of migrations into and through the 414-km² Budongo Forest (which is harvested for several species of hardwood, including mahogany) and the farming regions south of the study area, because the future of the elephant population in the Bunyoro region depended on policies regarding relationships of elephants to forestry and agriculture.

The average elevation of the land is 732 m, rising from a low of 620 m at Lake Mobutu to a high of 1,292 m at Rabongo Hill, which stands out as a monadnock in the center of the study area. Igisi Hill (1,274 m) forms another conspicuous landmark at the southern boundary of the park. The escarpment, which is about 305 m above Lake Mobutu, fades into the level landscape in the central part of the study area, providing an excellent topographic feature for orientation in regard to distribution and migration of elephants. The study area is well defined topographically by Lake Mobutu on the west and the Nile River on the north. The river enters Lake Mobutu at its northern end and immediately flows out northward. Since only a few elephants have ever been observed swimming the Nile River, it appeared to be an effective barrier to northward movements. Apparently significant movements from the area were mostly southward.

Rainfall according to four weather stations at the edges of the area varies from 102 cm to 127 cm annually. The bulk of the rain comes mostly as thunderstorms during the "long rains" from April through

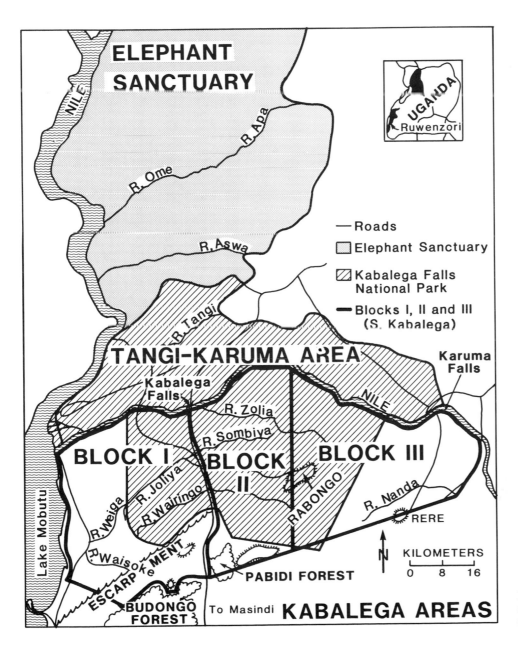

FIG. 3.2. Kabalega Areas showing Elephant Sanctuary bordering the park on the north.

June, and the "short rains" in September and October. A distinct long dry season occurs from late December to mid-March, and an inconspicuous short dry season occurs from late June to early September. Temperature is relatively uniform, from 21°C at night to 29°C at midday. Occasionally midday temperatures reach about 38°C during the driest season.

With moderate modifications, techniques of aerial counting were rather standard. Three types of aircraft were used; of these we liked the Stinson Voyager best. The additional seating capacity for extra observers, and slower speed of 105 km/hr for counting made this an entirely acceptable plane for aerial counting. Flying altitude ranged from 61 m to 224 m and averaged about 183 m.

In counting large herds (over 300 individuals), the pilot first circled in a climbing turn at low elevation and at low speed and then, for a better overall view, circled at a higher altitude. The largest herds were split into discernible groups and counted repeatedly, utilizing a mechanical hand-held counter, until reasonably close counts were obtained.

Beginning with the second count, the counting pattern was improved by dividing the area into three blocks, using natural features of topography as a means of orientation. Approximately 15 times we flew back over the region in which we had counted to check whether significant movements had taken place from areas where elephants were concentrated. Each verification of the location of large herds (100–1,000 individuals) showed that the animals had remained in the area where first seen. We were fortunate in finding no significant movement between blocks, for elephants are capable of moving distances of 32 km or more in one day. The counts showed that elephants were distributed in certain areas during different seasons, and we could predict where to find high concentrations (Table 3.1).

Although some small groups may have been recounted, this source of error probably was less important than failure to see groups. When viewing against the sun in early morning we found it difficult to see elephants that blended into long grass. Each count probably represents a minimum figure.

During the first count we photographed a herd of about 500 elephants and verified that our count from the air was accurate within 50 animals. In another check we counted 376 on photographs, compared with 386 from the air. To count such large herds we circled 5 to 10 times to ascertain the number of individuals in discrete parts of the herd identified by the concentration patterns of elephants within a big herd or by topograph-

ical features of the landscape. Exceptionally large herds (above 500 individuals) were seldom encountered, and there is a low probability that the difficulty of estimating the number in herds of such magnitude affected the results significantly. Herds of any size were counted more than once whenever we believed it necessary to satisfy our accuracy.

Our first three counts (4,153; 4,172; and 4,141) suggested accuracy greater than could have been achieved. Undoubtedly it was fortuitous that these counts fell within 31 animals of one another. The conspicuously lower level of the first three counts, compared with subsequent counts, suggests improvement of techniques and efficiency of counting with increased experience and greater familiarity with the landscape. However, our impression was that care exercised in the first three counts was equal to that of later counts and that we had enumerated not less than 90% of the elephants present. The frequency of distribution in herd size in each of the first three counts was similar to that of succeeding counts. Counts were made with increasing confidence in accuracy, but the degree of accuracy did not seem to improve progressively with each succeeding count. In all 12 counts combined, only 15 herds numbered more than 200. About half of the elephants were in herds of 50 individuals or less. Therefore, errors probably were not significant in determination of numbers within herds. The principal source of error among counts seemed to be in locating herds, and since the personnel on each flight was experienced in counting wild animals from the air, I believe that the

Table 3.1. Elephant counts by seasons, 1957–1959

Date	Number of Elephants			
	Block I	Block II	Block III	Total
Long dry season				
January 25–31, 1957	1,266	1,726	1,161	4,153
February 4–8, 1958	1,911	2,799	2,247	6,957
February 26–28, 1959	1,083	2,025	2,353	5,461
Long rainy season				
May 30–June 1, 1958	4,425	4,240	3,724	12,389
May 12–14, 1959	2,712	2,266	3,414	8,302
Short dry season				
July 19–21, 1957	1,618	1,235	1,319	4,172
August 23–25, 1957	1,616	967	1,558	4,141
August 1–2, 1958	3,699	2,033	3,000	8,732
August 6–8, 1959	3,178	2,418	2,867	8,463
Short rainy season				
September 28–30, 1957	1,942	1,398	2,216	5,556
December 7–9, 1957	2,554	3,427	2,337	8,318
October 24–26, 1958	3,301	1,966	1,496	6,763

data are accurate enough to reflect actual changes in numbers, distribution, and migratory behavior of the elephants.

NUMBERS, DISTRIBUTION, AND MIGRATION IN RELATION TO SEASONS.

Plotting elephants counted during the 32-mo period in relation to rainfall showed a stable population of elephants during the 7-mo period from January through August 1957. Migration into the study area apparently began in late September with the start of the short rains, and by early December the number of elephants was double that of the initial population. No counts were made in October and November because no aircraft was available. Despite this 2-mo lapse, the belief was that the increase that began in mid-September continued until it reached a peak about the first of December. The first five counts apparently reflect an actual increment in the population of elephants in the park and neighboring areas as a result of migration. The major migration seems to have occurred during the "long rains" in 1958, culminating in a peak of 12,389 on 1 June 1958. Over the succeeding 2 mo, egress probably resulted in a decline to 8,732 elephants, which continued until the end of February 1959, reaching a low point of 5,461 animals. Thereafter, the number increased to 8,392 by mid-May, remaining at that level until termination of the study in 1959.

Evidently ingress into the study area, beginning with the short rains in mid-September 1957, resulted in a permanent increase in numbers for the period of the study. In each of the 3 yr the number of elephants was at its lowest level during the long dry season. Major migrations into the park occurred during the long rainy season in 1958 and 1959; during most of the period from December 1957 to the termination of the early aerial counts, approximately 8,000 elephants were in the study area.

Despite the variation in population levels during the course of the early aerial counts, seasonal patterns of distribution were evident when the observations were plotted and studied.

Long Dry Season (December–March).

As soon as the grassy vegetation is combustible in mid-December (or earlier on the driest sites), fires are set by local people everywhere in Uganda until the whole countryside is burned over within a period of about 3 wk. Fires vary considerably in size, the largest covering about 130 km², and many fires are required to burn most of the vegetation in the entire region. Consequently, the larger

animals easily escape the fires and rarely suffer from a shortage of food. The basic purpose of burning seems to be to provide grassy vegetation and new growth for domestic and wild ungulates. At one time the assistant district commissioner set "burning days" allegedly to help control the Tsetse fly. Burned areas in the park soon became green with fresh growth of perennial grasses, attracting elephants, buffaloes, and antelopes. The concentration of elephants in the center of the study area in January 1957 resulted from advanced growth of grasses appearing as an island of green vegetation surrounded by a broad region of black, more recently burned vegetation.

In the western part of the study area, as part of the long dry season, January and February were characterized by comparatively few elephants along the Waisoke, Weiga, and Izizi rivers (Fig. 3.1) and the intervening areas between these rivers below the escarpment, which were favorite concentration places in other seasons. With the onset of the long dry season beginning about mid-December, most of the elephants migrated from the grasslands below the escarpment to the higher elevations of Budongo Forest and its contiguous wooded grasslands above the escarpment. During the period from late December to late March, the daily rhythm consisted of crepuscular and nocturnal movements to forage in open wooded grasslands surrounding the Budongo on the west, north, and east, with a diurnal return into the high forest. Wooded grassland most favored were a 5-km-wide strip between the Budongo Forest and the escarpment, and the area between the Budongo and Pabidi forests (Fig. 3.1). Failure to observe elephants in these areas during the height of the dry season very probably resulted from their daytime preference for the forest. The high incidence of 88% grass in the stomachs of 71 elephants, 57 of which were collected from the periphery of the Budongo Forest in the dry season (see Chapter 6 under "Analysis of Stomach Contents"), suggests that these movements were correlated with feeding.

Since rivers such as the Waisoke, Weiga, and Izizi provide permanent water throughout the year, movements over the escarpment to the Budongo Forest during the long dry season appear to be more closely related to forage supply than insufficient water. One obvious forage limitation results from the annual burning of grasslands, which occurs in early December on Mobutu Flats where the grasses dry sooner than in the more moist areas between the escarpment and the Budongo Forest. The relationship of early burning below the escarpment and later burning above it had probably prevailed for centuries.

During the long dry season, elephants were scarce east of the park and notably absent from the Nanda River swamp in Block III (Fig. 3.1).

Long Rainy Season (April–June). With the onset of the long rains in late March 1958 and 1959, elephants migrated back to Mobutu Flats and into the park in large numbers. In 1959 the timing of the movement from Budongo Forest to Mobutu Flats was noted and reported in the food habits studies. Between 18 and 23 March, four herds, each numbering at least 100 elephants, were observed between the Budongo and the escarpment, all traveling westward. On 25 March, about 400 elephants were seen feeding close to the Waisoke River and traveling downstream. Despite biweekly observations on Mobutu Flats from early January onward, these were the first elephants recorded between the Sonso and Weiga rivers on Mobutu Flats since 10 December 1958. By mid-April elephants were about as numerous below the escarpment as they were prior to the start of the dry season. During May–June 1958, and again in May 1959, about 500 elephants were observed in the wooded grasslands peripheral to Budongo Forest, indicating greater diurnal activity. Apparently there was not a complete exodus from the Budongo Forest to Mobutu Flats and the park during the long rains.

East of the park, elephants were more numerous during the rainy season, especially in the Nanda River swamps. The herd of about 1,000 observed at Rere Hill in May 1959 was traveling northwestward toward the park.

Short Dry Season (June–August). Distribution during the months of July and August differed from that at the end of the long rains, in having greater concentration along the main streams. Although numbers were somewhat reduced during the short dry season, elephants continued to utilize the study area east of the park boundary. Vigorous early growth of grasses, initiated by the long rains, fostered continued growth into the short dry period, providing an abundance of forage, which was associated with wide distribution of the elephants.

Short Rainy Season (September–October). Despite additional rainfall in September and October, elephants withdrew into the park from the eastern area; on the west side of the study area the animals concentrated in the Waisoke-Izizi-Weiga river area. Only a few elephants were seen between the escarpment and Budongo Forest. In 1957 a definite ingress into the study area occurred from September to November, and in 1958 there was an egress during the same period of the year. This reversal of behavior suggested that the short dry and short rainy seasons had little influence on movements. In 1958 there was, in fact, virtually no dry period in July and August, yet the numbers of elephants declined steadily in the study area from early June to the January–February 1959 dry season.

INFLUENCE OF THE PARK ON NUMBERS AND MIGRATION.

Before initiating the present study, we were informed by personnel of the Department of Game and by longtime local residents that elephants followed an annual pattern of migration involving movement out of the park in June and a return in November. The greatest number of animals occurred in the park during the long dry season from late December through March. That elephants seemingly concentrate in a predominantly grassland region during the driest period of the year is incongruous, especially where the grasses are burned annually. However, burning occurs in a spotty pattern, and some patches, particularly between water courses, remained unburned in the interior of the park until well into January or early February; some of the marshy areas did not burn at all. Moreover, water from permanent streams and some springs was within easy reach of elephants nearly everywhere in the park. An abundance of forage and water in proper distributional relationship probably is the attraction responsible for maintaining large numbers of elephants in the park during the dry season. (See also Chapter 6 under "Effects of the Dry Season".)

Southwest of the park, on Mobutu Flats where the elevation is somewhat lower, the area was drier; burning of the grasslands there occurred earlier in the year, and patches of unburned grass were infrequent. These conditions seemed to be related to the Mobutu Flats–Budongo Forest migration. In that part of the study area of the park, rainstorms drop less moisture than within the park, where generally higher elevation occurs and where Rabongo Hill forces storm clouds to rise, cool, and then release rain. The extreme eastern part of the study area, therefore, is also drier than the central park area; thus, elephants move from the driest areas to the central park areas during the long dry season.

Documentation of the original migratory pattern (presumably annual) is provided by Eggeling (1947), Buechner (1958), and Brooks and Buss (1962b). The pattern of migration and the distribution-abundance shown by the aerial counts were at considerable variance from the expected annual pattern described by earlier observers.

The counts suggested a stable population from January to July 1957, but because of the 6-mo gap between the first two counts one cannot be certain that the population did not fluctuate. There may have been an ingress with the beginning of the long rains, as in 1958 and 1959, with a subsequent egress prior to the July 1957 count. An October–November ingress was evident in 1957. The ensuing decline of about 1,400 elephants, occurring between the counts on December 1957 and February 1958, appeared to be related to the movement from Mobutu Flats to the Budongo Forest.

During the January–February dry season in both 1958 and 1959, about 1,500 elephants were conspicuously absent from Mobutu Flats. They returned with the onset of the long rains in late March. The additional increment from March to June 1958, beyond the numbers accounted for by the movement from the Budongo Forest to Mobutu Flats, seems to have resulted mainly from ingress across the Masindi-Matunda Road. Observation of a herd of about 1,000 elephants migrating northward close to Rere Hill on 14 May 1958 supports the probability of ingress along this pathway. Elephants may also have moved, however, into the study area from the 648-km² tract of uninhabited heavily wooded grassland between the southern boundary of the study area and the northern extent of cultivated lands. Because of the extreme difficulty of sighting elephants in the dense arboreal vegetation of this area, no systematic counts were attempted. A fortuitous observation of 300 elephants in a single herd on 18 July 1957 suggests that the area could conceal substantial numbers of animals. The Budongo and Pabidi forests may have been a third source of elephants migrating into the central part of the study area. Irrespective of the sources, which could not be determined accurately at that time, the influx of elephants, correlated in the study with the beginning of the long rains, did not fit the prescribed migratory behavior based on observations made prior to 1957.

Egress from the park apparently began in June 1958 as expected according to the observations of earlier observers, but it continued until the middle of the long dry season in January and February 1959. The November influx failed to materialize. The low point in February 1959 corresponds with the low in February 1958. About 1,500 elephants can be accounted for in the Mobutu Flats–Budongo Forest migration, but an additional 5,000 individuals emigrated from the study area between June 1958 and February 1959, some of which returned with the onset of the long rains in March 1959. The latter did not leave the study area in June, as expected from previous hypotheses, but remained at approximately the same level from May to August 1959.

In summary, the data from the series of counts showed that the migratory pattern of elephants during the period from January 1957 to August 1959 did not follow the annual pattern described for previous years. Whether the elephants changed their behavior or whether the earlier interpretation was inadequate is debatable. If there was a past annual pattern of migration, it had been disrupted by expansion of cultivation and by control of elephants by shooting to prevent damage to agricultural crops. Such changes in migratory behavior and drastic restriction in distribution in Uganda were reported by Brooks and Buss (1962b).

Frequency Distribution of Herd Size. Frequency distribution of herd sizes indicated that about 90% of the elephants occurred in herds of less than 20 individuals. Large herds of 800 to about 1,000 elephants were relatively rare. Although a herd of about 500 was seen on the first count, all herds were smaller in size during the five succeeding counts made over a 14-mo period. A herd of about 900 was seen on 1 June 1958 at the head waters of the Nanda River, southwest corner of Block III (Fig. 3.1), and a herd of about 1,000 was seen on 14 May 1959 close to Rere Hill, approximately 16 km east of the former observation. I observed a herd of at least 1,000 elephants near the Sonso River on Mobutu Flats on 19 November 1958.

During the December 1957 count, when 8,318 elephants were enumerated, 74% of the young were in groups of less than 40 individuals; during the June 1959 count when 12,389 elephants were recorded, 62% were in groups of less than 40 individuals. The difference between these percentages and the slight difference in frequency of distribution within the herd size-classes are not significant in view of additional data (see Chapter 4 under "Month of Parturition and Moisture Pattern").

Annual Increment. During two counts conducted by Longhurst and Buechner during the long rainy season of 1958 and the short dry season of 1957, a concerted effort was made to obtain accurate counts of young elephants in each herd. Elephants are able to walk under their mothers during most of their first year of life, and we used this criterion as well as we could to classify

Elephants that can walk under their mothers and have no visible tusks were considered not more than 1 yr in age. (*Photograph by Norman Meyers*)

young-of-the-year. Some individuals may have been over 1 yr of age. We flew as low as necessary to disturb and rout compact herds to obtain total counts, particularly of the young. Without this procedure young elephants could have been overlooked in the center of a compact mass. A few large herds, in which it was impossible to obtain an accurate count of the young, were not included in the enumerations. Comparison of the standard deviation calculated for the percent of young in each herd size-class indicated good precision between the two counts and reflects uniformity in technique and observation (Buss and Savidge 1966).

During the May 1959 count, Buss and Brooks (1961) made accurate counts of 2,067 calves or about 25% of the total number of elephants, in herds numbering up to about 100 individuals. Young were counted only in herds where the number and size could be determined positively. We concluded then that, on the basis of ground and aerial observations, the proportions of calves in this region of Uganda during 1959 was about 7.5%.

The percentage of young in the three aerial counts were 7.2%, 7.1%, and 7.3%, respectively. These figures represent remarkable precision. Accepting an annual in-

crement of 7–8% seems reasonable for the elephant population in Kabalega National Park and vicinity for that time.

Although data based on aerial counts suggested that breeding occurred throughout the year without significant peaks, later studies showed that such peaks did occur. After completing this study in 1959, I teamed up with one of my graduate students on a study of reproduction in which a relationship was shown to exist between rainfall and reproduction of elephants in western Uganda. There is an increase in breeding as the rainy seasons progress and a decrease as the drier seasons progress, suggesting that there is a lag in the response of the elephants to some changes in the environment induced by the rains (see Chapter 4, under "Month of Parturition and Moisture Pattern"). Laws and Parker (1968) and Laws (1969a) also found evidence for seasonal breeding in Kabalega.

Aerial Counts, 1963–1964

The 12 aerial counts conducted in the southern two-thirds of Kabalega between January 1957 and August

Table 3.2. Elephant counts by seasons, 1963–1964

Date	Location	Number of Elephants					
		Block I	Block II	Block III	Total	Tangi-Karuma	Sanctuary
Short dry season							
July 17–18, 1963	SK[a]	2,570	2,118	923	5,611		
July 2–8, 1963	RU[b]	217	887	654	1,758		
Long rainy season							
October 24–27, 1963	SK	1,467	2,105	2,554	6,126	1,170	2,339
October 29–31, 1963	RU	184	487	718	1,389		
Long dry season							
March 6–11, 1964	SK	2,009	2,996[c]	2,449	7,454	1,903	4,788
March 15–16, 1964	RU	323	592	380	1,295		
Short rainy season							
May 8–11, 1964	SK	2,153	2,673	2,989	7,815	1,894	5,284
May 14–21, 1964	RU	377	471	1,374	2,222		

[a] SK = South Kabalega.
[b] RU = Ruwenzori National Park.
[c] Mean of two counts (3,363 and 2,630).

1959 were continued; four aerial counts on the same area were conducted between July 1963 and May 1964 (Table 3.2). These additional counts were made primarily to show changes in numbers and annual increment of elephants that occurred during the 5-yr interim. Also, the aerial counts were expanded to include Ruwenzori National Park, also in Uganda, for comparative information on numbers, annual increment, seasonal distribution, and migratory behavior of elephants (Fig. 3.2). Hopefully this information, by emphasizing the deleterious effects of an excessively dense population, would provide a basis for better management of elephants, particularly in the parks and other similar areas of East Africa.

STUDY AREAS. The original study area, comprising that part of Kabalega Falls National Park south of the Nile River and adjacent tracts on the east and west, will be referred to as S. Kabalega. That part of the park north of the Nile is the Tangi-Karuma area, and adjoining it on the north is the Elephant Sanctuary. These three areas collectively comprise a single tract of land that will be referred to as the Kabalega Areas (Fig. 3.1). The other tract where comparative data were sought was Ruwenzori National Park in southwestern Uganda (Fig. 3.2).

Kabalega Areas. The S. Kabalega area, where 12 aerial counts were conducted in 1957–1959, is described under "Aerial Counts, 1957–1959."

The Tangi-Karuma area consists of about 1,658 km² of relatively flat land, and is similar to the S. Kabalega area in elevation, average rainfall, and tempera-

tures. In the eastern part, *Terminalia velutina* woodland differs from a forest in that the trees grow sparsely and form a single-layered canopy undergrown by a continuous stand of grass, except where laterite outcrops and erosion prevent grass cover. Aerial counts of elephants made on several reconnaissance flights over the terminalia woodland agreed closely with ground counts made in the same area.

In the central part of the Tangi-Karuma area, grasses (*Hyparrhenia* spp.) are associated with combretum (*Combretum* sp.) savanna. In the western part, the grass savanna is associated with borassus palm (*Borassus aethiopum*), tamarind (*Tamarindus indica*), and desert date (*Balanites aegyptiaca*).

The Elephant Sanctuary is approximately 3522 km² in size, extends north from the Tangi-Karuma area and east from the north-flowing Nile River. This tract is also similar in elevation, average rainfall, and temperature to the Tangi-Karuma area, and includes large tracts of rolling grasslands intersected by wooded streams. The western vegetation of the sanctuary is wooded savanna with scattered trees (mostly *Butyrospermum parkii* var. *niloticum*) and grasses. The eastern vegetation is wooded savanna with scattered combretum associated with grasses. Part of a *Vitex-Phyllanthus-Sapium-Terminalia* woodland projects into the northeastern corner of the sanctuary and an isolated "island" of dense tropical forest known as the Zoka Forest occurs in the north-central part. Except for this forest, the vegetation north of the river was sufficiently open to make counting feasible.

Ruwenzori National Park. Ruwenzori National Park consists of 1,986 km² of relatively flat land straddling the equator in southwestern Uganda (Fig. 3.3). This study area was also divided into Blocks I, II, and III for ease of reference. Included are large tracts of flat to gently rolling grasslands consisting of *Themeda* spp.

and *Hyparrhenia* spp., smaller tracts of dry acacia savanna, semideciduous thickets at the north side of Lake George and the east side of Lake Edward, a *Celtis-Cynometra* forest of about 233 km² known as the Maramagambo Forest, a relatively small swamp in the northeast corner, and an explosion crater area of about 155

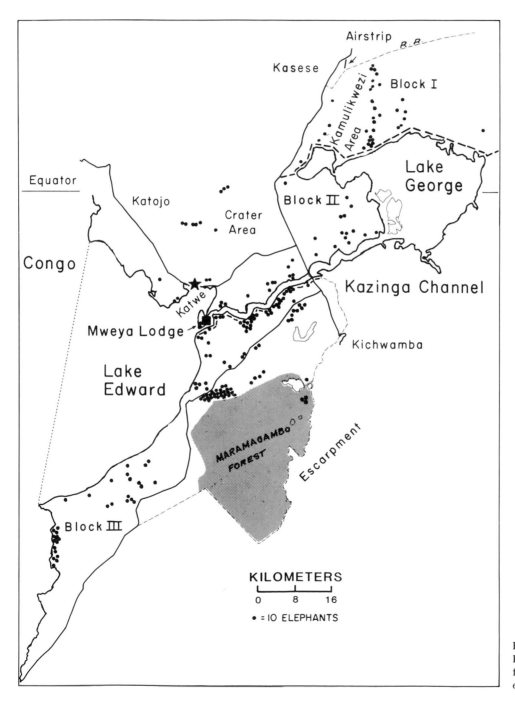

FIG. 3.3. Ruwenzori National Park also set off into three blocks for facilitating aerial counts, and ease of reference.

km² in the northwest. Except for Maramagambo Forest and part of the small swamp, vegetation was sufficiently sparse to make aerial counting practical.

Elevation of the land ranges from 913 m at Lake Edward to 1,061 m in the crater area and averages about 945 m. Rainfall varies from 76 cm to 114 cm annually, and lower rainfall occurs on rain-shadow areas near the lakes. Temperatures range from 16°C to 32°C, occasionally rising to about 38°C during midday of the dry seasons.

Wet and Dry Seasons. Accumulated rainfall data for Katwe near the center of Ruwenzori show that all areas (Kabalega Areas and Ruwenzori) typically have rains from mid-March through May (short, March–May rainy season) and another rain period from mid-August through November (long, August–November rainy season). These data also show all areas have dry seasons from December to mid-March (long, December–March dry season) and from mid-June into August (short, June–August dry season). Both dry seasons are more pronounced in the Kabalega Areas than in Ruwenzori.

Restriction of Elephant Movements. Movements of elephants into or out of the S. Kabalega area has been drastically restricted since Kabalega Falls National Park was established in 1952. Movement westward was always prevented by Lake Mobutu. Local movement between the park and Lake Mobutu has been seriously and progressively restricted by an upsurge in Ugandan occupation between the Weiga and Nile rivers and bordering Lake Mobutu (Fig. 3.1), and by establishment of the Bugungu Controlled Hunting Area in 1959 between the park and Lake Mobutu and south of the Nile River. Although a few elephants have been observed swimming the Nile, it evidently serves as an effective barrier to northward movements during most or all seasons. Local movements on the east have been curtailed by construction of a new highway through Rere Hill and Karuma Falls (Fig. 3.1) and by establishment of the Karuma Falls Controlled Hunting Area on the east boundary of the park. The Masindi-Paraa Road, skirting the south boundary of the park, was improved in 1959. This caused increased hunting pressure, which appears to have greatly reduced elephant movements in the area traversed by the road, and which was used heavily by elephants in 1958–1959, particularly during the long, December–March dry season. The restricted movements and burgeoning elephant population in the S. Kabalega area are obviously not conducive to a high rate of reproduction.

MODIFIED TECHNIQUES. Although the Stinson Voyager was the plane of choice for the 1957–1959 counts, a Piper Cruiser with a cruising speed of 153 km/hr was used on all the 1963–1964 counts. Generally, techniques were the same as those described for the counts in the 1957–1959 period, except that the flights made in 1963–1964 were flown at 183 m to 244 m except when elevation was reduced to drive out groups of elephants closely congregated under trees, or to split large herds into discernible groups. Parallel strips were maintained by adhering rigidly to cardinal points of the compass for flight headings. Strip interval was achieved by flying 2 min on a cross-leg over grassland (1 min over savanna woodland and brushy terrain) before starting the turn back on course for the next trip.

Accuracy of a particular count was probably influenced by climatic conditions that affected flying and visibility, and by differences in physical characteristics among the areas. On 7 March 1964 we surveyed Block II of the S. Kabalega area and counted 3,363 elephants. A recount of this block on 9 March resulted in 2,630 elephants, or a difference of 733 (nearly 2% fewer). Despite this difference, the percentages of calves were 5.3% and 5.8% for counts one and two respectively, and the frequency distribution of herd size for the two counts was nearly the same. Nearly midday (9:45 A.M. to 12:22 P.M.) on 7 March, turbulence and gusty winds caused the cruiser to drift and pitch on headings that quartered to the 24 km/hr to 32 km/hr southwest wind. Navigating was difficult despite our familiarity with the area and numerous good reference points. On at least two occasions distinct groups of elephants that had been counted previously were recognized close to the plane. When the count ended, our impression was that more elephants had been recounted than missed. Flying conditions were ideal without wind or turbulence during early forenoon (7:45 A.M. to 10:14 A.M.) of the second count. Some elephants had moved in the 2-day interim. On the first count a herd of about 260 on the upper Sambiya River near the center of Block II and two groups of about 50 each were observed near the escarpment's termination. Only a few elephants were seen at these sites during the second count, but a higher count was obtained in the woodlands along the Joliya and Sambiya rivers near the west edge of Block II. Since more elephants were probably missed in the woodlands than in open grasslands, I believe the second count was low. Consequently the average of these two counts is used in this report.

All other counts in 1963–1964 were conducted under more favorable climatic conditions than existed during the first count on Block II in March. With that exception, the counts in 1963–1964 were probably conducted no less efficiently than those in 1957–1959 when the impression was gained that not less than 90% of the elephants present had been enumerated. Flights started in the morning with the first good light, ceased during midday when winds and turbulence tended to be highest, and continued in late afternoon until good light waned. Flights were canceled during rain or during heavy smoke-haze from grass fires, which were numerous in the dry seasons.

In 1963–1964 a total of 92 hr 36 min flying time (66 hr 44 min counting time) was utilized to obtain a total count of 51,048 elephants on four areas of 11,052 km². Chiels Margach, who served as pilot for 28 hr 36 min flying time (22 hrs 1 min counting time), generally flew the same area for each count. Likewise, John Savidge served as pilot for 64 hr flying time (43 hr 53 min counting time) and flew the remaining areas for each count. Since the same two men used the same plane and served as pilots for nearly the same respective areas on successive counts, and since the personnel on each flight was experienced in counting elephants from the air and with the areas surveyed, I have high confidence that the data are accurate enough to reflect actual changes in numbers, distribution, and migratory behavior of the elephants.

NUMBERS, DISTRIBUTION, AND MIGRATION IN RELATION TO SEASONS.

Aerial counts for Kabalega Areas indicate a gradual increase on the S. Kabalega area from 5,611 elephants during the short, June–August dry season to 7,815 elephants during the short, March–May rainy season (Table 3.2). Evidently the June–August dry season of 1963, which began early in June and continued almost unabated into early November, caused an unusually early movement of elephants from the S. Kabalega area. Late in the long, August–November rainy season, a return movement apparently started, for the number of elephants in the area increased slightly over the previous season. The highest number (7,815) was counted during the rainy season in May, suggesting major immigration at that time and substantiating earlier observations during this season. The relatively high count of 7,454 during the long, December–March dry season on the S. Kabalega area was unexpected since this was the period during which the lowest counts were previously obtained (see discussion under "Aerial Counts, 1957–1959").

On the Tangi-Karuma areas the count was highest (1,903) during the December–March dry season; a relatively high count was also tallied on the Elephant Sanctuary during this dry period.

For Ruwenzori National Park the distributional and migratory pattern was different. Although the highest count (2,222) was recorded there during the March–May rainy season, the lowest count (1,295) was enumerated during the December–March dry season.

Interpretation of the counts obtained is as follows: (1) some elephants began to move into S. Kabalega area during the long, August–November rainy season; (2) major migrations into all study areas occurred during the short, March–May rainy season; (3) fluctuations are indicated by relatively high counts in the Kabalega Areas during the long, December–March dry season and the low count during the same period in Ruwenzori; and (4) during the 1-yr period of this study an average of approximately 6,750 elephants were in the S. Kabalega area, or about 1,000 fewer than the number reported for this same area between 1958 and 1959. The early counts of 1957–1959 are probably most representative of the numbers of elephants in the area during the earlier period of study.

Short Dry Season (June–August). In the S. Kabalega area during early and mid-July elephants occurred in average numbers and were distributed widely through Block II and in medium-sized herds along streams and close to the park boundary in Block I. Elephants were notably scarce in the eastern part of the area, and very few were seen between the escarpment and Budongo Forest. Ground observations obtained throughout July and August between Lake Mobutu and the escarpment disclosed many groups consisting of 9–75 elephants scattered between the Weiga and Waisoke rivers. By mid-August these groups had coalesced into a herd of about 1,240. During September this large herd split into several small herds; some of them migrated eastward over the escarpment. One herd returned northward into the park. Family units and small herds were observed during July and August above the escarpment, mostly east and north of Budongo Forest. Evidently the elephants had moved to these areas from open grasslands earlier than usual. In 1958 elephants were observed starting their migration from Mobutu Flats eastward over the escarpment during early November. Peter Hay, district ranger for the Game Department reported that a large herd (possibly 1,000) had moved into a woodland area east of Rere Hill in June 1963. He believed that they had migrated from the eastern part of the park. My interpretation of these observations suggests that the protracted and severe June–August dry season of 1963, ac-

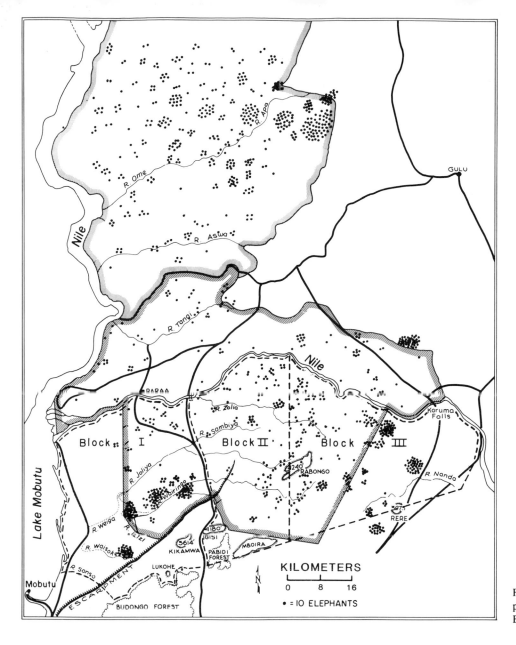

FIG. 3.4. Distribution of elephants in the Kabalega Areas and Elephant Sanctuary.

companied by extensive fires in the S. Kabalega area, caused an early and significant movement of elephants from the grasslands to the woodlands south and east of the park.

In Ruwenzori National Park, where the weather for the June–August dry season of 1963 was similar to the long-term pattern, vegetation appeared exceptionally green and dense. This condition possibly accounted for relatively high numbers of elephants in the open grasslands of the park at that time. In Block I (north of a line extended from the major bend in the highway between Kasese and Kichwamba to and along the north shore of Lake George), which includes considerable thicket, an acacia forest, a small swamp, and some grassland, most of the elephants occurred in grasslands. Also, in Block II (between Block I and the Kazinga Channel) and Block III (south of the Kazinga Channel) most of the elephants occurred in grasslands during the count in the June–Au-

gust dry season (Fig. 3.2). Thus, results of the aerial count during July in Ruwenzori suggest that the June–August dry season had little if any effect on the number and distribution of elephants in this area.

Long Rainy Season (August–November). In the S. Kabalega area temperatures were unusually high and practically no rain fell between mid-August and early November 1963. Three fires that started on 23 October near the west boundary of the S. Kabalega area swept eastward to the center of Block I and northward close to the Nile River during the night. No elephants were seen on burned-over areas when the aerial count was conducted the next day. They were concentrated along streams, particularly on the Wairingo and Waisoke rivers close to the escarpment in Block I and throughout Block II (Fig. 3.4). Herds were concentrated about Rabongo and southward to the park boundary. In Block III ele-

91

phants were also distributed along streams; one herd of about 430 occurred on the Nanda River a short distance from Rere Hill.

As a result of exceptionally dry conditions until early November, trophy hunters and live-animal catchers with jeep-type vehicles were able to operate on most of the land between Lake Mobutu and the escarpment and south of the Weiga River. These operations appeared to be extremely harassing to elephants in that area. While working intermittently from a field station on the Waisoke River between early July and late November, we observed single elephants, family units, and herds running from us when they heard our Landrover. These observations, the low count (1,467) in Block I where elephants were distributed mainly in two large herds close to the escarpment, and the increase in elephants reported by workmen in Budongo Forest, convinced us that many elephants were driven over the escarpment into the forest. There they interfered with experimental areas, and on 21 November officials of the Forest Department urgently requested a substantial increase in control operations to reduce the large number of elephants in the forest.

Relatively low counts were obtained in the Tangi-Karuma area and in the Elephant Sanctuary during the August–November Rainy Season. In the Tangi-Karuma area elephants were concentrated near the eastern end in woodlands where there was water, shade, and green vegetation. Similarly in the Elephant Sanctuary, elephants were most abundant near the east-central boundary at the edge of woodland, near the headwaters of numerous streams, and where vegetation was lush and green. This concentration of elephants near green vegetation and permanent water in the Kabalega Areas suggests that the unusually dry conditions between mid-August and early November 1963 markedly influenced their movements.

In Ruwenzori also, elephants were associated with trees and shrubs and water sources. The low count tallied in Block I suggests that some egress into nearby Kibale Forest to the northeast had occurred since the June–August dry season. Four herds seen north of Kichwamba and a herd of approximately 110 near the east side of Lake George were in woodland or wooded savannas where shrubs and vines were abundant. These herds probably represented transients migrating between Block III and Kibale Forest, since the elephants south of Kazinga Channel (Block III) migrate around the east side of Lake George and those north of the channel (Blocks I and II) usually migrate around the west and north side of Lake George (Brooks and Buss 1962a). During this season elephant numbers showed a slight in-

crease in Kibale Forest. The occurrence of elephants in wooded areas and their relatively low numbers on grasslands is similar to the pattern of the Kabalega Areas and suggests that some movement occurred during the August–November rainy season.

Long Dry Season (December–March). In the Kabalega Areas the dry conditions from early June until early November 1963 were followed by daily rainstorms that continued through the first week of December. A few rains followed, but by the third week in December the Kabalega Areas were very dry again.

I believe the intense rains of November and early December were responsible for ingress of elephants into the Kabalega Areas, where they concentrated along streams, in the eastern sector of the Tangi-Karuma area, in the east-central part of the Elephant Sanctuary, and in the center of the S. Kabalega area. Very few elephants were seen below the escarpment and outside the park in Block I, and elephants were scarce east of the park, in the western part of the Tangi-Karuma area, and in the western part of the Elephant Sanctuary. Although our count of elephants, which was completed at the very end of the December-March dry season of 1964, was unexpectedly high, the distribution of elephants throughout the Kabalega Areas appeared typical for this season.

In Ruwenzori intermittent rains fell between early December 1963 and early January 1964. Then the rains subsided and most herbaceous vegetation dried up. The low count of 1,295 elephant tallied for Ruwenzori during March 1964 was associated with a paucity of elephants in Block III. A relatively low estimate of elephants in Kibale Forest Reserve for the December-March dry season of 1964 and the scarcity of elephants in Ruwenzori during March suggest that elephants egressed from the park and forest to some other areas during this season. A westward migration from the forest through Blocks I and II into Zaire might be suggested by the distribution of elephants when plotted on a map for the March count, since approximately 70% occurred north of the Kazinga Channel.

Short Rainy Season (March–May). In the Kabalega Areas typical midday temperatures from 32°C to 37°C marked the approach of the rainy season in 1964. A thunderstorm with tornado-velocity winds blew down the radio antenna and roofs from several houses at park headquarters on the night of 11 March, indicating the beginning of the rains. Equally conspicuous was the large-scale migration of elephants into the Kabalega Areas. In our early studies of 1957–1959 we also observed that many elephants moved into the park when the rains began. On 14 March 1964 at approximately 9:00 A.M. while flying over Block I, we saw about 300 elephants in a herd immediately below the escarpment headed down the Waisoke River and a second herd of about 75–100 about 6.4 km farther down the river. The second herd was also moving downstream. In 1959 a similar movement of elephants from above the escarpment toward Lake Mobutu was also associated with the onset of rains.

Although elephants were widely distributed throughout the Kabalega Areas during the March–May rainy season, there were notable concentrations in Blocks I and III and also in the eastern part of the Tangi-Karuma area and the east-central part of the Elephant Sanctuary. Concentrations in the sanctuary were particularly impressive since concentrations were seen there during all three counts.

With two exceptions, data from our aerial counts on the Kabalega Areas show that the migratory pattern of elephants during the period from July 1963 to May 1964 followed the annual pattern described for the counts conducted between 1957 and 1959. High numbers of elephants tallied on the Kabalega Areas during the December–March dry season of 1963–1964 probably reflects increased migration to these areas during the intense rains of November and December. Apparently most of the elephants remained concentrated near streams in these areas throughout the December–March dry season, and were subsequently joined by still other migrants during the March–May rainy season. Natural movement of elephants from Block I, from the adjoining Bugungu Controlled Hunting Area, and into Budongo Forest probably resulted from a combination of protracted dry weather, shooting, and harassment by motor vehicles. East of Block III and south of the Nile River, and in Budongo Forest, control of elephants by shooting probably disrupted the annual migration pattern. Such disruption in natural migration and drastic restriction in distribution of elephants in Uganda were reported by Brooks and Buss (1962a).

In Ruwenzori Park elephants also increased in numbers during the March–May rainy season, particularly on the grasslands near Kazinga Channel (Fig. 3.2). The only observed exception to migration of elephants to savannas occurred in the crater area where elephants were scarce during this rainy season in 1964.

The most definite and probably most important conclusion that emerges from data on migratory movements obtained in 1963–1964 from the Kabalega Areas and from Ruwenzori National Park is that major elephant migrations occurred during the March–May rainy season. The importance of rain in stimulating migratory movements is emphasized by distinct migration of elephants into the Kabalega Areas between early November and early December 1963 when there were frequent and heavy rainstorms.

Annual Increment. In the Kabalega Areas, counts of calves, or young elephants not over 1 yr in age, were recorded during counts made in October 1963 and March and May 1964. Elephants that could walk under their mothers and had no visible tusks were considered to be approximately (and on an average) not more than 1 yr in age. Recognizing that a more objective technique for age estimation would be desirable and that estimating size under various flying conditions is subject to certain unknown error, we used these techniques because better ones were not available. Furthermore, errors inherent in these techniques were probably similar for each count; hence comparisons among aerial counts and between aerial and ground counts should be meaningful.

On the S. Kabalega area, the percentage of calves tallied during October, March, and May counts were 4.6%, 6.3%, and 6.4% respectively. When these percentages were compared to percentages of 7.2%, 7.1%, and 7.3% obtained during three aerial counts made between 1957 and 1959 and the average 7.5% obtained by Buss and Brooks (1961) by ground and aerial counts, a decrease in percentage of calves of approximately 1–1.5% becomes apparent. Further evidence of a decline in percentage of calves in this area during the 5 yr preceding the 1957–1958 counts is available from ground observations. Between 16 July 1963 and 11 May 1964 we classified 1,167 elephants by size into four categories (adult, subadult, intermediate, and calf). In the calf category we recorded 71 individuals, or 6.1% calves. Still further evidence relevant to this decline in annual increment was obtained in studying reproduction (see Chapter 4, under "Postpartum Conception Interval"), where the increased interval between birth of a calf to the onset of estrus resulted in increased calving interval during the highest population increase, 1953–1964. Is this trend now (1972–1986), under reduced population density, increasing in annual increment?

The percentages of calves enumerated during the October, March, and May counts on the Tangi-Karuma area and the Elephant Sanctuary were 7.1%, 6.9%, and 7.3% respectively. When these percentages are compared with those obtained on the S. Kabalega area, differences of about 1.0–2.5% are evident.

In Ruwenzori the percentage of calves enumerated

during the October, March, and May counts were 8.5%, 8.6%, and 8.3% respectively. There we also obtained ground observations on the percentage of calves based on the same criteria used on the S. Kabalega area. Between 1 July 1963 and 30 April 1964 we recorded 1,935 elephants in four size categories. In the calf category we recorded 180 individuals, or 9.3% calves. On the basis of the four figures, the annual increment for Ruwenzori National Park in 1963–1964 was approximately 8–9%, or about 2–2.5% higher than the annual increment for the S. Kabalega area.

Comparison of percentages of calves with elephant population densities on these areas shows that annual increment was inversely related to population density during the period of this study. The highest annual increment (8–9%) occurred in Ruwenzori where the average density was 2.2 elephants per 2.6 km². The second highest annual increment during the study period (7–7.5%) occurred on the Tangi-Karuma area and Elephant Sanctuary where the average density was 2.8 elephants per 2.6 km². The lowest annual increment (6–6.5%) was obtained on the S. Kabalega area where the average population density between July 1963 and May 1964 was 4.5 elephants per 2.6 km².

Here then is a good example of what we call in the United States "the Principle of Inversity" in operation. In discussing inversity, Elder and Rodgers (1968) in Luangwa Valley of Zambia, stated that "a density-dependent increase is released by a temporary reduction in numbers." Viewed another way, there is an inverse relationship between population density and reproductive gain. This principle was possibly first recognized by Malthus in 1798 (see Allee et al., 1949, 25). Later, Errington (1945) gave impetus to this principle by showing an inverse relationship between spring population density and summer rate of gain in populations of bobwhite quail. Cheatum (1947) also found this response in New York's white-tailed deer. In the northern high-density region 78% of the does were pregnant in contrast to 92% in the southern low-density agricultural region. Furthermore, about 1 in 24 of the Adirondack female fawns in the north was pregnant during its first fall of life, but in the southern agricultural region more than 1 in 3 were pregnant. Buechner and Swanson (1955) studied increased natality resulting from lowered population density among elk in southeastern Washington and found yearlings breeding. They concluded that "apparently the increase in natality reflects better nutrition through greater availability of forage . . ." After studying optimum yield in deer and elk populations, Gross (1969, 385) concluded that "fecundity rates and the net number of young produced per unit of breeding stock declines at high densities. . . . Net annual production of young by the population declines as the population size continues to increase . . ."

Reproduction in the African elephant is also inversely related to population density as shown above. Buss and Smith (1966) and Laws (1969a), working independently on elephants in western Uganda, reported evidence supporting this principle. All evidence associated with this change in natality suggests causative relationships very similar to those reported by Buechner and Swanson (1955) and by Gross (1969). Evidently reduced natality in elephant populations reflects inferior nutrition through reduction in availability of woody forage (Laws et al. 1970). An important conclusion is that "woody forage consumption by elephants is often as frequent, and occasionally more frequent, than that of herbaceous forage, but the total volume is considerably less. Evidently some woody material is consumed every day."

Movements

This study was conducted to obtain information on the movement of elephants between the Kibale Forest Reserve and Ruwenzori Park. Elephants were also studied directly and indirectly in other areas of western Uganda for comparative data on movements and associated behavior.

LOCAL, OR SHORT-RANGE, MOVEMENTS. In four different areas of western Uganda, local movement of elephants appeared to be diurnally rhythmic, but not synchronized among areas. From analyses of the direct and indirect observations secured in Kibale Forest Reserve, a pattern of movement emerged including the time of day when elephants moved into and out of forest cover-types. Evidently, elephants regulated their movements and associated activities by following changes in the thermal gradients within and among forest cover-types. On sunny days, elephants were never seen feeding in open grasslands between 10:30 A.M. and 3:30 P.M. They were frequently and consistently observed moving into shaded areas downhill and into swamps shortly after the morning sun became uncomfortably hot. Nighttime, early morning, and late afternoon feeding usually occurred at forest edges, on hillsides and tops, and in mostly open cover-types.

The movement of elephants into forest cover-types

during the morning and their return to grassland or relatively open areas during the afternoon in the reserve was very similar to elephant movements described near Kabalega Falls National Park. Between Budongo Forest and the southern boundary of Kabalega Falls National Park, elephants were concentrated in an area of interspersed woodlands and grasslands from mid-January to late March 1959. There the elephants usually retreated from savannas into woodlands soon after sunrise and started coming out of woodlands late in the afternoon. On 15 of 32 trips into this area to collect specimens for study, elephants were shot during the first hour after sunrise while they were feeding in grasslands near woodlands. On four of these occasions the elephants were disappearing into woodlands when they were first seen, and on three occasions groups were followed into woodlands to make collections. Elephants were seen on savannas at various times of the day on 13 trips, and on 4 occasions elephants were shot after sunset as they were coming out of woodlands.

In two other areas, however, the time of day when elephants moved into and out of forests was distinctly different. On the Kamulikwezi area in Ruwenzori National Park (Fig. 3.2), elephants had regular and predictable movements out of an acacia forest during morning hours. Between 4 October 1963 and 1 May 1964, I recorded 21 observations of elephants coming out of the forest at various times between 7:00 A.M. and 9:37 A.M. After coming out of the forest, most of these elephants were studied within 3.2 km of the forest edge. They drank and bathed at the north edge of Lake George, fed in the adjacent marsh, or loafed on the open shore of the lake. On six occasions between 9 September 1963 and 16 January 1964, elephants were seen traveling from the forest to the marsh between 10:45 A.M. and 1:05 P.M. Usually the elephants started back toward the forest in late afternoon. On 11 occasions from 4 October 1963 to 1 May 1964 elephants were seen heading back toward the forest between 4:15 P.M. and 9:00 P.M. Some individuals remained in the marsh until darkness, thus preventing sightings on the time of their return to the forest.

Between 22 and 26 March 1964, daily observations of elephant movements were recorded while working out of a field station operated by John Savidge (then scientific officer for the Uganda National Parks) near Rabongo Forest deep within Kabalega Falls National Park. These observations also indicated that elephants moved out of forest cover in the forenoon and returned to it in the afternoon. John Savidge informed me that this movement was typical for elephants in that locality.

Corroborating evidence of diurnal rhythm in local movement was obtained from radio-location experiments on two elephants through the assistance of R. M. Laws, then director of the Nuffield Unit of Tropical Animal Ecology, Ruwenzori National Park. During the March–May rainy season of 1965, two cows in the park were immobilized and fitted with radio collars. In addition to the radio collar, the first cow with long straight tusks had one ear painted silver. She carried the radio collar for between 30 and 40 hr after which it was found lying on the ground. Modification of the equipment resulted in a retention time of 11 days for the second cow that had a red nylon streamer as an auxiliary marker. According to Laws (personal communication) "both elephants showed very small-scale movements of a few miles, but there seemed to be a regular diurnal rhythm. One moved back and forth between a brushy savanna and a crater; the other one traveled up and down a small bush-filled valley. The cow with the painted ear and long straight tusks was identified 25 days after marking in the same valley, within a mile of the place of marking."

Regarding the different times of movement in and out of the forests, I believe that (1) temperature gradients among and within forests, (2) protective cover provided by forests in areas open to hunting, (3) availability and preference of foods, and (4) open areas with unrestricted winds to facilitate thermoregulation probably were involved in the differential movements.

To me the adjustment of times of movement to differences in local environments is an indication of the elephant's superior intelligence, a good example of flexibility of the matriarchal organization involving neural mechanisms of behavior.

Four observations of diagnostically marked individuals that occurred alone or in a group provided additional information on local or short-range movements. One of these groups, including a cow with crossed tusks in a family of seven elephants, was first seen on the bank of the Joliya River in Kabalega Falls National Park during midafternoon of 30 November 1963 (for details see Chapter 1, under "Bonding or Fidelity of Families"). This same group was seen 4 mo later, on 26 March 1964, in exactly the same spot. The cow with crossed tusks was unmistakable, even though the family now consisted of 12 individuals. All were feeding and meandering about slowly, suggesting occupance on their home range.

A second case of local movement involved a large solitary bull with both tusks broken off close to the gums. When first seen the bull was at a road junction 11.3 km south of Kabalega Falls and 22.5 km southeast

A large cow with crossed tusks and a tuskless cow with small calf distinguish this group from others. (*Drawing by R. W. "Mike" Carroll*)

of Paraa, headquarters of the park, on 3 December 1963 (Wing and Buss 1970). This same bull, with another large bull that carried heavy, well-developed tusks, was seen 3.2 km west of the first sighting on 22 December 1963.

A third record of local movement was obtained about 3.2 km south of Igisi Hill near Kabalega Falls National Park boundary in 1958. While collecting a sub-adult bull (No. 35) from a family of five elephants (adult cow, subadult bull, two subadult females, and a calf) on 5 December 1958, the leader (a very large cow) charged several times and gave a very impressive demonstration of devotion and protective behavior. The four surviving members of this family were collected within 0.62 km of the original site of observation on 22 December. Again the large cow showed extremely aggressive behavior and charged when danger was imminent. This behavior, plus the size structure of the elephants in the family unit, gave assurance of their identity.

A huge old cow that appeared near parturition was seen in a group of 12 elephants about 16 km south of Kabalega on 9 February 1959. The same cow was seen again on 4 March 1959 in a group of 12 elephants about 6.5 km from the site where she was seen 23 days previously. While studying this family on 4 March, the mem-

bers detected danger and stampeded. The large pregnant cow, however, walked slowly for about 60 m and stopped to rest while the other elephants ran out of sight. Her identity was definite.

SEASONAL, OR INTERMEDIATE-RANGE, MOVEMENTS. Elephants are able to sustain themselves in the Kibale Forest Reserve and Ruwenzori National Park areas throughout three of the four seasons of the year (Figs. 3.5–3.8). During the long dry season (December–March), however, the growth activity of forage in general is at its lowest point. Most plants undergo some degree of dormancy during this period, both in the reserve and the park. Dry grass abounds, burning is widespread, and most trees are dormant and many lose their leaves. Counts in both the reserve and the park indicate that the elephants migrate from the entire area during this period. Where they go is not definite. Possibly they go up into the Ruwenzori Mountains where rain still falls and the vegetation is actively growing, or they continue westward into the Congo (Zaire) (Fig. 3.5). By the end of February relatively few elephants remain; however, a nucleus of elephants stays in the reserve during this period, frequenting the swamps and major watercourses.

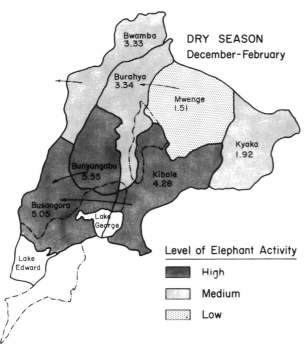

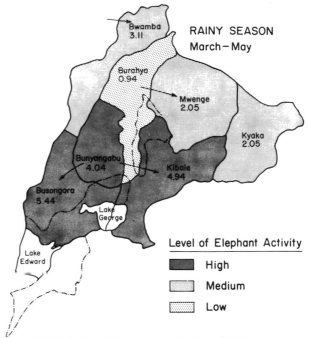

FIG. 3.5. December marks the beginning of a dry season and westward movement of the elephants from Kibale Forest Reserve and Toro District toward the Congo (Zaire).

FIG. 3.6. Population counts reached a peak in Ruwenzori National Park during May; elephants were scarce in the Kibale Forest Reserve, probably because they were still widely distributed in the grasslands.

With the onset of the short rainy season (March–May), when vegetation appears to be growing everywhere, elephant movement begins to change. Those in the Ruwenzori Mountains start downward, then disperse widely throughout the reserve; many leave the reserve entirely to feed in adjacent grasslands. The maximum regional and local dispersion of elephants is indicated at the onset of this season. Counts in both the park and the reserve are at their ebb. Good forage is available everywhere. As the season advances, elephants from the Ruwenzori Mountains gravitate to the expanses of protected grasslands in the park. By the end of this season, the park population is at its peak, but the reserve remains relatively empty (Fig. 3.6).

During the short dry season (June–August), which is often not extremely dry, physiological activity of most woody plants in the reserve attains its peak. Most woody plant species bloom and produce fruit during this period and growth in general is at its maximum while outside the reserve many plants dry up. Elephants, which were dispersed in adjacent grassland areas during the March–May rainy season, begin to move into the reserve from all sides (Fig. 3.7). Probably some of the park elephants move north into the

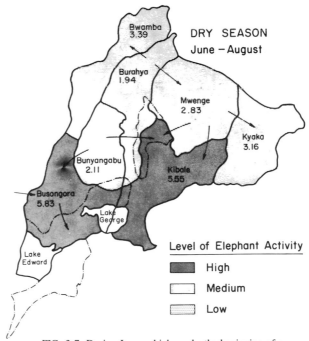

FIG. 3.7. During June, which marks the beginning of a dry season, elephants were attracted from all directions to the abundant, luxuriant vegetation in the Kibale Forest.

reserve during this time, particularly if the season is very dry and growth activity in grassland and savanna vegetation declines substantially. The dryness of this season appears to regulate largely the distribution of animals within the reserve. If the season is moderately dry, the elephants remain well dispersed throughout the reserve. Conversely, if the season is very dry, the relatively xeric South Block is avoided by the elephants in preference for the more moist Central Block. The maximum concentration of elephants in the Kibale Forest Reserve during this season probably is attributable to two factors: (1) the relative dryness of the season, which results in a general deceleration of growth activity in grassland and savanna plant species, particularly in low-lying areas such as Ruwenzori National Park, is sufficient stimulus to initiate elephant movements toward higher elevations and forested areas where plant growth has not been retarded; and (2) the attractiveness of the reserve is further enhanced by the fact that the woody vegetation attains its maximum growth activity during this season, and many fruits are mature.

With the onset of the September–November rainy season, vegetative growth is rejuvenated everywhere in the grasslands and savannas. As growth of the grasses and savanna vegetation accelerates, that of the woody

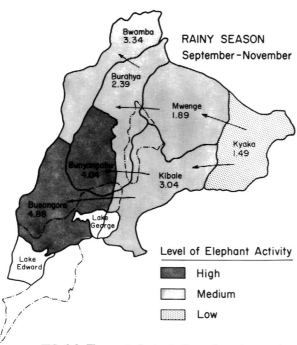

FIG. 3.8. The onset of rains in September rejuvenated plant life on grasslands, causing an exodus of elephants from the Kibale Forest.

forest vegetation probably begins to taper off; fruiting is completed in most species. Elephants respond accordingly, and many leave the reserve. Those that remain disperse widely making extensive use of its numerous grasslands. During the latter part of this rainy season and into the beginning of the December–February dry season, the animals again begin to migrate toward higher ground in the Ruwenzori Mountains and toward the Congo (Fig. 3.8). As always, some elephants remain in the forest, concentrated heavily in the swampy regions of the Central Block.

Ground and aerial observations obtained in and near Kabalega Falls National Park indicate that extensive migrations occur seasonally, particularly as a result of prolonged rain or protracted dry weather. Observations also show that elephants migrated into woodlands and concentrated near permanent water supplies during dry seasons. Likewise in Kenya the studies of Glover (1963) and Napier Bax and Sheldrick (1963) indicate extensive seasonal movements related to availability of water and foods. Brooks and Buss (1962a) indicate that drastic restrictions have been imposed on migration routes, migratory behavior, and distribution of elephants in Uganda. The magnitude of these seasonal movements generally appear to be up to 40 km or more.

I reflected on the above reports, and on those of Rodgers and Elder (1977). They found that 37 marked bulls in the Luangwa Valley of Zambia were very sedentary during the dry season but dispersed widely with the onset of rains. Thus I expected that elephants would move into the reserve during the dry seasons and return to the surrounding savannas when rains began. When eight estimated counts from the reserve were compared to four aerial counts from the park, however, they showed that elephants increased or decreased simultaneously on these two areas. On the basis of these data, I am forced to conclude that the pattern of seasonal movement was very similar on both areas, that is, egress and ingress tended to be synchronous. The similar trend in seasonal movement for the reserve and the park suggested that migration extended beyond the boundaries of these two areas. A westward migration from the reserve through the northern part of the park into the Congo was suggested by the distribution of elephants plotted on a map of the park from an aerial count of elephants conducted in March 1964. Approximately 70% of the elephants enumerated in the park during March occurred in the northern part. Such a migratory route, connecting these two areas to the Congo, was reported by Brooks and Buss (1962a).

LONG-RANGE MOVEMENTS. A long-range movement is indicated by what probably is the first return of a marked adult female elephant collected on 6 December 1963, at the southeast base of Igisi Hill near the south central edge of Kabalega Falls National Park. At the time of collection this female was pregnant and accompanied by a juvenile judged at that time to be between 2 and 3 yr of age. Dr. C. P. Luck (then from the Mulago Medical School, Kampala, Uganda, and who assisted in marking this elephant) was at the collection site on 6 December and recognized the four rectangular holes spaced equidistantly along the edge of her left ear. She was immobilized and marked in March 1961 on Semliki Plain of Toro District, about 185 km southwest of the collection site. When marked in 1961, she was accompanied by a yearling calf.

Long-range movements have also been reported by Melland (1938, 106), Rushby (1965, 27), Bere (1966, 75), and Pienaar et al. (1966); apparently the elephants were moving to areas of choice forage, mostly growth following rains.

Rodgers and Elder (1977, 60) state that "of the 14 rainy-period sightings, 7 occurred outside the marking area. One was downriver 25 km southwest; the other 5 were 25–42 km from the Luangwa River marking area and in all directions." They also state that "although distances from water were not indicated, Eltringham and Woodford (unpublished mimeo. 1968) recorded 32 sightings of marked elephants in Uganda with the farthest being about 11 km from the point of marking" (p. 59).

Following the 1970–1971 drought, which caused very heavy elephant mortality in Tsavo National Park in Kenya, Leuthold and Sale (1973) initiated a study there on home range and movements of individual elephants. Their data were obtained from two bulls and two cows radio-tagged in Tsavo (West) and two bulls and four cows tagged in Tsavo (East). Elephants in Tsavo (East) were more mobile than those in Tsavo (West). "The six elephants monitored in TsE had very much larger home ranges (mean = 1580 km²) and moved over substantially greater distances, producing a mean for the area of about 79 km, almost twice that for TsW." Movements for the six elephants of Tsavo (East) ranged from 45 km to 112 km, each based on from 22 contacts to 112 contacts. A preliminary and circumstantial conclusion suggested "that food is the proximal factor governing movements and distribution of elephants in the area. Food availability, in turn, is determined largely by the spatial and temporal pattern of rainfall (Leuthold and Sale 1973).

Their preliminary conclusion that food is the prox-imal factor governing movements and distribution is almost certainly correct. The capacity for long-range movements of elephants is still extant; the setting is nearly gone. Few people will again witness the very long migratory movements seen by Sir Samuel Baker in *Wild Beasts and their Ways* and other early writers. Also, the migratory movements, some very long, shown in one of my early joint publications (Brooks and Buss 1962a) have practically all been blocked in one way or another.

CONGREGATION AND BEHAVIOR OF LARGE HERDS. While conducting an aerial count of elephants on Mobutu Flats, adjoining the east side of Lake Mobutu, on 18 July 1963, a herd of 870 elephants was seen close to the north bank of the Waisoke River (Fig. 3.9, site 1). Four days later part of this herd was observed moving downriver about 3.2 km west of the site where they were seen originally. A careful study of the site where the 870 elephants were first seen showed broad and freshly made trails extending from the site in three directions. Evidently the herd had split; about

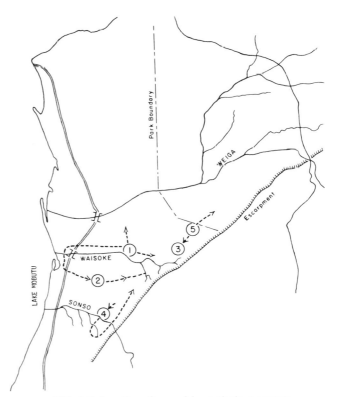

FIG. 3.9. Location of several huge elephant aggregations and movements observed on Mobutu Flats (bounded on the west by Lake Mobutu and on the east by Budongo Forest, above the escarpment) near the southwest boundary of Kabalega Falls National Park.

half moved downriver, about one-fourth moved upriver, and about one-fourth moved toward the Weiga River.

During the predawn hours of 25 July, elephants were heard trumpeting and bellowing as they moved eastward between the Waisoke and Sonso rivers toward the escarpment (Fig. 3.9, site 2). Later in the morning a broad trail and many fresh droppings were found near where the elephants were heard earlier that day. The back trail came from the Lake Mobutu Marsh and the mouth of the Waisoke River; the trail led to the upper Waisoke near the escarpment. The breadth of the trail and the number of droppings suggested a herd of about the size seen moving downriver three days previously. These observations led to the conclusion that this herd had spent about 3 days in the marsh and then returned to the river.

On 28 and 29 July 1963, many family units and herds of elephants numbering from 9 animals to 75 animals were seen north of the Waisoke River close to the escarpment (Fig. 3.9, site 3). Most of these groups were moving southward. One of the family units was identified by a large pregnant female that had a right tusk that pointed abnormally upward and a left tusk that pointed downward; thus they appeared vertically crossed when viewed from the side.

Evidently the many family units and small herds seen moving southward to the upper Waisoke on 28 and 29 July, and the large herd tracked to the upper Waisoke on 25 July, joined into an even larger herd and moved southward to the Sonso River. R. D. Fairrie, game warden, Uganda Game Department; R. Chipperfield, Chipperfield Circus, London; and Mr. Northcote, Uganda Wildlife Development, Ltd., reported that between 31 July and 18 August they saw a herd of 1,240 elephants on frequent occasions between the Waisoke and Sonso rivers, and that on 18 August they were milling about on the upper Sonso (Fig. 3.9, site 4). Chipperfield, who had seen the cow with vertically crossed tusks on 29 July, reported seeing her in the large herd.

The large herd moved northward at the foot of the escarpment and reached the Waisoke River where it was observed on several occasions between 20 and 27 August 1963. On 28 August a client of Uganda Wildlife Development, Ltd. shot a large bull from the herd, which had then reached a point near the park boundary north of the Waisoke River (Fig. 3.9, site 5). At that time the herd was reported as being split into two groups, one of about 500 elephants headed northward into the park, the other group headed southward to the Waisoke near the escarpment. This southward group was observed to split into several groups, one of which

stayed in the dense swampy cover of the Waisoke and another proceeded eastward over the escarpment.

Evidently the group that moved eastward over the escarpment disassembled into family units, one of which was seen about 11.3 km east of the escarpment and Waisoke Falls on 26 November 1963. This family of 12 elephants included the pregnant cow with vertically crossed tusks.

Four other herds of large size were also observed on Mobutu Flats east of Lake Mobutu. A herd of approximately 1,000 elephants was discovered south of the Sonso River on 24 October 1958 by I. O. Buss and C. D. Margach. Flights were made at 2- and 3-day intervals to trace the movement and ultimate destination of this herd, which was heading generally northward. By 31 October when they reached the Waisoke River, they had split into two nearly equal-sized groups. By 3 November the elephants in both groups had dispersed into smaller groups (probably family units) and were headed up the tributaries of the Weiga River or had already reached their destination within the park. Another herd of approximately 1,000 elephants was observed near the Sonso River on 19 November 1958 by I. O. Buss and J. B. Heppes, then of the Uganda Game Department. About 13 km northward and near the Weiga River a herd of about 1,200 elephants was seen by Brooks (personal communication, 1960) during the last week of November 1959. Still another large herd of approximately 600 elephants was observed on Mobutu Flats south of the Waisoke River by W. M. Longhurst, a former Fulbright Scholar engaged in wildlife investigations in Uganda, between 26 October and 5 November 1961.

The congregation of some large herds probably is a prelude to intended migration. The observations by Longhurst on the herd of approximately 600 elephants in 1961 were particularly suggestive of such behavior. On 26 October, when Longhurst began his observations, game guards of the Uganda Game Department, stationed on Mobutu Flats primarily to control elephants in areas where their activities conflict with human activities, reported seeing this herd in the Sonso-Waisoke area for about 2 wk before Longhurst's arrival. Two elephants had been shot from this herd on 21 October, and at least 20 calves had been live-captured during the previous dry season for commercial sale. Longhurst's aerial observations of the elephants' movements show that the herd meandered circuitously in this area until 4 November, when three elephants were shot from the herd, which was chased with an airplane to obtain photographs. That afternoon or night the herd moved northward; by morning of 5 November they had crossed the Sonso and Waisoke rivers and was moving toward the park.

The effects of shooting and chasing on congregation and movement of elephants on Mobutu Flats are speculative. During the nights of 2 and 3 November the herd moved southward and fed close to the Mobutu-Masindi road. Conceivably the elephants might have crossed this road and continued southward if they had not been disturbed. Brooks and Buss (1962a) reported that a widely known movement of elephants on Mobutu Flats south of the Mobutu-Masindi road was arrested in the late 1930s. Although the southward movement was arrested before World War II by intensified control operations, elephants re-established their movements over this route since 1957. The resumption of elephant migration was attributed to the increase and intraspecific competition in Kabalega Falls National Park. The drastic restriction of the main migratory routes from Mobutu Flats where these large herds congregated, and the elephants' continued circuitous meanderings over rather protracted periods, suggest restraint of migration. While working in the park with David Sheldrick, then warden of Tsavo National Park (East), during February 1964, he informed me that some of the large herds in Tsavo also meandered and moved circuitously about an area without migrating. The extent of restriction to the migratory routes of the Tsavo elephants was not ascertained.

Herds of the size that assembled on Mobutu Flats, which is adjacent to Kabalega Falls National Park, are evidently indicative of high density. John Savidge and I studied the size of elephant groups in three areas in Uganda and found a direct relationship between group size and density. The largest groups occurred in Kabalega south of the Nile River where a density of 4.5 elephants per 2.59 km^2 was recorded. The second largest groups occurred on two adjoining areas north of the Nile River that had a density of 2.8 elephants per 2.59 km^2. The smallest groups were found in Ruwenzori National Park where a density of 2.2 elephants per 2.59 km^2 was ascertained. In Tsavo National Park (East), which covers some 12,950 km^2, Glover (1963) obtained a count of 9,413 elephants in September 1962, or approximately 1.9 elephants per 2.59 km^2. That density, which is lower than those obtained in Uganda, is evidently excessively high for the more arid ranges in Tsavo, since Glover (1963, 38) concluded that "one elephant per [2.59 km^2] is apparently about the highest stocking rate possible in the Park." The three largest herds observed by Glover (1963, 34) consisted of 191, 289, and 700 elephants respectively. Herds of those sizes are not common and have not been reported in areas of low population density.

4

Reproduction

THE RANGE of the African elephant continues to dwindle at an ever accelerated rate with the inexorable increase in human population, which destroys habitat, disrupts migratory pathways, changes distribution, and alters behavior patterns. The net effect is that perhaps at least 90% of Africa's elephants are crowded into parks and other sanctuaries where much of the habitat is overpopulated (Brooks and Buss 1962a; Simon 1962; Buechner et al. 1963; Sikes 1971; Cobb 1980). Also, as a result of escalated ivory prices, which stimulated unusually heavy poaching (Cameron 1981; Eltringham 1982), elephant populations today are but a fraction of those preceding about 1972; thus the opportunity to secure quantitative or qualitative biological data on the African elephant has been critically reduced. The dense populations of 1950–1970, particularly in the national parks of East Africa, probably are a matter of history.

All management programs should be based on sound knowledge gained from research. Knowledge of elephant reproduction is especially critical; this facet of our knowledge has been gradually expanding and is now rounding out. Anatomy and development of the female reproductive system have been reported by Perry (1953, 1964) and Amoroso and Perry (1964). Early reports on age at sexual maturity and duration of gestation of the Asian elephant (*Elephas maximus*) were made by Seth-Smith (1932), Hundley (1934), Burne (1943), and Flower (1943); Hill (1953) included general information on reproduction of elephants.

The African elephant breeds throughout the year, at least in those areas for which data were available by mid-1960: Krumbiegel (1943) and Ansell (1960) observed calves throughout the year; Perry (1953) noted fetuses of variable age in cows collected throughout the year in Uganda; Buss and Brooks (1961) and Buechner et al. (1963) found no evidence of seasonal peaks in parturition and concluded that breeding occurred throughout the year in Uganda. Considering that environmental conditions within the African elephant's extensive range are highly variable and that information had been secured from a limited part of this range, the possibility of seasonal breeding in some areas could not be ruled out.

Norman S. Smith, one of my former graduate students, conducted field studies in Uganda for 2 yr; we then teamed up on the laboratory study of reproduction. This included a study of the structure of 120 pairs of ovaries from elephants collected in Uganda and considered to be of potential breeding age, mating behavior of wild elephants in the field, mating behavior of Asian elephants in captivity, and structure of ovaries sent to us from Zambia where additional elephants were collected.

Most of the data were collected from areas situated in Bunyoro and Toro districts of western Uganda, all outside but in the vicinity of Kabalega Falls and Ruwenzori National parks. The geography, vegetation, and precipitation patterns are described by Buechner et al. (1963) and Buss and Savidge (1966). Data were also collected in the Luangwa Valley in Zambia. A description of the vegetation, geography, and weather of this area is given by Trapnell (1953) and Feely (1965).

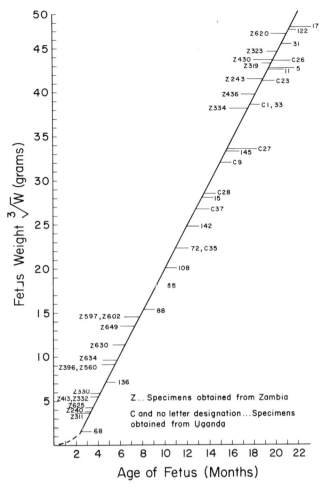

FIG. 4.1. Age-weight curve of 42 fetal African elephants, calculated from the Huggett and Widdas (1951) formula $W = a(t - to)$: W = weight of fetus (average weight at birth is approximately 124.5 kg; $a = 0.0746$ (constant); t = age in days (gestation is assumed to be 22 mo, or 660 days); $to = 0.1t$.

selected and sent to us. The age of fetus, date of collection, status of lactation, estimated age of mother, and ovarian measurements were recorded. Though elephants were collected during all months of the year, some months were better represented than others because travel and hunting conditions were variable.

Ages of the 146 females were estimated by a technique based on dental characteristics, and for most of them weight, height, and body length regressions were also used. For the few animals for which dental information was lacking, ages were estimated by using an equation based on regression of weight, on shoulder height, and on body length (see Chapter 2). There was at least one animal in each year class from 1 yr to 55 yr. Molariform replacement rate, which would seem to have a higher correlation with age than anatomical size, probably does not vary significantly between sexes. Although an average difference in body size probably occurs between males and females of the same age, this difference is less during early than late life. Accuracy is probably within a year for elephants up to 15 yr of age; thereafter accuracy becomes progressively less.

The gestation period of the African elephant is generally accepted to be 22 mo, and the average weight of the fetus is 124.5 kg. A formula propounded by Huggett and Widdas (1951) was used to estimate age of fetuses (Fig. 4.1). This formula has been used by numerous investigators. Although subject to error, this is presently the most practical method of fetal age estimation.

For macroscopic and microscopic study, routine procedures were followed in preparation of most materials (Smith and Buss 1973). In addition to the classification of cell types and vascular spaces, the amount of connective tissue, vacuolation, or any other unusual features were noted.

There is no general theme in this chapter other than to present information on various facets of reproduction that appeared to lack data or appeared to be incorrect.

Mating Observations and Seasonal Distribution

Elephants were observed copulating on 11 occasions in Uganda between August 1958 and October 1964. Additional observations of behavior related to mating were obtained during this time, and the first copulation was observed on 1 August (see Chapter 1, under "Influence of an Estrous Cow").

On 13 July 1963, at about 7:30 P.M., while watch-

Most of the 146 female elephants used in this study were collected in 1957, 1958, 1959, 1963, and 1964 in Bunyoro and Toro districts of Uganda. Field observations were recorded for these animals, and then numerous materials were obtained, preserved, and shipped to Washington State University. Ovaries were preserved in 9% buffered formalin. Various weights and linear measurements taken of the elephants are described in Chapter 2, under "Age Estimation." During 1967 the Zambia Game Department killed 374 elephants in the Luangwa Valley. Of these, 294 were examined. From 49 pregnant cows, 23 pairs of the best formalin-fixed ovaries were

ing a group of 14 elephants, a bull mounted a cow but weak light prevented assurance that coitus was achieved. The cow did not stand still and probably was not receptive. The bull kept following the cow and attempted to mount several times, but probably was not successful. During midafternoon of the following day, in almost the same place, copulation was completed. The similarity of size classes among the 14 elephants, which comprised the only group in the immediate area during both days, indicated that the same elephants were involved.

A rather loosely assembled herd of 75 elephants was clearly observed from early morning until 12:50 P.M. on 28 July 1958. Family units were recognized as they detached themselves temporarily from the herd and fed independently or moved away. Throughout the forenoon no estrous cow was seen, and there was no evidence of precopulatory play, defense of a particular cow, or close following of any cow. Among the 11 large bulls distributed widely throughout the herd, none showed antagonism or demonstrated dominance toward other bulls.

At 1:10 P.M. a medium- to large-sized bull mounted a large cow at the edge of the herd 35 m from us. Once again there was no courtship behavior. The bull suddenly raised his head above the cow's rump, lowered his trunk and tusks in typical fashion onto her back, mounted, and

in slightly less than a minute achieved coitus. The cow continued to feed throughout the interaction. When a second cow with a 1- to 2-yr-old calf inadvertently approached within about 9 m, the bull charged her but stopped abruptly as he neared her.

Another copulation was observed on this same day at 1:30 P.M., approximately 0.4 km away. Among a herd of 40–50 elephants feeding and moving slowly through tallgrass, a bull of approximately 4,082 kg was seen chasing a small cow. She ran rapidly from near the center to approximately 50 m from the herd. The bull pursued her closely, bellowed several times, and finally succeeded in getting his tusks on her back. She stopped and the bull raised his forelegs, seized her in a copulatory embrace, and copulation followed quickly. As soon as he dismounted, the cow returned slowly to the herd with her tail held nearly straight back and her back humped slightly more than usual. The bull also walked slowly back to the herd. Other elephants in the herd, including several large bulls, showed no aggression or interest toward either of the pair.

Mating behavior observed during 13 and 14 September 1963 differed widely from the behavior recorded on 28 July. In the morning of 13 September five family units, including four large bulls, were converging on a

Olfactory detection of estrus and close following by bull is the first phase of the mating sequence. (*Photographer unknown*)

Placing tusks and trunk on back of the female without taking front feet off the ground is the second phase of the mating sequence. (*Photographer unknown*)

narrow, flat strip bordering a channel where they came to drink. Two family units joined up in a mud wallow about 800 m from the channel. The elephants in the other units were grazing and moving toward the flat strip. As one of the converging units reached the strip, a bull joined the unit and examined the genitalia of three cows with his trunk without provoking any reaction from them. The bull did not examine the oldest-appearing cow with a young calf; a subadult bull in the unit showed no excitement. After his brief and perfunctory examination, the intruding bull moved about 150 m to another family unit and repeated his examination. Failing to find a cow in estrus, the bull walked to the mud wallow and rolled with some of the elephants from the two units that had assembled there. According to Kühme (1963, 117) when elephants were excited "sexually by members of their own species, and had not been able to find a satisfactory outlet, they preferred to roll in damp hollows."

The following day (14 September) the same five family units and attendant bulls were observed drinking from the channel. At 10:15 A.M. they started toward an area of shortgrass and scattered shrubs, and at 11:30 A.M. two adult males and one adult female in a family unit of nine became involved in a fight. The bulls appeared equal in size and both carried about 12-kg tusks. One lighter colored bull seemed to dominate the other; the cow occasionally butted either one. Fighting subsided, but 5 min later it began with renewed vigor between the bulls. The cow began to feed, but after 4 min she stopped feeding and approached the fighting bulls. The dominant bull soon mounted her but was promptly "unseated" by the other. Fighting was renewed and the subordinate bull driven away. He retired about 25 m and had a dust bath, leaving the light-colored bull and the cow facing each other butting heads and entwining trunks. The light-colored bull now had his penis extended and erect. The cow seemed only partially receptive; however, the bull finally positioned his tusks lengthwise along her back and, after following her about 10 paces, mounted and achieved coitus. Within 2 min the entire family unit was feeding peacefully. The six elephants not involved in the interaction remained passive.

Just before noon a bull at the edge of the channel repeatedly attempted to mount a small cow that would not stand still. After pursuing the cow for about 4 min, the bull gave up and began to drink. The cow moved rapidly away from the water toward the embankment. Part way up the slope she met another bull coming toward her. This second bull also attempted to mount her but she fled. He then chased her for about 2 min during which time he made several semimounts. At this point, a third elephant of unknown sex intervened. This elephant was probably a female since no extended penis

Lifting front feet off the ground and onto female's back places most of the male's weight on the ground and completes the mating sequence. (*Photographer unknown*)

was visible. She chased the second bull away from the small cow, which then escaped. After the bull left, the intervening elephant became passive.

Dr. William M. Longhurst observed elephants mating about a half hour before dark on 22 September 1961. Longhurst had moved to within approximately 50 m of a long file of about 300–350 elephants strung out against the skyline beyond the edge of a patch of forest. Cows, relatively young elephants, and adult bulls appeared to make up the herd. No precopulatory behavior was seen, yet a brief 5- to 10-sec copulation occurred. The elephants were walking slowly, and the receptive cow continued her slow gait throughout the event. The other elephants seemed to pay no attention; however, from Longhurst's position he could observe the file of elephants for a space of perhaps only 30 m through an opening in the trees, and so missed any pre- or post-copulatory behavior that might have occurred.

Promiscuity of sexual behavior in the cow elephant was clearly demonstrated by an observation reported (personal communication 1965) by Roger Wheater, superintendent of Kabalega Falls National Park. On 7 May 1964 a familiar family unit of three cows and a calf was observed searching through the waste bins near the main

lodge at Paraa. The calf, which belonged to the largest cow, had very small tusks and was estimated to be 15 mo of age. This family was seen frequently near the lodge, having become "waste-bin happy." Five and a half months later, the same family unit again was seen approaching the main lodge at Paraa. A bull from a nearby group of three bulls followed closely behind the family unit, mounted the large cow, and copulated, remaining mounted for 45–60 sec. Soon another bull from the same group arrived and, after easily driving off the first bull, mated with the same cow. Since the calf's mother was observed 5.5 mo previous when her calf was estimated at 15 mo of age, the cow came into estrus approximately 20.5 mo following parturition.

The next observed mating occurred on 29 November 1963. During a steady rain, a herd of 25–40 elephants was observed moving slowly through a stand of 3-m combretum. Low visibility prevented an accurate count of the various-sized animals as they fed and moved about in the screening vegetation. Observations had nearly ended when directly ahead of us a large bull mounted an average-sized cow. The cow did not move, and judging from the position assumed by the bull during the last moments of the mount, copulation was successful. The other elephants in the herd, including at least two other large bulls, appeared passive.

In midafternoon of 20 December 1963, a herd of 24 elephants was observed during feeding. The herd included two large bulls and a relatively small adult bull, who moved freely and amicably within the herd. At approximately 4:30 P.M. one of the large bulls in the herd rose on his hind legs and mounted a cow. She remained still throughout the 50-sec copulation. As on former occasions when large bulls were nearby, these bulls, as well as the other nonparticipants, nearly always appeared entirely passive.

On 9 May 1964 a herd of 338 elephants was observed during an aerial count. From an altitude of 200 m the herd appeared to be moving very slowly, probably feeding and resting. At 11:30 A.M. from an altitude of 135 m, a bull well within the herd was seen to mount a cow. She remained still during the brief interaction. The bull moved slowly away from the cow after dismounting. At a distance of approximately 50 m he stopped, raised his head, and pointed his trunk upward. The receptive-appearing stance of the cow, the typical copulatory position assumed by the bull, and the bull's deliberate departure after dismounting, suggested that copulation was successful.

The observations on variable behavior of large bulls in groups of elephants where an estrous cow was mated by a single bull are important. Why were these large bulls variable in their behavior toward estrous cows? This certainly fits studies of testosterone levels. Short (1966) followed and observed an estrous African female elephant mated by many different bulls with little competition among them for the cow. However, fighting finally broke out among the bulls, and one eventually established dominance, driving the others away. This bull showed no discharge from its temporal glands as did musth bulls, which have been reported to have a high testosterone level. Poole (1982) reports for the African elephant, the musth bull is always dominant over the nonmusth bull when they compete for an estrous female.

DISTRIBUTION OF BREEDING DATES. Breeding dates for 43 elephants from western Uganda were tabulated for study purposes. Eleven of these dates were from observed copulations, and 32 were based on conception dates extrapolated from ages of fetuses and calves of collected females; Dr. Norman S. Smith and I estimated the ages of the fetuses and calves. There was some evidence of breeding in all months except October.

Mean monthly precipitation data for 1957–1959

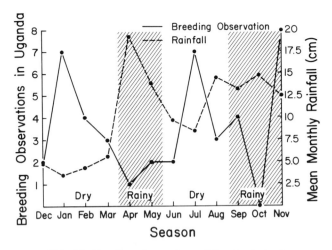

FIG. 4.2. Breeding observations of Uganda elephants and annual rainfall pattern.

from weather stations in or near Kabalega Falls National Park were calculated from data given by Buechner et al. (1963) and plotted with the number of breeding observations (Fig. 4.2). There appears to be an inverse relation of breeding and precipitation for a given month; however, the correlation coefficient value of 0.419 is not significant at the 0.05 level.

As Laws (1969a) points out, single-station precipitation records are difficult to correlate with population phenomena of wide-ranging animals. By using average annual rainfall for drainage areas, he showed good agreement between major long-term rainfall cycles and elephant age distribution of his Uganda sample, indicating a positive effect of precipitation on breeding success.

Even though copulation may not result in conception, recent information on duration of estrus (Hess et al. 1983) indicates that only promiscuous breeding would result in error. There may also be errors in estimation of fetal age, which would reflect on breeding dates. Nevertheless, breeding obviously occurred throughout the year. This observation has also been made by Krumbiegel (1943), Perry (1953), Ansell (1960), Brooks and Buss (1962a), Buechner et al. (1963), and Buss and Smith (1966). Perry, however, suggested that there was a seasonal peak of breeding during the early part of the year. This peak would include one of the two dry seasons for Uganda. Laws and Parker (1968) give evidence for seasonal breeding in Kabalega Park. The typical precipitation patterns of Ruwenzori and the southern part of Kabalega are rains from mid-March through May, dry from June to mid-

August, rains from mid-August through November, and dry from December to mid-March. Even though there is no direct correlation of breeding to rainfall in these data, a pattern is evident. There is an increase in breeding as the rainy seasons progress and a decrease as the drier seasons progress, suggesting that there is a lag in the response of the elephants to some change in the environment induced by the rains (Fig. 4.2).

In Tsavo National Park, Kenya, where the environment is relatively more harsh than in Uganda, Laws (1969a) claims that the best relationship between rainfall and recruitment is 2 yr later. He also discusses some reasons why a perfect correlation between rainfall and fertility is difficult to demonstrate even though it may exist. Principally, when a year of high reproductive success is followed by 2–3 yr of excellent climatic conditions, fewer adult females would be able to take advantage of it because many would be either pregnant or in lactation anestrus.

Extrapolation of breeding dates from ages of fetuses collected in Zambia showed that seasonal breeding is evident (Fig. 4.3). The usual rainy season in the Luangwa Valley is from November to April; most of the conceptions took place during the latter part of the rainy season and the first part of the dry season. These data also indicate that there is a lag time from the onset of the rains until the animals respond reproductively. Laws and Parker (1968) noted that conception dates of elephants from Uganda were skewed to the right, suggesting a gradual increase in fertility.

In Kruger National Park, South Africa, Smuts (1975) found that "on an average (n = 7 years) 70 per-

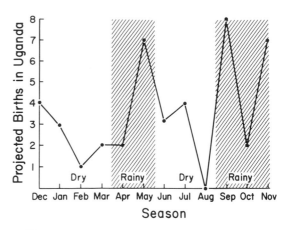

FIG. 4.4. Projected birth dates of Uganda elephants in relation to annual rainfall pattern.

cent of all conceptions took place from November to April when 81 percent of the rain fell."

Hanks (1969) found that of 150 embryos and fetuses taken from elephants of the Luangwa Valley 88% had been conceived during a period when 95% of the rain had fallen. His data indicated that conceptions continued after cessation of rain in a manner similar to that shown in Figure 4.4, suggesting a carry-over effect of the rain.

If a seasonal pattern of reproduction is to exist, it must have some cue, either from the environment or endogenously, in order to maintain synchrony. The most apparent cue in the tropical African environment is the seasonal alteration of wet and dry seasons. Other equatorial animals such as the wildebeest, which have definite seasonal peaks in breeding, have their reproductive cycle attuned to precipitation cycles (Talbot and Talbot 1963), mostly through the effect of rain on vegetation.

Possibly the elephant's physiological status changes at some time after the rains have fallen and habitat conditions have ameliorated, that is, grass and other vegetation become lush and more readily available. One of the first vegetative responses of the elephant's habitat is for grass to green up, and this improved condition will frequently last for some time into the next dry season. Grass has been shown to comprise the major part of the elephant's diet in Uganda as shown by the study conducted in Kibale Forest by Larry Wing and me. A similar response to improved habitat conditions is illustrated by the common practice of "flushing" in domestic animals, which may increase ovulation rates (Day 1962; Terrill 1962).

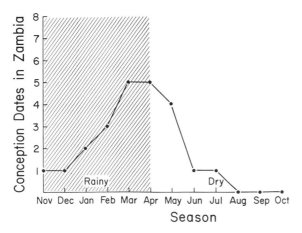

FIG. 4.3. Conception dates of elephants in Zambia in relation to annual rainfall pattern.

Hart and Guilbert (1933) and Miller et al. (1942), among others, noted that ovulation may be delayed or even prevented by a deficiency of Vitamin A and protein. Since green vegetation is the only natural source of Vitamin A, and is also high in protein, it may influence the reproductive cycle of wild populations. There are many examples of the influence of nutrition on reproduction of wild animals. A particularly appropriate one is by Newsome (1965), who developed an "index of aridity" to describe intensity of drought conditions and vegetational changes in Australia. His index took into consideration pasture response, estimated soil evaporation, and rainfall. With this index he showed that the proportion of female red kangaroos in anestrus increased significantly as the drought conditions became more severe, even though red kangaroos normally breed throughout the year. However, in severe droughts there were still kangaroos that were in breeding condition.

MONTH OF PARTURITION AND MOISTURE PATTERNS. If the dates of conception are advanced 22 mo and converted to parturition dates and plotted by month (Fig. 4.4), another interpretation of seasonal breeding can be envisioned. When the number of elephants that would have given birth during the month of the rainy season are compared to those that would have given birth during months of the dry season, 25 would have given birth in the rainy season and 18 would have given birth in a dry month.

There is evolutionary advantage to a population for the young to be born during the most propitious season, that is, when forage is most plentiful and climate is most favorable. This phenomenon is witnessed every spring in temperate climates. Except for the danger of flooding during years of exceptionally heavy rains, the most favorable seasons for most wild animals

in tropical Africa are those in which there is rain. Dasmann and Mossman (1962) state that impala in southern Zaire breed at the beginning of the dry season; as a result, their parturition dates are during the start of the rains. Laws and Clough (1966) showed that most young hippopotami are born during months of high rainfall and that the frequency of conception is highest during the dry seasons.

In Uganda the timing of the elephant's gestation period and the timing of the usual rainy seasons are such that if an elephant conceived 2 mo after the rains started, birth would generally occur during a rainy season (Fig. 4.5).

Assuming that several months are required after the beginning of the rains for the physiological condition of the elephant to reach reproductive readiness, there would be greater than normal amounts of breeding during June, October, and November (Fig. 4.5). If the condition of the habitat, and consequently the condition of the animal, carried over 2 mo after the rains stopped, then July, December, and January would be added to the above three.

The monthly average for breeding observations in this study was 3.5 mo; January, February, July, September, and November had 4 or more breeding observations. The most breeding occurred in January, July, and November, with February and September only slightly greater than normal (Fig. 4.2). Using the combined data from this study, Perry's study (1953), and Short's study (1966) for 62 observations with a monthly average of 5.0, January, June, July, October, and December had breeding in excess of the average. These findings fit closely the hypothesis that there is more breeding during the months that follow the onset of rains for 2 mo and extend 2 mo after the rains cease (January, June, July, October, November, and December) than in other months.

Month of Breeding	(Dec)	(Jan)	Feb	Mid Mar	Apr	May	(Jun)	(Jul)	Mid Aug	Sep	(Oct)	(Nov)
Month of Birth	Oct	Nov	Dec	Jan	Feb	Mid Mar	Apr	May	Mid Jun	Jul	Aug	Sep

Rainy [///]   Dry [ ]

191   FIG. 4.5. Relationship of breeding month to subsequent month of birth and annual
192   rainfall pattern. Months in parentheses are those 2 mo after the onset of the rains
193   and 2 mo after the cessation of the rains.

POSTPARTUM-CONCEPTION INTERVAL. The interval between parturition and the next conception was deduced by two methods. If a cow attended a calf whose age could be estimated and the cow's reproductive status could be ascertained, then the postpartum-conception interval could be calculated. The cow's lactational status and protective behavior were used to confirm the relationship of dam and progeny. The evidence thus obtained from 11 animals showed that the postpartum-conception interval can be at least as long as 54 mo and as short at 8.5 mo. The fact that elephants suckle from more than one female (Laws 1969a) may introduce error when using this method.

A second method of deducing the postpartum-conception interval is to compare the number of pregnant to nonpregnant cows in the population, assuming that the sample is representative of the population. Of the 142 animals collected, 120 were sexually mature: 25 were pregnant, 92 were not pregnant, and 3 were in estrus. Considering the distribution of pregnant to nonpregnant as the binomial ($n_1 + n_2 = 1$), where n_1 is the ratio of pregnant:gestation period (22 mo) and n_2 is the ratio of nonpregnant:interval from parturition to conception, the best estimate of this interval is 77.0 mo (6.4 yr). These data were previously published by Buss and Smith (1966), but since that time two nonpregnant females were reclassified—one as in estrus and one as pregnant. We then reported an interval of 81.8 mo.

Perry (1953) used this technique on a sample containing 31 pregnant and 34 nonpregnant animals collected in Uganda during 1947–1950. With these data the interval was estimated to be 24.1 months. On the basis of 23 females collected in Kabalega Falls National Park by Savidge and reported by Laws (1966), the interval of lactation anestrus was 62 mo.

By adding 22 mo, the normal gestation period, to the estimated average postpartum-conception interval, a mean calving interval can be estimated. Apparently the calving interval had increased from 4 yr in 1950 (according to Perry) to about 8 yr in 1964. For elephants of North Kabalega, Laws (1969a) gives a mean calving interval of 6–7 yr and 8–9 yr for those of South Kabalega. Perry and I discussed (1966) the possible reasons for the increased interval and suggested that higher densities of elephants and competition from large numbers of buffaloes and hippopotami resulted in overutilization of the range (see also Buechner and Dawkins 1961), which was reflected in a lowered reproductive rate. Since all three of these species are grazers, their population interactions resulted in each population adversely affecting the other in their struggle for resources

in short supply (see Odum 1971).

The lowered reproductive rate suggested that the lengthening of the postpartum-conception interval functioned as a self-regulation of elephant populations. Laws (1966) independently reached this same conclusion at about the same time, and he also suggested that there was retardation of puberty, which would further depress the reproductive rate.

Having ascertained that placental scars from each pregnancy persist for about 30 yr, Laws (1967, 1969a) estimated the mean calving interval by comparing the difference in ages of females with one and two placental scars. He suggested that because of the small sample size, the estimate of 5.2 yr in North Kabalega and 4.9 yr in South Kabalega obtained in this manner was not incompatible with the mean calving interval of 7.0 and 8.9 yr he had calculated by the proportion of pregnant and nonpregnant elephants.

Laws and Parker (1968) reported a calving interval of 8.5 yr for elephants in the area of Kabalega that is adjacent to the area from which collections were made for this study. Their calving interval of 8.5 yr is very close to the 8.6-yr calving interval that is deduced when 22 mo (the normal gestation period) are added to the average postpartum-conception interval (6.8 yr), calculated by Dr. Norman Smith and me in 1966.

ASIAN ELEPHANTS MATING IN CAPTIVITY. Four female Asian elephants (*Elephas maximus*) were captured as wild juveniles in southeast Asia when they were approximately 1 yr of age. These females and a 20-yr-old Asian bull lived in Washington Park Zoo in Portland, Oregon, when these observations were obtained.

Female A mated when she was about 7 yr old and 635 days (21 mo) later gave birth to a 102-kg male calf. Female B mated in June 1960 and January, and February 1961 when she was approximately 10 yr old; she delivered an 84-kg calf in October 1962. The large bull copulated with Female C when she was 4 yr old and at irregular intervals thereafter, even after she was pregnant. Apparently Female C conceived between 6 yr and 7 yr of age, for she delivered her first calf, a 70-kg male, when she was approximately 8 yr old. Female D was about 6.5 yr old when she was first observed to mate; 6 mo later she mated again, and after 31 days was observed mating the third time. Since Female D delivered her first calf, a 109-kg female when she was approximately 9 yr old, she was between 7 yr and 8 yr of age when she conceived the first time.

These ages at first conceptions (6–7, 7, 7–8, and

10 yr) and observations of widely variable copulatory behavior by captive Asian elephants are very similar to our data for earliest breeding of wild African elephants. The observations of multiple copulations, and of the wide range in number (2–15) and size of corpora lutea during pregnancy, suggest that there could be a protracted estrous period during which these corpora lutea develop; development of a corpus luteum might stimulate copulation. Corpora lutea (CL) refers to the yellow structures formed from ovarian follicles that luteinize without ovulating. Perry (1953) suggested that where relatively large numbers of CL occurred, the successive generations were produced during a series of estrous cycles. Short and Buss (1965) studied 11 CL from six African elephants in various stages of the estrous cycle and pregnancy and reported that some CL developed prior to conception. Hanks and Short (1972) reported that the African elephant "may undergo a number of estrous cycles before conceiving; unlike other mammals, the CL persist from one cycle to the next."

The observations of captive Asian and wild African elephants indicate mating promiscuity. There was no prolonged male-female relationship, and typically there was no fighting by bulls over estrous females unless two or more bulls of similar size and testosterone level were nearby.

FIRST BREEDING. By the mid-1960s information on age at first breeding of the African elephant was limited. Perry (1953) was probably first to report on the age at which females reach puberty. Further information on this subject was reported about a decade later by Buss and Smith (1966) and Laws (1966, 1967, 1969a).

Evidence from this study suggests that the wild African elephant sometimes begins to breed at an age of about 7 yr. Such a case is described in detail in Chapter 1, under "Bonding or Fidelity of Families." Four savanna-appearing cows and their calves, varying in age from about 6 mo to 5 yr, provided additional information on first breeding. The age at first conception of these cows was deduced by subtracting a 22-mo gestation period and a calf's age from the mother's estimated age at the time of her collection. On this basis, the four cows conceived at about 8, 8, 9, and 10 yr old. Although a few cows conceived when they were only about 7 yr old, other early-in-life conceptions occurred approximately between 9 yr and 11 yr.

All females in this series that were at least 14 yr old either were pregnant, were lactating and nursing calves, or showed corpora rubra in their ovaries and were lactating, indicating that they had conceived at least once.

The sum of observations on first breeding for this study indicates that although a very few female elephants in Uganda begin to breed at approximately 7 yr, most females breed first between ages of 10 yr and 12 yr. These observations are based on nearly all *L. a. africana* and *L. a. cyclotis*. Perry (1953) reports that the wild African elephant may begin to breed at about 9 yr of age.

The 146 female elephants used in this study included 12 adults from Toro District, which were either forest subspecies, *L. a. cyclotis,* or which appeared to be savanna subspecies, *L. a. africana,* but probably were intergrades between these two subspecies. Appearance alone can be misleading since these polymorphic intergrades may look alike, but they need not necessarily breed alike.

Smuts (1975) studied reproductive characteristics of 2,528 female elephants shot between 1970 and 1974 in Kruger National Park of South Africa, and from these females obtained 353 embryos and fetuses. In discussing puberty and sexual maturity he states that "the female pubertal interval for the population extends from about 7 to 12 years of age and maturity is attained at between 7 and 15 years of age. . . . Although no 7-year-olds were pregnant . . . , three 8-year-olds were, indicating that they had conceived for the first time at about 7 years of age."

The Estrous Cycle

The aim here is to describe some of the characteristics of reproduction in the female elephant and to present recent information on the estrous cycle.

Information concerning the period during which CL are formed was obtained from three cows: (1) No. C44, savanna-type, 12 yr of age, not pregnant, not lactating; (2) No. 140, forest-type, 9 yr of age, not pregnant, not lactating; and (3) No. 68, savanna-type, 34 yr of age, pregnant, fetus 3 wk of age (3.5 g), lactating freely.

The 14 CL (6–27 mm in diameter) of No. C44, and the 6 CL (5–30 mm in diameter) of No. 140, must not have begun to develop simultaneously. Also, all the CL of these two elephants were, by their macroscopic and histological appearance, too recent to be construed as regressing or degenerate CL of the preceding pregnancy. Since neither No. C44 nor No. 140 was pregnant, all CL

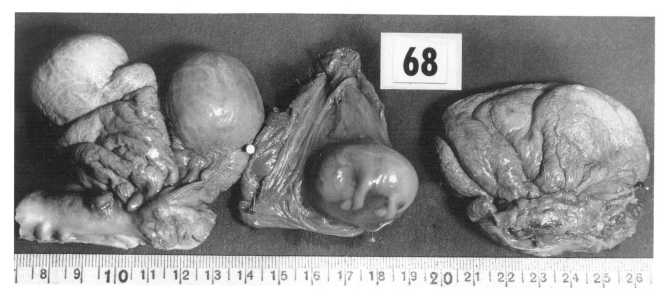

FIG. 4.6. Ovaries, and embryo (approximately 21 days old) from elephant No. *68*.

developed prior to conception, which supports the data reported by Short and Buss (1965), suggesting that some CL develop before conception. This may not always be the case, as suggested by the fact that No. 68 had two large, similar-sized CL, and a fetus of about 21 days old (Fig. 4.6). In this case, a fertile mating evidently occurred about when the CL were established.

The left ovary of No. 68 weighed 44.3 g, measured 66 × 53 × 23 mm, and contained no CL. The right ovary weighed 74.4 g, measured 68 × 63 × 30 mm, contained four follicles from 1 mm to 2 mm in diameter, and contained two light-yellow CL that measured 29 mm and 25 mm in diameter (Fig. 4.6). These CL will be referred to as *A* and *B* respectively.

Both *A* and *B* had a protuberance that Perry (1953) regarded as marking the point of rupture. Histological sections through the protuberances and the centers of the CL revealed luteal cells that stained a very pale color, even when the normal staining time was doubled. The general color of the CL was distinctly paler than a CL of similar size at or near the time of parturition. In comparing the histology of the two CL, no difference was detected in degree of vacuolation among luteal cells, they did not appear foamy, and they showed no evidence of fatty degeneration. In certain areas of the slides the luteal cells tended to be arranged radially in a linear order (Fig. 4.7A). The connective tissue formed a closely meshed reticulum surrounding the luteal cells, and near the center of the CL a fibrous central mass completely

obliterated the original cavity (Fig. 4.7B). Vascular ingrowths were apparent throughout but particularly conspicuous near and proximal to the protuberances (Fig. 4.7C). Blood cells were apparent in some vessels, but other vessels appeared as clear areas with a single-cell epithelial lining. The three largest blood vessels of *A* measured 0.11, 0.07, and 0.05 mm in diameter; the three largest vessels of *B* measured 0.95, 0.26, and 0.20 mm in diameter.

Collectively, these data indicate that (1) CL 68*A* and 68*B* were histologically indistinguishable, (2) both were relatively young but mature structures of similar age, and (3) both had developed from follicles that ovulated within a short period close to the time of conception.

ESTROUS CYCLE OF CAPTIVE ASIAN AND WILD AFRICAN ELEPHANTS.

There has been a discrepancy in the literature as to the length of the estrous cycle in both Asian and African elephants. Daily observations on bull-cow interactions of adult Asian elephants (*Elephas maximus*) at the Washington Park Zoo (WPZ) were obtained over a 7-yr period. These observations failed to confirm the reports of others who reported that the estrous cycle ranged from 16 days to 27 days based on bull-cow interactions or on morphological observations of material from the urogenital sinus of the female. Thus the animal health staff at the WPZ and the Oregon Regional Primate Research Center

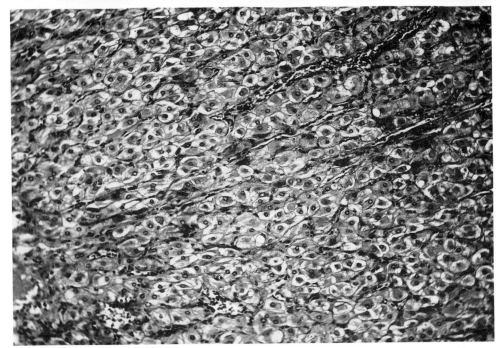

FIG. 4.7A–C. Sections through protuberances in the corpora lutea from a 34-yr-old, pregnant savanna-type African elephant (No. 68).

A. Linear arrangement of luteal cells.

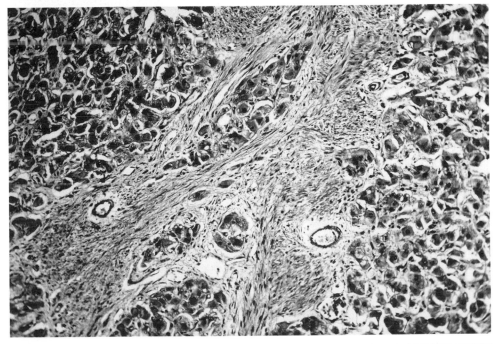

B. Connective tissue mass, surrounded by large nucleated luteal cells, near the center of the corpus luteum.

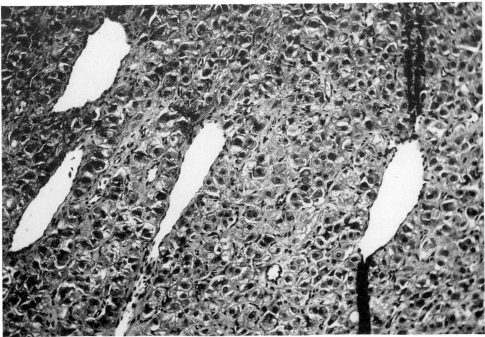

C. Developing vascular system among luteal cells near and proximal to the protuberance.

(ORPRC) cooperatively initiated and conducted a study based on serum hormone patterns in adult Asian elephants to determine the actual estrous cycle.

Dr. Michael S. Schmidt, WPZ veterinarian, reported to the American Association of Zoo Veterinarians in Seattle, Washington, October 1981, and Dr. David Hess, ORPRC endocrinologist, reported to the Society for Study of Reproduction in Corvallis, Oregon, August 1981, that "the estrous cycle of the Asian elephant has a duration of about 18 weeks with a follicular phase lasting about 6 weeks (range 3 to 14 weeks) and a luteal phase lasting about 11 weeks (range 8 to 13 weeks) based on the assumption that serum progesterone levels above 100 pg [picograms]/ml defines luteal function." Eisenberg et al. (1971, 222) reported that "the mean duration of estrous . . . for 6 females was 4 days."

Jainudeen et al. (1971) while studying captive Asian elephants, report that the range of "behavioral estrus" for 11 females was 2–8 days with 4 days being the most frequent period. Moss (1983) in a study of African elephants in Amboseli National Park, observed short periods of estrous behavior and estimated an average duration of 2–6 days. Watson and D'Souza (1975) reported an estrous cycle of about 16 days, based on one female African elephant. Bosman and Hall-Martin (1986) report the estrous cycle of African elephants as 2–3 wk.

Although the length of estrous cycle was determined to be 18 wk for the Asian elephant, the African elephant probably has a very similar length of cycle. Ovarian structures, particularly the distinct groups of CL, which have long intrigued and deluded scientists, need no longer be related to "silent heats" or "multiple cycles." Evidently the African elephant has an estrous cycle like or very similar to that of its Asiatic counterpart (Zarembka et al. 1987).

Graafian Follicles, Corpora Lutea, and Corpora Rubra

FOLLICLE SIZE IN RELATION TO SEASON OF PROJECTED BIRTH.

If there is more breeding 22 mo before a rainy season than before a dry season, and if females approaching estrus have larger developing follicles than those not near estrus, then Graafian follicles should be larger 22 mo before a rainy season than before a dry season. To test this hypothesis, the maximum diameter of Graafian follicles in the ovaries of 61 sexually mature, nonpregnant females were studied in relation to the season in which they would have given birth if they had been bred at the time of collection. Thirty-two animals would have given birth during a rainy season and 29 would have given birth during a dry season. The mean maximum follicle diameter for the projected rainy season birth was 5.56 mm, and for the dry season, 4.69 mm. The mean difference of 0.87 mm is significant at the 0.001 level of probability.

These data indicate that Graafian follicles are significantly larger 22 mo before a rainy season than they are at the same length of time before a dry season. Furthermore, this suggests that there is a tendency toward a synchronous rhythm of reproduction in the African elephant.

FOLLICLE SIZE IN RELATION TO STAGE OF PREGNANCY.

Thirty-four pairs of ovaries from 49 pregnant elephants (from Uganda and Zambia) had no developing Graafian follicles. In the pregnant elephants that did have Graafian follicles the mean number was 9.7 ranging from 1 to 43; the mean maximum diameter was 3.1 mm. The mean maximum diameter of Graafian follicles from nonpregnant animals was 5.0 mm; the difference of 1.9 mm was significant at the 0.01 level of probability ($t = 19.1$ and 47 df). Most of the pregnant animals that had Graafian follicles were those in the first half of pregnancy and only 4 out of 13 that were pregnant from 5 mo to 16 mo contained follicles. This is contrary to the findings of Perry (1953) and Laws (1969a); Laws states that by midpregnancy follicles were not evident in his samples from Uganda and Tsavo National Park.

In the study of 83 nonpregnant elephants from Uganda, 9 had no Graafian follicles in their ovaries. Of these, five had recently given birth; one was lactating profusely but the presence of a calf was not verified; one appeared to have lost a calf; one was sick; and one was very old.

To test if pregnancy significantly influences the number of Graafian follicles, a 2 by 2 contingency chi-square analysis of the data from 24 pregnant elephants (9 with follicles, 15 without follicles) and 83 nonpregnant elephants (74 with follicles, 9 without follicles) was used. If there was no influence, each of the four (pregnant, nonpregnant, with and without follicles) should have approximately the same frequency. The chi-square value of 30.562 indicates a significant variation at the 0.001 level of probability. I interpret this to mean that pregnancy, or the hormones associated with pregnancy, suppresses development of Graafian follicles.

Apparently the influence of lactation on presence or absence of Graafian follicles is not great; 33 of 46 lactating animals contained Graafian follicles as did 41 of 53 nonlactating animals. A chi-square value of 0.396 was calculated, which indicated no significant difference.

CORPORA LUTEA AND STIGMATA OF OVULATION.

There are three types of CL that may be encountered in the ovary: those that are formed by luteinization of granulosa cells of ovulated follicles; those that are formed by luteinization of granulosa cells of unovulated follicles; and those that result from luteinization of thecal and stromal cells, which invade atretic follicles. No attempt was made to distinguish among the different types unless a stigmata of ovulation was present. Most of the CL examined histologically were relatively large and probably of the first two types. There were some relatively small CL that probably were formed from small atretic follicles, but they were not used for comparison of cell types.

The term corpora rubra (CR) refers to the reddish brown structures that represent degenerate CL; CR is used rather than corpora albicantia because it is more descriptive of the pigmentation and because of precedence (Allen et al. 1939). At some later time CR may lose enough pigmentation to resemble corpora albicantia, but no attempt was made to follow the fate of these structures that long.

Ovaries of 22 pregnant elephants from Zambia were examined for presence of stigmata of ovulation, and the number of CL that were associated with these stigmata was recorded. The mean number of CL that appeared to have resulted from an ovulation was 2.2, and the mean number of those that had no stigmata of ovulation was 4.0. The mean diameter of CL of ovulation (those with stigmata of ovulation) was 25.5 mm and the mean diameter of secondary CL (those without stigmata of ovulation) was 12.5 mm. The mean difference of 12 mm was significant at the 0.01 level ($t = 8.51$ with 120 df).

The number of CL with stigmata in elephants in early stages of pregnancy was compared to those in elephants in late stages of pregnancy; the mean number for the first half was 2.4, and the mean number for the second half was 1.8. The mean number of secondary CL was 3.7 in the first half and 3.8 in the second half of pregnancy. A chi-square of 0.759 from a 2 by 2 contingency chi-square test indicated no significant difference in number of CL occurring in the ovaries of these pregnant elephants in the first or second half of gesta-

tion. The slight insignificant decline in number of CL with advancement of gestation might suggest that progesterone produced by these ovarian structures was starting its decline toward the ultimate level where parturition occurs. Hess et al. (1983), reporting on hormonal and behavioral components of the reproductive cycle in captive Asian elephants (*Elephas maximus*), report, among other findings, that "serum concentrations of [progesterone] fell dramatically before parturition, consistent with a role for this steroid in the regulation of gestational length." Early studies of the CL of the African elephant show either small quantities of progesterone or none (Edgar 1952; Short and Buss 1965; Short 1966; Smith et al. 1969).

LONGEVITY OF THE CORPUS LUTEUM.

Perry (1953) postulated that successive generations of CL may appear during the middle of gestation, but the following evidence tends to refute this idea. An indication of the longevity of the CL may be gained by tracing its size through time. In Figure 4.8 data are presented on maximum diameter of (1) CL from 24 pregnant elephants, (2) CL from 5 lactating cows collected with their calves up to about 6 mo postparturition, and (3) CR from 5 lactating cows collected with their calves from about 21 mo to 36 mo postparturition. All of these elephants were collected in western Uganda.

The upper end of each vertical line in Figure 4.8 represents the maximum diameter of the largest CL of both ovaries from a particular elephant and the CR of Nos. 73, 46, 38, 66, and 13; the lower end represents the maximum diameter of the smallest CL and CR from the same elephants. The lines in Figure 4.8 for the 24 pregnant elephants are arranged from left to right according to gestational stage, which was ascertained from fetal age by use of the formula propounded by Huggett and Widdas (Fig. 4.1). The lines representing the 10 postpartum females are arranged from parturition time to the right, according to the age of their calves.

The curve in Figure 4.8 (drawn near the maximum size of CL and CR) shows that CL were maintained throughout gestation and for a postpartum period of about 2 mo. By approximately 6 mo after parturition the CL had regressed conspicuously, and by about 21 mo after parturition only CR were found. Thereafter, the rate of involution was very slow. Two cows (Nos. 53 and 54, discussed under "Postpartum-Conception Interval"), collected about 4 yr after parturition, CR from 1 mm to 6 mm in diameter, which indicates that one set of CL lasts not only throughout pregnancy and

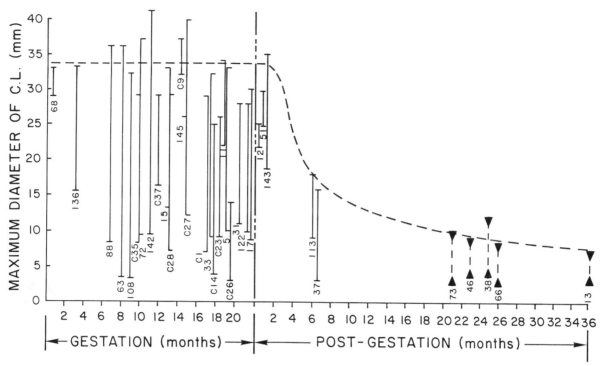

FIG. 4.8. Maximum diameters of corpora lutea from 24 pregnant and lactating elephants, and corpora rubra from 5 cows at approximately 21–36 mo following parturition.

for about 2 mo after parturition, but also that the degenerate CL persist for at least 4 yr postpartum. Short and Buss (1965) studied ovaries from six elephants and suggested that the CL persists structurally for a long time.

If Perry's statement regarding replacement of CL near midterm by a second set of these ovarian structures is valid, the degenerate remains of the first set should be readily distinguishable as CR in ovaries from young cows in the late stages of their first pregnancies, or in the early postpartum stages with their first calves. Animals that were apparently in these categories were a pregnant cow (No. C14) and two postpartum females (Nos. 12 and 37), estimated to be 8, 9, and 11 yr of age respectively. The calves of Nos. 12 and 37 were estimated to be 2 wk and 6 mo of age respectively (Fig. 4.8). Each cow was too young to have conceived more than once; their ovaries contained no CR. The right ovary of No. C14 contained seven CL, 4–21 mm in diameter; the left ovary contained five CL, 5–25 mm in diameter. The right ovary of No. 12 contained two CL, 25 and 22 mm in diameter; the left ovary had no CL. Additional information is provided by data from

postpartum female No. 66, which we estimated at 10 yr of age, and her calf, which was estimated at 26 mo of age when both were collected. Although No. 66 was not in an early postpartum stage and her ovaries contained no CL, there were only five CR (4–8 mm diameter) in her right ovary, and only three (2–6 mm diameter) in her left ovary. The small number of CR suggests that she had only one set of CL.

Evidence that a single set of CL is maintained throughout gestation may also be seen by comparing the average number of CL during the first half of gestation with those during the second half. Counts of CL were obtained for 24 pregnant elephants. The average number of CL for 7 females in the first half of gestation was 6.6; the average number for 17 females in the second half of gestation was 6.2. A 2 by 4 contingency chi-square test revealed no significant difference.

This evidence forces the conclusion that the CL present during early pregnancy are not replaced during any subsequent stage of pregnancy but are maintained throughout gestation and for about 2 mo after parturition.

116

MAXIMUM DIAMETER OF CORPORA LUTEA. The correlation coefficient of maximum diameter of CL and increasing fetal age calculated for the first half of pregnancy was not statistically significant. If a decrease or increase occurred in diameter of the largest CL as gestation progressed, some degree of correlation would be expected. Evidently the structural size as well as the number of CL are maintained throughout the gestation period (Fig. 4.9). This observation concurs with those of Short and Buss (1965), Hanks and Short (1972), and Smith and Buss (1973; 1975); all stated that the CL of elephants has a long structural life.

COMPARISON OF CELL TYPES IN CORPORA LUTEA OF EARLY AND LATE PREGNANCY. The mean number of cell types occurring in the sample of CL from elephants in early stages of pregnancy were calculated and compared with those of late stages. The means, differences, t values, and probabilities associated with the comparisons were tabulated and showed that Class I cells were significantly less abundant in late stages of pregnancy. There was an increase in Classes II, III, and IV in the late stages, but the differences were not statistically significant.

Spies et al. (1959) have shown that progesterone synthesis in swine was associated with large typical luteal cells (Class I) and that as regression induced by exogenous progesterone progressed, function of the luteal cells was lowered; at the same time, the number of regressive cells (Classes II and III) increased. Histological changes occur in bovine CL during the estrous cycle and are correlated with progesterone content. Large numbers of Class I cells were associated with the greatest quantity of progesterone (Hafs and Armstrong 1968). If Class I cells of the elephant are producing progesterone or a similar hormone, the data obtained in this study indicate a reduction in production by the CL in the late stages of gestation.

HOMOGENEITY OF CELL TYPES WITHIN INDIVIDUAL CORPORA LUTEA. A chi-square test for homogeneity of cell types (I–IV) and the amount of vascularity were considered together in each of 106 CL tests made. Chi-square values indicated that cell types and vascularity were not homogeneously distributed. In all 106 tests the computed chi-square value exceeded the tabular value of 74.5, which is the 0.05 level of significance with 56 degrees of freedom. In

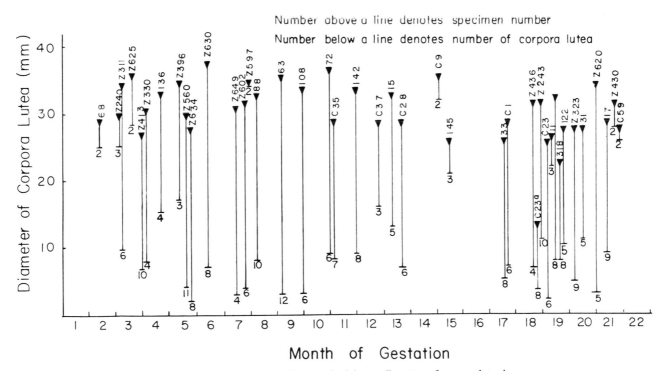

FIG. 4.9. Number and maximum and minimum diameters of corpora lutea by month of gestation in African elephants.

many CL there were clusters of certain cell types situated in various parts. The data indicate that cell types within a CL are distributed unevenly. Estergreen et al. (1968) concluded that there is heterogeneity of progesterone production within CL of the cow *Bos taurus*. If different cell types reflect a different functional stage or endocrinological activity and various areas of the CL are at different functional levels, heterogeneity would be expected. That certain cell types can be correlated with progesterone has been shown by Roy and Mullick (1964) in their paper on the endocrine functions of the water buffalo. They report a significant correlation of Foley and Greenstein's (1958) type I and II (Class I of this study) with progesterone production. Bjersing et al. (1970) found that the predominant cell type associated with progesterone production in sheep was a large luteal cell with a finely granular cytoplasm, vascular nucleus, and prominent nucleoli, which is similar to Class I of this study. Ultrastructural changes associated with steroid production in the granulosa cells of CL of various animals have been discussed by Richardson (1966). Ogle et al. (1973) described the fine structure of the CL of the African elephant. They state that cytoplasmic features of the luteal cells (Class I) are similar to steroidogenic cells of other species but with some variations, which include peripheral distribution of organelles, large stores of lipid and lipofuscin throughout pregnancy, and mitochondria sparsely populated with lamellar cristae. Ogle et al. (1973) state that luteal cell size reflected progesterone concentration in a general way; CL with the largest cells contain the greatest progesterone concentration.

In this study there was no conspicuous pattern of difference in the uneven distribution of cell types as the gestation period progressed.

HOMOGENEITY OF CELL TYPES AMONG CORPORA LUTEA OF THE SAME ELEPHANT. Chi-square

values associated with the test for homogeneity of cell Classes I, II, III, and IV among CL of the same elephant were calculated using the total numbers of each cell class in a 4 by M contingency table, where M equals the number of CL in an elephant. The totals used for these calculations and chi-square values are in Smith (1969).

Apparently there is usually a significant difference in the proportion of cell types of different CL of the same elephant at all stages of pregnancy. Some of the CL within an elephant appeared to have very similar ratios; however, when these were compared with all the CL of that elephant, a high degree of heterogeneity was

noted. If all CL were formed under the same hormonal conditions and were approximately the same age, all types could be homogeneous.

Even though there is much variation in the ratios of cell classes when all CL are considered, there are groups of CL that have similar cell compositions. Perry (1953) recognized differences among CL, and attributed these differences to successive generations that resulted from midterm ovulation and luteinization. I have already discussed the unlikelihood of Perry's hypothesis as have Laws (1969a), and Hanks and Short (1972).

HOMOGENEITY OF CELL TYPES BETWEEN CL OF OVULATION AND SECONDARY CL. A comparison

of the number of cell Classes I–IV was made between one CL of ovulation and one secondary CL from each of 15 elephants. A chi-square analysis was made, and significant differences were noted in 11 of the 15 animals. There is no apparent correlation of cell types between CL with stigmata or to those without stigmata. The inconsistency can be explained by the following assumptions: (1) if a CL of an ovulated follicle that did not result in conception was paired with a CL from a nonovulated follicle that was formed later in the estrous cycle, the calculated chi-square value might be high (as in 11 of the 15 elephants examined); (2) if the ovulated and nonovulated CL were formed at approximately the same time, however, and both were in the same functional state, the cell types would probably be similar and no significant difference would be detected by the chi-square method (as in 4 of the 15 elephants mentioned above); (3) if stigmata of ovulation were not detected, distinctions between CL of ovulation and secondary CL would also probably be obscured.

CYTOPLASMIC VACUOLATION. Each CL was examined histologically for cytoplasmic vacuolation. Animals thought to be in estrus displayed little or no vacuolation. After 13.5 mo there was diminution of this characteristic, which continued into the postpartum period.

The significance of vacuolation has been debated by numerous authors. Some suggest that vacuolation is the result or evidence of degeneracy of function. Others present evidence that correlates hormonal activity with vacuolation. Enders (1966) suggests that vacuolation in CL cells of the armadillo might be the result of glycogen and lipid extraction or shrinkage of the periphery of the cells. Rennels (1966) reported a high degree of lipid body vacuolation in active luteal cells of the rat. Deane (1958) suggested that lipid droplets represent stored precursors for steroid production and that luteal cells frequently fail to show any droplets when secreting most rapidly. Possibly, vacuolation results from the utilization of stored lipid precursors during active secretion of progesterone or other hormones. Ogle et al. (1973) relate that even during periods of maximum progesterone secretion there are large peripherally located lipid stores in the elephant CL and that they increase between 3 mo and 18 mo gestation.

Comparison of the luteal cells of elephants in this study with published accounts of other scientists with various mammalian species of known secretory activity strongly suggests that luteal cells of pregnant elephants are secretory until near termination of gestation at which time secretory activity declines significantly.

CORPORA RUBRA DIAMETER, NUMBER, AND PERSISTENCE IN RELATION TO REPRODUCTIVE STATUS.

Figures 4.9 and 4.10 illustrate the relationship of size and number of CL and CR to stage of pregnancy and time postpartum, respectively. The mean number of CR for 40 pregnant elephants, some pregnant for the first time, was 10.8 and the mean maximum diameter was 7.1 mm.

If CL regressed to CR during gestation there should be CR present in the late stages of pregnancy of all pregnant elephants, including those which were pregnant for the first time. There were four elephants that were pregnant from 9 mo to near full term that had no CR but from 3 to 13 CL. There also were two elephants that had recently given birth but whose ovaries contained no CR, but they contained 2 and 19 CL. These elephants provide positive information about formation and persistence of CL. Furthermore, if CR are formed from a first "crop" of CL during gestation, there should be an increase in the number of CR as gestation advances, especially in those animals that previously had been pregnant. This, however, was not true as the mean number of CR in the first half of pregnancy was 10.1 (range 0–20), and the mean number in the last half of pregnancy was 11.5 (range 0–25) with no statistically significant difference.

Of 110 female elephants, 78 had CR (20 pregnant, 58 nonpregnant) and 32 were without CR (4 pregnant, 28 nonpregnant). Of the 28 nonpregnant females in which no CR were found, 18 were less than 12 yr old, and probably had not yet been pregnant; 1 was in estrus; 2 had recently given birth and CR had not yet formed; 3 were 13–15 yr old; 1 was 20 yr old; 3 were not examined for CR. The animals that might possibly have been pregnant previously and had CR that had regressed to obscurity would include the 20-yr-old, the 3

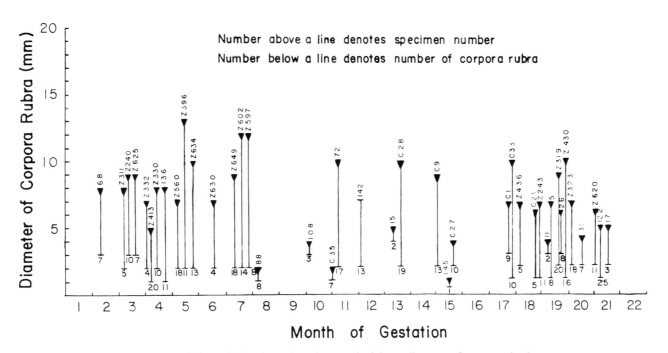

FIG. 4.10. Number and maximum and minimum diameters of corpora rubra by month of gestation in African elephants.

unexamined animals, and possibly the 3 that were 14–15 yr old. Of the corrected total of 65 nonpregnant animals (58 plus the above-mentioned 7), 58, or 89.2%, had CR. If at least 89.2% of the nonpregnant animals contained CR, the average time of persistence might approach or perhaps extend beyond the average post-partum-conception interval of 77 mo. The long time that CR persist after parturition suggests that if CL regressed to CR during gestation, they would remain visible at least until parturition. Thus it follows that one elephant that had given birth recently and had two large CL and no CR is evidence that the CL formed in late stages of the estrous cycle persist until term and do not regress to CR during gestation. Data on the number of CR in the first and second halves of pregnancy are consistent with this idea. If CR increased in number during gestation there would be more in the second half of pregnancy; this, however, was not found to be true in this study.

5

Forest Life

A 3-YR STUDY was conducted in Kibale Forest Reserve to obtain information on how elephants use the reserve and its importance to their survival. If elephant numbers were to be restricted in certain parts of the reserve, what impact might this have on elephants in nearby Ruwenzori National Park? Equally important, to what extent could control measures be applied to reduce or maintain elephant numbers without endangering their future in the reserve and in the park? These questions confronted us when we initiated the reserve study. The Uganda Forest Department already knew some of the impacts elephants exerted on the reserve.

Time and an assistant would be paramount to success. I was fortunate to obtain the services of Dr. Larry D. Wing as my assistant. We collected field data from October 1962 until June 1964, and the studies were then continued by the Uganda Forest Department personnel through August 1965.

The Reserve

Kibale Forest Reserve (Fig. 5.1) is in Toro District of Western Uganda near the western edge of the huge Uganda Plateau, extending between the eastern and western branches of the Great Rift Valley. The Ruwenzori Mountains, 24 km directly west of the reserve, interrupt the valley by rising to nearly 5,128 m. The plateau breaks off sharply to the northwest, and the eastern

escarpment plunges nearly 609 m to the valley floor. The scarp slope southwest of the reserve is less abrupt and the transition from plateau to valley bottom is more gradual.

The surface of the plateau containing the reserve undulates moderately and tilts slightly to the south. Elevation gradually decreases from an average of about 1,525 m in the northern extremity of the reserve to about 1,250 m in the south. Variation in relief is not extreme, with altitudinal differences among hilltops and valley bottoms seldom exceeding 150–180 m.

The reserve is roughly oblong, extends 56 km from north to south along its major axis, and encompasses a total of 547 km². The southernmost extension of the reserve is only 6.4 km from the Kamulikwezi Area in the northern extremity of the Ruwenzori National Park. This area, which was not publicly accessible until May 1964, is widely recognized as highly important for elephants. The Kamulikwezi Area's strategic location and its proximity to the reserve makes the area a gateway for elephants migrating between Ruwenzori and Kibale.

Water is abundant throughout the area with streams and swamps in nearly all of the numerous valleys. All of these watercourses eventually empty into either the Dura or the Mpanga rivers, the two major river systems that drain the area (Fig. 5.1). Because of these numerous and permanent water supplies the utility of the reserve for elephants is greatly enhanced.

The reserve is trisected by two major roads that divide the area into three unequal-sized sections or blocks

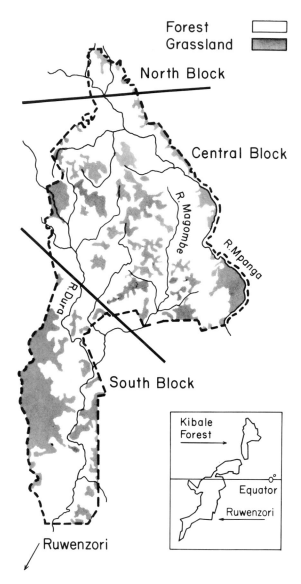

Forest ☐
Grassland ▨

North Block

Central Block

South Block

Kibale
Forest →

Equator
Ruwenzori ←

Ruwenzori

FIG. 5.1. Kibale Forest Reserve showing ideal distribution of forest, grassland, and water.

(Fig. 5.1), which have been designated by the Uganda Forest Department for descriptive purposes as the North, Central, and South blocks and have been subjected to vastly different levels of management. These three blocks comprise 13 km², 361 km², and 184 km² respectively. By the end of 1965 timber exploitation was limited to the North Block and the upper, or northern, third of the Central Block. The North Block underwent selective timber cutting from 1950 through 1956. Cutting operations in the northern part of the Central Block started in 1956 and was still in progress throughout the course of this study. Attempts were made to exclude elephants from these operational areas by regular patrols and

shooting, to try and protect forest regeneration and experimental silvicultural plots.

The vegetation of the reserve presents a complex interspersion of cover types and a huge variety of plant species. Grasslands and thickets are interspersed with forest, forming a complex and irregular mosaic of vegetation. Only 60% of the area is dominated by trees and can properly be referred to as forest. The remaining 40% contains various types of grassland, woodland-thicket, and colonizing forest. These all represent seral stages in the succession of natural forest, which in the absence of fire, will eventually occupy the entire reserve. The presence of fossil tree leaves in areas now dominated by grassland indicates that the entire reserve once supported high forest. Much of the area was probably destroyed by volcanic activity during recent times according to Henry Osmaston of the Forest Department. Clearings that originated in this way (perhaps of benefit to tsetse fly) probably have been maintained through habitation and cultivation by local Batoro tribesmen who inhabited the reserve until driven out by sleeping sickness in the early 1900s.

Osmaston described the forest in the reserve as tropical high forest, which he equated to the tropical rain forest. At maturity, it rises to over 30.5 m and exhibits a closed canopy of stratified tree crowns allowing little light to reach the forest floor. Undergrowth is sparse and consists of shade-tolerant shrubs and herbaceous plants. The forest is made up of a great profusion of broad-leafed tree species, which, with the exception of ironwood (*Cynometra alexandri*), seldom form pure stands but occur in various combinations or mixtures. The species composition of these mixed stands shifts from north to south in the reserve along an altitudinal gradient. Grey plum (*Parinari excelsa*) is the dominant species in the North Block but becomes progressively less conspicuous from north to south in the reserve. In the Central Block, white-star apple (*Chrysophyllum* spp.) and stinkwood (*Celtis* spp.) are the most prominent species. Ironwood and stinkwood are the most prominent constituents of the South Block; whereas forest of the North and Central blocks is classified as evergreen, that of the warmer and drier South Block is semideciduous.

For purposes of this study the vegetation of the reserve was classified according to its physiognomy, the drainage of the site it occupied, and its stage in plant succession. On this basis 12 classes or cover types were considered distinct enough to differentiate. The diagrammatic profiles of these cover types, arranged in the order of their usual relative positions in the sere, are illustrated in Figure 5.2.

Primary Hydrarch Succession

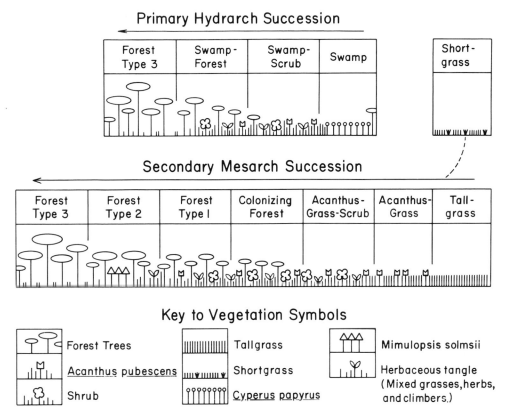

Secondary Mesarch Succession

Key to Vegetation Symbols

FIG. 5.2. Schematic presentation of plant succession in Kibale Forest Reserve.

SHORTGRASS. The shortgrass type occurs on shallow soils that are well drained and often rocky. Grasses up to 1.8 m, but generally less than 1.2 m in height, constitute the dominant form of vegetation, with trees and shrubs being widely scattered or absent. Perennial bunchgrass usually is dominant, with patches of bare ground occurring between tussocks. The predominant grass varies with locality, with *Cymbopogon afronardus* and *Imperata cylindrica* forming pure dense stands on areas where cultivation has recently been abandoned. In the south end of the reserve, *Themeda triandra* and *Hyparrhenia* spp. often are more prevalent. In the Central Block, the shortgrass type occurs most often on shallow well-drained soils of hillsides and tops. In the South Block it extends for many miles along all edges of the forest reserve. Soil drainage and total rainfall appear to be the principal factors that influence the distribution of this cover type. The successional status varies from north to south in the reserve. In the north end it probably is a seral stage in high-forest succession. In the extreme south end of the reserve it probably climaxes on the well-drained shallow soils. For purposes of this study, the shortgrass types are considered the poorgrass type described by Lang-Brown and Harrop (1962), the vegetation types classified by Langdale-Brown (1962) as moist *Acacia-Hyparrhenia* savanna, and the *Themeda* savanna.

TALLGRASS. Tallgrass occurs throughout the reserve on deep to medium-deep, well-drained soils and represents a very early seral stage closely following disturbance by fire, cultivation, or grazing. *Pennisetum purpureum* and *Hyparrhenia* spp. are the usual dominant species and form dense, impenetrable stands ranging in height from 1.8 m to 4.6 m. Availability of soil moisture appears to be the principal factor governing the relative abundance of these two species, both of which usually are present and often are codominant. *Pennisetum* is dominant on moist sites and is most common on deep soils in the Central Block. *Hyparrhenia* spp. is dominant where moisture is somewhat less abundant. In the Central Block *Hyparrhenia* spp. occupies medium-deep soils, but in the South Block where rainfall is lower, it dominates deep soil sites, almost to the exclusion of *Pennisetum purpureum* (Osmaston, 1959). *Beckeropsis uniseta* dominates the tops of the higher hills in the Central Block and belongs to what Lang-Brown and Harrop (1962) described as the hilltop tallgrass community. Except for an occasional seedling and isolated stems of the fire-resistant *Erythrina abyssinica*, woody species are absent. A few widely scattered stems of semiwoody *Acanthus pubescens* are sometimes present.

ACANTHUS-GRASS. This type is very similar to tallgrass, but it is a slightly more advanced seral stage. The tallgrasses *Pennisetum purpureum* and *Hyparrhenia* spp. are codominant with the semiwoody shrub *Acanthus pubescens*. Tree seedlings and small shrubs are more abundant than in the tallgrass type, but still do not form a conspicuous part of the community. *Securinega virosa, Bridelia micrantha, Vernonia* spp., *Hoslundia opposita, Hibiscus* spp., and *Triumfetta* spp. are some of the more common shrubs that begin to appear. Common tree seedlings include *Millettia dura, Dombeya* spp. *Olea welwitschii, Sapium ellipticum,* and *Celtis durandii*. On the successional gradient, this type is intermediate between the tallgrass type and the acanthus-grass-scrub type.

ACANTHUS-GRASS-SCRUB. Acanthus-grass-scrub is commonly found at the forest edge and is a slightly more advanced seral stage than the acanthus-grass type. This type is dominated by *Acanthus pubescens* and various mixtures of the woody and semiwoody shrubs and colonizing tree species that are listed for the acanthus-grass type. The tallgrasses, *Pennisetum purpureum* and/or *Hyparrhenia* spp., usually are prominent but are no longer dominant and are mixed with large tussocks of *Setaria chevalieri,* which attain diameters of 1–1.5 m and heights up to 3 m. This type maintains a rather uniform height of 3–4.5 m, with only a wide scattering of emergent tree canopies. The canopies of shrubby species such as *Bridelia micrantha* and *Securinega virosa* often are conspicuous and cover considerable areas, but seldom rise much above the average height of the community.

COLONIZING FOREST. Colonizing forest is a seral stage intermediate between the acanthus-grass-scrub type and young forest (type 1 forest). Tree and shrub species are dominant or codominant and, for the first time, emergent young tree canopies become conspicuous. Although herbaceous vegetation and shrubs

usually are prominent in this type, the physiognomy more closely resembles forest than grassland or shrubland. *Acanthus pubescens,* together with other less abundant semiwoody shrubs, vary in prominence from codominance to conspicuous constituents. The shrubby canopies of *Bridelia micrantha* and *Securinega virosa* may reach large proportions in these areas.

TYPE 1 FOREST. The type 1 forest is characterized by a dominance of herbaceous material in the understory. The principal influence in determining the status of this herbaceous vegetation is the quantity of light penetrating the overstory (canopy), so those forested areas with relatively open overstories exhibit the most luxuriant herbaceous understories. In general, two kinds of forested areas were classified as type 1 forest: (1) young forest well advanced from the colonizing stage, but with a very open overstory; and (2) older forest, which through heavy disturbance by cutting operations has had its overstory greatly reduced. Type 1 forest normally occurs between the colonizing forest and type 2 forest in the succession of seral communities.

TYPE 2 FOREST. Type 2 forest is thought to be a seral stage that is slightly more advanced than type 1 and is characterized by an understory in which herbaceous vegetation is prominent but not dominant. The overstory is more closed, but is still far from solid, with varying quantities of light reaching the understory. *Mimulopsis solmsii,* a heavily lignified herbaceous plant with tall stalks and broad leaves, commonly occurs mixed with the more succulent but less numerous climbers, grasses, and herbs.

TYPE 3 FOREST. Type 3 forest has a closed overstory with little or no herbaceous vegetation in the understory. The species composition, age, and stocking of the woody species varies considerably, but the morphological features of the community are strikingly similar. Characteristically there is a dense, high overstory and a generally weak understory with little or no herbaceous growth. This is the largest single cover type in the reserve and occupies almost 40% of the Central and South blocks.

FOREST OPENING. Clearings in an otherwise continuous stand of forest trees, which did not exceed 4 chains (80 m) across their longest diameters, were classified as forest openings. These forest openings are essentially isolated patches of acanthus-grass-scrub with nearly the same vegetation and, therefore, have not

Surrounded by woody forage, this bull is eating grass, an elephant's most frequently eaten food. (*Photograph by N. S. Smith*)

been diagramed separately in Figure 5.2. They receive more overstory shade than the acanthus-grass-scrub type and usually support fewer shrubs and more *Setaria chevalieri.*

SWAMP. Swamp is characterized by permanent standing water and the nearly complete absence of woody species. *Cyperus papyrus, Phragmites* sp., and various associated aquatic plant species are dominant forms of vegetation. Occasional palms (*Phoenix reclinata*) and widely spaced stems of *Mitragyna rubrostipulata, Macaranga* spp., and *Neoboutonia macrocalyx* occur around the edges and on the slightly elevated areas of ground within it.

SWAMP-SCRUB. The swamp-scrub type is seasonally to permanently flooded and supports a formidable tangle of herbaceous material mixed with thorny shrubs, *Acanthus pubescens,* and tree reproduction. It might otherwise be described as flooded acanthus-grass-scrub type and occurs mostly in narrow valley bottoms and on slightly higher areas adjacent to the

swamp type. Tree species listed for the swamp type also occur in the swamp-scrub type but are more widely scattered and do not form a canopy.

SWAMP-FOREST. The swamp-forest is a seasonally to permanently inundated forest type occurring along river banks and in valley bottoms of all sizes. The overstory is often open but varies considerably, depending mostly on the age of the stand. Herbaceous vegetation of the understory usually is prominent but may be noticeably sparse in the older stands with semiclosed overstories. The composition of tree species varies considerably and includes such water-tolerant species of *Pseudospondia microcarpa, Treculia africana, Symphonia globulifera, Cynometra alexandri,* and all the species listed for the swamp type.

UNGULATES. Kibale Forest Reserve supports a wide variety of ungulates, or grazing animals. Elephants, buffaloes, bushpigs, warthogs, and bushbucks are the most common grazing animals and occur throughout the Central and South blocks of the reserve.

125

Waterbucks and various other species of antelopes occur on the grasslands of the South Block, and hippopotami are widely scattered along the major water courses. Tiny blue duikers are found in the dense forest, and giant forest hogs frequent the swamps in the more remote parts of the reserve. Because of their size and relative abundance, elephants and buffaloes are the most conspicuous of the grazing animals and undoubtedly exert the greatest impact upon the forage resource.

FIRE. Although the reserve was uninhabited by people after the local Batoro tribesmen were driven out by sleeping sickness early in the twentieth century, local tribesmen have continued to hunt in the reserve and regularly burn many of the grasslands. The burning of the dense stands of tallgrass enables the hunter to see and move about more effectively. Burning also enhances hunter success, as bushpigs, warthogs, bushbucks, and buffaloes are attracted by the succulent regeneration of grasses that soon follows.

Although there is evidence that repeated burning of grasslands has retarded the succession of natural forest, no quantitative assessment of the overall impact of such burning has been made in the study area. Observations indicate that in general the forest is holding its own or is advancing throughout most of the area. In a few places, where repeated burning has occurred on areas that have also been used intensively by elephants, the forest edge appears to have receded. In such areas, small vestigial patches of forest and single relict stems of forest trees are isolated from the main body of forest by tallgrass and scrub.

Reserve Utilization Determined by Elephant Droppings

The object of this study was to determine the utilization of the reserve by elephants. Since dense vegetation in most of the reserve greatly limited direct observations from either the ground or the air, we had to rely almost exclusively on indirect evidence. This indirect evidence, therefore, provided most of the data for this study.

DROPPING COUNTS. To complete this study, it was necessary to estimate the number of elephants using the reserve seasonally and annually. Such an estimate probably could best be obtained by assessment of dropping counts; thus between July 1963 and August 1965 elephant droppings were counted as an index to annual and seasonal distribution in the reserve and as a means of identifying use geographically and by vegetative cover type. During these counts droppings were enumerated each season along a 323-km network of transects, which Larry Wing established throughout the reserve for studying elephant–woody plant relationships. To develop the technique, data were needed on defecation rates, deterioration rates of droppings, and the effects of cut transects on those rates.

If we were going to convert dropping counts into elephant–days use and finally into an index of elephant numbers, information was needed on the average number of times an elephant defecates during a 24-hr period. Since no such information was available when the project was initiated, a study was started in July 1963 and was conducted in Ruwenzori National Park, near the reserve where topographic and vegetative conditions permitted following and observing elephants. Observations were recorded to the nearest minute and converted to elephant-hours.

Defecation rates of elephants were studied for 400.6 hr between 11 July 1963 and 30 April 1964, during which time 284 total defecations were tallied, or an average rate of 0.7 defecations per hour. This rate multiplied by 24 hr gives a daily rate of about 17 defecations.

Unfortunately, only 6.8 elephant-hours of night observations were obtained as a result of cloudy weather during periods of full or nearly full moon. Although these night observations are insufficient for comparison with daytime observations, the five family units studied (6, 7, 9, 9, and 12 individuals) showed no unusual defecation rates or other unusual behavior. Also, a study of food habits conducted between 22 December 1958 and 7 May 1959 showed that elephants fed at various times during both day and night.

Defecation rates observed among individual elephants showed considerable variation. Among observations of 60 min duration or more, six elephants were seen to defecate twice with the following intervals between defecations: 33, 45, 50, 54, 82, and 85 min. Two elephants, at different times and places, defecated three times with the following intervals between defecations: (1) 53 and 42 min, and (2) 60 and 110 min during 4 hr under continuous observation. Two elephants were observed for 108 and 105 min, respectively, without defecating. During the first 60 min watching a herd of 24 elephants, 2 defecated twice, 9 defecated once, and 13 did not defecate at all.

The hourly rate of 0.7, based almost exclusively

on observations obtained during the elephants' waking hours, could not be corrected for sleeping time for several reasons. Experience showed that elephants slept almost exclusively during the night in some areas and during the day in others. In the Kamulikwezi Area in northern Ruwenzori National Park, elephant beds were found in a forest where elephants frequently spent the night; they were seen emerging from the forest during the forenoons with bits of vegetation and soil clinging to one of their sides, and the diurnally rhythmic movements to and from the forest provided evidence that these elephants slept during the night. In this same area no elephants were seen sleeping in approximately 393 daytime-hr of observations. In Kabalega Falls National Park, however, among 7,454 elephants counted during an aerial survey conducted between 7 and 9 March 1964, four adult-sized elephants were observed during daytime lying flat on their sides, and presumably sleeping. These were the only ones seen lying down in daytime between June 1963 and June 1964 during more than 60,000 elephant observations recorded from the ground and air in western Uganda. In reporting on the sleeping pattern of three African elephants about 11 yr of age, maintained unchained in an enclosure at Kronberg, Germany, Kühme (1964) reported that the times of sleep were intermittent and occurred between 9:00 P.M. and 6:00 A.M. Kühme stated that "on an average they slept 4 hours and 10 minutes in a night, about as long as chained elephants of the same age (Hedeger 1950; Gebbing 1959; Kurt 1960)."

As a further complication, we must accept that wild and captive elephants, particularly old individuals, probably do not develop the same sleeping habits. We observed apparently accelerated rates of defecation soon after elephants moved from sleeping sites or from resting sites under shade trees. Thus there may be compensation for nondefecation during sleeping and resting periods. In view of the unsolved problems associated with these defecation rates, the daily rate of 17 must be accepted as tentative for three reasons: (1) no random element was included in the sampling procedures, so no estimate of the statistical reliability of the mean can be made; (2) not enough data were obtained for validly comparing rates during the night with those during the day; and (3) the possibility that the defecation rate of the African elephant is greater than 17, at least under certain circumstances, is suggested by data reported by Dougall and Sheldrick (1964) who recorded 14 defecations in 11 hr and 35 min for a semidomestic African elephant in Kenya.

On the other hand, there are facts that suggest that

17 droppings per day is a reasonable approximation for elephants in the study area. Perhaps the strongest support comes from the fact that variation in average monthly defecation rates is rather small. The difference between the maximum (18.7) and the minimum (15.2) monthly averages over a year of observations was only 3.5. The limited records of nocturnal defecation rates suggested rates comparable to diurnal ones. Also, the fact that elephants were observed feeding at all times of day and night suggests that nocturnal defecation rates may be similar to diurnal rates.

Benedict (1936) studied frequency of defecation by a captive adult female Asian elephant for nine consecutive days. The total number of defecations per day ranged from 14 to 24 and averaged 19. The elephant was fed almost exclusively on hay, which possibly affected defecation rate. Nevertheless, the average rate of 19 increases our confidence in the average rate of 17 defecations for the wild elephants we studied in Uganda.

Coe (1972) found rates of 12.6, 15.6, 16.8, and 17.0 in four African elephants aged 10, 3, 1.5, and 1 yr respectively. The rate reported by Wyatt and Eltringham (1974) is somewhat lower at 11.3 for elephants studied in Ruwenzori, but they refer to these as minimum rates since some defecations were possibly overlooked.

MEASUREMENTS OF DROPPINGS. Soon after starting the study on dropping counts, the differences in size from various-sized elephants became obvious. Could these differences in size be applied to droppings for further classifying elephants into size classes if they lived in forests or other habitats that prevented direct observation? Certainly the average weight of droppings from a known number of elephants could be used to estimate the total weight of droppings deposited in the reserve for enhancement of the environment. Also these measurements might be difficult or impossible to obtain in the future for possible use in other studies.

Measurements were taken from 132 droppings on the Kamulikwezi Area. The elephants studied included single adult bulls, family units, and small herds. If any individual or group seemed disturbed, observations were stopped as a precaution against unnatural behavior. When possible, observations included size class and sex of elephant, number of boluses (a bolus is defined as a separate, intact, and basic unit of a dropping) per dropping, average diameter of boluses, and weight of dropping. For each dropping, the diameter of several boluses, which were intact and appeared not to be deformed, were measured to the nearest 7 mm and their average recorded. Droppings were then placed in a 15-L empty kerosene container and weighed to the nearest 0.5 kg on a spring scale.

Suboptimal viewing conditions caused failure to determine size class on 29 of the 132 elephants. Of the remaining 103 animals the average number of boluses for 60 adults was 6.1, with an average diameter of 15.3 cm and an average weight per dropping of 10.3 kg; for 21 subadults the average number of boluses was 6.6, with an average diameter of 12.5 cm and an average weight per dropping of 6.6 kg; and for 22 intermediate-sized elephants the number of boluses was 5.9, with an average diameter of 9.8 cm and an average weight per dropping of 4.4 kg. For all 132 elephants (including the 29 not classified to size) the average number of boluses was 6.0, with an average diameter of 13.4 cm, and an average weight of 8.0 kg.

DETERIORATION RATES OF DROPPINGS. If we were going to estimate the number of elephants in the reserve by counting elephant droppings, deterioration rates would be required. So a second special study was initiated aimed at getting this information. Between 21 July 1963 and 25 March 1964, the locations of 70 fresh droppings in the reserve were marked and subsequently revisited by 10-day intervals. Only droppings less than 48 hr old were selected for observation. On each revisit, the state of the droppings was recorded, and notes made on the general status of decomposition, dung beetle activity, and germination of seeds. Droppings were divided into the following four classes:

1. Easily recognized—little noticeable deterioration, boluses remaining essentially intact, and identification of dropping easy.
2. Recognizable—extensive decomposition, erosion, settling, and rearrangement of fecal materials may have occurred, but sufficient concentration of materials remains to identify the dropping.
3. Barely recognizable—decomposition and removal of materials is so extensive that only with care and examination of indirect evidence can the remaining materials be identified as components of an elephant dropping.
4. Not recognizable (gone)—removal or complete decomposition of fecal material is such that identification is no longer possible.

The 70 droppings were studied in various vegetative cover types throughout the reserve. The cover type in which each dropping occurred was recorded, as well as the degree of shading on the dropping and the presence or absence of dung beetle activity. Shade was classified as none, light, medium, and heavy, with numerical ratings or indices of 0, 1, 2, and 3 respectively. Droppings heavily shaded were those in shades at least 66% of the daylight hours; medium shade, 33–66%; light shade, 5–33%; and none, less than 5%.

General observations indicated, and the results of the deterioration rates corroborated, that most elephant droppings in the reserve deteriorated beyond recognition in a relatively short time. The sample size was not large enough and the study period too short to merit many definite conclusions, but enough observations were obtained to permit the following conclusions:

1. Some droppings may completely disappear in 15 days or less.
2. Most droppings can be easily identified for at least 20 days.
3. Few droppings can be easily identified after a 4-mo period.
4. Some droppings remain recognizable for 150 days or more.
5. Dung beetle activity appeared to be the main factor governing the amount of time required for a dropping to disappear. Trampling, weathering, shading, cover type, decomposition, and erosion were secondary influences.
6. Droppings in grassland cover types, which were lightly shaded, appeared to become unrecognizable more rapidly than those in other cover types. This conclusion is similar to that of Riney (1957).

Piles of elephant dung provide fertile germination beds for various plant seeds contained in them. Often the only evidence of the former presence of an elephant dropping was the dense clump of plant seedlings that had sprung from it; development of seedlings in these fertilized beds is very rapid. The seeds of the forest date (*Balanites wilsoniana*), which were often found in elephant droppings, were observed to germinate and grow to heights of 61 cm in 2 mo. Mitchell (1961) presented this idea in his forest studies in Zambia.

Data gathered from the survey suggested that dropping counts should be made every 3 mo, since the number of droppings that disappeared in less than 3 mo compensated for those persisting longer than 3 mo.

DISTRIBUTIONAL PATTERNS OF DROPPINGS. Tallying elephant droppings along previously cut transects could be expected to yield reasonable estimates of population numbers only if the dropping densities along the transects were representative of the reserve as a whole. Since the clearing of understory vegetation altered the original condition considerably, there was reason to suspect that the amount of time the elephants spent on the transects might differ significantly from the time spent in undisturbed areas of comparable size. In some areas the opening of the understory resulted in rapid invasion of various herbaceous plants, which might be attractive to elephants. In other areas the cutting of seedlings and sapling-sized woody plants created a formidable array of sharp, chisel-shaped stumps near ground level, which might cause elephants to avoid these areas. Before we began, therefore, an extensive presample was conducted for the purpose of estimating whether densities of droppings along the cut transects differed significantly from those on adjacent undisturbed areas.

Five counters were lined abreast at 1.6-m intervals to obtain the desired sampling rate. The man in the middle walked along the cut line-transect with four men flanking him (two on each side) in the undisturbed vegetation. The middle man tallied all droppings on a 3.2-m strip (two adjacent 1.6-m strips), and each of the four flankers tallied 1.6-m strips respectively. The belt-transect thus sampled was 9.7 m in total width. Seven different transects, totaling 32 km and scattered throughout the Central Block of the reserve, were sampled.

The average number of droppings per 1.6-m transect was determined for the undisturbed vegetation by dividing by four the total number of droppings tallied by the four flankers. A comparable average for the cut line-transect was obtained by dividing the middle man's total tally by two.

The averages for the flankers and middle man were made for each sampled transect. When checked statistically none of the differences was significant. Thus elephants did not spend significantly more or less time on previously cut line transects than they did on adjacent undisturbed areas of comparable size. The conclusion was that a forestwide count of droppings on previously cut line-transects would be as representative of the number of droppings as an enumeration on undisturbed areas.

SEASONAL INDEX OF POPULATION SIZE FROM DROPPING COUNTS.

The method used for this study was based primarily on the preceding preliminary investigations; however, the statistical details are reported by Wing and Buss (1970). The reserve was divided into 91 randomly located transects. Droppings were counted along 88 cut line-transects totaling about 323 m in the Central and South blocks. Three transects in the North Block were not sampled because elephants had been permanently excluded from that area.

All elephant droppings within 1.6 m of both sides of the line-transect were tallied, resulting in a belt-transect 3.2 m wide. The exact figure of 3.2 m was selected because it gave an even sampling rate of 0.002, or 0.2%. A stick 1.6 m long was held at right angles to the line-transect by the enumerator to assure which droppings were within the sample boundaries. Vegetation on each consecutive chain length (20 m) of sample transect was classified according to cover type. Each of these 20 m by 3.2 m areas was considered a single plot and marked with a numbered wooden stake. All droppings on each transect were recorded by plot number. Attempts were made to count droppings every 3 mo, near the end of each season; in practice, however, intervals between counts varied from 80 days to 130 days, depending on the variable length of seasons and the number of obstacles encountered in field work. Parts of most transects had become overgrown with herbaceous vegetation between counts and had to be recut for each enumeration, and plot stakes were sometimes destroyed or removed by elephants and had to be maintained regularly. Over a 2-yr period there were a total of eight counts. All droppings were removed from sample transects after they had been counted.

As a result of this testing, we found that the estimates of population size were unbelievably high when compared with elephant densities obtained in other areas in Uganda where damage to vegetation was considerably greater than in the reserve. The eight-count average of 1,713 elephants for the reserve (547 km^2) was equivalent to 7.9 elephants per 2.6 km^2. In Kabalega Falls National Park, Buss and Savidge (1966) calculated a density of 4.5 elephants per 2.6 km^2 from four aerial counts. This density, combined with annual fires, resulted in conversion of extensive tree and shrub areas to grassland (Buss 1961; Buechner and Dawkins 1961; Laws and Parker 1968). Based on four aerial counts in Ruwenzori, only 6.4 km from the southern tip of the reserve, Buss and Savidge (1966) found an average of 2.2 and a maximum of 2.9 elephants per 2.6 km^2.

After carefully considering the circumstances and examining the possible sources of distortion, including the strong negative relationship between population estimates and time intervals, we strongly suspected that the difference was primarily the result of counters mistakenly tallying boluses as droppings.

Mistaking boluses for an entire dropping is difficult to avoid since the variation in the amount of material voided during a single defecation is very large, not only between, but also within elephant size classes. For example, a single dropping may contain up to 16 boluses and weigh as much as 22.7 kg. Alternatively, a dropping may contain as few as 2 boluses and weigh as little as 3.6 kg. When material is deposited while an elephant is walking, as frequently occurs, boluses may be strung out for 4.6–9 m or more. Even when the animals are not walking, they often shift position while defecating, thus isolating many of the boluses. After a scattered dropping has been exposed to the deterioration process for several weeks, the original forms of the boluses are obscured and the material is reduced and scattered. Since the total volume of material present in one, two, or three boluses from the dropping of a large elephant is equal to or greater than that of an entire dropping of a smaller elephant, boluses often cannot be distinguished from droppings. A semiskilled laborer instructed to search carefully so as not to miss any droppings during an enumeration is particularly likely to record many boluses as different droppings. Parts of droppings probably were regularly mistaken as entire droppings throughout all eight enumerations. This error, I believe, was the principal cause for the overestimates of elephant numbers.

The only known means available for estimating the degree of bolus counting is to assume various magnitudes of error, correct for them, and compare the resultant figures for elephant density with what is considered a reasonable estimate for elephant density in the reserve. We assumed that the average density for the reserve would not differ greatly from the average annual density for the park, or 2.2 elephants per 2.6 km².

In making this adjustment we used six as the average number of boluses per dropping (see discussion under "Measurements of Droppings"), and assumed a relatively high level of error in bolus counting. For example, at error level 4, four boluses out of every dropping were erroneously recorded as droppings. Testing six different levels of error showed that levels 4 and 5 produced density estimates of 2.93 and 2.35 elephants per 2.6 km² respectively, which are most comparable to the average density for Ruwenzori National Park. This suggests that a minimum of four boluses, and perhaps more, out of every dropping were erroneously recorded as droppings.

Although the numbers of elephants based on forestwide counts of droppings are approximate, the relative magnitudes of these estimates should be valid and provide useful information about seasonal movements when compared to the aerial counts of the park. The knowledge gained during the course of this study should enable future investigators to avoid some of the problems inherent in such an endeavor. Based on information acquired by this study, the following set of suggestions is submitted for consideration of others confronted with the prospect of estimating elephant numbers by use of dropping counts.

1. Because of the difficulty in determining in the field what constitutes a dropping, counting boluses may be more feasible. Total counts could then be divided by the average number of boluses per dropping in estimating population size. If this approach is undertaken, additional information should be collected on the average number of boluses per dropping (random sample, statistical analysis, and determination of reliability levels).

2. Correction for deterioration of droppings should be made unless the time interval between enumerations is 30 days or less. Statistically reliable data are needed on deterioration rates of droppings.

3. Removal of droppings from sample transects is important (see Jackmann and Bell 1979).

4. A statistically reliable 24-hr defecation rate should be determined. Variation caused by differences in season, diet, age of elephant, and environment should be studied.

5. This study indicated that density of elephant droppings on cut line-transects did not differ significantly from undisturbed areas, but this might not be true under different circumstances.

These recommendations are based on conditions in Kibale Forest Reserve and surrounding localities in western Uganda and may not be directly applicable in other regions.

Elephant–Woody Plant Relationships

To determine the nature and extent of elephant utilization of woody plants (trees and shrubs) in the reserve, elephant use of those plants was studied and recorded on plots established along transects in the Central and South blocks. As mentioned earlier, Larry Wing cut 91 line-transects, totaling 338 km throughout the North, Central, and South blocks, but three transects in the

North Block were not used since elephants were restricted in that block. On the remaining 88 transects, which totaled 323 km, 118,618 woody plants were studied and recorded on 2,547 plots. These were .05-hectare (ha) plots measuring 20 m by 4 m distributed along the transects at 80.5-m intervals according to a stratified random sampling technique. This arrangement gave a sampling rate of 0.0005, or 0.05%.

To locate transects in the field, prominent landmarks, a map, a hand compass, and 20-m chain were used. Because of the density of vegetation, workers cleared an access area along each transect to allow passage and the sighting with the compass. Five-man cutting crews, using large machetelike knives, cleared about 1.6 km of transect per day. Sample plots were offset from the transect to ensure the sampling of undisturbed vegetation. The boundaries of each sample plot were marked by thrusting eight poles into the ground and connecting them with string. Since most of the major drainages and ridges in the reserve exhibit a predominantly north-south orientation, transects were established on east-west bearings; thus anticipated sources of variation in vegetation were intersected at right angles.

Within the transect all woody plants over 1.8 m in height or 1.3 cm in diameter at ground level were examined, classified, and recorded according to a letter and number code. For each stem enumerated, the following information was recorded: (1) species, (2) size class (based on the diameter at breast height, or dbh), (3) whether elephant use was discernible, (4) the type and intensity of elephant use, (5) the height or level at which elephant use occurred, (6) an estimate as to whether use was less than 1 yr old, and (7) a description of damage incurred by causes other than elephants.

Major environmental characteristics were rated at each sample plot site according to a detailed number and letter code. Evaluations of the following characteristics were recorded: (1) cover type, (2) aspect, (3) slope, (4) drainage, (5) shade, (6) size and stocking of trees, (7) prominence of herbaceous understory vegetation, (8) density of understory vegetation, and (9) general notes on evidence of elephant activity.

Since a sampling rate of 0.0005 was used, the 118,618 woody plants studied theoretically represent 1/2000 of all woody plants in the Central and South blocks of the reserve. Therefore, multiplying 118,618 by 2,000 yields a rough estimate of 237,236,000 total woody plants in the two blocks.

A total of 24,709 elephant-used plants, or 20.8% of all stems in the reserve, were studied and recorded during this survey. Extrapolating this figure to the reserve level yields an estimate of 49,418,000 elephant-used stems. (The term stem is used throughout the text of this report as a synonym for woody plant. An elephant-used stem is one that has sustained some recognizable form of elephant utilization. The percentages reflect incidence of use and not volume, although the two are likely correlated to some extent.) This estimate represents a cumulative effect, since it includes all forms and ages of recognizable use by elephants. Much of this use is visible for many years after it has occurred, particularly tusk-gouged trees; 34% of all recorded use was estimated to be more than 1 yr old. An average of 14.3% of all plants studied exhibited use that was estimated to be less than 1 yr old. This percentage closely approximates the fraction of total forest stems used during a 1-yr period.

TYPE OF WOODY PLANT UTILIZATION. A feeding elephant does not directly graze or browse plant parts with its mouth, but removes forage with its trunk and swings it back into its mouth. In utilizing woody forage plants, elephants consume terminal twigs and leaves and/or remove and eat bark from branches and trunks. The desired parts of the plant are utilized in one or more of three ways:

1. Breakage—terminal twigs and leaves are broken directly off the plant and eaten. Elephants sometimes break off branches 2.5–5 cm in diameter and chew the bark off them or they may eat only the terminal parts and discard the rest. At other times they break down large horizontal branches up to 30 cm in diameter and browse the terminal parts. On large, straight-boled trees where foliage is out of reach, the main stem or trunk may be broken, bringing the terminal twigs and leaves within reach. Trees up to 25 cm dbh can be broken down in this manner.

2. Pushed over—certain species of trees between 25 cm and 36 cm dbh frequently are pushed over or uprooted, and the crown foliage browsed.

3. Barking—elephants use their tusks to pry or gouge off bark, which they eat; sometimes the bark is only loosened with their tusks and then stripped high above their reach by holding the loosened bark with their teeth. This is usually limited to trees that are 10 cm dbh or larger.

The relative magnitude of these usages is in the same order as given; that is, breakage is by far the most common form of use and accounts for 97.3% of total utilization of woody vegetation. Very few plants are used lightly by elephants. They are used heavily or not at all. One notable exception is leaf stripping. Elephants regularly strip leaves of some woody forage plants, leaving the branches intact. We suspected that much leaf stripping went undetected during this survey because the evidence is rapidly obscured by regrowth of those leaves.

The relationship of the three types of utilization to the eight size classes of woody vegetation is illustrated in Figures 5.3, 5.4, and 5.5. These indicate that as the size class of forage increases, making one type of feeding behavior difficult or impossible, another type of feeding behavior more suitable to the size of forage being used is employed.

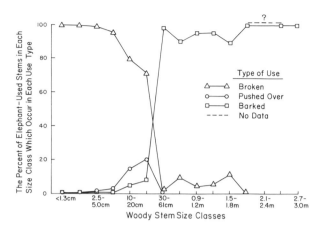

FIG. 5.5. Relative proportion of total elephant use in each of eight size classes accounted for by three types of use.

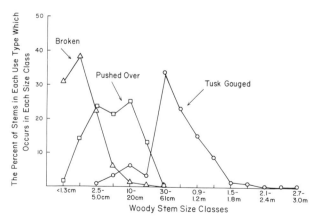

FIG. 5.3. Impact on vegetation in each of eight size classes by three types of use.

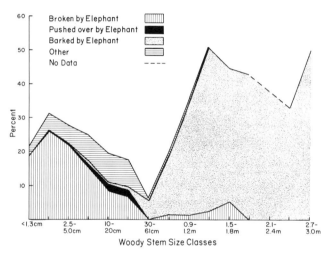

FIG. 5.4. Incidence of the three use forms relative to plant size within eight size classes.

UTILIZATION BY SIZE CLASS. The relative impact of use by elephants on each size class of woody vegetation and the importance of each size class to the elephant are presented along with the difference between observed and expected numbers of elephant-used stems in each size class (Fig. 5.6). A very striking preference by elephants for the smaller woody vegetation is apparent. Nearly 75% of all woody stems utilized by elephants were less than 2.5 cm dbh, and 97.5% were less than 10 cm dbh. The incidence of utilization of stems

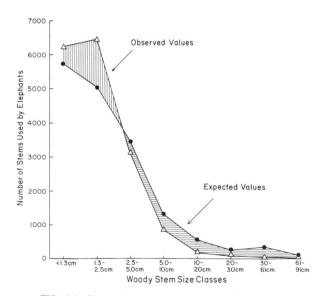

FIG. 5.6. Observed and expected numbers of elephant-used stems in eight size classes.

from 5 cm to 91 cm is noticeably lower than stems of smaller and larger size classes. For some unknown reason, the incidence of utilization of stems in the 30–61 cm diameter class is particularly low (Fig. 5.6).

UTILIZATION BY COVER TYPE. The relative impact of utilization by elephants on each type of vegetative cover and the importance of each cover type to the elephant were also analyzed. Considering the vast difference in total acreage and number of stems per acre in each cover type, there is a surprisingly small amount of variation in the average percentages of stems used within each cover type. This relatively constant percentage, however, created a greatly different number of total stems utilized from each cover type. Nevertheless, a study of the importance of various cover types showed that type 3 forest supplied two-thirds of all woody stems consumed by elephants.

The significance of the difference between observed and expected numbers of elephant droppings in each cover type was listed in an elephant preference index. Densities of droppings instead of incidence of woody plant utilization figures were used in constructing this preference index because droppings are considered a better guide to the amount of time elephants spend in a given cover type. Elephants can spend considerable time in an area without using much woody vegetation. The incidence of utilization would, in such cases, be a poor indicator of the amount of time spent there. The converse is also true; elephants can utilize the woody plants of an area intensively without spending a disproportionately greater amount of time there. This last situation is illustrated in Figure 5.7. Although dropping counts indicated that elephants spent significantly less time than expected in type 2 forest, the incidence of woody forage utilization was significantly higher than expected.

Elephants spent significantly more time in acanthus-grass-scrub and colonizing forest cover types than expected. The incidence of woody stem utilization is also significantly higher than previously believed (Fig. 5.7). Notwithstanding this apparent use, the average percentage of stems utilized in these two cover types is not much higher than in other cover types, which suggests that some factor other than the presence of woody forage makes these types attractive to elephants. All the data suggest, and field observations corroborate, the likelihood that herbaceous forage plants receive the bulk of elephant utilization.

Elephants utilize the woody vegetation of the swamp-scrub more intensively than any other cover

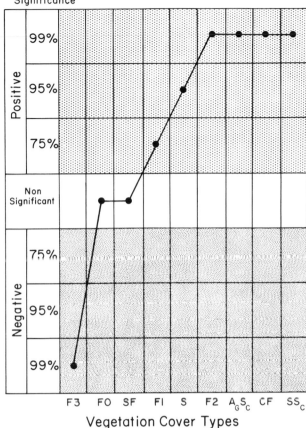

Incidence of Elephant-Used Woody Stems

☐ Significantly higher than expected

☐ Does not differ significantly from expected

☐ Significantly lower than expected

FIG. 5.7. Significance levels of use of woody stems. *F3* = type 3 forest; *FO* = forest opening; *SF* = swamp-forest; *F1* = type 1 forest; *S* = swamp; *F2* = type 2 forest; A_GS_C = acanthus-grass-scrub; *CF* = colonizing forest; SS_C = swamp-scrub.

type. Counts of droppings indicate that they spend more time there, and survey data indicate that they utilize more stems of woody vegetation and make use of a higher average percentage of total stems than in any other cover type.

ENVIRONMENTAL FACTORS. The relationship among various factors and the incidence of utilization of woody vegetation for elephants is illustrated in Figures 5.8A–H. As indicated by these figures, var-

FIG. 5.8A–H. Environmental factors influencing utilization of woody vegetation.

Slope Aspects

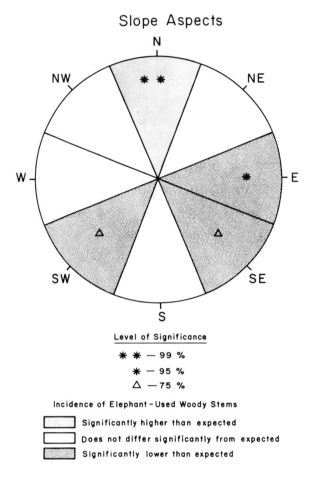

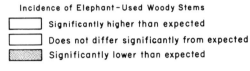

A. Direction of slope

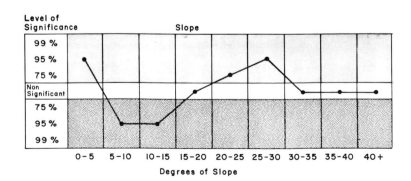

B. Degrees of slope

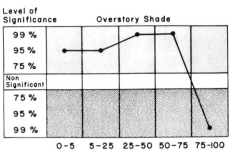

C. Shade

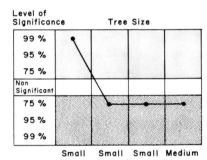

D. Tree size

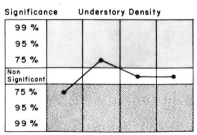

E. Understory density

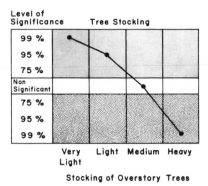

F. Overstory

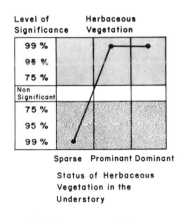

G. Herbaceous vegetation

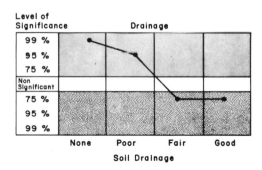

H. Drainage.

iations in the environmental factors measured have a pronounced effect on the incidence of woody plant utilization. Utilization is likely to be greatest in areas where the (1) understory herbaceous vegetation is prominent or dominant, (2) stocking of overstory trees is light, (3) soil drainage conditions are poor, (4) predominant tree size is small, and (5) total amount of shaded ground is less than 75%. There appears to be

little response to the density of understory vegetation as such, and no plausible explanation can be offered for the apparent preferential utilization of plots with certain directional aspects. Response to slope is variable, with flat sites and areas with moderate slopes showing maximum incidence of use.

GEOGRAPHICAL DISTRIBUTION OF USE. Tests were made for each of the 88 sample transects to estimate the significance of difference between observed and expected numbers of stems used by elephants. Transects were placed in three groups (following statistical tests) and plotted on a map of the reserve to illustrate the geographical distribution of the incidence of woody stem utilization (Fig. 5.9). This map shows the distribution of incidence of woody forage only, and does not necessarily reflect the distribution of the incidence of total utilization of forage resources of the reserve. Distribution of seasonal densities of droppings probably is a better relative index of total use by elephants.

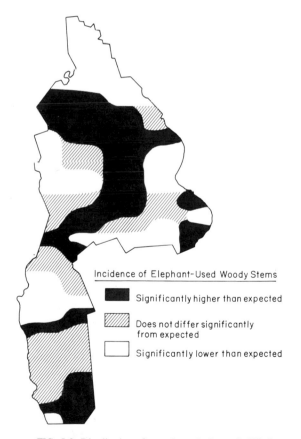

FIG. 5.9. Distribution of use of woody forage in Kibale Forest Reserve.

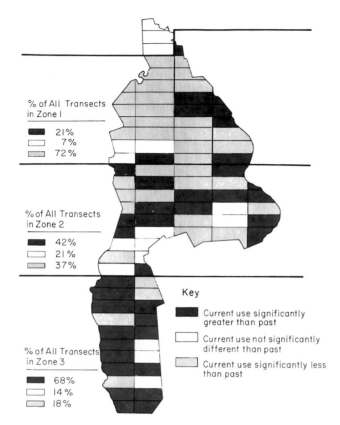

% of All Transects in Zone I

- ■ 21%
- □ 7%
- ▥ 72%

% of All Transects in Zone 2

- ■ 42%
- □ 21%
- ▥ 37%

Key

- ■ Current use significantly greater than past
- □ Current use not significantly different than past
- ▥ Current use significantly less than past

% of All Transects in Zone 3

- ■ 68%
- □ 14%
- ▥ 18%

FIG. 5.10. Geographical distribution of three groups of transects, Kibale Forest Reserve.

An estimate was made of the degree to which the incidence of recent use on each transect differed from old use. These estimates, based on statistical procedures, resulted in three use categories: (1) new use dominant and conspicuous, (2) new use nonsignificant, and (3) new use light or not visible. Geographical distribution of the three use categories was then plotted on a map of the reserve (Fig. 5.10). The map tended to be divided into three major sections, emphasizing regions in which evidence of recent use was conspicuous. Although considerable variation occurred within each of the three areas, a very definite north-south gradient was apparent, with the incidence of use increasing as one moved southward.

HEIGHT OF BREAKAGE AND BARKING. The average heights of breakage of all elephant-used stems in each size class were studied. In general the height of breakage increases as the size of the plant increases, with no breakage at all occurring in stems larger than 1.8 m dbh.

Tusk gouging or barking was recorded for various height classes. A single incidence of barking was recorded for every height class included within the barked area of a barked stem. Thus, 2,120 tallies were recorded for 421 stems. Actual barking seldom occurred higher than 2.4 m or 2.7 m, but bark was sometimes stripped to much greater heights. The bark of *Pterygota milbraedii* in particular was often stripped high up on the bole.

UTILIZATION BY SPECIES. A total of 255 species of woody plants representing 50 families was studied and recorded during this survey. Elephants utilized 227 of these species representing all 50 families.

Although elephants utilized to some extent nearly every species of woody plant in the reserve, some species were definitely more sought after than others. Thirty woody plant species provided the largest number of stems in the elephants' diet and made up 75% of all woody stems utilized. Some species that did not appear to be sought after nevertheless provided a substantial total amount of forage, apparently because of their great abundance and availability: *Uvariopsis congensis, Diospyros abyssinica,* and *Rinorea* spp. are species whose sheer abundance resulted in their frequent use. *Acalypha subsessilis* and *Acalypha* sp. supplied 12% of all stems utilized, and *Teclea nobilis* provided more total stems than any other single species. The forestwide distribution of these 30 species, as indicated by transect frequency, is relatively high. Two-thirds of these major food species are plants that seldom exceed 0.5 m dbh at maturity.

Although 19.7% of all stems used by elephants was provided by large trees, the total number of stems provided was significantly higher than would be expected if they had been utilized in direct proportion to their abundance. The significance of the generally high average percentage of utilization indicates that elephants preferentially utilize large species of forest trees. However, 80% of all woody stems in the elephant's diet is obtained from species of woody plants that seldom exceed 0.5 m dbh at maturity.

Elephant–Herbaceous Plant Relationships

The numerous patches of seral vegetation in the reserve produce large quantities of herbaceous forage used by elephants. Difficulty was encountered in assessing utilization of this vegetation, however, because of its ex-

Bark stripping on *Pterygota mildbraedii* frequently reaches 4 m. (*Photograph by Larry D. Wing*)

tremely rapid growth rate. During the wet seasons much evidence of elephant utilization was obscured because new growth appeared within several days.

To obtain a quantitative evaluation of the utilization of herbaceous plants, an enumeration program was initiated in which vegetation was surveyed within 48 hr of its use. When fresh elephant tracks were located, one was selected for sampling. The investigator proceeded along this track at 20-m intervals recording all utilization observed within 2 m of each side; thus each successive 20 m by 4 m area comprised one plot.

On each plot a record was kept of the plant species eaten, the parts used, and the cover type sampled. Coded ratings were recorded for the intensity and frequency with which each species was used. Species that were noticeably abundant but unused were also recorded. For each species utilized a percentage estimate was made of the amount of ground it covered within the plot. A forage-importance rating was estimated for individual herbaceous plant species by multiplying ratings for total cover, frequency, and intensity of use and dividing their product by 1,000 to reduce the figures to a convenient size.

Although the primary objective of this survey was to study the nature and extent of elephant utilization of herbaceous plant species, data on the use of woody species and elephant behavior in general were simultaneously collected. Observations on feeding behavior were made throughout the period of work and have been used to supplement the quantitative data.

Groups of elephants were followed in the Central and South blocks on eight different occasions for a total of 34.6 km; 12.1 km were traversed (600 plots) while following two different groups in the South Block in November in 1963 and the other 22.5 km were traversed (1,111 plots) while following six different groups in the Central Block in February and March 1964. Behavior in general, and feeding behavior in particular, were observed and recorded along these tracks, and forage utilization was studied and recorded.

SOUTH BLOCK

Observation 1. Between 11 and 19 November 1963, line-cutting crews worked throughout the southern end of the reserve, but found no sign of elephant activity, even though one crew was engaged full time in searching for evidence. On 20 November a group of about 10 elephants entered the southeastern corner of the reserve along a deeply worn game trail, which closely followed a high contour of the topography. Outside the reserve this game trail traversed the *Acacia-Hyparrhenia* savanna, which surrounds the southern tip; inside the reserve the trail passed through a small acanthus-grass-scrub cover and then continued almost due west through a shortgrass cover, right up to the edge of type 3 forest dominated by *Cynometra alexandri*. Inside the type 3 forest the trail led directly to a ford of the Dura River and continued in a northwesterly direction on the west side of the river.

On 21 November, these elephants were backtracked for 4.8 km along the trail from the point where it entered the type 3 forest. In this section, seven normally palatable herbaceous species were abundant, but no evidence of feeding was found other than on occasional seed heads of *Themeda triandra,* which were within trunk's reach of the trail. Nineteen droppings were found along the trail, indicating that the animals were traveling in single file without stopping to feed. The droppings were examined and estimated to contain 95% grass.

As the elephants approached the edge of the type 3 forest through the shortgrass cover, they removed terminal twigs and leaves of *Hibiscus fuscus, Hoslundia opposita,* and *Ocimum suave.* At the forest edge a *Triumfetta macrophylla* was uprooted and most parts above the root eaten. Between the forest edge and the Dura River ford, the terminal shoots and bark of four *Maytenus undatus* trees were heavily used. After fording the river, the elephants spread out and browsed woody forage species in the type 3 forest. Browsing continued for 2 km with the intensity of use decreasing as the animals progressed. During this time, 16 species of woody forage plants were used.

Ninety-five percent of all woody plants used were species of small trees and shrubs, which seldom exceed 0.5 m dbh. *Acalypha* spp. and *Maytenus undatus* were the most frequently used species and together comprised 60% of all woody stems used; *Acalypha* alone accounted for 40% of all utilized stems. Other species of woody plants utilized included *Alchornia hirtella, Celtis mildbraedii, Cleistanthus popystachyus, Coffea eugenoides, Craibia brownii, Cynometra alexandri, Dombeya mukole, Dovyalis macrocalyx, Drypetes* sp., *Markhamia platycalys, Oxyanthus* sp., *Pavetta acrochlora, Teclea nobilis,* and an unidentified climber.

Of all woody plants utilized, use was limited to the removal of terminal twigs and leaves in 9% and the removal of only the leaves in 13%. One stem was barked, and six plants were completely demolished. Leaf stripping was particularly common in *Maytenus undatus,* where this form of use occurred on one-third of all utilized plants.

Observation 2. On 26 November 1963, the trails of 16 elephants were discovered and followed for 5.2 km. These animals had entered the extreme southeastern tip of the reserve from the adjacent grassland less than 12 hr prior to the commencement of the enumeration. They proceeded north and then northwest through the reserve crossing the Dura River 5.2 km north of the point where they entered the reserve. Tracking was abandoned where they crossed the river. During the first 3.2 km of this traverse, the elephants fed actively as they passed through intermittent patches of acanthus-grass-scrub, colonizing forest, and type 3 forest. Intensive feeding was nearly continuous with woody and herbaceous species receiving heavy use. This was the longest distance over which elephants in the reserve were ever observed to maintain feeding activity of this intensity. Forage uti-

lization occurred on 58.1% of all plots along this initial section of track. Herbaceous species were used on 38.1%, and woody species on 40.6%. In all, 48 different forage species were utilized, 18 of them herbaceous and 30 of them woody. Intensive use of woody vegetation was made in the type 3 forest as well as in the acanthus-grass-scrub cover. The heaviest feeding occurred in the latter, where 14 different forage species were utilized in a 101-m interval. The herbaceous vegetation used included 11 grasses, 5 herbs, 1 sedge, and 1 climber. Although many of the smaller forage species were completely pulled from the ground, only the tops were eaten.

The use of woody forage was limited to terminal twigs and leaves on 97% of all plants. Barking occurred on only two plants, or 33% of all plants enumerated. Species of small trees and shrubs, which seldom exceed 0.5 m dbh provided 98% of all woody stems used. *Acalypha* spp. and *Triumfetta macrophylla* accounted for half, with *Acalypha* spp. being used most frequently. *Allophylus macrobotrys, Dichrostachys cinerea, Dovyalis macrocalyx* were the next most frequently used woody species, in the order listed. Other woody species utilized included *Acacia* sp., *Acanthus pubescens, Bridelia micrantha, Celtis africana, Chaetacme aristata, Cissus adenocaulis, Clausena anisata, Coffea eugeniodes, Dasylepis eggelingii, Dombeya mukole, Dracaena steudneri, Drypetes* sp., *Erythrina abyssinica, Ficus* sp., *Glyphaea brevis, Kigelia moosa, Leptonychia milbraedii, Maytenus undatus, Millettia dura, Sapium ellipticum, Securinega virosa, Teclea nobilis, Uvariopsis congensis,* an unidentified climber, and an unidentified shrub. At the end of the 3.2 km the animals stopped feeding and marched through type 3 forest to the Dura River.

CENTRAL BLOCK

Observation 1. On 11 February 1964, five elephants were followed for 2 km through mixed patches of type 3 forest, shortgrass, and acanthus-grass-scrub. The track had to be abandoned when the elephants headed northwest across a deep swamp and the Mgombe River. These elephants did not feed on herbaceous plants even though normally palatable species such as *Beckeropsis uniseta, Pennisetum purpureum, Digitaria* sp., and *Hyparrhenia* spp. were available. The terminal twigs and leaves of one *Coffea canephora* and one *Teclea nobilis* stem were browsed in passing. The animals stood under and barked a *Trichilia prieureana* tree near the swamp.

Observation 2. On 14 and 15 February 1964 a group of elephants (more than 10) was followed for 5.2 km, as they traveled through a complex interspersion of seven vegetative cover types. On the 5.2-km track the animals passed from one cover type into another on 31 occasions. Moderate feeding occurred in a recently burned shortgrass cover and adjacent type 3 forest. The elephants then fed heavily and bedded down in an acanthus-grass-scrub area. On the last two-thirds of the track they fed very lightly as they traveled through a large block of type 3 forest that was interspersed with occasional patches of other cover types. Of the 255 plots enumerated along this track 50% were in type 3 forest, 24% in recently burned shortgrass, 20% in acanthus-grass-scrub, and the remaining 6% distributed among swamp-scrub, swamp-forest, colonizing forest, and forest openings.

In the recently burned shortgrass, the elephants utilized a total of 16 forage species including 8 grasses, 2 herbs, and 6 woody species. *Themeda triandra, Imperata cylindrica,* and *Brachiaria* sp. dominated the shortgrass type, but were little used. *Beckeropsis uniseta* and *Pennisetum purpureum* were not abundant, but were fed upon whenever encountered. *Digitaria scalarum* was common and was used frequently. *Paspalum* sp. was used occasionally. In a few places the dominant grasses were lightly used where the elephants had fed on *Beckeropsis uniseta* and *Pennisetum purpureum*. In one place the roots of *Themeda triandra* were consumed. The elephants ate large quantities of an unidentified herb in the shortgrass, and frequently utilized the herb *Geniosporum paludosum. Triumfetta macrophylla* and *Ocimum suave* were the most frequently used woody species in the shortgrass type, with *Acanthus pubescens, Erythrina abyssinica, Hibiscus cunescens,* and *Vernonia camponea* receiving only light use. In the type 3 forest adjacent to the burned shortgrass, the elephants browsed the terminal twigs and leaves from the woody species *Dasylepis eggelingii, Drypetes* sp., *Lasiodiscus mildbraedii,* and *Funtumia latifolia.*

The elephants bedded down in an acanthus-grass-scrub type and spent some time standing about. In this area they made intensive use of three woody and three herbaceous forage species. The terminal twigs and leaves of *Dichrostachys cinerea* and *Securinega virosa* were browsed. *Triumfetta macrophylla* was used both frequently and very intensively, often pulled from the ground with nearly all aboveground parts being consumed. *Melanthera scandens* was pulled from the ground and eaten; the tops of *Beckeropsis uniseta* and *Hyparrhenia* spp. were broken and eaten.

After leaving the acanthus-grass-scrub, the elephants entered type 3 forest cover with an understory dominated by *Coffea canephora.* The animals traveled through this forest and small patches of other cover types for 3.2 km. During this time, very little feeding occurred. The leader or terminal growth was snapped off one *Coffea canephora* plant and twigs were nipped from *Acalypha bipartita.* One stem of *Blighia unijugata* and *Albizia grandibracteata* was barked. In a swamp-scrub type, the fruits of *Phoenix reclinata* were consumed.

Observation 3. On 14 March 1964, a large group of elephants with young was followed for 1.6 km through tallgrass, acanthus-grass-scrub, and small patches of colonizing type 2 forest. During this trek the elephants bathed in a nearby swamp, rubbed on trees, stood about, laid down, and leisurely fed on both woody and herbaceous forage species. *Pennisetum purpureum* was abundant and was the most-used herbaceous species, the roots being eaten as often as the tops. *Hyparrhenia* sp. was common but was unused except in bedding and loafing areas where it was used as heavily and as often as *Pennisetum purpureum. Panicum* sp. was used lightly on one occasion. Terminal leaves and twigs of *Allophyius macrobotrys, Dombeya mukole, Dovyalis macrocalyx, Maytenus undatus, Pterygota mildbraedii,* and *Teclea nobilis* were browsed, with *Pterygota mildbraedii* and *Teclea nobilis* used most frequently. *Triumfetta macrophylla* was also used heavily wherever encountered.

Observation 4. On 16 March 1964, a large group of elephants was followed for 5.2 km through a complex interspersion of grassland, scrub, and forest cover types. These animals advanced in a northwesterly direction along a deeply worn game trail, stopping at various places to feed. Not much time was spent in any one place, however, and the intensity of feeding was only light to medium. On three separate occasions they traveled through type 2 forest for a distance of 0.8 km without feeding.

The elephants stopped to feed in an area of mixed shortgrass, tallgrass, and acanthus-grass-scrub and used both woody and herbaceous species. *Pennisetum purpureum* (elephant grass) was the most frequently used species, both the tops and the roots being consumed. *Hyparrhenia* sp. was used on only one occasion, and *Triumfetta macrophylla* was heavily used when encountered. The terminal twigs and leaves of *Sapium ellipticum* were browsed on one occasion.

In a shortgrass area the elephants pulled *Themeda triandra* plants from the ground and ate the roots. *Imperata cylindrica* (cotton grass) was also used highly.

The elephants used *Triumfetta macrophylla* whenever they encountered it and often stopped to feed on it during marches when they were not eating any other species.

At one place in the type 2 forest, the elephants left the game trail and spread out to feed on herbaceous climbers and woody forage plants. The terminal leaves and twigs of *Dasylepis eggelingii*, *Phyllanthus discoideus*, and *Millettia dura* were removed and eaten and a large *Chaetacme aristata* was overturned and fed upon.

Observation 5. On 17 and 18 March 1964 at least 10 elephants with young were followed for 7.6 km. The largest part of this track (5.6 km) meandered through type 3 forest adjacent to swamp-scrub and swamp-forest. The elephants spent their time bathing, rubbing on trees, standing, and feeding on mostly woody vegetation. The other 2 km of track passed through tallgrass, acanthus-grass-scrub, and acanthus-grass areas where intensive feeding on herbaceous vegetation occurred.

In the swampy cover and adjacent forest, elephants utilized 23 species of woody vegetation. They browsed the terminal twigs and leaves of *Allophyius macrobotrys*, *Celtis africana*, *Celtis mildbraedii*, *Chrysophyllum* sp., *Clausena anisata*, *Dasylepis eggelingii*, *Dictyandra arborescens*, *Dovyalis macrocalyx*, *Drypetes* sp., *Fagaropsis angolensis*, *Phyllanthus discoideus*, *Pterygota mildbraedii*, *Strychnos mitis*, and *Teclea nobilis*. Of these species, *Teclea nobilis*, *Pterygota mildbraedii*, *Fagaropsis angolensis*, and *Dovyalis macrocalyx* were the most frequently used and collectively accounted for one-third of all stems browsed. *Albizia grandibracteata*, *Chrysophyllum albidum*, *Lovoa swynnertonii*, *Monodura myristica*, and *Strombosia scheffleri* were barked. Relatively little use was made of herbaceous vegetation in the swamp and forest cover, with *Aframomum sanguineum*, *Cyanthula achyranthoides*, *Setaria chevalieri* and unidentified climbers being the only species for which utilization was recorded. On one site, the roots of *Aframomum sanguineum* were eaten after it had been pulled from the ground.

During the period of intensive feeding in the tallgrass, acanthus-grass, and acanthus-grass-scrub cover, *Pennisetum purpureum*, *Beckeropsis* sp., and *Hyparrhenia* sp. were all used frequently, with *Pennisetum purpureum* being used most often. *Brachiaria* sp. was used moderately, *Digitaria* sp. lightly, and *Imperata cylindrica* not at all. *Triumfetta macrophylla* was used intensively throughout this feeding period, *Sapium ellipticum* was browsed once, and *Erythrina abyssinica* twice.

Observation 6. On 20 March 1964, a small group of elephants was followed for 0.6 km through type 3 forest and swamp-scrub. The elephants browsed the terminal twigs and leaves of woody plants and occasionally fed on herbaceous plants. Woody species utilized included *Chaetacme aristata*, *Dasylepis eggelingii*, *Dovyalis macrocalyx*, *Funtumia latifolia*, and *Sida* sp. Herbaceous species eaten included *Achyranthes aspera*, *Aframomum sanguineum*, *Chloris* sp., and *Setaria chevalieri*. Unfortunately, these elephants were disturbed while feeding, and the track was abandoned.

EVALUATION OF DATA. Estimates of the relative importance of common herbaceous forage species in the elephants' diets indicate that the order of importance was much different in the South Block than in the Central Block. Part of this difference probably resulted from the big difference in the relative abundance and availability within the blocks; part of the difference may also have been the result of seasonal fluctuations in the elephants' preference for certain forage species. The Central Block was sampled at the end of the December-February dry season and the South Block near the end of the September-November rainy season.

In the Central Block there were extensive stands of nearly pure *Pennisetum purpureum* with varying proportions of *Beckeropsis uniseta* and *Hyparrhenia* spp.; thus these three species ranked high above all other herbaceous species in importance. In the South Block differences in species importance were not so extreme, and no single species or group dominated; nearly all grassland vegetation included a wide mixture of species, and pure stands of one or more species were not extensive.

The average intensity of elephant utilization was recorded for common herbaceous forage species of the Central and South blocks. In most, a rather high proportion of the entire plant was consumed. Almost all herbaceous plants that elephants utilized were heavily damaged, even when only small parts of them were consumed. Small grasses and herbs frequently were pulled completely out of the ground, even when only the tops were eaten. Usually only the tops were broken from larger plants like *Pennisetum purpureum*, *Beckeropsis uniseta*, and *Hyparrhenia* spp., leaving the rest of the plant firmly rooted in the ground. On occasion, however, even large species were uprooted and their basal parts eaten. During the wet seasons, mostly aboveground parts of herbaceous plants were consumed. During the dry seasons, seed heads were eaten

Tusk gouging on *Pygeum afri-cana*, Kibale Forest Reserve. (*Photograph by Larry D. Wing*)

and plants were often uprooted with the basal parts being eaten.

Although *Pennisetum purpureum, Beckeropsis uniseta,* and the tall species of *Hyparrhenia* were not as abundant in the South Block as in the Central Block, they were preferred forage species and often selectively utilized. Elephants often traveled several hundred meters through stands of *Themeda triandra, Cymbopogon afronardus, Imperata cylindrica,* and *Brachiaria* sp. without stopping to feed. However, whenever *Pennisetum purpureum, Beckeropsis uniseta,* or tall *Hyparrhenia* spp. were encountered, they stopped and fed. While feeding on these choice grasses, they often ingested smaller amounts of other species. Since the choice grasses, particularly *Pennisetum purpureum,* require relatively moist soil conditions, all species growing on such sites probably are succulent and perhaps more nutritious than forage on adjacent drier sites. Also, some of the less preferred forages probably were eaten inadvertently along with the choice. On recently burned areas, elephants were less discriminating in their selection of forage species, and an increase was noted in the incidence of utilization of species that nor-

mally were low in palatability or unused; even *Acanthus pubescens* was eaten on such areas.

On some occasions, normally palatable herbaceous vegetation was bypassed in favor of woody forage. Such instances occurred in the South Block and were described earlier in this section, under "Observation 1" and "Observation 2." These observations recorded the highest incidence of sustained utilization of woody forage observed during any of our studies. When these rates were compared with those in the Central Block, the reasons for the great difference between the two blocks was not even suggested. Since the elephants observed in the South Block had just entered the reserve, they probably craved certain nutrients in the woody vegetation that were lacking or difficult to obtain in the grasslands and savannas from which they had come. The fact that the observations in the South Block were made during a different season than those in the Central Block is not thought to be the reason for the difference in rates, since other observations indicate that the rate of woody forage utilization in general is higher during the dry seasons. The rate of tree barking, for example, is higher at the end of the dry seasons and at the start of the wet seasons than at the end of the wet seasons. The suggestion that elephants consume woody forage at a greater rate upon first arriving in the reserve is also supported by other data. Geographic distribution of relative rates of woody plant utilization by elephants shows that the southern tip of the reserve receives a significantly higher incidence of utilization than expected (Fig. 5.9). Since the southern tip is the area where northward migrating elephants first encounter high forest, one might expect to view heavier use than on other areas, particularly if it offers a source of nutrients not easily obtained elsewhere.

Observations made throughout our field work in the reserve indicated that the *incidence* of woody forage consumption by elephants was often as high, and occasionally higher, than that of herbaceous forage, but that the total volume consumed was considerably lower. Evidence indicated that some woody material was consumed every day, sometimes during periods of rest.

These findings are at slight variance with the statement of Hanks (1979, 30) in his caption to Plate 5, which reads, "In the wetter summer months they [elephants] graze on fresh green grass, but in the dry season most of their food is browse, often taken high up in the taller trees." Plate 5 shows three elephants under large trees with practically no herbaceous or shrub foods in sight. Hopefully Hanks wanted to convey the idea that during dry season(s) elephants utilize woody vegetation more frequently, rather than their usual food.

In his discussions of elephant food habits studies by other researchers, Hanks (1979) briefly sums up differences among these studies and their impacts on habitats (Lawton 1966; Verboom 1968; Coe 1972; McCullagh 1973; Western 1973; Croze 1974a, b; Wyatt and Eltringham 1974; Anderson and Walker 1974; and Thomson 1975). Perhaps any study conducted on this subject at a specific time and place will vary with other studies on the same subject conducted elsewhere at the same or other time. Environments are dynamic, not static, with or without elephants.

Observations made during the elephant–herbaceous plant relationships study in Kibale Forest Reserve brought out the fact that leaf stripping is a very common form of woody forage utilization. Probably much utilization of this type went undetected because of the rapid rate at which evidence of use, which is subtle to begin with, is obscured by growth of new leaves. Leaf stripping was particularly common in *Dasylepis eggelingii, Maytenus undatus, Pancovia turbinata, Rawsonia ugandensis, Rinores* spp., and *Teclea nobilis.*

The importance of several semiwoody grassland and scrub forage species was learned during the survey on feeding behavior. *Triumfetta macrophylla* and, to a lesser extent, *Ocimum suave* were discovered to be very palatable and were regular constituents in the elephants' grassland-scrub diet.

Rarely was an elephant group followed for more than 0.4 km without some type of feeding activity being recorded. Even when the animals were moving between areas without stopping to feed, they usually removed bits of forage with their trunks as they passed.

Various plants known to be utilized by elephants were noted, but no utilization percentages of their use were obtained. The leaves and bark from small-diameter stems were utilized from woody climbers and *Triumfetta macrophylla;* only small terminal tips of herbaceous tissue were removed from *Acanthus pubescens;* fruits, seeds, and the leader of *Phoenix reclinata* were all observed to be utilized. Sikes (1971, plate 23) shows an unusual picture of an "African elephant bull shaking a doum palm vigorously in an attempt to dislodge the ripening fruit. Kenya 1965."

6

Food Habits and Feeding Behavior

THIS STUDY was conducted primarily to obtain information on food habits of elephants during and soon after the dry season from the Kabalega population, to record observations on behavior that appeared to be related to their food habits, and to supplement the work described in Chapter 5 on "Elephant–Woody Plant Relationships" and on "Elephant–Herbaceous Plant Relationships." This information was secured by vegetation surveys, analyses of stomach contents, and analyses of droppings; all three techniques help to overcome weaknesses inherent in each technique. To rely solely on any one technique would result in inadequate and very probably inaccurate conclusions. Supplementary observations from other areas in western Uganda at various times are also included.

Stomach contents from 71 elephants provided most of the data used in this study. These elephants were collected between December 1958 and May 1959 along the Masindi-Paraa road south of the Kabalega National Park, except 14, which were taken from Mobutu Flats along the Sonso, Waisoke, and Weiga rivers (Fig. 6.1).

Scientific names of trees and shrubs, and most of their common and local names, follow Eggeling (1958); those of other plants are from various sources including local lists (a complete guide to flora does not exist).

Habitat Vegetation

Lake Mobutu Marsh (elevation about 620 m) is at the east edge of the lake, near the mouths of the Waisoke

and Weiga rivers. East of the marsh is a nearly flat area about 6–13 km widely known as Mobutu Flats, a semi-arid savanna dominated by secondary pyrophytic vegetation. Shantz and Turner (1953, 139) state that on the slopes of the escarpment at the south end of the flats, "intensive annual burning undoubtedly destroys the larger non-sucker-forming trees and selects for smaller, rapid-growing sucker-forming types . . ." Desert date (*Balanites aegyptiaca*), desert thorn (*Acacia* spp., probably mostly *A. hockii*), tamarind (*Tamarindus indica*), candelabra (*Euphorbia candelabrum*), *Harrisonia abyssinica, Commiphora abysinica* var. *simplicifolia, Aloe* sp., and *Sansevieria* sp. are common locally or widely scattered. The sausage tree (*Kigelia aethiopica*) grows commonly along watercourses with other trees and shrubs, providing shade and cover.

At the east edge of the flats the land rises steeply for over 305 m to the top of the escarpment, and the land east and above the escarpment undulates on the gentle upper slopes of the watershed where the Weiga, Waisoke, and Sonso rivers originate. These rivers flow westward across the flats and into Lake Mobutu. The vegetation above the escarpment and north of Budongo Forest consists of extensive grasslands on which scattered trees and numerous woodlands occur, many of them less than 4 hectares (ha) in size. Most of the grasslands are dominated by dense stands of thatching grass (*Hyparrhenia dissoluta* and *H. filipendula*). *Andropogon gayanus*, which attains a height of 3.7 m, and *Loudetia arundinacea* are mixed with thatching grass on the hills.

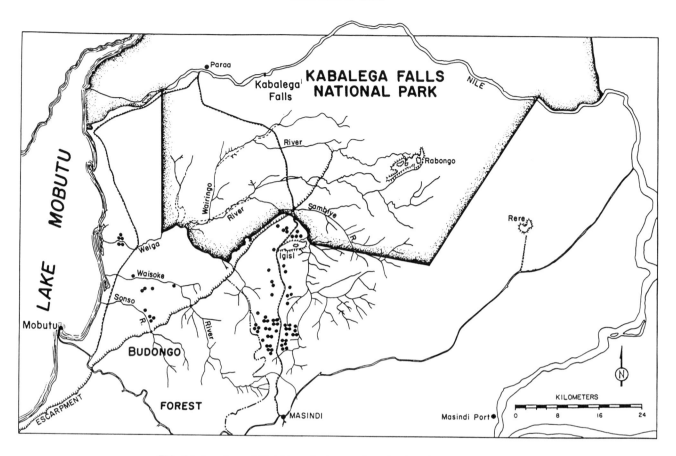

FIG. 6.1. Locations of 71 African elephants collected and used partly for study of food habits (each dot represents one elephant).

Elephant grass (*Pennisetum purpureum*) and guinea grass (*Panicum maximum*) are dominant in low areas and along watercourses. Other common grasses include *Setaria sphacelata, S. longiseta,* palisade grass (*Brachiaria brizantha*), *Paspalum commersonii,* "cotton grass" (*Imperata cylindrica*), spear grass (*Heteropogon contortus*), and rush grass *Sporobolus* sp.). Generally the growth of grass is less luxuriant near the escarpment where soil is poorer and the climate drier than it is farther east (Eggeling 1947). The two most common trees of the grasslands are the small *Combretum binderanum,* which occurs in nearly thicketlike stands on some sites, and the larger *Terminalia velutina,* which attains a height of about 11 m. A few desert date occur near the escarpment, and black plum (*Vitex doniana*) is scattered locally through the grasslands. Throughout most of the grasslands there are termite mounds.

The woodlands above the escarpment are in various stages of development or recession; these stages are very similar to three chief types of forest described by Eggel-

ing (1947) for Budongo Forest. The presence of *Maesopsis eminii, Olea welwitschii, Caloncoba schweinfurthii, Albizia coriaria,* and *Dombeya mukole* in two-storied woodlands, which contain trees characterized by a relatively low height class (21–30 m) and small diameters, few or no buttresses, a scarcity of mosses and lichens, and many small climbers, indicate pioneering or colonizing woodlands of early seral stage. Intermediate and rich woodlands of many seral species include *Alstonia congensis, Khaya anthotheca, Entandrophragma cylindricum, E. utile,* and several species of *Chrysophyllum* and *Celtis.* These trees are recognizable in three or four stories, vary in height up to about 37 m, and have relatively large diameters and well-developed buttresses. Many vascular epiphytes occur on the trees. Near Rabongo Hill, isolated woodlands represent remnants of Rabongo Forest; according to Buechner and Dawkins (1961) these woodlands are in a recessive stage and are dominated by *Cynometra alexandri,* an indicator of climax (Eggeling 1947). At various other places in the area, tall individual forest trees with smooth trunks measuring up to about 30 m from ground level to the crown collar provide evidence of former climax or intermediate woodlands.

VEGETATION CHANGES. Evidence has been recorded for some of the vegetational changes that occurred in previous years north of Budongo Forest to the Nile River and west of the east boundary of Kabalega Falls National Park to Lake Mobutu. The magnitude and time of most of these changes are unknown.

Buechner and Dawkins (1961) studied vegetational changes in the park, and in speculating on the vegetation that occurred south of the Nile River a century ago state that "it seems likely that high *Cynometra alexandri* forests were at one time more extensive, although limited to the area in the vicinity of Rabongo Hill, and that gallery forests were numerous along streams and around springs." In discussing the occurrence and historic significance of elephant grass in the area, Eggeling (1947, 36) states that "pure stands of elephant grass usually indicate a man-made condition which persists, because of fire, even after man's activities have ceased. If burning can be prevented, the density of the stand diminishes, light enters, woody species regenerate and the slow process of forest formation begins." Worthington (1958) expresses the view that in Uganda the large areas of elephant grass were once high forest; his views support those of Thomas (1940), who believes that "elephant grass should be regarded as a man-made degradation of forest." Eggeling (1947, 36) points out that "it is possible that at the time when the original lateritic blanket over Bunyoro eroded, elephant grass competed successfully with forest for the colonization of the freshly formed soils, and that with the aid of fire the grass had held its gains ever since."

The area north of Budongo Forest to the Nile River, and west of the forest to Lake Mobutu was closed to settlement as a Sleeping Sickness Area in about 1912; the area has served as a game reserve since then. Assuming that the high elephant population then in the area developed since 1912, I infer that the greatest damage to forest vegetation by elephants should have occurred in the past 50 yr. However, the widespread occurrence of old termite mounds, which are not generally constructed in forests of Bunyoro, and numerous old *Terminalia velutina* (a savanna tree) in the grasslands of the area do not support such a conclusion. Eggeling (1947) expresses the belief that north, northeast, and northwest of Budongo Forest elephants and fires slowed down and possibly prohibited the spread of the forest. However, he concluded (p. 38) that "an examination of the areas of Colonizing Forest shows conclusively that within the last thirty years Budongo has spread considerably. The evidence includes the presence of relict *Terminalia velutina* and of derelict termite mounds of a grassland type well within the forest, and is confirmed by a comparison of old and present-day maps."

The high elephant population of this area is concentrated inside Kabalega Falls National Park where the animals are involved in a high rate of destructiveness to trees. The elephant uses its tusks with amazing dexterity in rending bark from trees, and when trees at the edge of a forest are damaged, the exposure of the cambial layer and other living tissues to fire eventually kills many trees. Buechner and Dawkins (1961) concluded that death of these trees allows more light to penetrate into the forest edge, permitting the invasion of grasses that carry the fire from adjacent grasslands progressively deeper into the forest. Since the amount of fire destruction at the forest edge is directly related to the extent of tree damage by elephants, it appears that the elephants are destroying the forests. Actually, elephant depredations to trees act as a catalyst to fires, which are directly and primarily responsible for changing woodlands to grasslands. Buechner and Dawkins (1961) state that "it is through the basic influence of fire that vegetation in the Park south of the [Nile River] is now primarily treeless grassland."

Shantz and Turner (1953) documented changes in vegetation that occurred in the southern part of Mobutu Flats between 1920 and 1957. They refer to the work of Eggeling (1947) and state that he "may be correct that elephants *and* fire were responsible for the original destruction of a 'closed forest' and its replacement by open savanna and grassland on the Mobutu Flats, but certainly it seems clear from the photographic evidence that fire is the most important factor in maintaining that dis-climax today." Closed, high tropical forest (similar to Budongo Forest) would probably not develop on Mobutu Flats even if fires and elephants were eliminated since annual rainfall is now only 76 cm (Lands and Surveys Dep. 1959).

Regardless of the comparative effects that fires and elephants had many years ago in initiating destruction of forests on Mobutu Flats or above the escarpment, most of the evidence obtained during the past 50 yr indicates that fire is the dominant ecological force inhibiting natural development and regeneration of forest communities and in maintaining extensive grasslands. Evidently suppression of grassland fires, particularly where remnant forest and shrub species still persist, would help these species regenerate and establish extensive stands. There remains the possibility that if elephant populations escalate above those of 1955–1970, elephants could become dominant in destroying remnant forests, for there is "evidence that . . . experimental exclusion of elephant, or substantial reduction in elephant density, is followed by regeneration of woody vegetation, even in the presence of regular burning" (Laws 1970b, 8).

According to Stephen Cobb (1980) Phil Glover set up a series of elephant-proof exclosures in Tsavo (East) in 1971. In 1975 Willem van Wijngaarden arrived in Tsavo and used the exclosures to demonstrate that the woodlands were quite capable of remarkably rapid recovery from the assaults of elephants and subsequent ravages of fire. In 1977

a herd of buffalo was chased by lions over the ditch into the Ndara exclosure . . . and annihilated the woody vegetation, as well as the grass. . . . The Irima exclosure had no such trouble from animals and contained a flourishing woodland three and more metres high *after eight years of protection.* But then the high rainfall of 1977–79 increased grass cover in Tsavo and thus the incidence of brush fires. When a fire burned in the Irima area in late 1979, it was easily able to jump the ditch into the exclosure. The young trees were severely damaged and have not yet shown signs of recovery.

METHODS FOR DETERMINING USE OF VEGETATION.
Direct observations of feeding habits and food utilized by elephants were recorded in the field on every possible occasion. When an elephant was shot, the stomach and contents were weighed in the field on a government-tested spring scale having a capacity of 272 kg. The contents were removed, the empty stomach was weighed, and the net weight of the contents was recorded. The stomach contents were then spread on the ground to a uniform thickness of about 5 cm and divided into four approximately equal parts to facilitate percentage estimates. The items in each part were identified, and the percentage occurrence of each item was estimated and recorded (Table 6.1). Items not identified in the field were preserved and subsequently identified with the aid of reference materials. The moisture content among stomachs was conspicuously similar regardless of the amount of material in a stomach or the distance from a source of water at which an elephant was collected. The total net weight of the stomach contents was multiplied by the percentage of each item to ascertain its relevant net weight. Items weighing less than .45 kg were recorded as traces.

Table 6.1. Stomach contents of 71 African elephants examined during a dry season in Uganda

Item	Net Weight Consumed (kg)	Occurrence (%)
Mature grass[a]	3793	99
Young grass[a]	479	56
Combretum binderanum (combretum)	266	35
Vitex doniana (black plum)	59	9
Afromomum sp. (wild ginger or masasa)	tr.	8
Stereospermum kunthianum (mulemangundu)	17	7
Sansevieria-Aloe (sansevieria-aloe)	83	6
Kigelia aethiopica (sausage tree)	16	4
Trichilia roka (makaku)	4	3
Piliostigma thonningii (camel's foot leaf tree or mugali)	tr.	3
Harrisonia abyssinica	73	1
Portulaca (purslane)	0.5	1
Cissus quadrangularis (ivy)	0.5	1
Balanites aegyptiaca (desert date)	tr.	1
Terminalia velutina (terminalia)	tr.	1
Khaya grandifoliola (African mahogany)	tr.	1
Entandrophragma sp. (Budongo mahogany or muyovu)	tr.	1
Ficus sp. (fig tree)	tr.	1
Hoslundia opposita (nkibibi)	tr.	1
Tinnea aethiopica (kanyahira)	tr.	1
Sticks (6, 8, 11 cm long)	tr.	1
Stones (35, 28, 25, 20 mm in diam.)	tr.	1
Unidentified woody material	27	30

[a] Includes *Hyparrhenia dissoluta, H. filipendula, Pennesetum purpureum,* and probably *Heteropogon contortus, Brachiaria brizantha,* and *Sporobolus* sp.

Analyses of Stomach Contents

GRASSES. Grasses were the most prevalent food of the 71 elephants collected. One or more species of grass occurred in 70 stomachs (99%) and comprised from 25% to 100% of the stomach contents by weight. The stomachs contained 4,272 kg of grass (Table 6.1), or an average of about 61 kg each. Thatching grass was eaten more frequently and in larger quantities than any other grass. Elephant grass and guinea grass were eaten occasionally; some stomachs appeared to have spear grass, palisade grass, and rush grass, but these three grasses were not positively identified. Although cotton grass was common in the area, there was no evidence of its utilization by elephants. The one elephant that had no grass in its stomach, a 3,765-kg bull shot on Mobutu Flats, had a trunk 0.6 m shorter than other bulls its size. Apparently its trunk had been severed by a snare, which probably prevented the animal from reaching the relatively short grass available at that time. Leaves and twigs

This bull's shortened trunk prevented feeding on shortgrass, but shrubs and emergent aquatic vegetation could be utilized. Adjustment must have been extremely painful and difficult, but he was well developed and of good weight. (*Photograph by Roger Wheater*)

of *Harrisonia abyssinica*, a shrub growing abundantly on the nearby plain, comprised 98% of the food materials in its stomach; the other 2% consisted of pieces from the fruit coat of the sausage tree. In the Kibale Forest Reserve in 1963 elephants were observed feeding on elephant grass and cattails (*Typha latifolia*).

TREES AND SHRUBS. Although there is wide recognition that the activities of elephants are not regularly nocturnal, diurnal, or crepuscular, they apparently adjust the time of their activities to different circumstances. Elephants above the escarpment frequently retired from savannas into woodlands soon after sunrise, and usually started coming out of woodlands late in the afternoon. On 15 of 32 trips I made into this area, elephants were shot during the first hours after sunrise while they were feeding in grasslands near woodlands. On 4 of these occasions the elephants were disappearing into woodlands when they were first seen, and on 3 occasions I followed groups into woodlands to make collections. Elephants were seen on savannas at various times of the day on 13 trips, and I shot them on 4 occasions after sunset as they were coming out of woodlands.

Evidence of small trees and shrubs being broken down does not always indicate that feeding was taking place. On 18 March 1959 I was following close behind a band of about 60 elephants in a woodland attempting to collect one of the animals. At least three different individuals were observed at less than 20 m breaking down or damaging saplings about 3.7 m to 7.6 m in height. Apparently these animals were trying to rid themselves of ectoparasites by rubbing their heads on the saplings, particularly the base of their tusks where ticks tend to concentrate. The vertical head movements, with tusks generally straddling or close to the saplings, resulted in many broken limbs and frequently a broken trunk of the saplings. During these "bashing" operations no part of the saplings was eaten. Evidently *Lonchocarpus laxiflorus* was damaged more frequently than other species. This observation suggests (1) that elephants do not damage young trees for feeding purposes only, and (2) why people commonly and erroneously believe that elephants "feed" nonselectively on all young trees of certain size classes.

Although elephants spent considerable time in woodlands, trees and shrubs provided a low percentage of their food. Only 10% (462 kg) of the total food ma-

147

Combretum spp. appears to be a choice elephant food in Uganda and South Africa. This burned-over area dominated by grass and C. binderanum is a favorite feeding site for elephants northeast of Budongo Forest and south of Kabalega Falls National Park. (*Photograph by I. O. Buss*)

terial in the 71 stomachs consisted of leaves, twigs, and fruit of trees and shrubs. Leaves and twigs from *Combretum binderanum,* which occurred in 35% of the stomachs, were eaten more frequently than any other woody food (Table 6.1). Elephants appeared to prefer combretum about 1.2 m to 4.6 m in height; these young trees grew profusely on lands where annual fires had obviously occurred regularly for many years. Elephants were collected while feeding from combretum of this size class, and on numerous occasions they were seen feeding on both grass and combretum where the latter species was in this size class.

Leaves, twigs, and many mature fruits of black plum were found in 7, or 9%, of the stomachs; the stomach of a 2,649-kg female collected on 29 December 1958, contained about 4 L of ripe black plums. Small quantities of leaves and twigs from *Stereospermum kunthianum,* which is a common tree where these elephants were collected, occurred in 7% of the stomachs. Pieces from the fibrous fruit coat of the sausage tree were found in three stomachs, leaves from the makaku tree (*Trichilia*

roka) were identified in two stomachs, and several leaves from the camel's foot leaf tree (*Piliostigma thonningii*) occurred in two stomachs. Although fruits of desert date were found in only 1 of the 71 stomachs, I noted that three elephants shot near the Waisoke River on Mobutu Flats between 17 and 19 December 1958 had fed extensively on the fruits of this tree; 1 stomach contained over a thousand fruits. A few leaves of terminalia occurred in only 1 stomach. This is a very common tree that sustains extensive bark damage by elephants, whereas desert date receives very little or no bark damage. Since both trees are common in the area, elephants apparently damage terminalia selectively. A few green leaves and a fruit of African mahogany were found in 1 stomach, several leaves from Budongo mahogany were eaten by one elephant, and part of the fruit from a fig tree occurred in 1 stomach. Unidentified woody material totaling 27 kg occurred in 30% of the stomachs; combretum probably comprised a high percentage of this material. Direct field observations and the contents of the stomachs examined force the conclusion that elephants use the woodlands primarily for daytime concealment and shade, not as a principal source of food.

In Kibale Forest Reserve the bark of *Alangium chinense, Pterygota mildbraedii, Trichilia prieureana, Albizia grandibracteata, Chrysophyllum albidum, Lovoa swynnertonii, Monodura myristica,* and *Strombosia scheffleri* was selectively stripped and sometimes eaten.

FORBS AND MISCELLANEOUS MATERIALS.

Herbaceous plants, including sansevieria, aloe, and a vine, and sticks and stones comprised 3% of the total material in the 71 stomachs (Table 6.1). Fruits and seeds of wild ginger, or masasa (*Aframomum lutealbum*), occurred in 8% of the 71 stomachs. Evidently these fruits are very palatable to the elephant since the fruit grows close to the ground and is frequently completely hidden by surrounding vegetation.

Five bulls collected near the Weiga River on Mo-

This bull is feeding on *Combretum imberbe* in Kruger National Park, South Africa. (*Photograph by Anthony Hall-Martin*)

butu Flats in February had all eaten from the fleshy and succulent basal leaves of aloe and the leaves of sansevieria. The stomach contents from four of these bulls were analyzed; leaf material from these two plants comprised from 10% to 30% of the total weight of food in their stomachs. Aloe and sansevieria occur on the plain between the escarpment and the marsh, growing most abundantly at the east edge of Lake Mobutu Marsh and close to the rivers. There the elephants fed on these plants during the night and generally returned to the tall, dense vegetation of the marsh very early in the morning. There is a wide and general belief that elephants chew the leaves of aloe and sansevieria for moisture, spitting out the masticated fiber balls. A. M. H. Henley, a former employee of the Game and Fisheries Department of Uganda, informed me that he had witnessed elephants utilizing these plants in this manner on Mobutu Flats. Also, George A. Petrides, who conducted various big-game studies in East Africa as a Fulbright Research Scholar, informed me that these discarded sansevieria "chews" were common in the Northern Frontier District of Kenya where moisture is very scarce. The leaf material eaten by the four Weiga River bulls evidently had not been masticated more than the other food materials in their stomachs, and at the many sites that I observed on Mobutu Flats where elephants had fed on these plants, I found no masticated fibrous balls that suggested this type of feeding. Since there is no shortage of water in the large Lake Mobutu Marsh and the area close to the Weiga River, there was no necessity for these bulls to utilize aloe and sansevieria for moisture only.

In 1963 in Tsavo National Park (East), Kenya, however, I watched elephants chewing the leaves of these plants and rejecting the fibrous material (balls) during early February. This was a time when temporary rain pools were scattered throughout the park supplementing the permanent water supplies. Evidently these plants provided something else besides moisture, or the elephants in Tsavo are so completely habituated to utilizing them for moisture during the dry seasons that this habit is carried throughout all seasons.

Among the 71 stomachs, each of the following plants was represented once by small quantities of leaves and stems: purslane, or *Portulaca*; ivy, *Cissus quadrangularis*; nkibibi, *Hoslundia opposita*; and kanyharia, *Tinnea aethiopica*. An adult female that weighed 2,672 kg was shot in a woodland on 12 March 1959. Her stomach contained three dry sticks that were 6, 8, and 11 cm long and 1.3 cm in diameter. An adult cow that weighed 3,524 kg had four stones in her stom-

Bark of *Terminalia velutina* damaged from 1 m to 4 m above ground, near Weiga River, Kabalega Falls National Park. (*Photograph by H. K. Buechner*)

ticularly when the bolls start to open. Unfortunately, where cotton fields are available to elephants, depredations occur frequently and control of the marauders is necessary.

Along the Kazinga Channel near Ruwenzori National Park grass was eaten in the highest volume, and *Acacia* spp. were second in volume consumed. Also along the channel, elephants fed extensively on *Grewia similis,* a medium-sized shrub, and the mature fruits (and possibly the young tips) of *Capparis erythrocarpus,* a dominant and fragrant shrub. *Albizia coriaria, Tamarindus indica,* and both *Cissus quadrangularis* and *C. rotundifolia* also provide food in the vicinity of the channel. In the park near Lake George, leaves and stems of *Commelina* sp. were eaten, although again grass was the principal food. In the same vicinity elephants were feeding on the spiny shrub *Azima tetracantha.* An old cow pulled the whole shrub from the ground, bashed it against her knee several times to get

Aloe sp. in normal condition near Weiga River, Mobutu Flats. (*Photograph by I. O. Buss*)

ach measuring 20, 25, 28, and 35 mm in diameter. There is a common belief among natives living in elephant country in Uganda that elephants accidentally suck stones into their trunks when drinking and then deliver both stones and water into their mouths.

OTHER FOODS. About 50 km south of Kabalega Falls National Park observations were recorded on the food habits of elephants in Toro District in southwest Uganda, between August and November 1958. The fruits of borassus palm (*Borassus aethiopum*) and the leaves and twigs (including spines) of the desert thorn (probably *Acacia sieberiana*) are highly favored food items.

Cotton has a special attraction for elephants, par-

Aloe sp. after being fed on by elephants near the Weiga River. (*Photograph by I. O. Buss*)

rid of the soil, and ate the roots and most of the leaves and terminal stems.

Cyperus papyrus is also consumed. The stomach of a 4,037-kg bull shot on 1 May 1959 contained 85% papyrus and 15% grass. Before shooting this bull in a large papyrus swamp bordering the Chambura River and Ruwenzori National Park, I saw it skillfully select the newly grown tips of the papyrus and reject the old tops. In October 1963 bulls were encountered feeding on papyrus in the Nile River near Buligi in Kabalega Falls National Park. Two bulls were belly-deep digging up huge tuskloads of papyrus roots and debris from under water and heaving them to the surface where they ate only selected parts. Apparently they were eating young papyrus roots that were probably developing at that time since they were of moderately red color in contrast to the discarded dead parts, which were black. All the vegetative parts above water were dead and had fallen to the water's surface. Another occasion of feeding on papyrus in the Nile was observed in December 1963, when 11 large bulls shuffled through the bush to the water's edge and without stopping to drink, 8 of them waded out to a 0.2-ha patch of papyrus. In about a half hour every visible stem plus underwater parts were eaten. The other 3 bulls remained near shore eating what appeared to be young developing papyrus roots, in a manner similar to that of the Buligi bulls.

Eight bulls waded to a papyrus patch in the Nile River and ate every visible stem in about a half hour. (*Photograph by I. O. Buss*)

Analyses of Droppings

The digestive system of the elephant is relatively inefficient (Benedict 1936, and many others), and much coarse, undigested material in droppings facilitates identification. Most of the material in undisturbed and recently deposited droppings can be classified as herbaceous or woody, and individual species frequently can be identified. The analyses and direct observations on droppings were conducted to obtain supplemental data for enhancing the vegetative surveys and stomach analyses. Specifically, the purpose was to estimate relative proportions of woody and herbaceous materials in droppings examined at various times and places, collect information on seasonal use of plants, particularly fruits and bark of trees, and record direct observations on feeding behavior.

During the last week in April 1959, I examined more than 50 sets of elephant droppings from the Kibale Forest Reserve and along the Kazinga Channel near Ruwenzori National Park. All these droppings contained at least 90% grass. Five droppings examined from near the Mpanga River, deep within the reserve where grass was scarce and woody foods were abundant, still consisted of 98% grass. Those examined from along the channel showed that grass was eaten in greatest volume and that *Acacia* spp. was second in volume consumed.

HERBACEOUS VS. WOODY MATERIAL

Kibale Forest Reserve. Data from 108 droppings examined from the center of the reserve during mid-August indicated that about 93% of the materials consisted of grass and herbs, and approximately 7% of the materials was woody material (mostly leaves and twigs). From nine droppings near the edge of the reserve during late August, analysis showed 86% grass and herbs and 14% was woody material. An abundance of grass and woody material was available at both sites. Examination of the area surrounding the droppings found at the forest edge revealed extensive feeding on bark, pith, and leaves of *Alangium chinense*.

From 1 to 22 fruits of *Balanites wilsoniana* (desert date) occurred in 52 of the 117 droppings examined. By mid-August an anastomotic pattern of trails connected all observed balanites trees in the reserve, and practically all vegetation was trampled flat under these trees where elephants had fed and searched for fruits. On the afternoon of 13 August, many balanites fruits were found under trees where elephants had obviously fed on fallen fruit during the previous night. Several fruits fell from the trees while the ground under them was being studied.

Although the fruits of *B. wilsoniana* were highly preferred when they matured and became available, no evidence was obtained of elephants feeding on any vegetative parts of this tree. Near Kabalega Falls National Park, elephants fed extensively on the fruit of *B. aegyptiaca*, a savanna tree that sustained very little or no bark damage.

Seeds from the large fruits of *Landolphia florida*, a woody clambering plant of the forest edge were found in at least eight droppings.

The 108 droppings studied from near the center of the reserve during mid-August and the 9 droppings examined from near the forest edge in late August provide information restricted by time and area. Data representing a more extensive area and collected over a relatively long period of time were obtained in the South Block of the reserve between 28 November 1963 and March 1964. These data are from 88 droppings: herbaceous material in 65 of them ranged from 5% to 100% and averaged approximately 68%. A high proportion of the herbaceous material consisted of grass. In 19 of the 88 droppings, grass was distinguished from other herbaceous materials and averaged about 64%. This estimate for grass is low since some of the unidentified material certainly contained some highly masticated grass, which could not be distinguished among the unidentified fibrous material.

Woody material in 40 of the 88 droppings ranged from 0% to 95% and averaged approximately 31%. This material included stems, leaves, seeds, and pieces of wood and bark. One dropping contained a piece of the fruit from the sausage tree, *Kigelia aethiopica*, and 10 droppings contained distinguishable parts from the Phoenix palm tree, *Phoenix reclinata*. Two droppings contained what appeared to be papyrus seeds, probably *Cyperus papyrus*. If indeed these were papyrus seeds, they represent the second known record of elephants feeding on this plant in the Kibale Forest. Although small pieces of wood were identified in six droppings, bark was found in only four.

Budongo Forest. Data from 13 droppings examined from Budongo Forest at the south edge of Kabalega Falls National Park on 21 November 1963 contained an average of approximately 60% herbaceous material and 40% woody material.

GRASS VS. WOODY MATERIAL

Kabalega Falls National Park. Forty-eight elephant droppings examined in Kabalega Falls National Park in August contained an average of approximately

97% grass; the 3% woody material included pieces of leaves, bark, roots, and vines. During late November and early December, 25 droppings that were examined in this park contained approximately 93% grass. The 4% difference in the amount of grass eaten during these two periods appears insignificant.

Ruwenzori National Park. In 1963 data were gathered from 25 droppings examined in the Kamulikwezi Area of Ruwenzori in September and from 27 droppings examined there during early October for comparison of foods utilized during these two months. The 25 droppings examined in September contained about 95% grass and 5% woody material. The woody material was mostly acacia (probably *Acacia sieberiana*) stems and leaves. Two droppings contained small pieces of vine material and two contained small pieces of papyrus stems. By comparison the 27 droppings examined during the first two weeks in October contained approximately 91% grass and 9% woody material. The higher utilization of woody material (mostly acacia stems and leaves) during October probably is insignificant. Napier Bax and Sheldrick (1963) studied foods of elephants in Tsavo National Park (East) of Kenya and stated that "bark and leaves of bushes and trees also became more important in the dry season." They also stated that "the eating of bark and the resultant destruction of trees by elephants may be partly the result of a search for calcium."

Do large and small elephants eat the same or similar proportions of woody and herbaceous food materials? The study of "Family Units," which is discussed below, showed that the kinds and amount of food (considering individual size) utilized by individual elephants within a family group are conspicuously similar; thus one would expect little or no difference in proportions of woody and herbaceous food materials eaten by various-sized elephants. This is exactly what was found from direct observations obtained by following elephants in the Kamulikwezi Area between 10 April and 1 May 1964 and studying the droppings of 132 various-sized elephants. Sixty adults utilized only about 1% more woody materials than 21 subadults, and the subadults utilized only about 1% more woody material than 22 intermediate-sized elephants. Obviously those differences are insignificant. Most of the woody materials consisted of leaves and twigs from acacia trees that dominate among tree species in the Kamulikwezi Area. Every dropping contained some woody materials; one contained an intact 5-cm acacia spine.

Grass ranged from approximately 60% to 99%

among the 132 droppings, and averaged about 94%. Forty of the 132 droppings (30%) contained seeds of *Capparis erythrocarpus;* one contained 305 seeds of this fragrant shrub. On numerous occasions the elephants were observed concentrating under capparis shrubs. By the end of April the ground under practically every capparis shrub observed in the Kamulikwezi Area was trampled heavily and littered with droppings. During this period elephants were sighted on many occasions feeding intensively on papyrus and the broad-bladed cotton grass *Imperata cylindrica;* both occurred in abundance in the Kamulikwezi Area. When imperata appeared mature and tending to become dry, elephants ate only the basal parts of stems. The high percentage of grass estimated in droppings probably was somewhat higher than the proportion actually eaten. Some leaf or succulent food materials may have been digested more quickly or completely than grass (Talbot and Talbot 1962), or these materials might have been nearly indistinguishable from grass when masticated thoroughly and mixed with grass materials. If an error of 5–10% is attributed to these sources, the average utilization of grass is practically the same as the 88% observed in the stomachs of elephants collected near the south edge of Kabalega Falls National Park and described above.

Whenever elephants were observed feeding since this research was started in 1957–1958, grass was eaten with impressive frequency. An example of the elephants' preference for grass was demonstrated by an adult bull feeding near the north shore of Lake George in October 1963. In his meandering the bull came upon a recumbent dead tree about 2.5 m in length, which he tossed aside with his trunk, and ate the grass that had grown under the tree's protection; he spent at least 20 min, ate and searched carefully where the tree had lain, circled the spot three times, and cropped practically every stem of grass from the newly exposed site.

Feeding Behavior

In addition to the observation made on 475 droppings reported above, records were secured on other foods and behavior related to feeding in western Uganda between July 1963 and June 1964. Elephants were observed along the Kazinga Channel in Ruwenzori National Park during July feeding on grass and papyrus roots, which they washed by holding the uprooted material in their trunks and swishing it back and forth in the water several times before eating it.

Bark gouging starts by loosening bark with the tusk.

If bark strips, the elephant grasps loosened bark with its trunk or teeth and strips upward. If bark does not strip, gouging continues.

As previously noted, imperata is eaten very extensively in the Kamulikwezi Area of Ruwenzori National Park, and papyrus is eaten extensively in both Ruwenzori and Kabalega parks. However, our evidence indicates that elephants rarely utilized either of these plants in the Kibale Forest Reserve where both occur commonly. I believe that low utilization of these plants in the reserve results from availability of foods that are preferred to imperata and papyrus.

In Budongo Forest on 22 November 1963 I watched a large female elephant eat bark that she had gouged from a 0.76 m by 1.1 m patch of an African mahogany (*Khaya grandifoliola*), leaving only several bits of bark about .5 cm by 8 cm at the base of the large tree. Extensive bark damage to *Terminalia velutina* by elephants in Kabalega Falls National Park, primarily during the dry season, killed many of these trees throughout the park.

An elephant also uses its front foot with amazing dexterity in pawing out rootlets, pulling out deeply rooted plants, or scuffing off vegetation close to the ground. Fresh elephant pawings were found on numerous occasions in Kibale Forest Reserve during August (near the end of the dry season). In October 1963 I watched a large bull attempt to pull a 61-cm acacia from the ground with his trunk, which kept slipping off the young tree. After four unsuccessful attempts, he grasped the tree with his trunk, tilted the hind part of his right front foot about 5 cm above ground by bending the lower

Bark stripping continues by upward and downward pulling of bark, eventually leaving a large damaged area. (*Drawings by R. W. "Mike" Carroll*)

154

joint of his leg, scuffed off the root just perceptibly below the surface with the leading edge of his foot, and ate the entire tree. Three other adults were seen using this same technique to remove and eat small acacias in the Kamulikwezi Area in May 1964.

FAMILY UNITS. There were 19 groups of from two to five elephants that were studied. Each group was collected at one site from a particular unit. These 19 groups, totaling 54 elephants, were studied to ascertain (1) whether these groups represented closely related or family units, (2) whether individuals in these groups showed high fidelity, (3) whether the food habits and behavior of individuals within each group were similar, and (4) whether these groups were made up of closely related individuals that governed behavior of an elephant population. The sex, total weight, weight of stomach contents obtained at the time of necropsy, and the approximate occurrence of the most prevalent food items that occurred in each stomach were recorded (see Table 6.2). Each group was collected on a different day between 7:25 A.M. and 6:45 P.M. local time. The groups are arranged from the earliest to the latest time of day collected to show possible relations between time of day during which elephants were collected to the volume of food in their stomachs; individuals within a group are arranged in descending order of total body weight to further facilitate comparisons.

At the time of collection of the 19 groups of elephants, certain elephants within a group frequently disclosed behavior that indicated that these groups were closely related or family units. This behavior was most conspicuous among females and individuals in groups of at least four animals. The individuals of Group 5 were notable in this respect. They were part of a herd comprising at least 25 elephants that was encountered before daylight. The animals were feeding on green grass, about knee height, on a savanna that was burned over about 3 wk previously. The abundance of fresh droppings and recent tracks indicated that this area had been visited frequently and recently by elephants. Evidently the new grass was very attractive and palatable, but direct observations of this herd, plus similar observations for Groups 6, 8, and 16, suggested that the animals did not remain very long on such areas. They moved continually while feeding and appeared restless and unusually vigilant. When the same animals encountered stands of tall, mature grass or woodlands they appeared to relax, moved more slowly, and even stopped frequently in their meandering. This difference in behavior gave an impression of security and of protective concealment to the elephants while they fed in the tall vegetation, and it probably affected the proportions of mature and young grass that the elephants ate (see Table 6.1). By 7:30 A.M. the herd was leaving the burned-over area and entering tall, mature grass, mostly thatching grass.

The animals reorganized into three rather distinct groups; five individuals (Group 5) moved farthest into the mature grass and were feeding upon it at 7:40 A.M. when the first three individuals (Nos. 51, 52, and 53) were collected. At the sound of shooting, the other two groups immediately ran out of sight, but the two remaining individuals of Group 5 (Nos. 54 and 55) refused to leave. The behavior of No. 54, which proved to be a large old cow, indicated that she was the mother of No. 55, a young, 816-kg male that stayed close beside the large cow for 40 min while she "defended" two of the dead elephants. The cow was furious. She trumpeted, screamed, pawed the ground, and tried alternately to lift the two dead animals with her tusks or bury them with debris gathered with her trunk. On four occasions she made short, vicious charges in the direction from which the shooting occurred. Shooting above her head and into the ground close to her feet failed to drive her from the dead elephants, and at 8:20 A.M. both animals were shot. On the basis of the maternal and defensive behavior of the large cow (No. 54) to the two dead elephants, I concluded that she was their mother. Examination of these two dead animals showed that No. 52 was a small male and No. 53 was a medium-sized, lactating female. Since No. 51 was 821 kg, of nursing size, and remained close to the medium-sized female while the group was observed feeding, I further concluded that she (No. 53) was the mother of No. 51. These family relationships are shown in Figure 6.2A. The behavior of individuals in Group 14 was also notable in revealing the close relationship of elephants (Fig. 6.2B) within the group. A 2,767-kg male (No. 35) was shot in the vicinity of Igisi Hill (see Chapter 1 under "Matriarchal Organization," "Bonding and Fidelity" for details). The family relationships of Group 14 are presented in Figure 6.2B.

Data in Table 6.2 show that the kinds and amounts of food (considering individual size) utilized by individual elephants within a family group are conspicuously similar. This relationship, however, is not apparent between families, suggesting that feeding is on a family basis.

Stomach contents of the five elephants in family Group 5 were exceptionally low in volume, weighing about 8.2 kg. Although their stomach contents were not

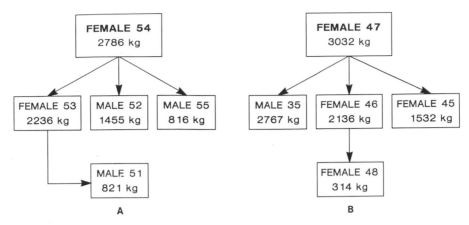

FIG. 6.2A, B. Family relationships of two elephant groups shot in Kabalega Falls National Park. **A.** Group 5. **B.** Group 14.

analyzed, I noticed that young grass occurred in each stomach, and the proportions of young to mature grass among individuals appeared similar. Evidently each elephant in this family group had fed for about the same length of time on approximately the same kinds of food; a similar pattern of feeding is evident for each family group shown in Table 6.2, indicating further that feeding is based on family group behavior. This fits the behavior pattern of young elephants learning for long periods under the leadership of their mothers. This learning starts early in life and includes the acquisition of the family feeding patterns.

TIME OF FEEDING AND AMOUNT OF STOMACH CONTENTS. The weight of stomach contents, the percentage of stomach/items, and the time of collection for 54 elephants are presented in Table 6.2. (The food analyses of these elephants, except Groups 5, 14, and 17, are included in Table 6.1.)

The nine fullest stomachs (those weighing 4.9–6.0% of the live weights—see Groups 6, 7, 8, 11, and 16) were from elephants collected between 7:40 A.M. and 10:15 A.M. Other elephants that were collected early (Groups 1, 4, 13, and 15) also contained relatively full stomachs. The interpretation here is that these elephants with relatively large amounts of food in their stomachs in the morning had fed during the night and early morning; Benedict (1936) reports the minimum elapsed time before items fed to a captive Asian elephant appeared in feces varied from 21 hr to 30 hr. The time required for food to pass through the gut of two African elephants born in the wild was between 21 hr and 46 hr (Rees 1982).

Evidence was obtained indicating that elephants fed at night. Before sunrise (6:20 A.M.) on Mobutu Flats on 18 February 1959, fresh elephant droppings and tracks near partly eaten bushes of sansevieria and aloe indicated that elephants had been feeding on these plants during the night; the tracks were followed until 7:30 A.M. when two large bulls were collected (Group 2) as the bull herd of five elephants was retiring into Lake Mobutu Marsh. On the following morning, three bulls (Group 3) were tracked down and collected within a mile of the Group 2 collections, under practically the same conditions. On 26 March 1959 at 7:15 P.M. John B. Heppes and I saw 19 large elephants (probably all bulls) by moonlight feeding and meandering eastward from the marsh between the Weiga and Waisoke rivers; backtracking indicated that these animals had been in the marsh during the day.

Some elephants that were collected early in the day (Groups 2, 3, 5, 9, 10, 12, and 14) had relatively small amounts in their stomachs; most of them were collected while they were feeding. Nearly all elephants collected in the afternoon (Groups 17, 18, and 19) had relatively small amounts of food in their stomachs.

These observations indicate that feeding occurred most frequently during early morning, but some elephants fed at various times of the day and night. Benedict (1936) concluded that the only time when the Asian circus elephant is not eating during the 24 hr when hay is available is when the animal is lying down, and since the period of lying is relatively short, the elephant is eating almost constantly. He also stated that the wild elephant eats a good part of the day. Direct observations of wild African elephants indicated that they

Table 6.2. Volume of stomach contents related to time of collection, group behavior, and total weight in 19 groups of elephants

Group No./ Time	Spec. No.	Sex	Weight of Elephant (kg)	Weight of Stomach Contents (kg)	Stomach Contents[a] (%)
1/7:25 A.M.	92	F	2436	97.9	Old grass, 97; combretum, 3
	93	F	2073	78.5	Old grass, 95; new grass, 4; combretum, 1
	94	M	1194	39.0	Old grass; 95; combretum, 5
2/7:30 A.M.	84	M	4496	114.3	Grass, 70; aloe and sansevieria, 30
	83	M	4121	120.2	Grass, 80; aloe and sansevieria, 20
3/7:30 A.M.	85	M	3237		Grass, 85; aloe and sansevieria, 15
	86	M	3015	67.6	Grass, 80; aloe and sansevieria, 20
	87	M	2690	112.0	Grass, 90; aloe and sansevieria, 10
4/7:30 A.M.	107	F	3513	147.4	Old grass, 80; new grass, 20; terminalia leaves, tr.
	109	F	2650	111.1	Old grass, 92; combretum leaves and twigs, 8
	108	F	1990	73.9	Old grass, 60; combretum leaves and twigs, 40
	110	F	1919	78.5	Old grass, 60; combretum leaves and twigs, 40
5/7:40 A.M.	54	F	2781	8.2	(Stomach contents not analyzed; entire family feeding in grass about 3 wk of age.)
	53	F	2232		
	52	M	1452		
	51	M	821		
	55	M	816		
6/7:40 A.M.	97	F	1430	54.4	Old grass, 85; new grass, 15
	89	M	1287	63.9	Old grass, 85; new grass, 15
7/7:40 A.M.	113	F	2774	136.0	Grass, 92; combretum, 8
	111	F	2233	124.3	Old grass, 75; combretum leaves and twigs, 25
	112	F	1157	39.0	Old grass, 82; new grass, 15; combretum, 3
	114	F	1069	64.4	Old grass, 75; combretum leaves and twigs, 25
8/8:00 A.M.	62	M	2214	83.5	Old grass, 75; unidentified, 1
	61	M	2045	99.8	Old grass, 75; unidentified, 1
9/8:00 A.M.	63	F	2312	67.6	Old grass, 56; new grass, 14; combretum, 30
	64	M	1473	49.8	Old grass, 68; new grass, 17; combretum, 15
10/8:10 A.M.	65	F	2869	112.9	Old grass, 95; new grass, 5
	66	F	2053	58.1	Old grass, 89; new grass, 10
	67	F	368	8.6	Old grass, 100
	101	F	2662	112.0	Old grass, 85; new grass, 15
11/8:30 A.M.	100	F	1675	82.6	Old grass, 98; unidentified woody material; 2
	103	F	1589	93.4	Old grass, 90; new grass, 8; unidentified woody material, 2
	102	F	765	38.1	Old grass, 95; new grass, 4; unidentified woody material, 1
12/8:45 A.M.	71	F	3251	77.1	Old grass, 90; new grass, 5; mulemangundu, 5
	72	F	2790	58.9	Old grass, 93; new grass, 5; mulemangundu, 2
13/8:45 A.M.	121	M	3905	109.7	Old grass, 88; new grass, 10; unidentified, 2
	122	F	2922	117.9	Old grass, 60; new grass, 30; mulemangundu, 10
14/9:45 A.M.	47	F	3021	87.9	(Stomach contents not analyzed; entire family collected.)
	46	F	2130	76.2	
	45	F	1528	48.1	
	48	F	311	7.3	
15/9:45 A.M.	68	F	2582	90.2	Old grass, 60; new grass, 20; combretum, 20
	69	F	2146	81.2	Old grass, 86; new grass, 9; combretum, 5
16/10:15 A.M.	105	F	2794	122.9	Old grass, 57; new grass, 38; combretum, 5
	106	M	1070	53.5	Old grass, 98; unidentified, 2
	38	F	2538	69.9	(Stomach contents not analyzed)
17/3:00 P.M.	37	F	2217	40.8	(Stomach contents not analyzed; part of family collected.)
	36	M	1884	39.9	
	39	F	1519	28.1	
18/5:00 P.M.	117	F	2643	58.1	Grass, 99; unidentified woody material, 1
	118	M	1546	31.3	Grass, 98; unidentified woody material, 2
19/6:45 P.M.	81	F	1901	64.9	Old grass, 99
	82	F	797	21.3	Old grass, 99

[a] All stomach contents (except those from Spec. No. 85 and Groups 5, 14, and 17) are from elephants included in Table 6.1.).

A calf learns to eat grass by taking bits from its mother's mouth. (*Drawing by R. W. "Mike" Carroll*)

were searching almost continually for food with their trunks, but frequently they appeared to select only very special items for eating. At other times they appeared to engage primarily in feeding and consumed large quantities of food in relatively short periods of time. Collectively, these observations of the African elephant's food habits and its inefficient digestion (Benedict 1936; Rees 1982) indicate that its life must virtually be one continuous meal or the animal dies of starvation.

When the weights of stomach contents for the nine fullest stomachs were plotted graphically against the live weight for these elephants, the points showed a linear regression (Fig. 6.3).

The regression line *AB* can be considered as a moving average determined by the points among which it passes, and the best estimate of maximum weight of stomach contents (expectation value) per live weight falls on the regression line.

Six of the nine fullest stomachs (67%) were from females (Nos. 100, 102, 103, 111, 113, and 114) with

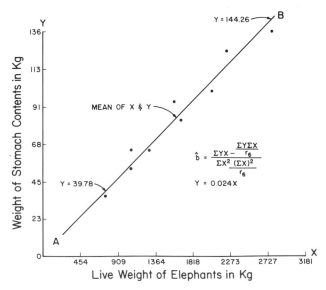

FIG. 6.3. Linear regression based on observations of nine elephants having relatively full stomachs.

a mean percentage of 5.4%, compared to the three males with a mean of 4.9%. Laws and Parker (1968) studied stomach contents of 180 elephants from the North bank of the Nile River in Kabalega and reported similar results except their sample was big enough to show that females with maximum stomach fills had a mean of 5.1% and males had a mean of 3.2%. From a sample of 197 elephants from the South bank of the Nile they report the "mean maximum" stomach fill for males was 3.0% of live weight, and the mean maximum for females was 3.8%. Thus the conclusion that females have heavier stomach contents when at maximum fill than males seems well established.

EFFECTS OF THE DRY SEASON. Soon after the dry season began in early November 1958 on Mobutu Flats, savanna vegetation matured and became dormant, and natives resorted to their traditional practice of starting fires wherever grass and forbs appeared dry enough to burn. At about this same time the elephants on Mobutu Flats began to assemble into herds for their migration upstream over the escarpment to the headwaters of the rivers. Within a month fires swept over practically all of Mobutu Flats and many of the well-drained grasslands above the escarpment. Although the vegetation on various sites did not mature and burn simultaneously, there was a continual diminution of old-growth vegetation as the season advanced. By the end of the season in late March 1959, practically all grasslands on the area were burned over at least once; some mature grass persisted in low, damp areas. By early December most of the elephants had dispersed and emigrated from the flats. An aerial reconnaissance over the area on 16 December 1958 revealed a herd of about 40 elephants in Lake Mobutu Marsh and several smaller groups close to the Weiga River and the escarpment; no elephants were seen south of the river on the flats on this flight.

In their migrations from and back to the flats, some elephants move through the Budongo Forest where they pause and live temporarily in seclusion. Their feeding habits, and frequently their mere presence, interfere with logging operations, and as a consequence many animals are shot by officials of the Game Department on control assignments. In the calendar year 1957, 24% of the 912 elephants shot on control operations in Uganda were recorded at Masindi (Game and Fisheries Dep. 1959); most of them were shot in Budongo Forest.

Throughout the dry season of 1958–1959, elephants were concentrated in the interspersed grasslands and woodlands (which remained unburned) above the escarpment at the headwaters of the Weiga and Waisoke rivers and between Budongo Forest and the park boundary; this was ideal range for elephants at that time. Between 22 December 1958 and 21 March 1959, I made 32 trips to this area, saw from 1 to 35 elephants on all except two of these trips, and shot 57 elephants. Each morning there were many fresh droppings on the road and many fresh trails crossing the road, attesting further to the presence of many elephants.

With the onset of the rainy season in late March 1959, many of the elephants above the escarpment were congregating into large herds preparatory to their emigration from the area. Between 18 and 23 March, I saw four herds on the area above the escarpment, each consisting of at least 100 elephants; all were traveling westward toward Mobutu Flats. On 24 March, John B. Heppes saw three herds totaling 189 elephants migrating down the banks of the Waisoke River on the flats. The following day I saw nearly 400 elephants feeding close to the river and traveling downstream. Although we had made biweekly safaris to the flats searching for elephants after 6 January 1959 and conducted an aerial reconnaissance over this area on 26 February 1959, these were the first elephants that we recorded between the Sonso and Weiga rivers on the flats since 10 December 1958. By mid-April, the migration of elephants to the flats apparently had ended, very few were seen above the escarpment, and the numbers were about as high as those preceding the dry season.

Direct field observations, and the distribution records obtained by aerial counts conducted in October 1958 and February 1959 (Buechner et al. 1963), indicated that some elephants showed a strong tendency to congregate during the dry season in Lake Mobutu Marsh and along the south banks of the Nile River below Kabalega Falls. An aerial count conducted during the wet season in May 1959 showed very few elephants at these locations. Based on ground observations made at these permanent water supplies, the concentration of elephants during the dry season resulted in overutilization of some food plants thus limiting the kinds of foods available near these sites, particularly in Lake Mobutu Marsh. Soon after the rainy season began water became available throughout most of the elephants' range, and they quickly dispersed from Lake Mobutu and the Nile River to the better and more extensive food supplies on the open savannas. In some cases these migrations were probably many miles in length; in others they were relatively short. I believe this wet-dry season relationship is very important in governing some of the food habits and migratory behavior of the elephants in Uganda.

ENVIRONMENTAL EFFECTS. Since the elephant's droppings contain a high percentage of grass and since counts of droppings in the Kibale Forest Reserve show that they were distributed throughout all habitat types, elephants evidently transport considerable fecal material from grasslands into the reserve. An approximation of the daily and annual deposition by an elephant in the reserve can be gained by multiplying the average weight of droppings, 7.98 kg, by the average daily or annual defecation rate. With a daily number of 17 droppings, the average daily rate per elephant is 136 kg. Using 413 as the average number of elephants (excluding calves) inhabiting the 547-km² Kibale Forest Reserve annually, 56,051 kg of droppings are deposited daily by these elephants. Annually this amounts to about 20,458,743 kg (20,459 metric tons) of material deposited in the reserve.

Movement of 136 kg of material through an elephant in one day requires much plant material, indicating a high rate of conversion. Deposition and distribution of this material by an elephant in a single day suggests a profound environment-enrichment activity. The only comparative information we found was reported by Riney (1957), who observed dry weight of 455 kg of droppings in one area in a national park compared to 227 kg in an adjacent cattle-grazed area. Grass measured at the same time in both areas was twice the height in the area of greatest droppings as in the one of least droppings. This is not the only environment-enrichment activity of the elephant. By their nomadic meandering while feeding and their large drum-shaped feet, elephants trample down much vegetation. Like elephant droppings this trampled vegetation serves as fertilizer and helps to develop a protective mat of litter and duff, which shades the soil (Vesey-Fitzgerald 1963), reduces runoff and leaching, and builds up (develops) a soil fauna conducive to a richer biotic community. Thus feeding behavior of this huge mammal can be particularly valuable to the senile lateritic soils in many parts of the elephant's range in East Africa.

A notable example of habitat enrichment by elephants and other large mammals was reported for northern Rhodesia (Zambia) by Mitchell (1961) who combined historic data with ecologic deductions to show where and how large mammals played an important role in creating and maintaining forests. When these large mammals were destroyed, forests disappeared, land became parched, and the rich biotic community disappeared.

Where elephant populations exceed their forage supply (where they eat more in a given year than is grown that year), and particularly where their migration routes are blocked, these same feeding habits soon result in degradation of environment. This situation prevailed in Kabalega during the 15 yr prior to about 1972. Actually the entire physical and biotic environment was rapidly undergoing progressive retrogression. Interspecific feeding competition among overpopulations of elephants, buffaloes, and hippopotami, combined with destructive fires, frightfully devastated the flora, fauna, and soils of the park. Buss and Smith (1966) reported that "elephants south of the Nile River in the [then Murchison Falls National Park] are hemmed in closely by the Nile River, Lake Albert, two controlled hunting areas, and highways used by continually increasing numbers of hunters. . . . The continual constriction of this elephant range appears to approach pen conditions."

Such destructive interactions caused Curry-Lindahl (1968, 26) to state that "except for man there is no other animal in Africa that is able to alter a habitat so drastically as does the elephant." Laws (1978) after long experience in Tsavo and Kabalega National parks came to much the same conclusion: "In a world with finite resources, the elephant is second only to man in its capacity to inflict long-term irreversible damage on the food environment—reducing the diversity and complexity of the habitat (as well as its own food base) by converting forest and woodland into grassland and desert."

Another example of environment-destroying activity by elephants is suggested by Simon (1962) in his records of elephant hunting in Kenya. During the heyday of the slave trade and the ivory-hunting era in East Africa, elephant hunters from the coast near Mombasa made long overland treks to the east side of Lake Rudolph for big tuskers. En route they passed through the area that is Tsavo National Park, but no mention is made in the literature of elephants in Tsavo. Since then the situation has changed very markedly. The desolate area east of Lake Rudolph is marginal elephant range and harbors few elephants. In Tsavo, however, overpopulations of elephants drastically altered their range until a very severe drought from the middle of 1970 until 23 November 1971 took a heavy toll of more than 5,000 elephants and 300 black rhinos (Sheldrick 1972). Although Glover (1963) published a report giving an estimate of 10,799 elephants in the park during 1962, Laws (1970b) soon after starting work in Tsavo during 1967 estimated 23,000 in the park with an additional 12,000 in the peripheral areas. One can readily understand and believe that large numbers of elephants near

Lake Rudolph were primarily responsible for changing and reducing the vegetation to a threshold of uninhabitability. The only practical way known to prevent or halt such destruction is through scientific control of population numbers. Sikes (1971, 230) points out that "the slave trade and the ivory trade grew up hand in hand in Africa . . ." and concluded that "the drastic culling of the elephant populations in those days was also somewhat advantageous to the elephant populations, by maintaining them well within the carrying capacity of the environment." Likewise, the First International Conference on National Parks held in Seattle, Washington, in the United States during 1962 adopted the policy that "where animal populations get out of balance with their habitat and threaten the continued existence of a desired environment, population control becomes essential." Finally, the International Affairs Committee of the U.S. Wildlife Society has recommended that for the control of wildlife populations in African reserves the authorities "support the controlled harvest of wild animals in those parks where habitats are being adversely affected by excessive animal numbers, i.e., populations which exceed carrying capacity over an extended period." No wonder then that professional wildlifers in the United States are advocates of this policy.

As agriculture creeps ever forward engulfing habitat like streaming ameboid protoplasm, as migration routes dwindle and become permanently blocked, as forests shrink and foresters proclaim areas closed to elephants, the elephants are irreversibly forced into smaller ranges. These shrinking ranges are not only in danger of being reduced to uninhabitable ecologic units, but they also demand continual monitoring and scientific study to assure that environment-enrichment activity does not become degrading to environments by failing to detect them or by ignoring excessive population densities. To allow overpopulations of elephants, or to fail to recognize environment-enrichment activities of a properly managed elephant population is, as stated by Darling (1964), "to squander natural resources for a pipe dream."

Is the elephant an efficient herbivore in utilization of its available food? This is no simple question since the word utilization has several connotations. For example, Darling (1960) visited the Kasanka Reserve at the southern end of the great Northern Province in 1957. He observed (p. 39) that

the ecotone between swamp and woodland, possibly a quarter of a mile deep, bore ample sign not only of usage by the ele-

phants, but of presence of food plants which please them in season. . . . Yet there was no sign here of overbrowsing or overgrazing. Watching the elephants one was conscious afresh that no other animal has such a wide and varied food range; no other animal can occupy so many habitats. . . . Equally, one might say, no other animal can equal the elephant in efficient utilization of the vegetation of Africa.

In other words, by its wide and varied food range the elephant has a high capacity to exploit the food resource of its environment. In this respect the elephant is indeed an efficient herbivore.

Efficiency of utilization might also refer to digestibility or percentage of matter or energy in food that does not appear in feces. Benedict (1936) studied digestibility of hay fed to an adult female Asian elephant. He reported (p. 196) that

the apparent digestibility of the energy content of the food was 40 percent. . . . Comparison of the percentage of digestibility of dry matter and energy noted with the elephant and with other animals demonstrates what was surmised for the general appearance of the feces, namely, that the elephant makes an extraordinarily poor utilization of the ingredients of the hay.

When viewed in this way the elephant is an inefficient herbivore.

Still another way of viewing efficiency of utilization is demonstrated by studies of productivity and energy relations of animal populations, such as the study conducted in Ruwenzori by Petrides and Swank (1964). Their study included a comparison of the efficiency of productivity of the African elephant with that of two smaller herbivores, the meadow mouse and white-tailed deer, studied in Michigan. From this comparison they found (p. 839) that

the elephant population exists as a very high biomass standing crop. On equal areas of their native ranges, the elephant biomass supported is more than five times greater than for the deer population, yet the rate of protoplasmic growth is only about half as much. The energy value of food consumed by the standing crop of elephants is only slightly higher than that consumed by the much lower standing crop of deer. As also evidenced by the general appearance of elephant droppings, however, much food passes through the elephant in a relatively undigested form. It is not surprising, therefore, that the proportion of food which is assimilated (growth plus maintenance) by an equivalent weight of elephants is considerably less than half that assimilated by the deer. Per unit of standing crop, the elephant population eats only one-fourth as much and assimilates and adds growth at only about one-tenth the rate of deer.

Meadow mice produce 2.5 times their average standing

crop weight each year; the growth production of elephants, on the other hand, is only one-twentieth of the standing crop. The absolute growth of elephant protoplasm, despite the vastly greater biomass standing crop, is only 68 percent that of meadow mice.

In comparison with cattle, Petrides and Swank (1964, 840) reported that "for a given caloric intake . . . steers produce about thirteen times as much growth as elephants." In conclusion they stated "that the elephant eats relatively little per unit of body weight and its assimilation is poor, yet it maintains a high standing crop. On the study area, the observed elephant population comprised 16 percent of the total biomass standing crop of large herbivores present . . . , yet it consumed only about 9.6 percent of the available forage." From the view of productivity and some energy relations, therefore, the elephant does not appear to be a highly efficient herbivore.

Beyond the above views on food utilization by the elephant as a species, elephant feeding behavior is tremendously important in its effects on the entire biotic community. One of these effects is well recognized by Smuts (1982, 166) who states that "elephants also open dense areas, both through their feeding and the trampling action of their huge feet." Additional effects are recognized by Petrides and Swank (1964, 841) who point out that "elephants enable other large herbivores to live where they might not otherwise exist. Elephants make the upper strata of vegetation available to other herbivores when they push over and tear down trees. . . . They often maintain a relatively early successional stage of plant community development as a habitat for those species."

The magnitude of effect on successional stages depends on several factors of which elephant density and degree of burning appear to be most important. The modus operandi of these factors has been described in part above and by Buechner and Dawkins (1961) in Kabalega where an excessively high density of elephants and annual burning resulted in conversion of much forest and woodland to grassland. There elephants gouged and tore bark from trees, and when trees at the forest edge were damaged, the exposure of sensitive living tissues to fire killed many trees. Dead trees allowed more light to penetrate the forest edge and fostered invasion of grasses that carried fire from adjacent grasslands progressively deeper into the forest. Since the amount of fire destruction at the forest edge was directly related to the extent of tree damage by elephants, elephants appeared to be destroying the forests. Actually, the elephant depredations to trees acted as a catalyst to fires, and Buechner and Dawkins (1961) concluded that "it is through the basic influence of fire that vegetation in the [Kabalega National] Park south of the Nile is now primarily treeless grassland."

The proportion of grassland to forest that comprises optimum range for the African elephant probably varies by both time and place, and with freedom of migration. Wherever the elephant lives, large amounts of grass are evidently consumed in all seasons. The early observations of Nicholson (1954) showed that elephant grazing was a widespread habit in Tanganyika (Tanzania) and that grass comprised about 75% of the diet during early rains in December, January, and in some areas as late as February. Napier Bax and Sheldrick (1963) studied elephant foods during an 18-mo period in Tsavo where there usually is less than 10 in. of rain annually. There, too, grasses were a major item in the diet.

The study of food habits conducted off the south boundary of Kabalega in the dry season of 1958–1959 and based on stomach contents of 71 elephants showed that grass comprised 98% of the total food material. Subsequently, a decline in the elephant population became evident (Buss and Savidge 1966). Soon after, Laws and Parker (1968) reported grass as the main component of stomachs averaging 84% and 95% for two populations studied inside Kabalega. Also, Laws and Parker (1968, 351) suggested "that reduction of available browse, leading to dependence on grass, particularly in the dry season, is a contributory factor to decline." Their suggestion may be correct, for it is supported by some of the studies conducted in Kibale Forest Reserve.

In the reserve the proportion and interspersion of cover types probably approach optimal range conditions for elephants. Although the actual number of elephants living in the reserve needs further study, the density was conspicuously lower than in Kabalega where annual damage to trees was vastly higher. Relatively few trees were being pushed over or damaged by tusk gouging, and annual fires burned only to the forest edge without advancing into the forest. Under these conditions the cover types became relatively stable.

Grazing succession, tiered in the grasslands of the reserve, is similar to the pattern of grazing described by Vesey-Fitzgerald (1963) for grasslands in the Rukwa Valley of Central Africa. That is, in Kibale Forest Reserve heavy animals (elephants and buffaloes) do the initial trampling and feeding, then animals of medium weight (waterbucks and bushbucks) follow and concentrate on the shorter grass. Finally small animals (warthogs, bushpigs, and several species of small antelopes)

Large straight-boled trees up to 41.0 cm dbh may be broken down to reach foliage.
(*Drawing by R. W. "Mike" Carroll*)

concentrate on the shortgrass areas resulting in a well developed and efficient grazing mosaic. Even during the two dry seasons, green grass is available along many watercourses and in swamplands, and shade is not far from the grasslands. With the onset of rains most animals need not move far to fresh grasslands, and when they do move, temporary respite is given to areas where grazing had been concentrated.

Reader and Croze (n.d.) sum up behavioral effects of elephant feeding in completely natural (unaffected by humans) environments on a basis of energy flow through ecosystems.

In its continuous "predation" on plants, the elephant tears branches from trees, pulls great tufts of grass and roots from the earth, gouges huge holes in baobabs and pushes over Acacia and Commiphora trees. Is this destruction? Not really; it is modification, perhaps even enrichment of the habitat. For a rich habitat is not one which simply makes a pretty picture, but one in which energy is flowing through numerous pathways, and . . . materials are changing form continuously.

Considering that a large elephant can ingest some 300 pounds [136 kg] of green matter a day, we might wonder how the habitat can take it. Yet far from being demolition agents, elephants are in fact the greatest natural construction crew in Africa, contributing more to the change and variety in local habitat than any other species. Nowhere, not even in regions of apparent over-population where habitat destruction might be expected, has it yet been demonstrated that elephants by themselves degrade habitats to the point of creating deserts. They change them certainly, but they do not destroy.

Today there are very few places left where elephants by themselves can change habitats without destroying them; parks and elephant sanctuaries certainly are not natural areas. Establishing a park boundary, building a fence, creating artificial watering facilities, constructing roads and dams, and adding parcels of land adjacent to overpopulated elephant sanctuaries are palliatives fostering unnatural habitats that become vulnerable to degradation. Sikes (1971) recognized the status of natural environment left at that time and attempted "to achieve a balance between the data emerging from recent ecological studies carried out in the semi-artificial envi-

163

ronments of the national parks, and data on the genuine *natural* environment of which isolated pockets still exist unchanged in some parts of Africa."

Functionality of an ecosystem involving elephants is at least a 26-yr-old concept. Vesey-Fitzgerald (1963) pointed out that

a grass association cannot be evaluated by itself. . . . The whole range of associations which any particular assemblage of animals utilizes is the important unit; it is quite essential that the fauna should have access to all the component plant associations which are needed to satisfy the needs of each species through the seasons. In order that the range may be fully and efficiently utilized, without damage to the pastures, the fauna must be in tact, and maintained in this condition at all times. Because it is only then that the grazing succession [among] the species is operative, and the range's optimum carrying capacity maintained.

If the elephant population in Kibale Forest Reserve were allowed to increase appreciably above its 1958–1965 level, the forest area very probably would start shrinking. That is, the tree-dominated area that comprised 60% of the reserve would gradually decrease, and the remaining 40% occupied by grasslands, woodland-thicket, and colonizing forest would increase. Eventually, a status would be reached similar to the biotic degradation that was so dramatically portrayed in Kabalega Falls National Park, during the 15-yr period preceding about 1972.

Suppression of fire or drastic reduction of elephants would very probably cause grasslands in the reserve to revert to forest. Edward (1942, 229) studied the effects of fire on grasslands of East Africa and stated that "the protection of these areas by the exclusion of fire will, in most cases, involve the cessation of grazing and the return of the area to brush or forest." Reversion of grasslands to forest in Kibale very probably would cause grassland-associated herbivores to decline significantly or even disappear. Maintaining the present population level of elephants would allow their feeding behavior to help maintain the present diversity of cover types and assure a multispecific animal community probably greater in productivity than any component of the community. Although an increase in number of species in the community does not always assure increased total productivity, "such a result would be expected if the greater diversity of secondary producers represented a broader capacity to consume and convert organic matter and thereby to speed up the turnover rate within the system" (Evans 1967, 13). Viewing Kibale Forest Reserve as an ecosystem, the elephant population with its feeding be-havior appears to be the key component in continued high total productivity of the entire reserve.

Mineral Utilization

The International Union for Conservation of Nature and Natural Resources met at Arusha in northern Tanganyika (Tanzania) in early September 1961. There I met Sir Julian Huxley who told me about a roadside site on the south slope of Ngorongoro Crater where elephants had tusked out soil and had eaten it. Sensing my interest in this biological phenomenon, Huxley very kindly arranged to have my good friend Major Bruce Kinloch, at that time Tanganyika's chief game warden, drive me to the elephant "digs." Bruce called his district warden, Bill Moore-Gilbert, who set up a camp at the bottom of the crater for our visit.

Arriving at the south base of the crater in late afternoon, we speculated about the possibility of seeing a "jumbo" or two on our trip up the winding unimproved road of the crater's side. We agreed our chances were slim, but about three-fourths of the way to the rim, and rounding a bend, we came upon five large elephants close to the bank side of the road and less than 35 m ahead. We stopped and watched. The elephants were at a long, high trench that had evidently been grubbed and gouged out over a long period of time. To reach the back of the trench, the elephants stretched forward and pushed with their hind legs. Occasionally an elephant turned its head to facilitate probing into hard-to-reach recesses. Soil was gouged out with the tusks and transferred by the trunk to the mouth.

We drove on noting several extensive excavations where elephants had grubbed soil from the exposed profile at the high side of the graded road, but we saw no more elephants. At the rim of the crater we followed the road perhaps another 3.2 km until we arrived at Bill Moore-Gilbert's home. After introductions Bill assured us that proper arrangements were complete for our overnight trip into the crater; we turned to elephant discussions. Bill told of several elephants that came to his yard regularly, and one of them, a rather large bull, carefully selected the tender young shoots of asparagus. After finishing his delicacy, the bull stepped carefully over a picket fence about 1.2 m in height without even moving it. This surprised me considerably; I would have guessed that any elephant would have walked right through the fence leaving a gaping opening wide enough for several elephants to leave abreast.

We transferred the gear into Bill's Landrover and descended the steep and tortuous road down the north-facing side of the crater to the campsite near a stream. What a wonderful spot for sleeping!

Hooves rattling against rocks launched me from bed in the gray of early morning. A quick squint through the mosquito netting over our doorway revealed countless wildebeest moving downstream in long strings to their feeding areas out in the crater. After a hasty breakfast we toured the crater's 16-km floor seeing 31 lions, hordes of wildebeest and zebras, and three black rhinos. Bill reported up to 60 elephants using the crater sporadically during the year but mostly in March, April, and May. During their visits the elephants bashed over acacia trees, eating terminal twigs and small limbs along with bark from the larger limbs.

I received a letter dated 8 January 1963 from H. A. Fosbrooke, conservator, Ngorongoro Conservation Area. He wrote that

you will be interested to know that . . . 90 elephants were observed in the Crater the other day. Although this was not in the critical habitat of the Lerai Forest where elephant damage is considerable, it may well be an indication that increased agricultural development on the outer rim of the Crater, Oldeani via Karatu to Mbulambulu, is penning in the elephants which would normally migrate to the area below the Rift at certain times of the year.

Back at camp we packed and prepared for our return from the crater. Retracing our track we drove to the elephant excavations. The size and number of excavations told us that elephants had visited there over many

Bill Moore-Gilbert amidst acacias on Ngorongoro Crater floor; these trees 25–36 cm dbh are pushed over or uprooted and the foliage of the crowns browsed. (*Photograph by I. O. Buss*)

I. O. Buss studying destructive feeding on an acacia tree, Ngorongoro Crater floor, September 1961. (*Photograph by Bill Moore-Gilbert*)

Adams suggested conducting a semiquantitative spectrographic analysis, which would provide a reasonably close estimate of the percentages of elements in the samples.

The results of the analyses are presented in Table 6.3 as percentages of metallic oxide found in each of five samples obtained from the original samples. All samples with the exception of Sample 2 are similar and can be classed as average silicate mineral. As indicated by the Halvorson tests, the samples showed no potassium and a relatively low calcium content. Sample 2, however, which contained black inclusions in light-colored rock (like paint spattered on a wall), contained 6.7% manganese oxide (MnO_2) and 0.38% cobalt oxide (CoO_2). Both are conspicuously higher concentrations than occurred in the other samples, and higher than usually occurs in soils elsewhere.

I pondered the analyses while conducting further research on the elephant; I wanted to return to the elephant diggings at Ngorongoro. In 1971 I was able to

years. I obtained a half-dozen soil samples from the site where we had seen the elephants eating bits of soil. I carefully packed the samples into my briefcase, guarding them closely until I was back home in Pullman, Washington.

Initial tests on the soil samples conducted in the Soil Testing Laboratory, Washington State University, by A. R. Halvorson in October 1961 showed pH 7.5, potassium 10 parts/ml, phosphorus 5.6 parts/ml, calcium 0.75 ml equiv/gr, salt 1.2 mmho, and a trace of organic matter. These measurements showed nothing unusual except very low quantities of potassium and calcium. The pH value is nothing more than a convenient way of expressing degree of acidity or alkalinity; a pH of 7.0 indicates neutrality. Higher values indicate alkalinity and lower values acidity; thus pH 7.5 was slightly alkaline.

After studying the results of the initial tests, I decided that more detailed analyses were needed, so I consulted Dr. Mark Adams, Division of Industrial Research in the Institute of Technology at Washington State University. Certainly the samples harbor some clue as to why elephants endangered their lives migrating considerable distances over semiopen terrain, peppered with hostile poachers, just to locate and eat this soil! Dr.

Bill Moore-Gilbert at elephant excavation on Ngorongoro Crater wall where soil samples were taken, September 1961. (*Photograph by Bruce Kinloch*)

166

Table 6.3. Analysis of Ngorongoro Crater soil samples

Metallic Oxide	Sample 1	Sample 2	Sample 3	Sample 4	Sample 5
			(% of oxide)		
Fe_2O_3	Major	Major	Major	Major	Major
Al_2O_3	"	"	"	"	"
SiO_2	"	"	"	"	"
MgO	.0044	.004	.0096	.0084	.0074
MnO_2	.42	6.7	.50	.50	.60
CoO_2	.0085	.38	.01	.01	.02
NiO		.001	.003	.002	.004
Cr_2O_7			.0085	.00515	.003
CuO	.00009	.00009	.00009	.00009	.00009
PbO		.10			
AgO		.003			
Na_2O	.08	.40	.74	.18	.14
SrO	.07	.13	.17	.007	.07
TiO_2	1.35	.85	1.20	1.60	1.10
V_2O_5	.01	.04	.04	.02	.02
ZrO_2	.02	.02	.03	.03	.04
BaO	.007	.07	.10	.002	.05
CaO	.30	.18	.40	.26	.30

Note: Five samples, obtained from two original samples submitted and analyzed by the "semiquantitative" spectrographic method, were designated as follows: (1) gangue material from light-colored rock; (2) black material for light-colored rock; (3) buff-colored material from dark-colored rock; (4) gangue material from dark-colored rock; (5) black material from dark-colored rock.

return to Africa and the crater road. Were elephants still migrating to this site for manganese- and cobalt-laden soil? Yes indeed they were! I found the diggings considerably extended both up and down the roadside; some of the previously used excavations were now too deep and inconvenient for easy access. The elephants had deserted these old worn out mines and opened new ones. Fresh dung littered the road, particularly by the new diggings, attesting to recent use. From all appearances there were more elephants using this site than ever before.

After returning to the United States I reviewed and discussed the soil-eating proclivities of elephants with one of my close friends Dr. James A. Kittrick of Washington State University's Department of Agronomy and Soils. He suggested asking Dr. Ronald K. Sorem, who specializes in studying manganese nodules on the ocean floor, to conduct an x-ray diffraction test on the black inclusions of Sample 2. He tested the sample, and his report states in part that the

microsample of black coating from small cavity gives a powder pattern of very fine-grained lithiophorite. General formula is $(Al,Li)MnO_2(OH)_2$, but Li is often minor and may be as low as 0.2% or even absent. Many other ions have been reported: Co, Ni, Cu among them. Lithiophorite is common in the zone of weathering in some places. Known localities are Umurup

(SW Africa), Tennessee (SE USA), Brazil, and Australia. Many similar Mn oxides are known as localizers of cobalt and other metals in soils.

The x-ray diffraction test corroborated the spectrographic analysis on the relatively high manganese content. My interpretation of this information is that elephants migrated to the south rim of Ngorongoro Crater primarily for the manganese- and cobalt-laden soil, utilizing woody foods en route that are important but which alone would probably not motivate migration. Very likely these elephants could obtain woody food closer to or on their home ranges thus precluding exposure to severe poaching hazards.

One might logically ask whether manganese is essential in the diet of elephants, and what symptoms result from manganese deficiency. According to Mertz (1981)

an element is essential when a deficient intake consistently results in an impairment of a function . . . and when supplementation with physiological levels of this element . . . prevents or cures this impairment. . . . The following trace elements are now considered essential in animals: silicon, vanadium, chromium, manganese, iron, cobalt, nickel, copper, zinc, arsenic, selenium, molybdenum, and iodine.

Although research findings from laboratory animals cannot be applied directly to elephants living in natural environments, such findings might suggest whether manganese might be important to elephants, as well as other wild mammals with self-selective feeding opportunities. Evidence of such importance is summarized by Mortvedt et al. (1972) who point out that laboratory studies conducted in the Department of Biochemistry at the University of Wisconsin in 1931 were the first to show that manganese is an essential element in animal nutrition. With a diet composed exclusively of milk, the poor growth and poor reproduction that occurred in mice could be partially corrected by supplementing the diet with manganese. They also point out that in 1931 other reports were published showing that manganese is also required by the rat, and that high mortality, testicular degeneration, and poor lactation accompany manganese deficiency.

Mortvedt et al. (1972) state that

symptoms of Mn deficiency in mammals (rats, mice, and rabbits) are similar but not identical. The nature and severity of symptoms depends upon the previous nutritional history of the experimental animals, especially upon carryover of Mn from the mother and the Mn content of the diet prior to being placed on Mn-deficient diets. Manganese deficiency . . . is character-ized by reduced growth, slightly reduced mineralization, de-fective structure of the bones, and decreased reproductive per-formance in both males and females.

In summarizing studies on rats and guinea pigs, Mortvedt et al. (1972) list numerous impacts from man-ganese deficiency: ataxia, bone changes, lowered thresh-old to electric shock, stillbirths, poor viability, and abnormal electrocardiographic patterns. Congenital manganese deficiency also produces animals that with-stand stress poorly, have decreased resistance to infec-tion, and suffer ataxia (including a late-developing Par-kinsonianlike twitch).

Leach (1978) states that "manganese deficiency greatly impedes skeletal growth and development" in hu-mans. In summarizing impacts of manganese deficiency in humans, Waslien (1976) concluded that "the majority of the studies indicate intakes in excess of 2 mg/day for most adults. Such intakes would represent 10 to 25% of the total body pool of manganese which is about 20 mg."

The most impressive report on manganese defi-ciency that I found was that of Lucille S. Hurley (1981). After long-term study she concluded that (1) "ataxia is the most striking effect of manganese deficiency and has been seen in every species in which manganese defi-ciency has been produced," (2) "another system influ-enced by manganese deficiency is the skeleton," (3) "manganese deficiency also produced ultrastructural ab-normalities," and (4) "manganese deficiency also leads to abnormal brain function."

The summary of impacts from manganese defi-ciency is impressively long. Their criticality to highly variable life functions and the variety of laboratory mammals experimentally involved (mice, rats, guinea pigs, rabbits, and humans), makes one wonder how ele-phants could possibly escape all these impacts. In other words, manganese does indeed appear to be an essential element in the diet of all mammals including humans and very probably elephants.

According to Smith and Carson (1981) the litera-ture on cobalt has not been treated as exhaustively as that on other metals with less voluminous data. In discussing cobalt Mortvedt et al. (1972) state that

problems of lack of appetite, poor growth, and poor reproduc-tion in cattle and sheep had been recognized since colonial times in parts of eastern USA. The cause of these problems was unknown, and the difficulties were variously termed. . . . In the Saco River Valley of New Hampshire, the problem was attributed to a "curse" put on the area by the Indian Chief,

Chocorua, in revenge for mistreatment by early settlers.

Regardless of such beliefs, the essentiality of cobalt for ruminants was discovered during field investigations of problems of livestock in Australia in 1935. "Following this discovery, affected animals were supplemented with cobalt in USA experiments. Dramatic improvements in their general health resulted. In this country [America] cobalt deficiency is now commonly corrected either by adding cobalt to the salt licks or to mineral supple-ments."

Smith and Carson (1981, 980) state that "the nutri-tion literature has consistently held that cobalt has one essential function in mammals and that is in the B_{12} mol-ecule;" in other words, B_{12} is dependent on cobalt for its synthesis. They go on to state that "both epidemiologic and laboratory studies from USSR have suggested a pos-sible role for cobalt in addition to its B_{12} function." No-vikova (1963) in Russia using 120 male rats found that either excessive or deficient intakes of cobalt "renders a decrease in absolute content and concentration of iodine in the thyroid gland."

In discussing terrestrial food chains of temperate versus tropical ecosystems, Cole and Carson (1981, 825) point out that "the tropical moist forest chain rep-resents the largest natural system studied, as well as a unique environmental situation favoring cobalt accumu-lation (for that matter, all minerals). . . . Tropical forest animals are exposed to higher levels of cobalt in their diet than are their counterparts in temperate forests, and apparently there is a larger accumulation of cobalt in their bones than in their soft tissues." To some this might suggest that the soil-eating elephants at Ngorongoro Cra-ter do not really need cobalt to supplement their diet. The difficulty is, does anyone know whether these ele-phants have access to a tropical moist forest?

The combination of sandy soil, high rainfall, and high temperatures promote both relatively low man-ganese and cobalt, primarily because of rapid leaching. Trace metals like manganese and cobalt are relatively heavy thus being subject to rapid leaching. Considering the heavy rainfall and high temperatures in large parts of Africa, there probably are vast elephant ranges there with very low inclusions of these trace metals. They probably are there but too deep to be available to plant roots or even detectable by elephants. At the roadside extending up the side of Ngorongoro Crater, these trace metals were exposed by road construction, which was not planned to benefit elephants. Their benefits were co-incidentally contingent upon road construction for ac-cess into the crater. The soil there is very dense, almost rocky, and of a gray color, and at least part of this gray soil probably came from well below the soil surface at the time of crater formation.

The recent report by Redmond (1982) of elephants going deep within a cave on Mount Elgon in western Kenya to eat salt-laden rock is certainly unusual and noteworthy. More than a few readers will probably question whether the elephants went there only for salt. Perhaps if several samples of this rock were obtained from the site and a detailed and scientific analysis made and published, the record might be surprising.

Very little has been published on mineral utilization by wild elephants, either African or Asian. The director of the National Museum in Ceylon, P. E. P. Deraniyagala, gave a report to the Ceylon Association for the Advancement of Science in 1950 on "Extinct Elephants, Their Relatives, and the Two Living Species," which includes a few empirical statements on mineral utilization by Asian elephants.

The elephant's mineral requirements are considerable, and periodically it betakes itself to areas of saline earth which it often swallows in sufficient quantity to act as a purgative. When the first showers after a long drought wet certain rocks, elephants visit these for the salty liquid, for during the dry season both capillary attraction and disintegration cover the surface of such rocks with a deposit of mineral salts. Not only does the elephant eat such earth but it also scours the exterior of its body by rolling and rubbing itself in it.

The elephant, however, does not readily accept ordinary sodium chloride, always preferring earth from a "lick" as this contains a high percentage of iron salts, nitrates, nitrites, and so great is the animal's craving for such salts that in forest villages in the eastern province it is known to exhume from their shallow graves corpses when nearly reduced to skeletons, and to devour them.

Could the animal's craving for such salts, as claimed by Deraniyagala, be related to the elephants carrying bones of dead elephants? Possibly, but because

Elephants are attracted to bones of many mammalian species. Does this reflect a nutritional shortage? (*Drawing by R. W. "Mike" Carroll*)

Sketched from a photograph of a cow carrying her putrified calf in Ruwenzori National Park. The two medium-sized elephants in the background might be the cows' first-born calves, and the small living calf and dead calf might be their second-born calves. (*Drawing by R. W. "Mike" Carroll*)

evidence is lacking the idea must remain as a postulate. Ian and Oria Douglas-Hamilton (1975) show elephants carrying bones and displaying considerable interest in them, but they offer no clue for such behavior. Willock (1965) cites an example of "elephant child-love" when referring to Bere's (1966, 77) observation of a cow elephant carrying a putrified calf for several days in Ruwenzori National Park.

Sutcliffe (1973) in Norway studied similarity of bones and antlers gnawed by deer to human artifacts and states that osteophagia (chewing of bones) is widespread. Blood and Henderson (1968) point out that "in herbivores it is often a symptom of phosphorus deficiency. This habit is widespread in natural conditions and has a distinct geographical distribution which depends principally on the phosphorus content of the parent rock on which food plants are growing, but also on other factors such as excessive calcium, aluminum or iron, which can reduce the availability of phosphorus to plants." Fraser-Darling (1947; 1968) described how, even before modern advances in the understanding of animal nutrition, the inhabitants of Atlantic townships of the Hebrides ground the backbones of fish (accumulated byproducts of the fishing industry) to make a meal consisting largely of calcium phosphate, which was fed to the cows during winter. In this way the lime-rich and phosphorus-poor soils of the machair (phosphate-poor soil type between sandy beaches and rocky grazing land above) were able to support cattle.

Would blocking migration routes and thus preventing elephants from obtaining manganese and cobalt result in their acquiring some of the innumerable maladies associated with deficiency? There is no scientific evidence proving that this would occur, and there is an extremely remote probability that anyone ever will obtain such evidence. Nevertheless, blocking an elephant migration route would not be scientifically or politically prudent. Just because no one has demonstrated that lack of certain mineral (or metallic) elements is harmful to elephants, it may be dangerous to assume these elements are not needed. With or without proof of danger, we had better not block their routes because of high potential danger and widespread apprehension of harm. I am reminded of a statement that Aldo Leopold once made when discussing management of wildlife: "The hope of the future lies not in curbing the influence of human occupancy—it is already too late for that—but in creating a better understanding of the extent of that influence and a new ethic for its governance."

Gallstones

Among the many records published on the formation of gallstones, or cholelithiasis, only one reported gallstones in an elephant. Decker and Krohn (1973) examined a 10-yr-old female Asian (*Elephas maximus*), partly trained, circus elephant weighing 1,500 kg and found 11 faceted gallstones, the largest measuring about 2 cm in diameter. My observations on gallstones in elephants were all from wild African elephants (*Loxodonta africana*) collected off the south edge of Kabalega Falls National Park.

Since an elephant has no gallbladder, my crew of seven, who were trained for a particular necropsy assignment, was very excited about discovering four relatively large gallstones in an old female, the twentieth elephant collected. The stones, measuring from 60 mm to 108 mm in major diameter and weighing 66, 67, 210, and 430 g respectively, were found in the bile duct system (Table 6.4). In the 95 elephants collected off the south edge of the park, 19 had from 1 to 110 gallstones; in other words, 20%, or one out of every five, had cholelithiasis. All except 3 of the elephants with gallstones were adults; 2 were intermediates, and 1 was a subadult (Table 6.4).

Initially I was intrigued by finding concretions between 95 mm and 109 mm in diameter (Table 6.4) in ducts normally less than 6 mm in diameter. Seemingly, this would cause considerable pain. Examination of duct tissue over a large gallstone, however, revealed tissue no less in thickness than that of the same duct located proximally to the site of the gallstone. Furthermore, the tissue over a large gallstone showed no inflammation or swelling. Assuming that gallstones increase in size very slowly and that their formation and increase does not involve movement, in an elephant with relatively large gallstones pain probably is minimal or does not occur.

In addition to the elephants collected close to Ka-

Table 6.4. Gallstones in 19 African elephants, Kabalega Falls National Park

Specimens			Gallstones		
No.	Sex	Age[a]	No.	Major Diam. (mm)	Weight (g)
20	F	Ad	4	60–108	66, 67, 210, 430
22	F	Ad	9	103 (largest)	0.8, 1, 2, 4, 5, 6, 7, 7.5, 37
23	M	Ad	2		
32	F	SAd	2	(Trapezoidal, medium size, shriveled)	
34	M	Int	1	60	
35	M	Ad	1	14	
49	F	Ad	4	43, 47, 50, 95	25, 32, 52, 225
59	F	Ad	4		4, 5, 8, 17
71	F	Ad	4	15 (largest)	
77	F	Ad	2	10, 10	
83	M	Ad	26		
89	M	Ad	Many		
99	F	Ad	110	85 (largest)	104 (largest)
101	F	Ad	3	5, 8, 8	
104	M	Ad	37	10 to 38	185 (all 37)
105	F	Ad	3	20, 8, 8	
118	M	Int	1	10	
120	M	Ad	2	10, 10	
123	M	Ad	1	20	

[a] Ad = adult; SAd = subadult; Int = intermediate.

Four gallstones, weighing 25, 32, 52, and 225 g, from adult female No. 49, Kabalega Falls National Park. (*Photograph by I. O. Buss*)

171

balega Falls National Park, I collected 23 additional ones from Toro District (7 from the eastern outskirts of Ruwenzori National Park, 16 from Semliki Plain), none of which had gallstones. The most notable difference between the elephants close to Kabalega Falls National Park and those from the outskirts of Ruwenzori National Park and Semliki Plain was in respect to migratory movements. The elephants of Kabalega were restricted from movements in nearly all directions, but those of Toro District had few if any such restrictions; their migratory routes were still not blocked, allowing wide movements. In the food habits studies, important differences in foods utilized occurred between elephants restricted in movements and those not restricted.

Diets are important in gallstone formation. In rabbits Borgman (1965) found that gallstones can be induced in 12–24 wk by diets high in fats (15% olive oil) and high in proteins (40% casein). More recently Lee et al. (1986) found that a carbohydrate diet induced calcium bilirubinate sludge and pigment gallstones in the prairie dog. Pellegrini et al. (1986) also studied gallbladder filling and emptying during cholesterol gallstone formation in the prairie dog.

Powell (1985) published a report on a 2-yr-old human female with cholelithiasis. Preoperative work-up revealed no etiology, and an analysis of the stones revealed the content to be pure calcium carbonate. The mother had taken a calcium carbonate supplement during the last 4 mo of pregnancy. The most unusual case of gallstones I found reported involved the unstable form of calcium carbonate, vaterite. Filippich et al. (1984) reported vaterite gallstones in a canary.

Cosenza (1984) reported finding a large stone in a hepatic duct of a sedentary, overweight dog; the stone probably had its formation in the duct rather than in the gallbladder for "reflux of large stones into the hepatic duct is considered unlikely. However, there are no valves in the biliary system, and bile can flow in either direction." Cosenza (1984) also states that "bacterial infection of the bile is considered one of the causes of biliary stone formation in human beings." That could very well be the cause for stones in elephants as well.

The variation in color of gallstones reported by different writers is probably the result, at least partly, from bile pigments. Villee et al. (1963) state that "the color of bile (green, yellow, orange, or red in different species) results from the presence of bile pigments, excretory products derived from breakdown of hemoglobin in the liver." Heidner and Campbell (1985) found "numerous dark green, gritty stones . . . in the gallbladder and bile duct" of a cat. The gallstones that we found in the elephants were a rich brown.

7

Looking Ahead

THE ELEPHANT POPULATION in Kabalega Falls National Park remained high into 1973, during which year 14,309 elephants were counted by S. K. Eltringham and R. C. Malpas (1976). According to Norris (1977) the real destruction of elephants by poaching started in 1973. By 1974 the count had plunged to 6,030, then dropped to 2,246 in 1975, and apparently leveled off at 2,448 in 1976. This precipitous drop resulted from more than ordinary or usual poaching. Highly escalated ivory prices, former president Idi Amin's henchmen, and a political upheaval of governments that unleashed a veritable horde of poorly fed and clothed soldiers into Uganda played a major role in the destruction. Agreed, when a hungry soldier armed with a lethal weapon meets an elephant that can provide both a year's salary and a feast of protein-rich elephant meat, few would blame him for succumbing to such a temptation! If apprehended, however, his penalty would probably not be mitigated.

Kabalega was not the only site of major poaching operations during this period. In Tsavo the situation was not much different, including skyrocketing ivory prices and political storms similar to those in Uganda. Stephen Cobb (1980) in writing an early historic record of Tsavo, stated that "in a decade [1970–1980], 6,000 elephants have died in a drought; perhaps 20,000 have died in the hands of poachers. . . . The question is simply, how to keep the remaining elephants and rhinos alive?" Should we recriminate over the past problems, or should we forget all about the messy business and try again? We can do better if we conduct a comprehensive analysis of the entire problem. Were there early warnings that elephants were above carrying capacity? Yes indeed, there were many gross warnings that were either turned aside or left to nature. In Kabalega and Tsavo the warnings were basically the same: trees that were debarked by elephants were dead, and the extent of the damage everywhere in both parks proclaimed to the world that something was wrong.

Shantz and Turner (1958) and Buechner and Dawkins (1961) clearly indicated the cause of the problem in Kabalega, which was well advanced at that time, but politics and deaf ears prevented action. A tour group from New York City passing through Tsavo in 1971 was appalled by the dead trees throughout the park and asked whether there was a way to stop the continuation of the catastrophe. These were concerned, intelligent people, none of whom was a biologist, yet they saw overutilization almost everywhere they went in Tsavo.

Maintenance of forage is the key to carrying capacity. Emphasis should be directed to better studies of vegetation. Such studies should be designed to estimate whether, under current use, as much vegetation is grown as is utilized in a given time period. If this is the case, all is well, but too often this is not the case, and reduction of herbivores becomes necessary. Herbivores will not, by themselves, reduce their numbers; if they do the reason clearly is that their range is already badly overused.

Elder and Rodgers (1968) clearly stated a historic fact when they wrote: "Once an elephant has found sanc-

173

tuary in a park it is essentially doomed to overpopulate it." As time moves on, restriction of elephants into their sanctuaries will become progressively more acute. Migration routes will be blocked, sanctuary boundaries adjacent to agricultural lands will require elephant-proof fences, artificial watering devices will be required in some preserves, and ultimately all elephants will live only in sanctuaries where they will be completely restricted. Under such restriction more frequent monitoring of vegetation utilization and elephant numbers will be necessary. Once overutilization begins, control or scientific management is necessary, otherwise other animals coexisting with elephants on the same ranges will begin to decline or disappear completely; a decline in these animals is not easily detected.

Under ideal conditions some of the smaller coinhabitants with elephants serve as prey for larger animals, thus assuring maintenance of a healthy ecosystem. Maintenance of a diverse fauna is an excellent goal for any wildlife management program.

I agree with Sikes (1971), who obviously had full knowledge of this problem.

The outlook is gloomy, but man has such difficulty in maintaining his own populations within the carrying capacity of his planet that it seems unrealistic to expect that there will be much room in the future for African elephants as well. The best that may be hoped is that Africa's own national governments will conserve realistically as a part of their own natural heritage at least a viable remnant of the finest elephant stock available within well-run ranch-type national parks.

After Laws (1970b) had studied elephant populations in five different ranges, with regard to management he concluded that

in most of the case studies described the habitat changes can only be halted or reversed by reducing the elephant populations to densities at which their natural regulatory mechanisms can operate effectively. The situations which had led to the development of the problems are essentially man-made, whether by his alienation of land, control shooting measures, rapid elimination of poaching without substituting rational cropping, direct change of habitat by forest management, or indirectly by burning. Even the creation of National Parks has led to artificial concentration of elephants within their sanctuary. It is therefore irrational to argue that human intervention to manage elephant populations, involving reduction cropping, cannot be contemplated because it represents unnatural interference. Action is essential to ensure the survival of many elephant populations, and of other animal and plant species, as well as to conserve the unique habitats and landscapes. Knowledge is now available which, properly applied, offers a good prospect

of success, but in any case no enhanced danger to the ecosystems.

The final suggestions of Bere (1966) are still sound and appropriate:

The future of the elephant in Africa depends on man who has the power to conserve as well as to destroy. The old balance has gone. No longer can man and wild animals live in harmony throughout vast areas of the continent as was possible in days gone by, for man's needs have increased as well as his numbers. . . . Conservation, if it is to be effective, must be a positive constructive act and it is wishful thinking to imagine otherwise, particularly in the case of the elephant; and if this is not yet true of the whole of Africa it soon will be, for the upsurge of the human population is almost universal. Where man and wild animals find themselves in competition with one another, the animals will lose. Even if there appears to be room enough for both, man will not tolerate for long a situation in which elephants and other creatures make even occasional raids upon his fields of food or economic crops. For many years this has been a major cause of conflicting interests and the reason why so many elephants have had to be shot on control.

Survival of the elephant in the wild state is absolutely contingent upon sufficient land being set aside for its conservation, and on this land being managed in such a way that the animal populations are not allowed to destroy their own environment. It is probable that existing national parks and reserves, together with a few other wild land areas which man is unlikely ever to exploit, are adequate for the purpose, in spite of certain obvious limitations, provided that they are well managed. In any case it is extremely unlikely that much more land will be set aside for wildlife conservation though certain well-stocked areas may yet be given higher status than they now enjoy. It is vital, of course, that existing areas should not be reduced for any reason; and this can only be assumed by the widest possible appreciation of the need and purpose of conservation.

The most important factor in securing a future for the elephant is that the leaders of the new African nations should accept the principles of conservation. Of these the most fundamental is the sanctity and permanence of the conservation areas. It is a complicated problem involving full appreciation of an incomparable natural heritage as well as land use and the economics of the tourist trade. On the whole, signs are hopeful, for the argument can be presented in economic terms. There are obvious advantages to the tourist trade in having wild elephants in places accessible to the public. Even so, one hopes that the elephant will not be reduced by man to the status of a tourist attraction and nothing else.

Bere has recognized and recorded the necessary principles for scientific management of the African elephant. These principles have remained unchanged throughout the 24 years since he set them down in his book; they may be modified by new scientific findings, but the basics will never change. Whether we refer to the use of these principles as "ranch-type" or other terminology makes little difference; the tools by which elephants can be managed are available. If we really want to conserve that incomparable heritage Bere refers to, we need to adhere strictly to these principles without letting sentiment interfere with management.

Laws (1970a, b) has clearly pointed out human mistakes to good elephant management, and Bere (1966) outlined a management program that has stood the test of 24 years without criticism insofar as I can ascertain. I believe his program could serve very well for management of nearly all large wild mammals in Africa. In addition, considerable information on elephants has been published in the last two decades. Why are we continuing to study without applying more of what has been learned about the African elephant?

Pienaar in Kruger National Park of South Africa is one of a very few who has done an outstanding job managing elephants. In 1980 I published a report on African elephant management, which included most of the salient activities conducted on elephant management in Kruger National Park. The important conclusions reached included the following:

By holding elephants at the logarithmic phase of population growth, fertility and reproduction are maintained at a high rate and age composition typically remains younger than populations held at any other phase of growth. Equally important, chances of survival have increased, high biotic diversity is fostered, there is increased flow of energy through the ecosystem, and an opportunity has been established for human utilization of the resource.

Let us not forget that wildlife cannot be stockpiled.

An example of maintaining fertility and reproduction was published by Smuts (1975) who worked in Kruger National Park. Among other population characteristics, he found that some elephants bred as early as 7 yr of age, whereas in Kabalega Falls National Park first breeding for most females began between the ages of 10 yr and 12 yr, under high population density (see Chapter 4 under "Mating Observations and Seasonal Distribution," "First Breeding"). Why not compare reproductive rates reported above with rates from some of today's low population densities reported from some of the better elephant ranges in Africa?

Also, why not establish a new area or two and test some of the findings? I suggest that Kibale Forest Reserve, close to Ruwenzori National Park, be considered

for such a test area. When and IF such an area becomes a reality, there should be not only a few progress reports but a steady and comprehensive series of reports letting everyone know what is being achieved. Without such reports some enterprising, commercially minded individual or group can and very well might "muscle in" on the land and set up a plant, pointing out how many local people will eventually be employed and what this will mean dollarwise to the community and district. As pointed out by Bere (1966), seldom is a wild animal a winner over humans when the two sides meet in court. Yes indeed, "where man and wild animals find themselves in competition with one another, the animals will lose" (Bere 1966). We must regard elephants as "an incomparable natural heritage" of inestimable value! Once lost in any area, they will never again be rehabilitated to that area.

Importance of Kibale Forest Reserve to Regional Elephant Management

Kibale Forest Reserve in its vegetational status at the time of this study was of paramount importance to the elephant. There in the reserve the elephant had a diversity and richness of foods found only on the best ranges. Solid stands of mature trees are not conducive to diverse and rich foods for elephants, but Kibale Forest Reserve was not grown solidly to mature trees; about 60% of the entire reserve was forest interspersed with various types of grassland, woodland-thicket, and colonizing forest. These cover types, consisting almost exclusively of seral plants, provided the bulk of the elephant's food. In addition to the vast supply of quality foods, many permanent streams and swamps distributed throughout the reserve assured ready availability of water, and the extensive cover in the Central and South blocks provided seclusion from humans.

Thus Kibale served as the nucleus to an elephant range having natural boundaries far beyond those of the reserve. Extensive local and seasonal movements occurred within and extended beyond the reserve, giving respite to the forage within. Less frequently there were long-range migrations involving large numbers of elephants from the reserve and nearby areas. Although highway contruction and agricultural development imposed restrictions on migratory routes connected with the reserve, elephants could still travel to the Ruwenzori Mountains, to Ruwenzori National Park, and to the Congo. Maintenance of these migratory routes was, and

175

always will be, very important because they allow the elephant population to spread out and utilize a large and more heterogeneous range while providing still further respite to the forage within the reserve. Hence there is more efficient utilization of the total range, less danger of overutilization in certain areas during critical periods, higher assurance that the elephant's nutritional requirements will be fulfilled, and a greater potential for maintaining the elephant population compatible with other natural resources.

An ecologically complete unit of range for elephants and other large mammals can be achieved by maintaining Kibale Forest Reserve and Ruwenzori National Park as integral components of a scientific managment program. Maintaining migratory routes connected to the reserve would greatly enhance the unit's utility for elephants. Such a unit, even under past elephant numbers, would allow for more intensified commercial use of forest products. If such a program is established, timber harvest like or similar to the rotation plan used in Budongo Forest is strongly recommended; elephants use mature timber primarily for shade and protective cover, but very little food is obtained from mature trees. Elephants probably influence species composition with their marked preference for certain species and apparent distaste for others. The elephants surely are a long way from overusing the forest habitat, however, when only about 20% of all trees and shrubs show some degree of usage, and only about 14% show some degree of usage annually. Probably more trees are dying annually than show elephant use during the same time.

The scientific management program should include maintenance of an up-to-date inventory of elephants so that possible changes will be indicated in population numbers. Such changes are related to forage utilization and to environment-enriching (or -destroying) activities of the elephant. Thus there would be a sound basis for regulating the elephant population and assuring perpetuation of a diverse and rich biota, including elephants and forests.

If the above outlined management plan were followed in detail, how long might it function successfully? This plan would provide adequate habitat for elephants and other wildlife, but what about villager attitude toward such a program?

Big ranches that previously supported herds of animals such as eland, impala, kob, and even elephants, have been divided into smaller farms and the new settlers promptly killed off all the herbivores. Why? Because they are good to eat and there is no financial advantage in keeping them alive. Ranchers and farmers will seldom tolerate non-profit making wild animals which are in direct competition with their crops and livestock. There are, therefore, ranchers who instruct their armed cattle guards to shoot on sight any wild animal of any species whatsoever if it sets foot on their property (Cheffings 1986).

Additional recent writers can be cited; perhaps two will be adequate. Kaiza-Boshe (1985) raises the question, "Do developing African countries take enough heed of the legitimate desires and needs of their people when trying to develop effective wildlife conservation strategies?" Boshe (1986), who studied wildlife at the University of British Columbia, Canada, and at New Mexico State University, United States, answers that question very well.

Perhaps the saddest part of the story is that many of the villagers living near protected areas are starving and the law does not permit them to harvest any of the thousands of wild animals roaming next door. The village officers are on constant patrol, often with their guns and the silent but implicit message: "Whether you are hungry or not, the wildlife must remain untouched." This . . . has created a strong antagonism between the public and conservation officers, the former always believing that wildlife is only for the benefit of the conservators and tourists. In this context it is hardly surprising that many people are happy to support, directly or indirectly, the extermination of wildlife.

Of the numerous recent reports published by people who have lived or worked with wildlife, I like Cheffings's (1986) best. He starts his report with a quote from Dr. Norman Myers.

For much of emergent Africa the only long-term hope for the big mammals of the savannahs depends in part on a new line of thought; you either use wildlife or you lose it. If it is not economically self-sufficient there is little point in saving its space. If it pays its own way some of it will survive, if it can't, it won't.

This sums up the new line of thought clearly and succinctly, which is not as new as some might believe from reading recent literature on African growth related to wildlife. In 1958 I worked part-time with William Pridham, then in charge of wildlife in Toro District, Uganda. This was an important elephant area of Uganda, and Bill had become well educated with the problem of villager attitude toward wildlife preservation. Our discussion on this problem included Bill's plan that seemed like a reasonably good way to get such a program started.

Each of the district supervisors would announce

when and where a wild animal would be collected in their district. All meat would be divided among villagers living in the collection vicinity. Where certain species were scarce others could be taken (buffalo, waterbuck, kob or other antelope). If a depredation problem occurred at a particular site, collection could be made there. The number and time of collection could be adjusted to fit a particular situation. As good as it sounded to me, I don't believe it was ever tried.

Still another problem with this or any other management plan for the African elephant concerns me very deeply. Henry Fairfield Osborn in 1936 and 1942 described over 300 different kinds of elephants that once lived on practically every land area of the world. Today there are two genera of elephants extant: *Elephas maximus,* the Asian elephant, and *Loxodonta africana,* the African elephant. Carrington (1958) reminds us that the two kinds of elephants are the only survivors of a huge order of animals, with over 300 different branches, which during the past 60 million years was spread over almost the whole land surface of the globe. No one proposed a management plan for any of the elephants; they survived through this extremely long period by evolution. Considering this 60-million-yr period of evolution, the two living forms may not be able to continue the evolutionary process much longer, if at all.

The plight of the African elephant is finally drawing worldwide attention. Dana Lauren West (1990) reports that a decision was reached in October 1989 by 92 members of the Convention on International Trade in Endangered Species (CITES) that "a total ban on international trade in elephant ivory will take effect on January 18, 1990. . . .Celebrated anthropologist Richard E. Leakey, joined by U.S. senators Patrick J. Leahy (D-VT) and Robert W. Kasten, Jr. (R-WI), and WWF staff spoke at a special briefing on elephants sponsored by WWF in Washington, D.C., on November 15. At that meeting, Leakey, who directs Kenya's Wildlife Department, stated that since June, when bans on ivory imports were imposed and anti-poaching efforts stepped up, no elephants have been killed in Kenya. Senators Leahy and Kasten have championed elephant conservation in the U.S. Congress this past year and sponsored legislation to appropriate $2 million for elephant conservation."

Kathryn S. Fuller states for the World Wildlife Fund, of which she is presently the president, that "Protecting the environment has become the dominant issue of the day in the United States and around the world. We must marshall WWF talents at this critical juncture for conservation, a time when world political and financial leaders are listening. Now is the time to make a strong stand; it is a chance we cannot afford to miss."

References

Adams, A. B., ed. 1962. *First World Conference on National Parks*. Natl. Park Serv.

Allee, W. C., A. E. Emerson, O. Park, T. Park, and K. P. Schmidt. 1949. *Principles of Animal Ecology*. Philadelphia: W. B. Saunders Co.

Allen, E., C. H. Danforth, and C. A. Dorsey. 1939. *Sex and Internal Secretions*. Baltimore: Williams and Wilkens.

Amoroso, E. C., and J. S. Perry. 1964. The foetal membranes and placenta of the African elephant. Philos. Trans. R. Soc. London, Ser. B, Biol. Sci. 248:1–34.

Anderson, G. D., and B. H. Walker. 1974. Vegetation composition and elephant damage in the Sengwa Wildlife Research Area, Rhodesia. J. S. Afr. Wildl. Manage. Assoc. 4(1):1 14.

Ansell, W. F. H. 1960. The breeding of some larger mammals in northern Rhodesia. Proc. Zool. Soc. London 134:251–74.

Benedict, F. G. 1936. *The Physiology of the Elephant*. Washington, D.C.: Carnegie Institution.

Bere, R. M. 1966. *The African Elephant*. London: Arthur Barker Ltd.; New York: Golden Press.

Bjersing, L., M. F. Hay, R. M. Moor, R. V. Short, and H. W. Deane. 1970. Endocrine activity, histochemistry, and ultrastructure of bovine corpora lutea. Z. Zellforsch. 111:437–57.

Blood, D. C., and J. A. Henderson. 1968. *Veterinary Medicine*. 3d ed. London: Bailliere, Tindall and Cassell.

Bolk, L. 1919. Over de ontwikkeling van het gebit van *Elephas africanus*. Amsterdam Versl. Wis. Nat. Afd. K. Akad. Wet. 27:1056–70.

Borgman, R. F. 1965. Gallstone formation in rabbits as affected by dietary fat and protein. Am. J. Vet. Res. 26:1167–71.

Boshe, J. 1986. Wildlife law enforcement in Africa. Swara 9(2):8–10.

Bosman, P., and A. Hall-Martin. 1986. *Elephants of Africa*. Foreshore, Cape Town, S. Afr.: C. Struik (Pty) Ltd.

Bourliere, F., and J. Verschuren. 1960. Introduction a l'ecologie des ongules du Parc National Albert. Explor. Parc Natl. Albert Miss. F. Bourliere J. Verschuren, fasc. 1.

Brooks. A. C. 1957. Elephant food habits. Game and Fish. Dep., Entebbe, Uganda. Mimeo.

Brooks, A. C., and I. O. Buss. 1962a. Past and present status of the elephant in Uganda. J. Wildl. Manage. 26(1):38–50.

———. 1962b. Trend in tusk size of the Uganda elephant. Mammalia 26(1):10–34.

Buechner, H. K. 1958. Elephant census II. Aerial counts of elephant in Murchison National Park and vicinity, Uganda. Uganda Wild Life and Sport 1(4):16–25.

Buechner, H. K., and H. C. Dawkins. 1961. Vegetation change induced by elephants and fire in Murchison Falls National Park, Uganda. Ecology 42(4):752–66.

Buechner, H. K., and C. V. Swanson. 1955. Increased natality resulting from lowered population density among elk in southeastern Washington. Trans. 20th N. A. Wildl. Conf., pp. 560–67.

Buechner, H. K., I. O. Buss, W. M. Longhurst, and A. C. Brooks. 1963. Numbers and migration of elephants in Murchison Falls National Park, Uganda. J. Wildl. Manage. 27(1):36–53.

Burne, E. C. 1943. A record of gestation periods and growth of trained Indian elephant calves in the southern Shan states, Burma. Proc. Zool. Soc. London, Ser. A 113:21–27.

Buss, I. O. 1961. Some observations on food habits and behavior of the African elephant. J. Wildl. Manage. 25(2):131–48.

———. 1980. Management suggestions for the African elephant. Elephant Interest Group, Wayne State Univ., Am. Soc. Mammal. (Suppl.):19–35. Modified from Management of big game with particular reference to elephants, specially invited Malayan Natl. J. 31(1):59–71.

Buss, I. O., and A. C. Brooks. 1961. Observations on number, mortality, and reproduction in the African elephant. Proc. IUCN, Arusha, Tanganyika, Sept. 1961. French trans. in La terre et la vie, Rev. Ecol. Appl. 1962, 2(April–June):175–82.

Buss, I. O., and O. W. Johnson. 1967. Relationships of Leydig cell characteristics and intratesticular testosterone levels to sexual activity in the African elephant. Anat. Rec. 157(2):191–96.

Buss, I. O., and J. M. Savidge. 1966. Change in population number and reproductive rate of elephants in Uganda. J. Wildl. Manage. 30(4):791–809.

Buss, I. O., and N. S. Smith. 1966. Observations on reproduction and breeding behavior of the African elephant. J. Wildl. Manage. 30(2):375–88.

Cameron, Sara. 1981. Caught in the crossfire. Africana 8(1):17–18.

Carrington, R. 1958. *Elephants.* London: Chatto and Windus, Hogarth Press.

Cheatum, E. L. 1947. Whitetail fertility. N.Y. State Conserv. 1(5):18, 32.

Cheffings, J. 1986. Use wildlife or lose it? Swara 9(1):8–11.

Cobb, S. 1980. Tsavo National Parks: Their first thirty years (also the next thirty years). Swara 3(4):12–17, 20–23.

Coe, M. 1972. Defaecation by African elephants (*Loxodonta africana africana,* Blumenbach). E. Afr. Wildl. J. 10:165–74.

Cole, G. E. D., E. R. Downer, and E. Parker. 1962. *Atlas of Uganda.* Entebbe: Dep. of Lands and Surveys.

Cole, J. C., and Bonnie L. Carson. 1981. Cobalt in the food chain, pp. 777–924. In *Trace Metals in the Environment.* Vol. 6, *Cobalt.* Ann Arbor, Mich.: Ann Arbor Science.

Colyer, F., and A. E. W. Miles. 1957. Injury to and rate of growth of an elephant tusk. J. Mammal. 38:243–47.

Cosenza, S. F. 1984. Cholelithiasis and choledocholithiasis in a dog. J. Am. Vet. Med. Assoc. 184(1):87–88.

Croze, H. 1974a. The Seronera bull problem. I. The elephants. E. Afr. Wildl. J. 12:1–27.

———. 1974b. The Seronera bull problem. II. The Trees. E. Afr. Wildl. J. 12:29–47.

Curry-Lindahl, K. 1968. Zoological aspects on the conservation of vegetation in tropical Africa, pp. 25–32. In *Conservation of Vegetation in Africa South of the Sahara.* Acta Phytogeographica Suecica 54. Ed. I. Hedberg and O. Hedberg. Uppsala, Sweden: Almqvist and Wiksells Boktry Chri Ab.

Darling, F. F. 1960. *Wildlife in an African Territory.* London: Oxford Univ. Press.

———. 1964. Conservation and ecological theory. J. Ecol. 52(Suppl.):36–45.

Dasmann, R. F., and A. S. Mossman. 1962. Population studies of impala in southern Rhodesia. J. Mammal. 43(3):375–95.

Day, B. N. 1962. The reproduction of swine, pp. 255–65. In *Reproduction in Farm Animals.* Ed. E. S. E. Hafez. Philadelphia: Lea and Ferbiger.

Deane, H. W. 1958. Intercellular lipids: Their detection and significance, pp. 227–63. In *Frontiers in Cytology.* Ed. S. L. Palay. New Haven: Yale Univ. Press.

Decker, R. A., and A. F. Krohn. 1973. Cholelithiasis in an Indian elephant. J. Am. Vet. Med. Assoc. 163(6):546–47.

Deraniyagala, P. E. P. 1963. Tusk and tail variations in *Elephas maximus* and *Loxodonta africana.* Spolia Zeylandia 30:85–86.

Dillman, J. S., and W. R. Carr. 1970. Observations on arteriosclerosis, serum cholesterol and serum electrolytes in the wild African elephant (*Loxodonta africana*). J. Comp. Path.

80:81–87.

Dougall, H. W., and D. L. W. Sheldrick. 1964. The chemical composition of a day's diet of an elephant. E. Afr. Wildl. J. 2:51–59.

Douglas-Hamilton, I. 1973. On the ecology and behavior of the Lake Manyara elephants. E. Afr. Wildl. J. 11:401–3.

Douglas-Hamilton, I., and Oria Douglas-Hamilton. 1975. *Among the Elephants.* New York: Viking.

Driak, F. 1937. Anatomical and histological examination of the structure and development of the elephant molar. J. Dent. Res. 16:73–80.

Edgar, D. G. 1952. Progesterone in body fluids. Nature 170:543–44.

Edward, D. C. 1942. Grass-burning. Emp. J. Exp. Agric. 10:219–31.

Eggeling, W. J. 1947. Observations on the ecology of the Budongo rain forest, Uganda. J. Ecol. 34(1):230–87.

———. 1958. *The Indigenous Trees of the Uganda Protectorate* (with corrigenda and addenda). Entebbe: Gov. Printer.

Eisenberg, J. E., G. M. Mckay, and M. R. Jainudeen. 1971. Reproductive behavior of the Asiatic elephant (*Elephas maximus maximus* L.). Behavior 38:(3–4):13–225.

Elder, W. H. 1970. Morphometry of elephant tusks. Zool. Afr. 5:143–59.

Elder, W. H., and D. H. Rodgers. 1968. Age and growth of elephants: A study in the Luangwa Valley, 1965–1967. Afr. Wild Life 22:281–93.

———. 1975. Body temperature in the African elephant as related to ambient temperature. Mammalia 39(3):395–99.

Eltringham, S. K. 1982. *Elephants.* Poole, Uganda: Blandford Press.

Eltringham, S. K., and R. C. Malpas. 1976. Elephant slaughter in Uganda. Oryx 13(4):344–55.

Eltringham, S. K., and M. H. Woodford. 1968. Excerpts from Annual Report 5 July 1967–June 1968, Nuffield Unit of Tropical Ecology. E. Afr. Wildl. Soc. Sci. Tech. Comm. Bull. 27. Mimeo.

Enders, A. C. 1966. The reproductive cycle of the nine-banded armadillo (*Dasypus novemcinctus*), pp. 195–204. In *Comparative Biology of Reproduction in Mammals.* Ed. I. W. Rowlands. New York: Academic Press.

Errington, P. L. 1945. Some contributions of a fifteen-year local study of the northern bobwhite to a knowledge of population phenomena. Ecol. Monogr. 15:1–34.

Estergreen, V. L., Jr., D. W. Holtan, and S. N. Smith. 1968. Heterogeneity of progestin distribution in bovine corpus luteum. J. Diary Sci. 51(Abst.):948.

Evans, F. C. 1967. The significance of investigations in secondary terrestrial productivity, pp. 3–15. In *Secondary Productivity of Terrestrial Ecosystems.* Krakow: Inst. Ecol., Polish Acad. Sci., Intern. Biol. Programme.

Fatti, L. P., G. L. Smuts, A. M. Starfield, and A. A. Spurdle. 1980. Age determination in African elephants. J. Mammal. 61(3):547–51.

Feely, J. M. 1965. Observations on *Acacia albida* in the

REFERENCES

Luangwa Valley. Puku 3:67–70.

Filippich, L. J., C. H. Kennard, and J. J. Mines. 1984. Vaterite gallstones in a canary (*Serinus canarius*). Aust. Vet. J. 61(9):298.

Flower, S. S. 1943. Notes on age at sexual maturity, gestation period and growth of the Indian elephant, *Elephas maximus*. Proc. Zool. Soc. London, Ser. A 113:21–26.

Foley, R. C., and J. S. Greenstein. 1958. Cytological changes in the bovine corpus luteum during early pregnancy, pp. 88–96. In *Proceedings Third Symposium on Reproduction and Infertility*. Ed. F. X. Gassner. Fairview Park, N.Y.: Pergamon Press.

Frade, F. 1955. Ordre des proboscidiens. Ed. P. P. Grasse. Traite de Zoologie 17:715–83.

Fraser-Darling, F. 1947. *Natural History of the Highlands and Islands*. London: Collins.

———. 1968. *In the Future of the Highlands*. Ed. D. S. Thompson and I. Grimble. London: Collins.

Game and Fisheries Dep. 1959. Annual report of the Game and Fisheries Department, 1 July 1957 to 30 June 1958. Entebbe, Uganda: Gov. Printer.

Gebbing, T. 1959. Beobahtungen uber den Schlaf der Elefanten. Z. Saugetierkunde. 24:85–88.

Geist, V. 1975. *Mountain Sheep and Man in the Northern Wilds*. Ithaca, N.Y.; London: Cornell Univ. Press.

Glover, J. 1963. The elephant problem at Tsavo. E. Afr. Wildl. J. 1:30–39.

Gross, J. E. 1969. Optimum yield in deer and elk populations. Trans. 34th N. A. Wildl. Conf., pp. 372–87.

Hafs, H. D., and D. T. Armstrong. 1968. Corpus luteum growth and progesterone synthesis during the bovine estrous cycle. J. Anim. Sci. 27:134–41.

Hanks, J. 1969. Seasonal breeding of the African elephant in Zambia. E. Afr. Wildl. J. 7:167.

———. 1972. Aspects of dentition of the African elephant, *Loxodonta africana*. Arnoldia 5(36):1–8.

———. 1979. *The Struggle for Survival*. New York; Cape Town, S. Afr.: Mayflower Books.

Hanks, J., and R. V. Short. 1972. The formation and function of the corpus luteum in the African elephant, *Loxodonta africana*. J. Reprod. Fert. 29:79–89.

Hart, G. H., and H. R. Guilbert. 1933. Vitamin-A deficiency as related to reproduction in range cattle. Univ. of California Agric. Exp. Stn. Bull. 560.

Hediger, H. 1950. La capture des elephants au Parc National de la Garamba. Bul.Inst. Royal Col. Belg. 21:218–26.

Heidner, G. L., and R. L. Campbell. 1985. Cholelithiasis in a cat. J. Am. Vet. Med. Assoc. 186(2):176–77.

Hess, D. L., Anne M. Schmidt, and M. J. Schmidt. 1983. Reproductive cycle of the Asian elephant (*Elephas maximus*) in captivity. Biol. Reprod. 28:767–73.

Hill, W. C. O., ed. 1953. *The Elephant in East Africa: A Monograph*. London: Rowland Ward Ltd.

Huggett, A. St. G., and W. F. Widdas. 1951. The relationship between mammalian foetal weight and conception age. J.

Physiol. 114:306–17.

Humphreys, H. F. 1926. Particulars relating to the broken tusk of a wild Indian elephant. Brit. Dent. J. 47:1400–1407.

Hundley, G. 1934. Statistics of height increments of Indian calf elephants. Proc. Zool. Soc. London 104:697–98.

Hurley, Lucille S. 1981. Trace metals in mammalian development. Johns Hopkins Med. J. 148:1–10.

Jackmann, H., and R. H. V. Bell. 1979. The assessment of elephant numbers and occupancy by means of droppings counts in the Kasungu National Park, Malawi. Afr. J. Ecol. 17:231–39.

Jainudeen, M. R., J. F. Eisenberg, and N. Tilakeratne. 1971. Oestrous cycle of the Asiatic elephant, *Elephas maximus*, in captivity. J. Reprod. Fertil. 27:321–28.

Johnson, O. W. 1964. Histological and quantitative characteristics of the testes, observations on the teeth and pituitary gland and the possibility of reproductive cyclicity in the African elephant (*Loxodonta africana*). Ph.D. diss., Washington State Univ., Pullman.

Johnson, O. W., and I. O. Buss. 1965. Molariform teeth of male African elephants in relation to age, body dimensions and growth. J. Mammal. 46(3):373–84.

Kaiza-Boshe, T. 1985. Conserving wildlife in developing Africa. Swara 8(3):27–29.

Kinloch, B. 1972. *The Shamba Raiders*. London: Collins and Harville Press.

Krumbiegel, I. 1943. Der Afrikanische elefant. Monogr. Wildsäugetiere 9:1–152.

Krumrey, W. A., and I. O. Buss. 1968. Age estimation, growth, and relationships between body dimensions of the female African elephant. J. Mammal. 49(1):22–31.

Kühme, W. 1963. Ethology of the African elephant. Int. Zool. Yearb. 4:113–21.

Kurt, F. 1960. Le sommeil des elephants. Mammalia 24:259–72.

Lands and Survey Dep. 1959. (Map) of Uganda mean annual rainfall. Lands and Surveys Dep., and E. African Meteorological Dep., Uganda Region, E. African High Commission.

Lang, E. M. 1980. Observations on growth and molar change in the African elephant. Afr. J. Ecol. 18(2–3):217–34.

Lang-Brown, J. R., and J. F. Harrop. 1962. The ecology and soils of the Kibale grasslands, Uganda. E. Afr. Agric. For. J. 27(4):264–72.

Langdale-Brown, I. 1962. Vegetation, p. 24. In *Atlas of Uganda*. Entebbe: Dep. Lands and Surveys.

Lark, R. M. 1984. A comparison between techniques for estimating the ages of African elephants. Afr. J. Ecol. 22(1):69–71.

Laws, R. M. 1966. Age criteria for the African elephant, *Loxodonta africana*. E. Afr. Wildl. J. 4:1–37.

———. 1967. Eye lens weight and age in African elephants. E. Afr. Wildl. J. 5:46–52.

———. 1969a. Aspects of reproduction in the African elephant, *Loxodonta africana*. J. Reprod. Fert.,

6(Suppl.):193–217.

———. 1969b. The Tsavo research project. J. Reprod. Fert., 6(Suppl.):495–531.

———. 1970a. The Tsavo research project. Oryx, 10(6):355–66.

———. 1970b. Elephants as agents of habitat and landscape change in East Africa. Oikos, Copenhagen, 21:1–15.

———. 1978. Back-up from the former Tsavo Research Director, In A time for sense not sentiment on culling the game, W. L. Robinette and L. H. Blankenship, Africana 6(10):12–15.

Laws, R. M., and G. Clough. 1966. Observations on reproduction in the hippopotamus, *Hippopotamus amphibius* Linn. Symp. Zool. Soc. London 15:117–40.

Laws, R. M., and I. S. C. Parker. 1968. Recent studies on elephant populations in East Africa. In *Comparative Nutrition of Wild Aniamls*. Ed. M. A. Crawford. Symp. Zool. Soc. London 21:319–59.

Laws, R. M., I. S. C. Parker, and R. C. B. Johnstone. 1970. Elephants and habitats in north Bunyoro, Uganda. E. Afr. Wildl. J. 8:163–80.

Lawton, R. M. 1966. A survey of part of the Luangwa Valley, Zambia, to ascertain the causes of erosion and the relationship between erosion, vegetation type, game population and fire. Roneoed Report, Mount Makulu Research Station, Chilanga, Zambia.

Leach, R. M. 1978. Manganese deficiency—Man, pp. 259–60. In *CRC Handbook Series in Nutrition and Food, Nutritional Disorders*, West Palm Beach, Fl.: CRC Press.

Leakey, L. S. B. 1969. *Animals of East Africa*. Washington, D.C.: Natl. Geographic Soc.

Lee, S. P., C. Tasman-Jones, and V. Carlisle. 1986. Oleic acid–induced cholelithiasis in rabbits. Changes in bile composition and gallbaldder morphology. Am. J. Pathol. 124(1):18–24.

Leuthold, W. 1976. Age structure of elephants in Tsavo National Park, Kenya. J. Appl. Ecol. 13:435–44.

Leuthold, W., and J. B. Sale. 1973. Movements and patterns of habitat utilization of elephants in Tsavo National Park, Kenya. E. Afr. Wildl. J. 11:369–84.

McCullagh, K. G. 1972. Arteriosclerosis in the African elephant. Pt. 1. Intimal Atteroschlerosis and its possible causes. Atteroschlerosis 16:307–35.

———. 1973. Are African elephants deficient in essential fatty acids? Nature 242:267–68.

McCullagh, K. G., and M. C. Lewis. 1967. Spontaneous arteriosclerosis in the wild African elephant: Its relation to disease in man. Lancet(ii):492–95.

McLachlan, G. R., and R. Liversidge. 1958. *Roberts Birds of South Africa*. Cape Town, S. Afr.: Cape Times Ltd.

Melland, F. 1938. *Elephants in Africa*. London: Country Life, Ltd.

Mertz, W. 1981. The essential trace elements. Science 213:1332.

Miller, R. F., G. H. Hart, and H. H. Cole. 1942. Fertility in sheep as affected by nutrition during breeding season and pregnancy. Univ. of California Exp. Stn. Bull. 672.

Mitchell, B. L. 1961. Ecological aspects of game control measures in African wilderness and forested areas. Kirkia 1:120–28.

Morrison-Scott, T. C. S. 1947. A revision of our knowledge of African elephants' teeth, with notes on forest and "pygmy" elephants. Proc. Zool. Soc. London 117:505–27.

Mortvedt, J. J., P. M. Goerdano, and W. L. Lindsay, eds. 1972. *Micronutrients in Agriculture*. Madison, Wis.: Soil Sci. Soc. Am.

Moss, C. J. 1983. Oestrous behaviour and female choice in the African elephant. Behaviour 86:167–96.

Napier Bax, P., and D. L. W. Sheldrick. 1963. Some preliminary observations on the food of elephant in the Tsavo Royal National Park (East) of Kenya. E. Afr. Wildl. J. 1:40–53.

Newsome, A. E. 1965. Reproduction in natural population of the red kangaroo *Megaleia rufa* in Central Australia. Aust. J. Zool. 13:735–59.

Nicholson, B. D. 1954. The African elephant (*Loxodonta africana*). Afr. Wildl. 8(4):313–22.

Norris, T. 1977. Further facts on Uganda's elephants. Africana 6(4):21.

Novikova, E. P. 1963. Effect of different amounts of dietary cobalt on iodine content of rat thyroid gland. Vopr. Pitan. 22(2): FASEB(1964)23(Trans. Suppl.)T459–60.

Odum, E. P. 1971. *Fundamentals of Ecology*. Philadelphia: W. B. Saunders Co.

Ogle, T. F., H. H. Braach, and I. O. Buss. 1973. Fine structure and progesterone concentration in the corpus luteum of the African elephant. Anat. Rec. 175:707–723.

Osborn, H. F. 1936–1942. *Proboscidea. A Monograph of the Discovery, Evolution, Migration, and Extinction of the Mastodonts and Elephants of The World*. 2 vols. New York: Amer. Mus. Press.

Osmaston, H. A. 1959. Working plan for the Kibale and Itwara Forests. 1st Rev. Entebbe: Uganda For. Dept.

Owen-Smith, N. 1966. The incidence of tuskless elephants in Mana Pools Game Reserve. Afr. Wildl. 20:69–73.

Parker, I., and M. Amin. 1983. *Ivory Crisis*. London: Chatto and Windus, Hogarth Press.

Pellegrini, C. A., T. Ryan, W. Broderick, and L. W. Way. 1986. Gallbladder filling and emptying during cholesterol gallstone formation in the prairie dog. A cholescintigraphic study. Gastroenterology 90(1):143–49.

Perry, J. S. 1953. The reproduction of the African elephant, *Loxodonta africana*. Philos. Trans. R. Soc. London, Ser. B, Biol. Sci. 237:93–149.

———. 1954. Some observations on growth and tusk weight in male and female African elephants. Proc. Zool. Soc. London 124:97–104.

———. 1964. The structure and development of the reproductive organs of the female African elephant. Philos. Trans. R. Soc. London, Ser. B, Biol. Sci. 248:35–52.

REFERENCES

Petrides, G. A., and W. G. Swank. 1964. Estimating the productivity and energy relations of an African elephant population, pp. 831–42. In Proceedings Ninth International Grassland Congress, Sao Paulo, Brazil.

Pienaar, U. de V. 1961. A second outbreak of anthrax amongst game animals in the Kruger National Park. Koedoe (4):4–18.

————. 1963. The large mammals of Kruger National Park: Their distribution and present-day status. Koedoe 6:1–37.

Pienaar, U. de V., J. W. Niekerk, E. Young, P. Van Wyk, and N. Fairall. 1966. The use of oripavine hydrochloride (M-99) in the drug-immobilization and marking of wild African elephant (Loxodonta africana Blumenbach) in the Kruger National Park. Koedoe 9:108–24.

Poole, J. H. 1982. Musth and male-male competition in the African elephant. Ph.D. diss., Cambridge Univ., Eng.

Powell, R. W. 1985. Pure calcium carbonate gallstones in a two year old in association with prenatal calcium supplementation. J. Pediatr. Surg. 20(2):143–44.

Reader, J., and H. Croze. n.d. Pyramids of Life. New York; Phila.: Lippincott.

Redmond, I. 1982. Salt-mining elephants of Mount Elgon. Swara 5(4):28–31.

Rees, P. A. 1982. Gross assimilation efficiency and food passage time in the African elephant. Afr. J. Ecol. 20(3):193–98.

Rennels, E. G. 1966. Observations on the ultrastructure of luteal cells from PMS and PMS-HCG treated immature rats. Endocrinology 79:373–86.

Richardson, G. S. 1966. Ovarian Physiology. Boston: Little, Brown and Co.

Riney, T. 1957. The use of faeces counts in studies of several free-ranging mammals in New Zealand. N. Z. J. Sci. Technol. 38B(6):507–32.

Rodgers, D. H., and W. H. Elder. 1977. Movements of elephants in Luangwa Valley, Zambia. J. Wildl. Manage. 41(1):56–62.

Roy, D. J., and D. N. Mullick. 1964. Endocrine functions of corpora lutea of buffaloes during the estrous cycle. Endocrinology 75:284–87.

Rushby, G. G. 1965. No More Tuskers. London: W. H. Allen.

Seth-Smith, D. 1932. Remarks on the age at which the Indian elephant attains sexual maturity. Proc. Zool. Soc. London 102:816.

Shantz, H. L., and B. L. Turner. 1958. Vegetational changes in Africa over a third of a century. Univ. Arizona Bull., 158 pp.

Sheldrick, Daphne. 1972. Death of the Tsavo elephants. Sat. Rev. Sci. (Sept.):27–36.

Sherry, B. Y. 1975. Reproduction of elephant in Gonarezhou, southeastern Rhodesia. S. Afr. Wildl. J. 27:1–13.

Short, R. V. 1966. Oestrous behavior, ovulation and the function of the corpus luteum in the African elephant, Loxondonta africana. E. Afr. Wildl. J. 4:56–68.

Short, R. V., and I. O. Buss. 1965. Biochemical and histological observations on the corpus luteum of the African elephant, Loxodonta africana. J. Reprod. Fert. 9(1):61–67.

Shoshani, J. 1982. On the dissection of a female Asian elephant (Elephas m. maximus Linneaus, 1758) and data from other elephants. Elephant 2(1):3–94.

Sikes, Sylvia K. 1966. The African elephant (Loxodonta africana): A field method for estimation of age. J. Zool. London 150:279–95.

————. 1968. The African elephant (Loxodonta africana): A field method for the estimation of age. J. Zool. London 154:235–48.

————. 1971. The Natural History of the African Elephant. London: Widenfeld & Nicholson; New York: Elsevier Publ. Co.

Simon, N. 1962. Between the Sunlight and the Thunder: The Wildlife of Kenya. London: Collins.

Smith, I. C., and Bonnie L. Carson, ed. 1981. Trace Metals in the Environment. Vol. 6, Cobalt. Ann Arbor, Mich.: Ann Arbor Science.

Smith, J. G., J. Hanks, and R. V. Short. 1969. Biochemical observations on the corpora lutea of the African elephant, Loxodonta africana. J. Reprod. Fert. 20(1):111–17.

Smith, N. S. 1969. The persistence and functional life of the corpus luteum in the African elephant. Ph.D. diss., Washington State Univ., Pullman.

Smith, N. S., and I. O. Buss. 1973. Reproductive ecology of the female African elephant. J. Wildl. Manage. 37(4):524–34.

————. 1975. Formation, function, and persistence of the corpora lutea of the African elephant (Loxodonta africana). J. Mammal. 56(1):30–43.

Smuts, G. L. 1975. Reproduction and population characteristics of elephants in the Kruger National Park. J. S. Afr. Wildl. Manage. Assoc. 5(1):1–10.

————. 1982. Lion. Johannesburg, S. Afr.: MacMillan.

Spies, H. G., D. R. Zimmerman, H. L. Self, and L. F. Casida. 1959. The effect of exogenous progesterone on formation and maintenance of the corpora lutea and on early embryo survival in pregnant swine. J. Anim. Sci. 18:163–72.

Spinage, C. A. 1962. Animals of East Africa. London: Collins.

Sutcliffe, A. J. 1973. Similarity of bones and antlers gnawed by deer to human artefacts. Nature 246:428–30.

Talbot, L. M., and M. H. Talbot. 1962. Food preferences of some East African wild ungulates. E. Afr. Agr. For. J. 27(3):131–38.

————. 1963. The wildebeest in Western Masailand, East Africa. Wildl. Monogr. No. 12.

Temple-Perkins, E. A. 1955. Kingdom of the Elephant. London: Andrew Melrose.

Tennent, J. E. 1867. The Wild Elephant. London: Longmans, Green, and Co.

Terrill, C. E. 1962. The reproduction of sheep, pp. 240–54. In Reproduction in Farm Animals. Ed. E. S. E. Hafez. Philadelphia: Lea and Ferbiger.

Thomas, A. S. 1940. Grasses as indicator plants in Uganda. Pt. I. E. Afr. Agr. J. 6(1).

Thompson, D. 1942. *On Growth and Form.* Cambridge: Cambridge Univ. Press.

Thomson, P. J. 1975. The role of elephants, fire and other agents in the decline of *Brachystegia boehmii* woodland. J. S. Afr. Wildl. Manage. Assoc. 5(1):11–18.

Trapnell, C. G. 1953. The soils, vegetation and agriculture of northeastern Rhodesia. Lusaka, Rhodesia: Gov. Printers.

Verboom, W. C. 1968. Report on the visit to the vegetation plots laid down by Mr. W. L. Astle in the Luangwa South Game Reserve. Roneoed Report, Dep. of Agric., Lusaka, Rhodesia.

Verheyen, R. 1960. Sur la morphogenese et le remplacement des molaire chez l'elephant d'Afrique (*Loxodonta*). Bull. Inst. Sci. Nat. Belg. 36:1–19.

Vesey-Fitzgerald, L. D. E. F. 1963. Ecosystems and biological productivity. Int. Union Conserv. Nat. Resources (Vaud), Switzerland.

Villee, C. A., W. F. Walker, and F. E. Smith. 1963. *General Zoology.* Philadelphia: W. B. Saunders Co.

Waslien, C. L. 1976. Human intake of trace elements, pp. 347–70. In *Trace Elements in Human Health and Disease.* Vol. 2. Ed. A. S. Prasad. New York: Academic Press.

Watson, P. F., and F. D'Souza. 1975. Detection of oestrus in the African elephant (*Loxodonta africana*). Theriogenology 4:203–9.

West, D. L. 1990. CITES bans all trade in elephant ivory. World Wildlife Fund, Special Report 1990, p. 1.

Western, D. 1973. The changing face of Amboseli. Africana 5(3):23–27.

Williams, J. G. 1963. *A Field Guide to the Birds of East and Central Africa.* London: Collins.

Williamson, B. R. 1976. Reproduction in female African elephant in the Wankie National Park, Rhodesia. S. Afr. J. Wildl. Res. 6:89–93.

Willock, C. 1965. *The Enormous Zoo.* New York: Harcourt, Brace and World, Inc.

Wing, L. D., and I. O. Buss. 1970. Elephants and forests. Wildl. Soc., Publ. 19.

Worthington, E. B. 1958. *Science in the Development of Africa.* Great Britain: Stephen Austin and Sons, Ltd.

Wyatt, J. R., and S. K. Eltringham. 1974. The daily activity of the elephant in the Rwenzori National Park, Uganda. E. Afr. Wildl. J. 12:273–89.

Zarembka, F. R., E. D. Plotka, U. S. Seal, L. G. Simmons, A. Teare, L. G. Phillips, and K. C. Hinshaw. 1987. Luteinizing hormone and progesterone cycles in African and Asian elephants. Biol. Reprod. 36(Suppl.)1:1–129.

Index

INDEX

INDEX